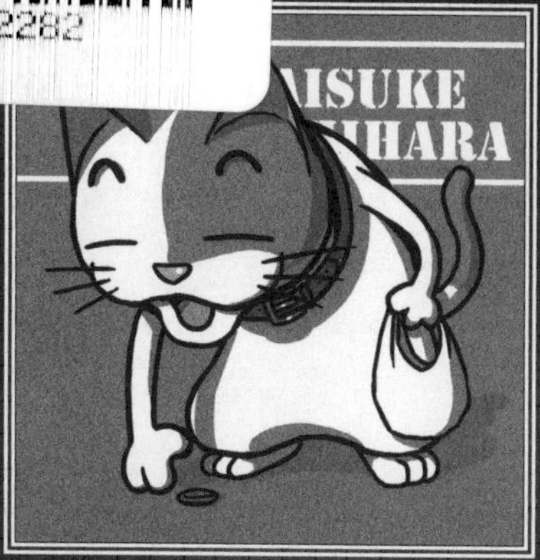
AISUKE
HIHARA

Reading my own manga is almost never sentimental to me, but when I read fan mail, I get to experience my own manga "through the eyes of the reader," and I get unexpectedly emotional. Here's ***World Trigger*** volume 7.

—Daisuke Ashihara, 2014

Daisuke Ashihara began his manga career at the age of 27 when his manga ***Room 303*** won second place in the 75th Tezuka Awards. His first series, ***Super Dog Rilienthal***, began serialization in ***Weekly Shonen Jump*** in 2009. ***World Trigger*** is his second serialized work in ***Weekly Shonen Jump***. He is also the author of several shorter works, including the one-shots ***Super Dog Rilienthal***, ***Trigger Keeper*** and ***Elite Agent Jin***.

WORLD TRIGGER VOL. 7
SHONEN JUMP Manga Edition

STORY AND ART BY DAISUKE ASHIHARA

Translation/Lillian Olsen, Sarah Tangney, Christine Dashiell
Touch-Up Art & Lettering/Annaliese Christman
Design/Sam Elzway
Weekly Shonen Jump Editor/Hope Donovan
Graphic Novel Editor/Marlene First

Printed in the U.S.A.

Published by VIZ Media, LLC
P.O. Box 77010
San Francisco, CA 94107

10 9 8 7 6 5 4 3 2 1
First printing, October 2015

SHONEN JUMP MANGA EDITION

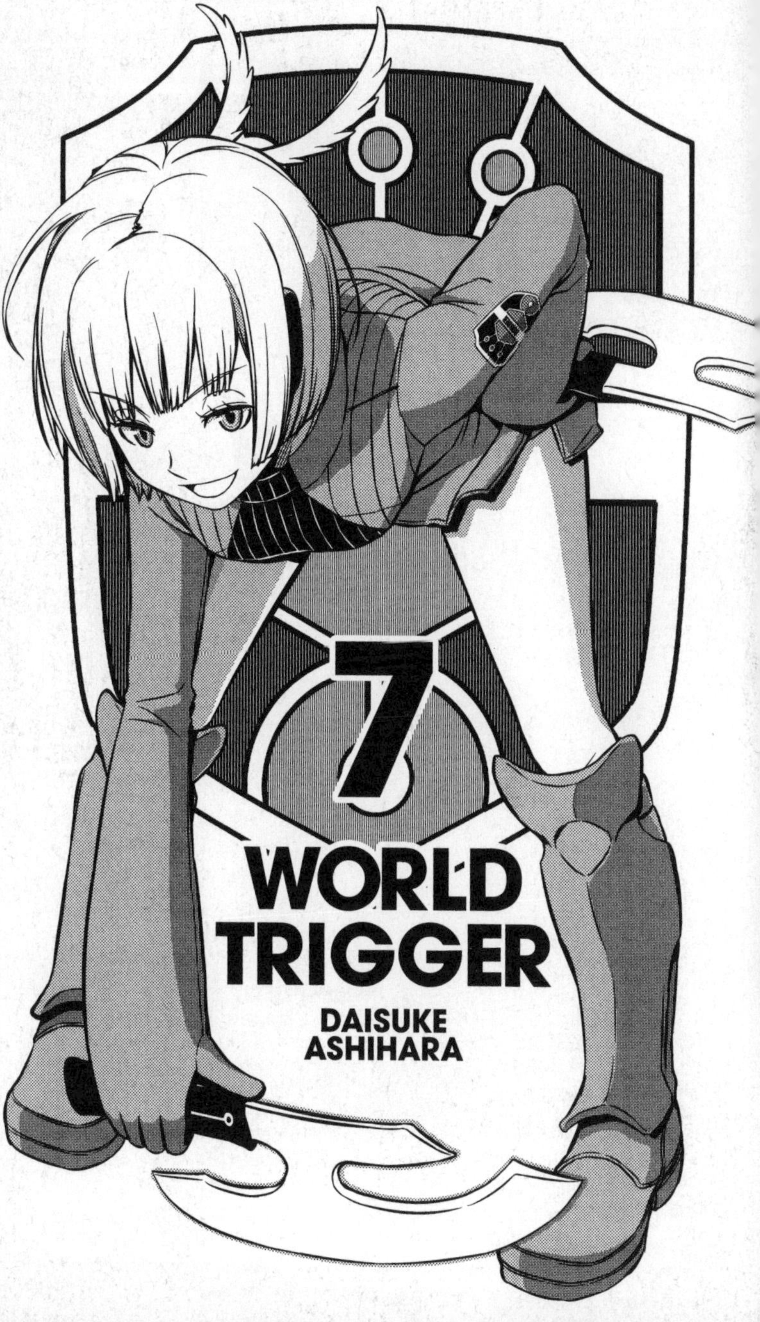

7

WORLD TRIGGER

DAISUKE ASHIHARA

WORLD TRIGGER DATA BASE

NEIGHBOR

Invaders from another dimension that enter Mikado City through Gates. Most "Neighbors" here are Trion soldiers built for war. The Neighbors who actually live on the other side of the Gates are human, like Yuma.

RRMN
H-HEY, IT'S COMING THIS WAY!!
WHOA...
WAAA

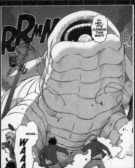

Trion solider built for war. ▶

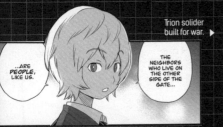

THE NEIGHBORS WHO LIVE ON THE OTHER SIDE OF THE GATE...
...ARE PEOPLE, LIKE US.

NEIGHBORHOOD

The Neighbor world. Mostly the darkness of space, with individual countries floating like stars.

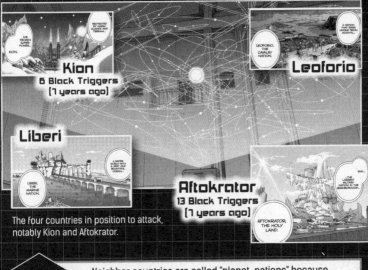

PROTECTED BY HARSH CLIMATE AND TERRAIN...
THE FROZEN SUPER-POWER...
KION.
Kion
6 Black Triggers
(7 years ago)
A NATION THAT RIDES UNIQUE TRION MOUNTS...
LEOFORIO, THE CAVALRY NATION.
Leoforio
Liberi
A WATER WORLD WITH A VAST AND BOUNTIFUL OCEAN...
LIBERI, THE MARINE NATION.
AND...
...THE LARGEST MILITARY NATION IN THE NEIGHBORHOOD...
AFTOKRATOR, THE HOLY LAND.
Aftokrator
13 Black Triggers
(7 years ago)

The four countries in position to attack, notably Kion and Aftokrator.

Planet-Nations

Neighbor countries are called "planet-nations" because they traverse the darkness on their own orbits. Many of them brush by this world as they travel along their paths. Some, called "errant nations," fly about freely, without determined orbits.

BORDER

An agency founded to protect the city from Neighbors. Agents are classified as follows: C-Rank for trainees, B-Rank for main forces, A-Rank for elites and S-Rank for those with Black Triggers. A-Rank squads get to go on away missions to the Neighborhood.

Resistan

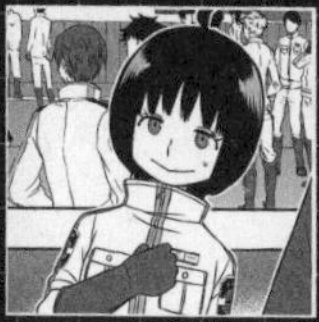

C-Rank: Chika

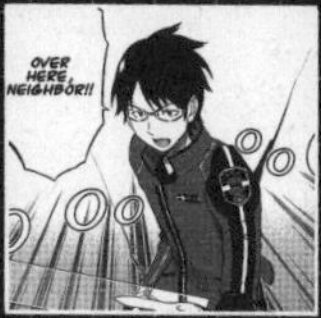
OVER HERE, NEIGHBOR!!

B-Rank: Osamu

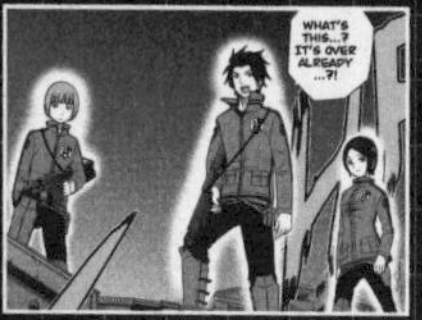
WHAT'S THIS...? IT'S OVER ALREADY ...?!

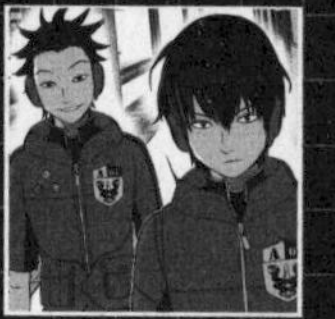

A-Rank: Arashiyama Squad, Miwa Squad

Trigger

A technology created by Neighbors to manipulate Trion. Used mainly as weapons, Triggers come in various types. Border classifies them into three groups: Attacker, Gunner, and Sniper.

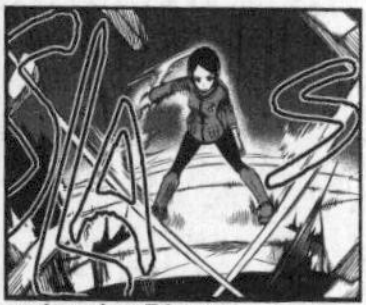

▲Attacker Trigger

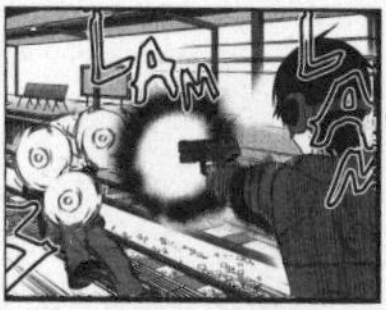
LAM

▲Gunner Trigger

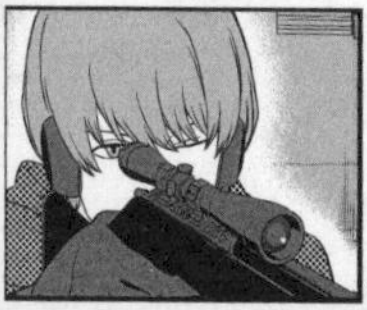

◀Sniper Trigger

Black Trigger

A special Trigger created when a skilled user pours their entire life force and Trion into a Trigger. Outperforms regular Triggers, but the user must be compatible with the personality of the creator, meaning only a few people can use any given Black Trigger.

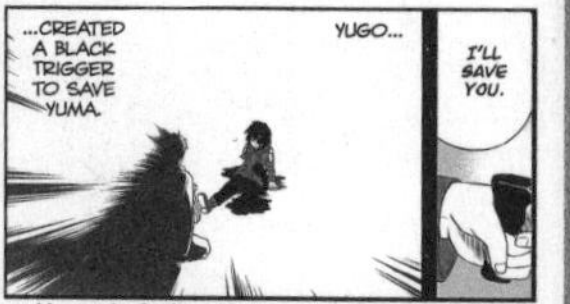
I'LL SAVE YOU.
YUGO...
...CREATED A BLACK TRIGGER TO SAVE YUMA.

▲Yuma's father Yugo sacrificed his life to create a Black Trigger and save Yuma.

STORY

About four years ago, a Gate connecting to another dimension opened in Mikado City, leading to the appearance of invaders called Neighbors. After the establishment of the Border Defense Agency, people were able to return to their normal lives.

Osamu Mikumo is a junior high student who meets Yuma Kuga, a Neighbor. Yuma is targeted for capture by Border, but Tamakoma Branch agent Yuichi Jin steps in to help. He convinces Yuma to join Border instead, then gives his Black Trigger to HQ in exchange for Yuma's enlistment. Now Osamu, Yuma, and Osamu's friend Chika work toward making A-Rank together.

As predicted, a large-scale Neighbor invasion begins. New-model Trion soldiers called Rabits capture agents. Osamu and Kitora go to rescue the trainees, but are driven back by an onslaught of enemies! And then, they learn the goal of the attack is to capture the trainees!

WORLD TRIGGER CHARACTERS

TAMAKOMA BRANCH

Understanding toward Neighbors. Considered divergent from Border's main philosophy.

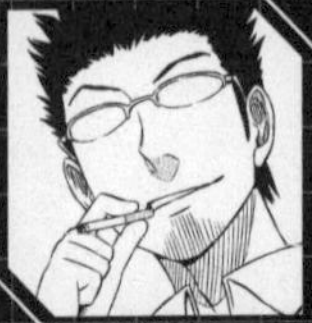

TAKUMI RINDO

Tamakoma Branch Director

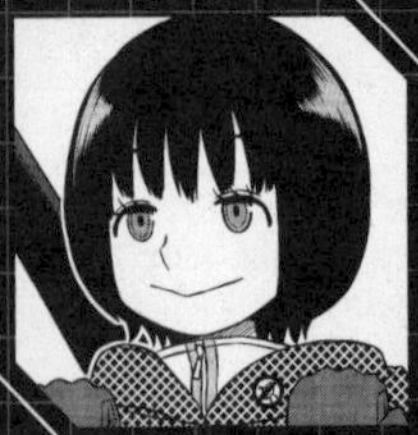

CHIKA AMATORI

Osamu's childhood friend. She has high Trion levels.

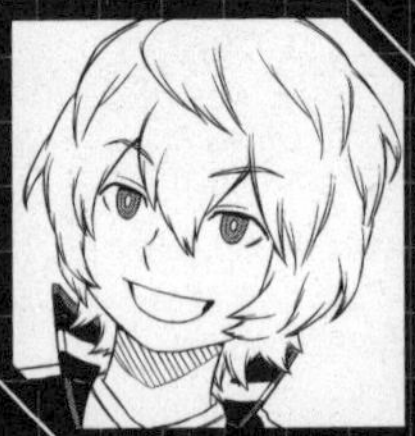

YUMA KUGA

A Neighbor who carries a Black Trigger.

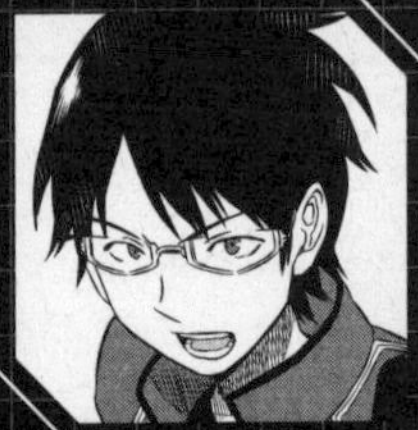

OSAMU MIKUMO

Ninth-grader who's compelled to help those in trouble. B-Rank Border agent.

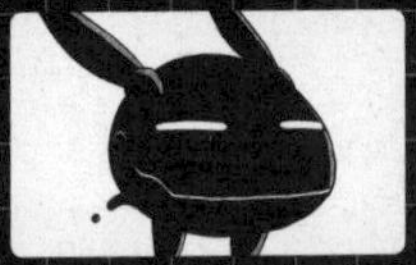

REPLICA

Yuma's chaperone.

TAMAKOMA-1

Tamakoma's A-Rank squad.

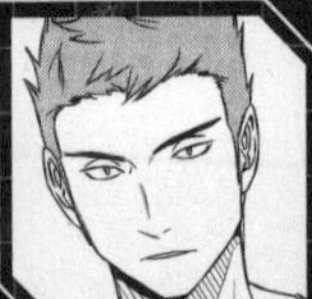

REIJI KIZAKI

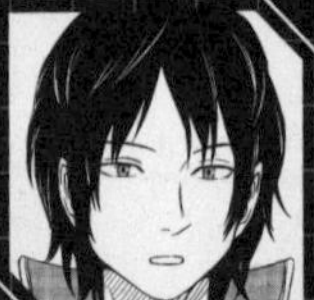

KYOSUKE KARASUMA

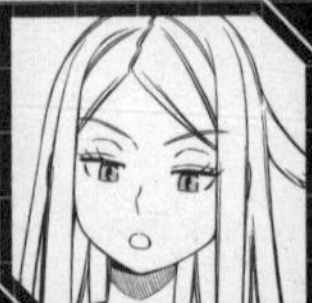

KIRIE KONAMI

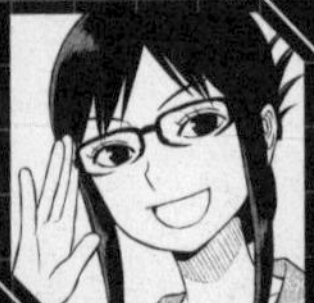

SHIORI USAMI

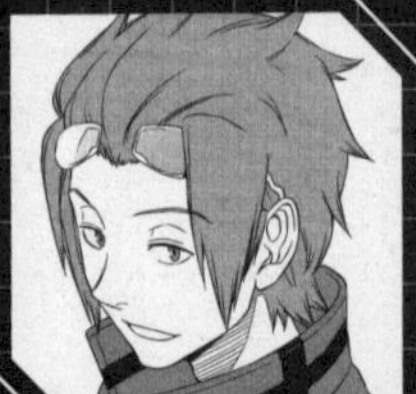

YUICHI JIN

Former S-Rank Black Trigger user. His Side Effect lets him see the future.

BORDER HQ

A-RANK AGENTS

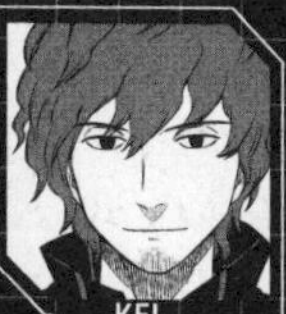
KEI TACHIKAWA
Captain, A-Rank #1 squad.

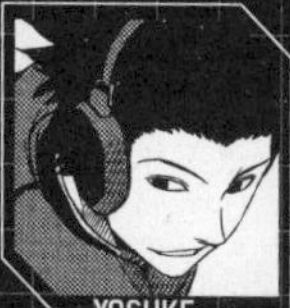
YOSUKE YONEYA
A-Rank #7 Miwa Squad Attacker

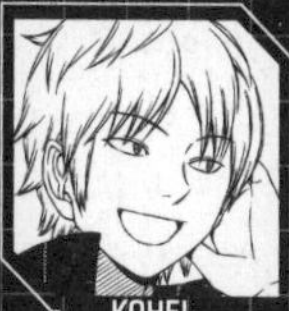
KOHEI IZUMI
A-Rank #1 Tachikawa Squad Shooter

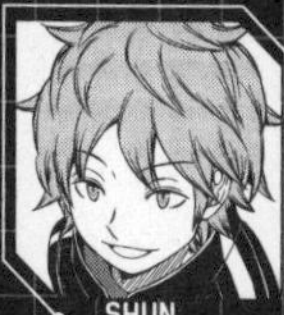
SHUN MIDORIKAWA
A-Rank #4 Kusakabe Squad Attacker

KAZAMA SQUAD

A-Rank #3 squad.

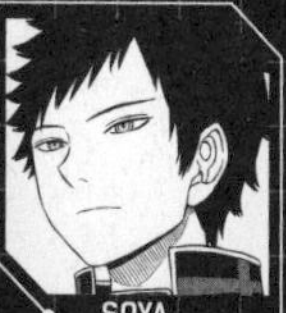
SOYA KAZAMA

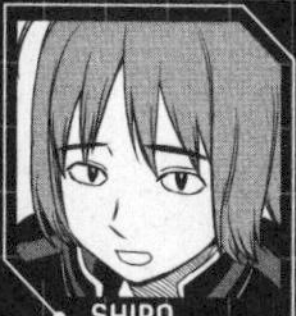
SHIRO KIKUCHIHARA

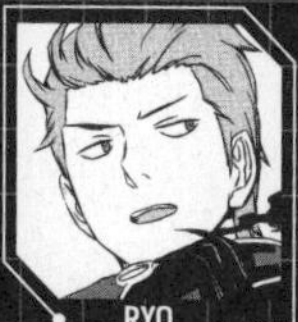
RYO UTAGAWA

B-RANK AGENT

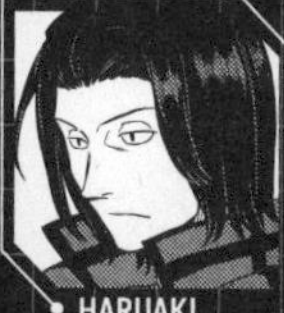
HARUAKI AZUMA

BORDER SENIOR OFFICERS

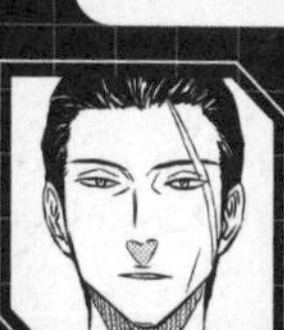
MASAMUNE KIDO
HQ Commander

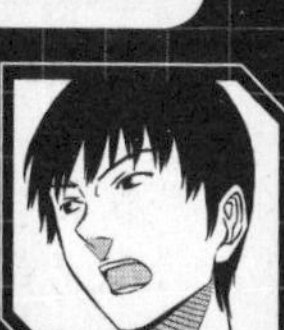
MASAFUMI SHINODA
HQ Director, Defense Force Commander

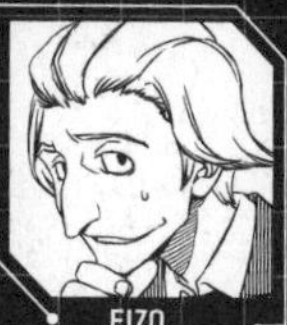
EIZO NETSUKI
PR Director

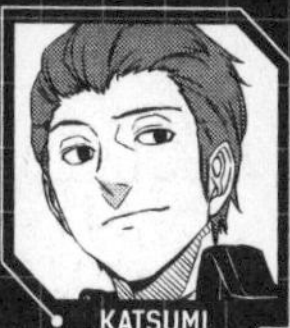
KATSUMI KARASAWA
Business Director

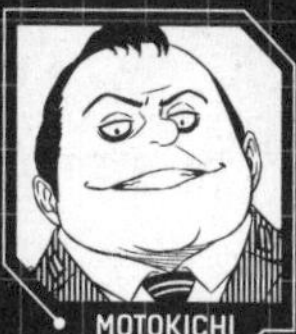
MOTOKICHI KINUTA
R&D Director

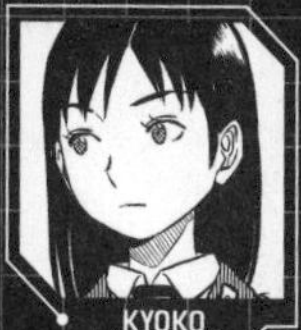
KYOKO SAWAMURA
HQ Assistant Director

C-RANK TRAINEE

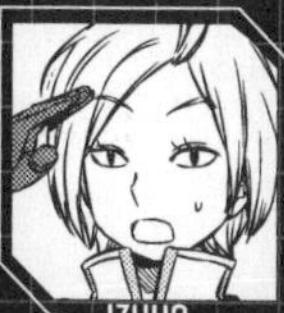
IZUHO NATSUME
Aspiring sniper and Chika's friend.

WORLD TRIGGER

CONTENTS

7

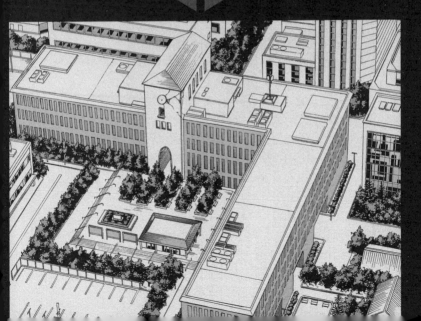

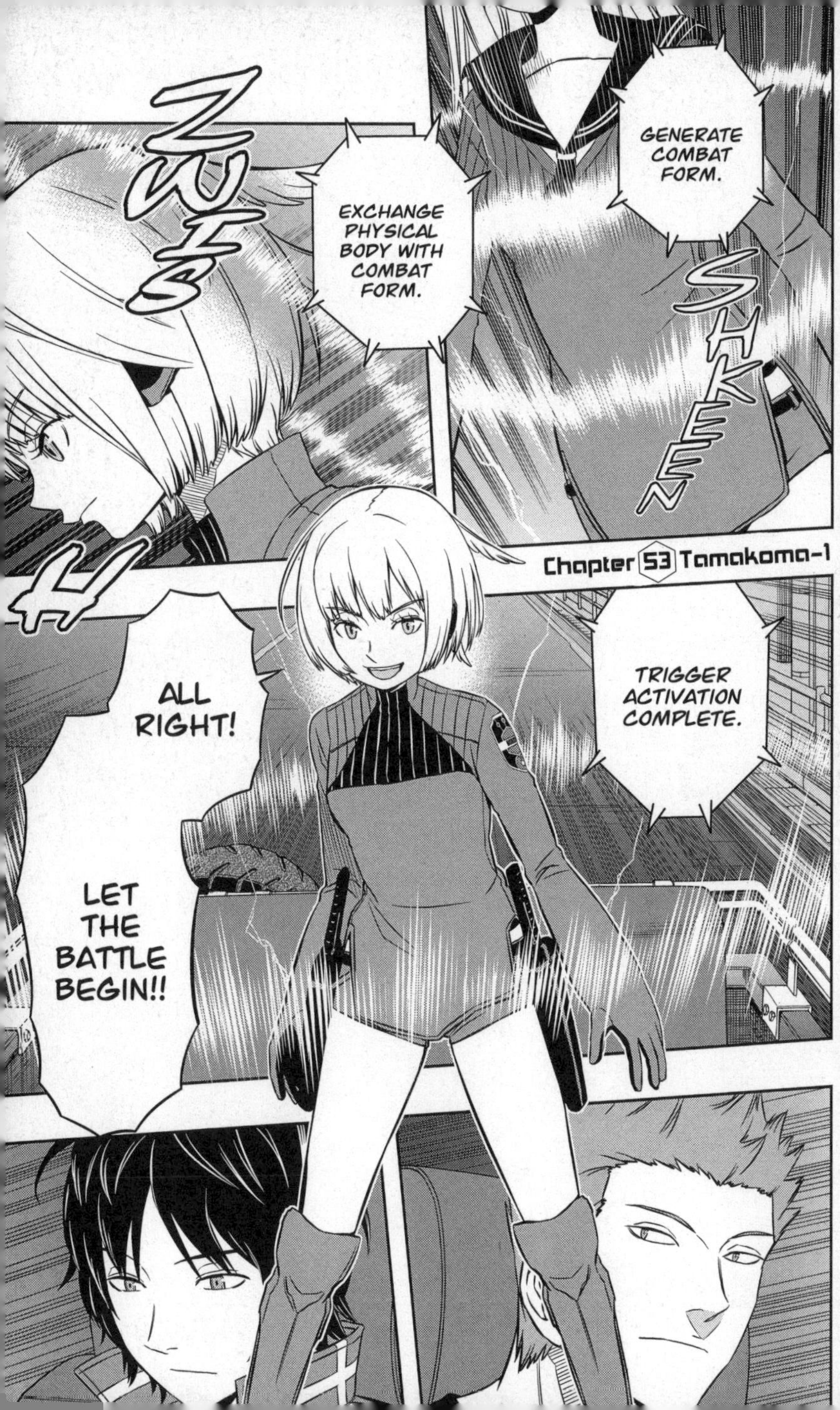
GENERATE COMBAT FORM.
SHKEEN
EXCHANGE PHYSICAL BODY WITH COMBAT FORM.
ZUISSH
Chapter 53 Tamakoma-1
TRIGGER ACTIVATION COMPLETE.
ALL RIGHT!
LET THE BATTLE BEGIN!!

Chapter 53 Tamakoma-1

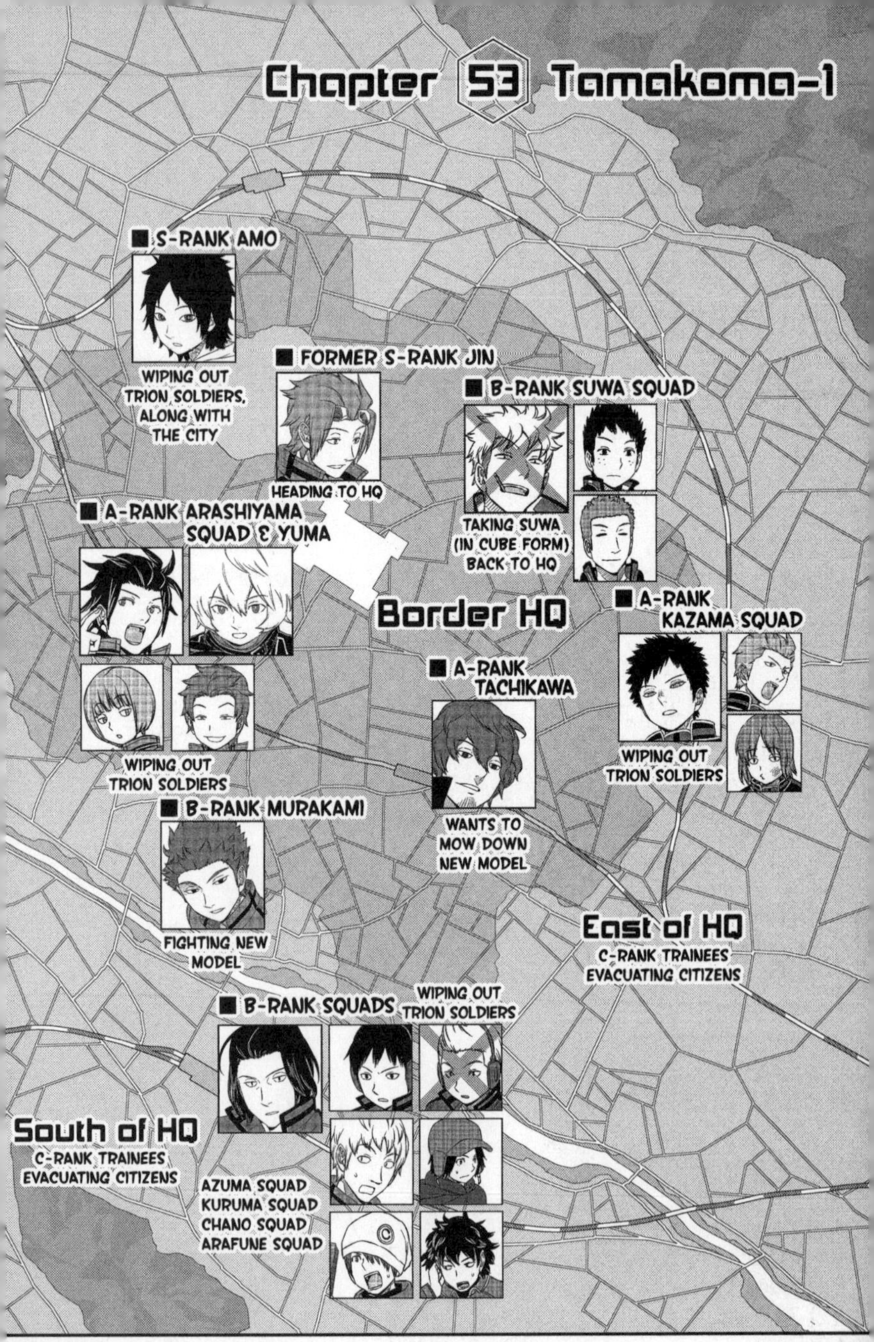
■ S-RANK AMO
WIPING OUT TRION SOLDIERS, ALONG WITH THE CITY
■ FORMER S-RANK JIN
HEADING TO HQ
■ B-RANK SUWA SQUAD
TAKING SUWA (IN CUBE FORM) BACK TO HQ
■ A-RANK ARASHIYAMA SQUAD & YUMA
WIPING OUT TRION SOLDIERS
Border HQ
■ A-RANK KAZAMA SQUAD
WIPING OUT TRION SOLDIERS
■ A-RANK TACHIKAWA
WANTS TO MOW DOWN NEW MODEL
■ B-RANK MURAKAMI
FIGHTING NEW MODEL
East of HQ
C-RANK TRAINEES EVACUATING CITIZENS
■ B-RANK SQUADS
WIPING OUT TRION SOLDIERS
AZUMA SQUAD
KURUMA SQUAD
CHANO SQUAD
ARAFUNE SQUAD
South of HQ
C-RANK TRAINEES EVACUATING CITIZENS

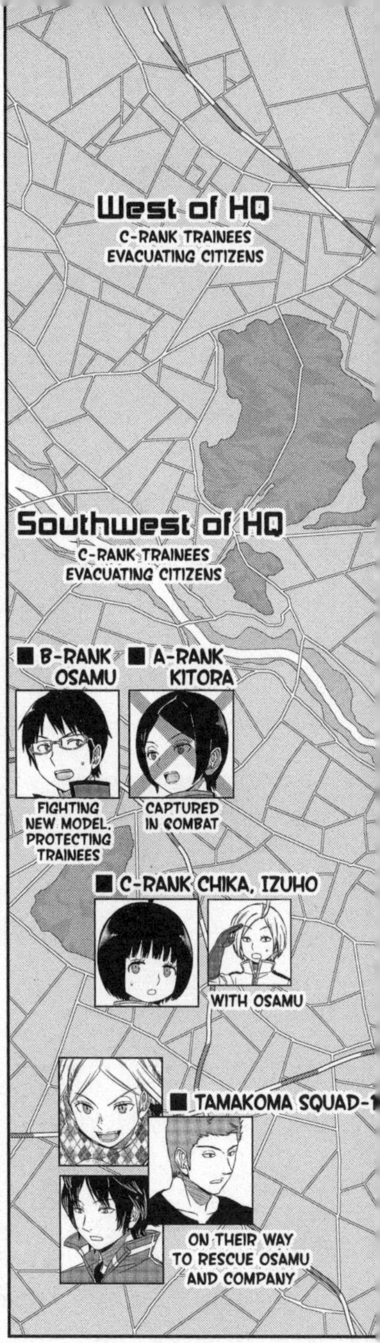
West of HQ
C-RANK TRAINEES EVACUATING CITIZENS
Southwest of HQ
C-RANK TRAINEES EVACUATING CITIZENS
■ A-RANK KITORA
CAPTURED IN COMBAT
■ B-RANK OSAMU
FIGHTING NEW MODEL, PROTECTING TRAINEES
■ C-RANK CHIKA, IZUHO
WITH OSAMU
■ TAMAKOMA SQUAD-1
ON THEIR WAY TO RESCUE OSAMU AND COMPANY

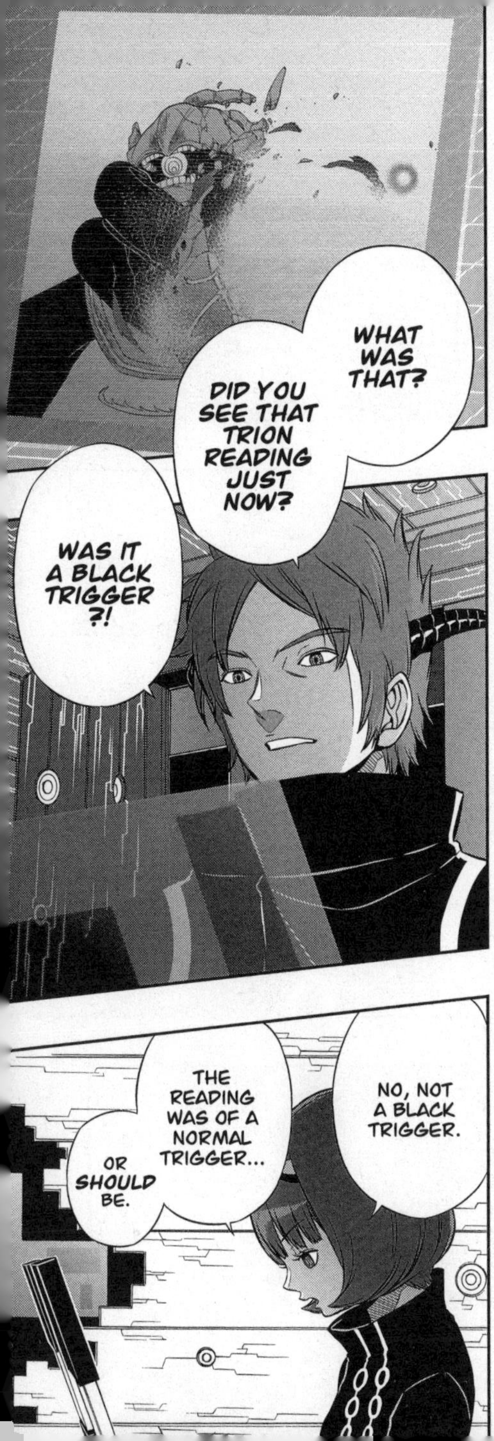
WHAT WAS THAT?
DID YOU SEE THAT TRION READING JUST NOW?
WAS IT A BLACK TRIGGER ?!
NO, NOT A BLACK TRIGGER.
THE READING WAS OF A NORMAL TRIGGER...
OR SHOULD BE.

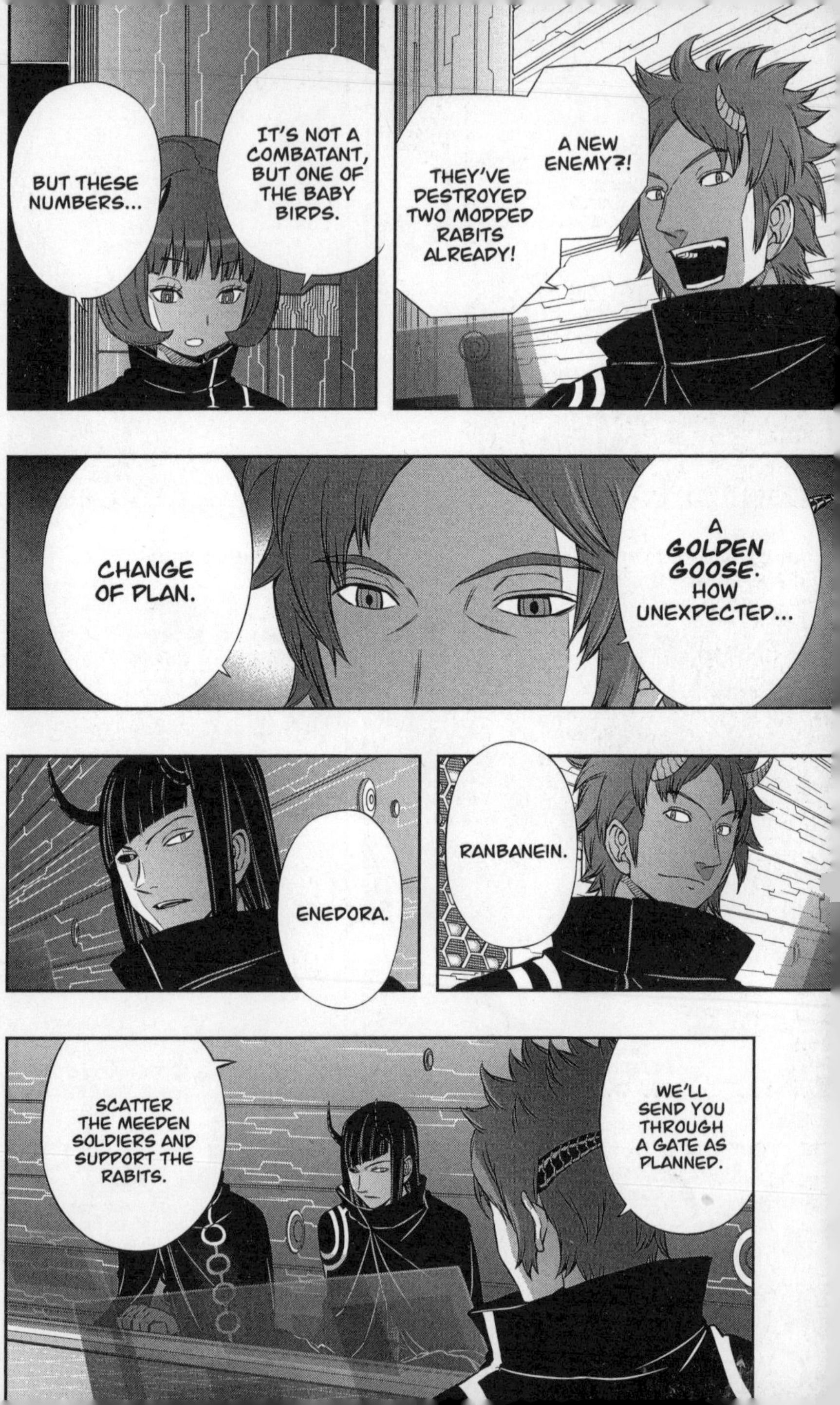
A NEW ENEMY?!
THEY'VE DESTROYED TWO MODDED RABITS ALREADY!
IT'S NOT A COMBATANT, BUT ONE OF THE BABY BIRDS.
BUT THESE NUMBERS...
A GOLDEN GOOSE. HOW UNEXPECTED...
CHANGE OF PLAN.
RANBANEIN.
ENEDORA.
WE'LL SEND YOU THROUGH A GATE AS PLANNED.
SCATTER THE MEEDEN SOLDIERS AND SUPPORT THE RABITS.

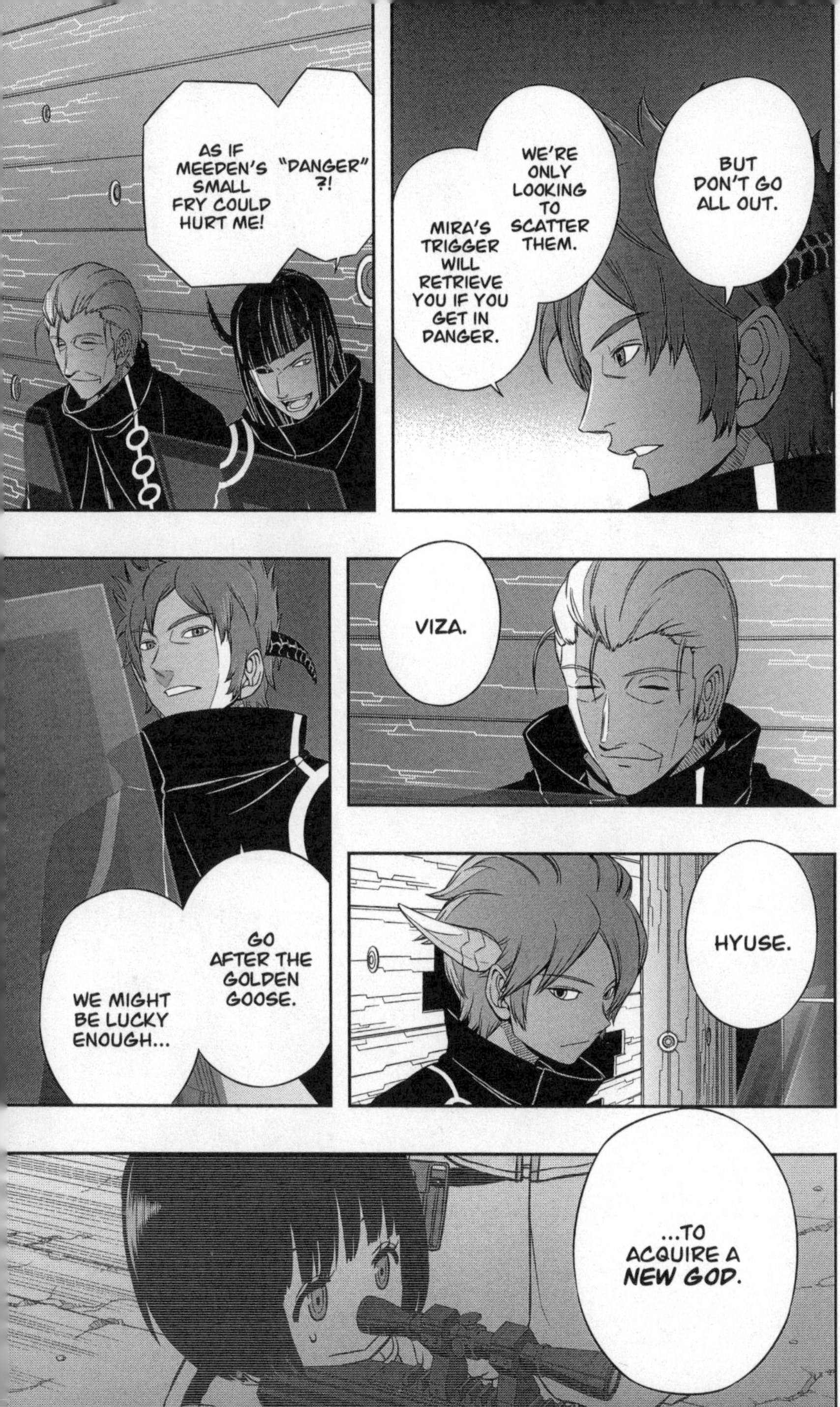
BUT DON'T GO ALL OUT.
WE'RE ONLY LOOKING TO SCATTER THEM.
MIRA'S TRIGGER WILL RETRIEVE YOU IF YOU GET IN DANGER.
"DANGER"?!
AS IF MEEDEN'S SMALL FRY COULD HURT ME!
VIZA.
HYUSE.
GO AFTER THE GOLDEN GOOSE.
WE MIGHT BE LUCKY ENOUGH...
...TO ACQUIRE A NEW GOD.

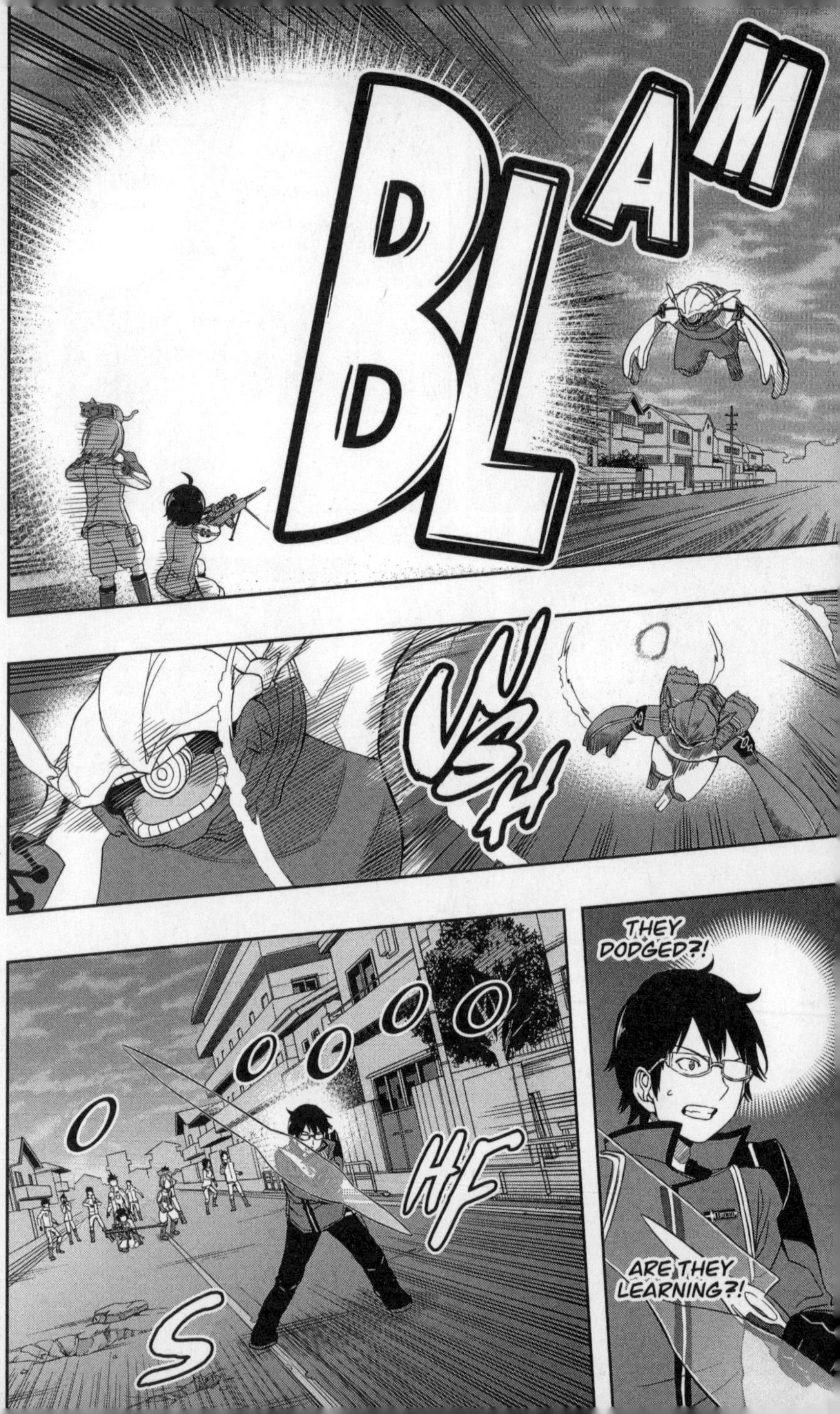
BLAM
VSH
THEY DODGED?!
ARE THEY LEARNING?!
SHOOOOOO

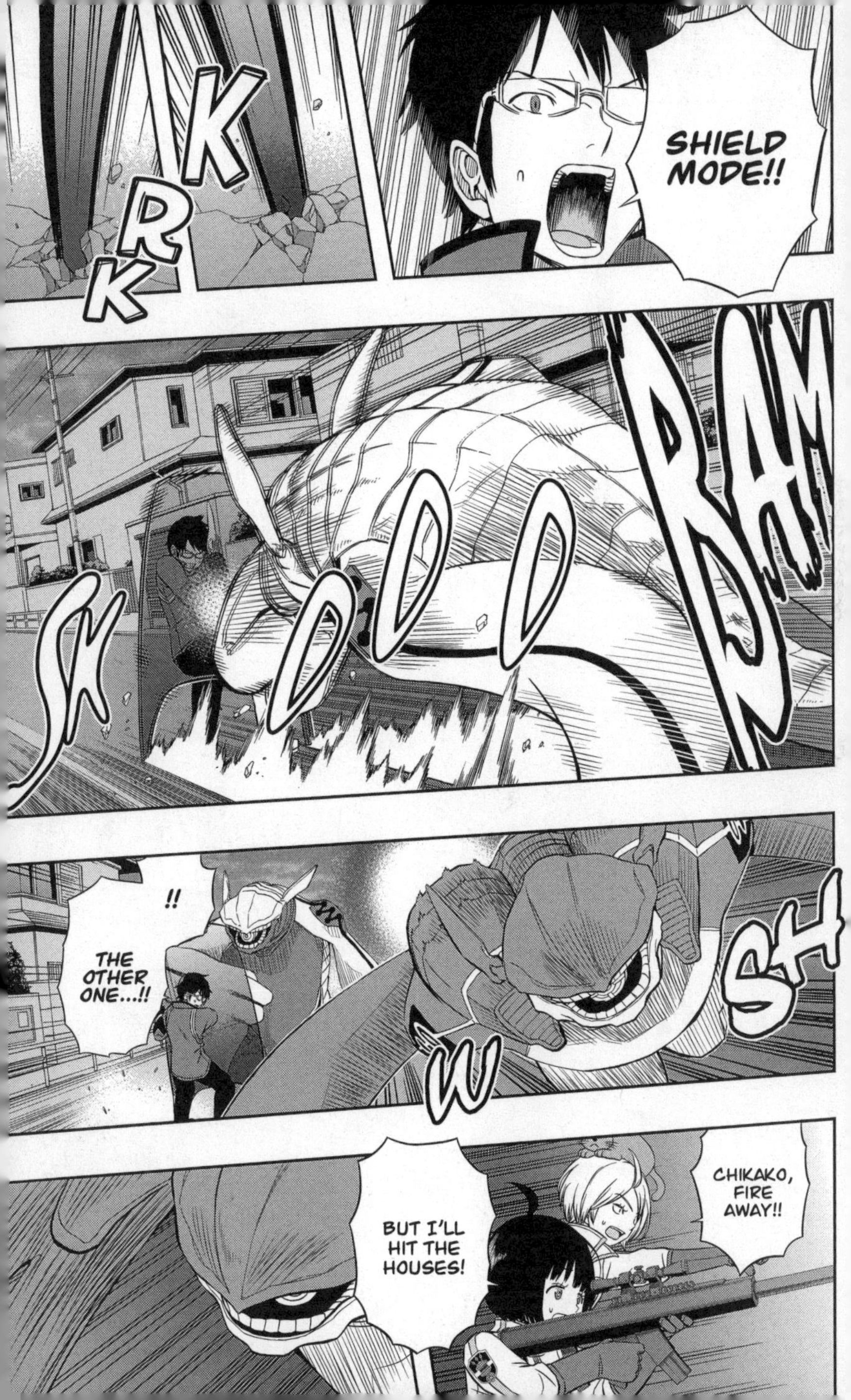
SHIELD MODE!!
KRK
BAM
DDDD
SK
SH
W
!!
THE OTHER ONE...!!
CHIKAKO, FIRE AWAY!!
BUT I'LL HIT THE HOUSES!

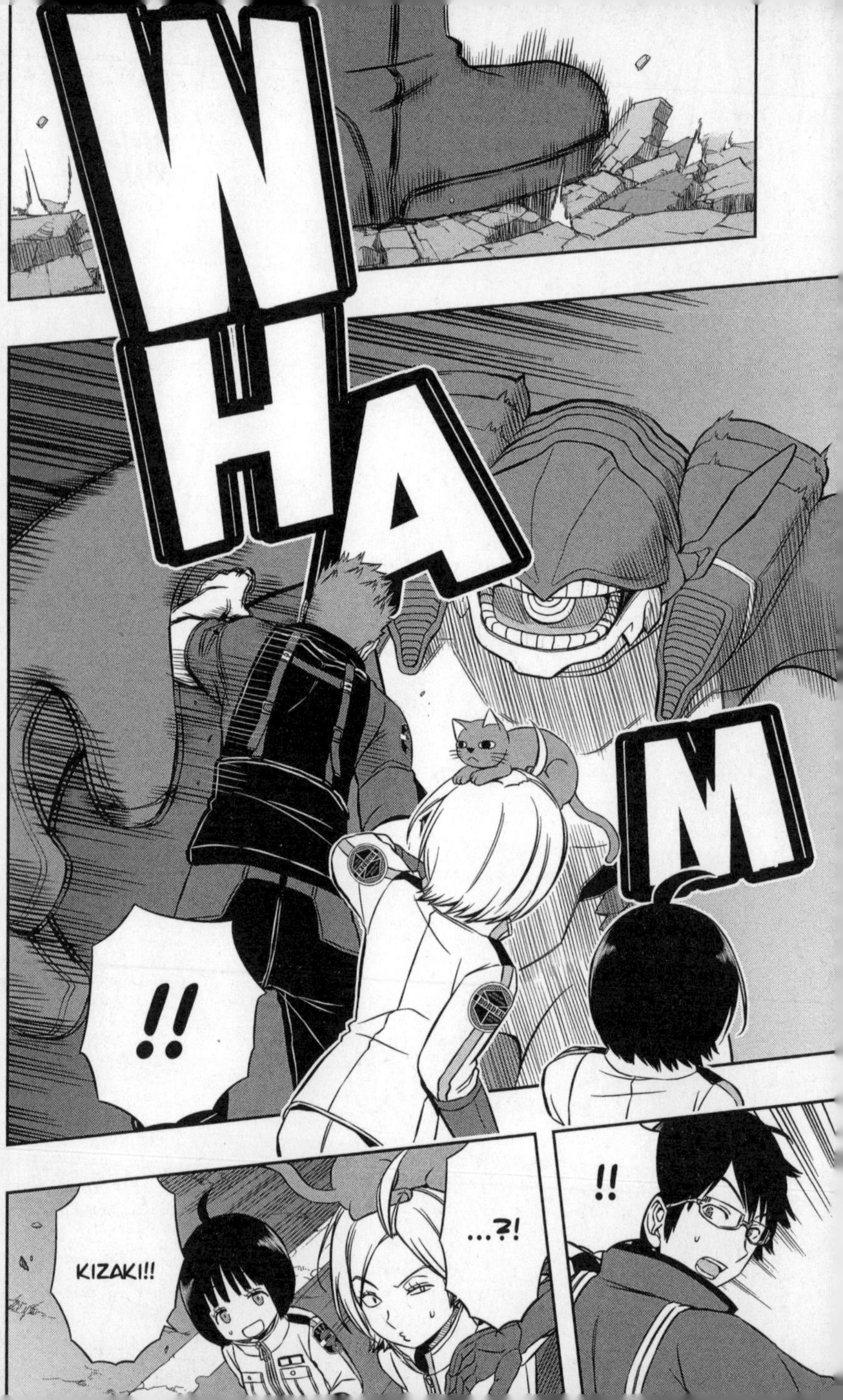
WHAM
!!
!!
...?!
KIZAKI!!

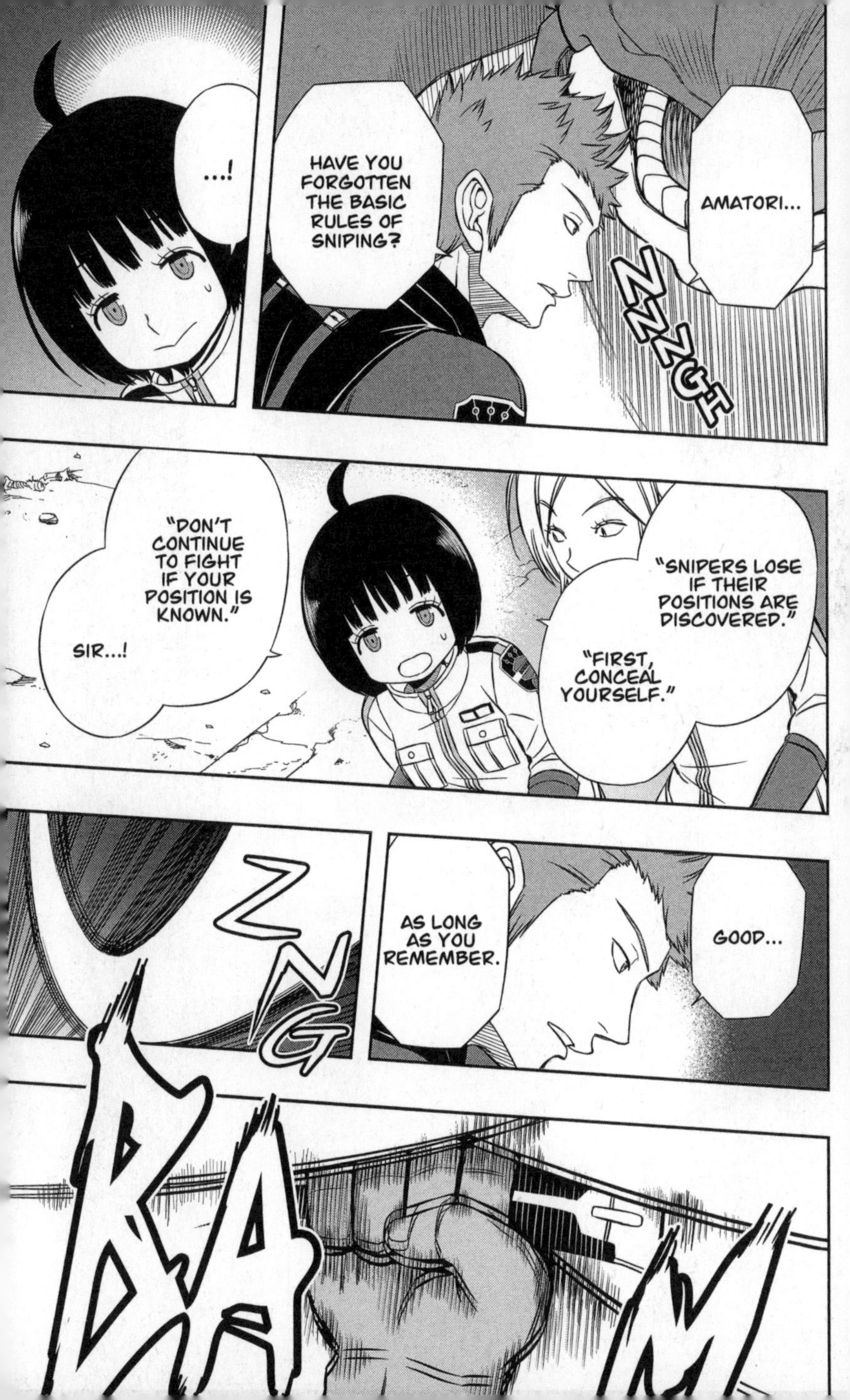
AMATORI...
HAVE YOU FORGOTTEN THE BASIC RULES OF SNIPING?
ZZZGH
...!
"SNIPERS LOSE IF THEIR POSITIONS ARE DISCOVERED."
"FIRST, CONCEAL YOURSELF."
"DON'T CONTINUE TO FIGHT IF YOUR POSITION IS KNOWN."
SIR...!
GOOD...
AS LONG AS YOU REMEMBER.
ZNG
BAM

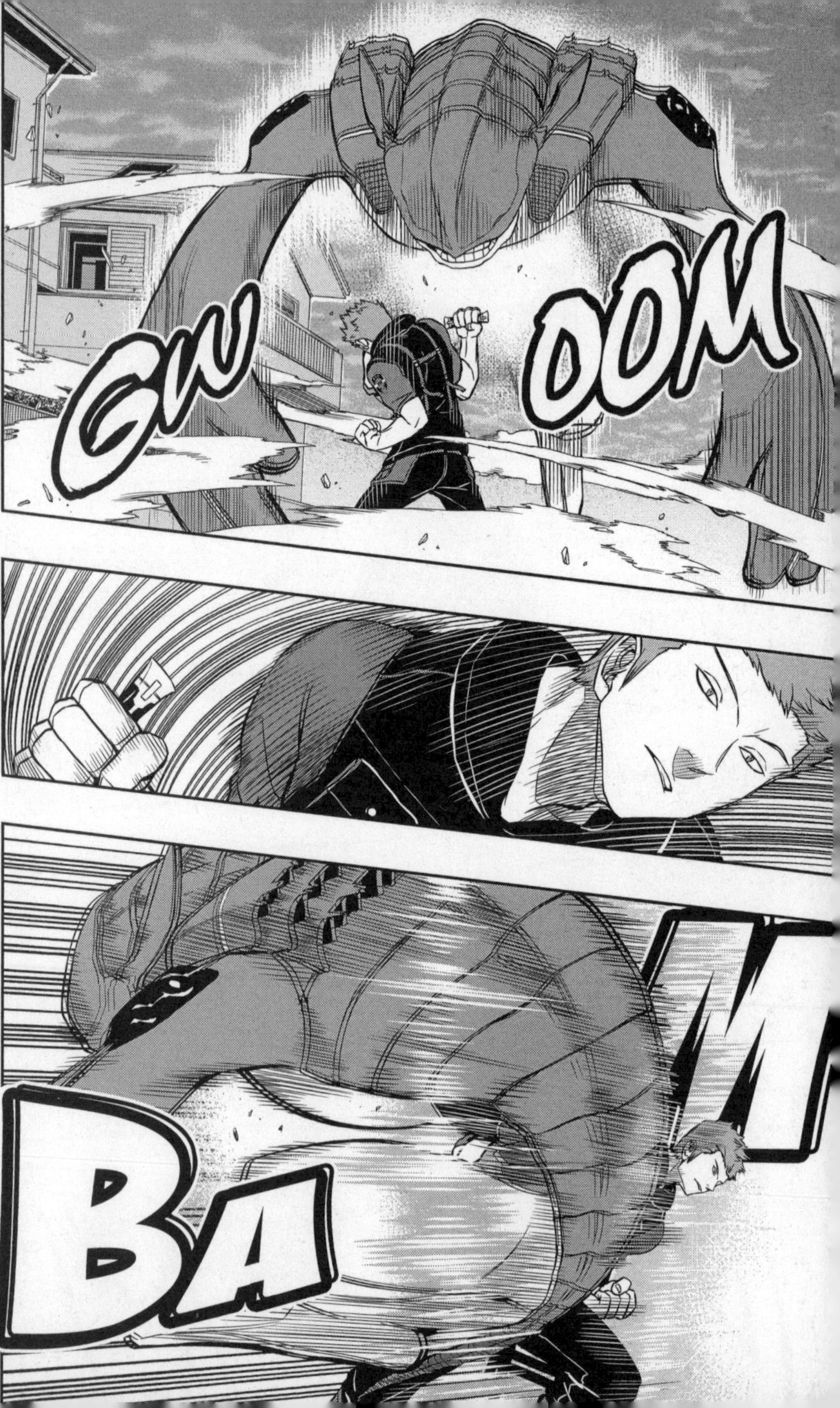
GW OOM
BA M

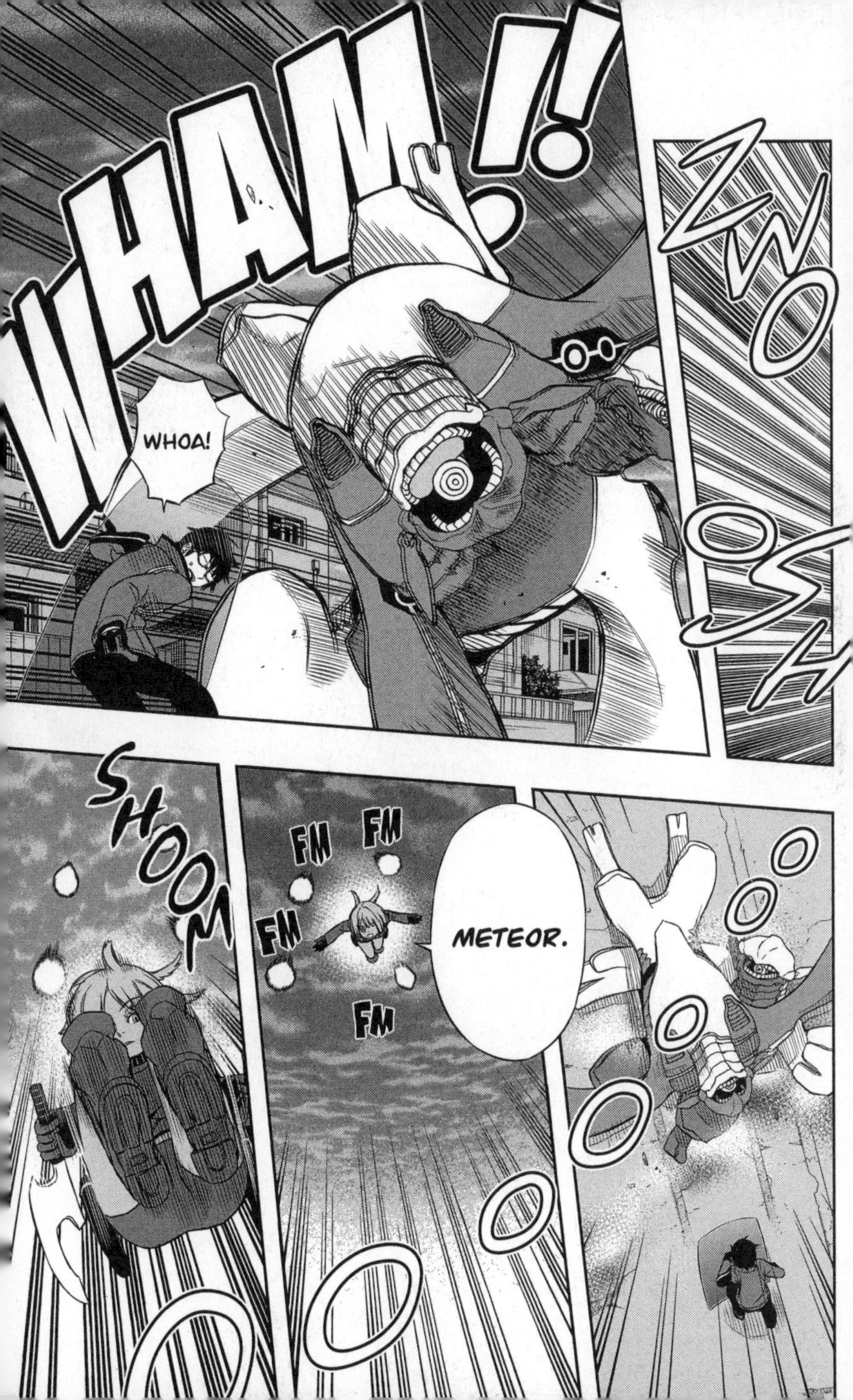
ZWOOSH
WHAM!!
WHOA!
OOOOOO
METEOR.
FM FM
FM
FM
SHOOOM

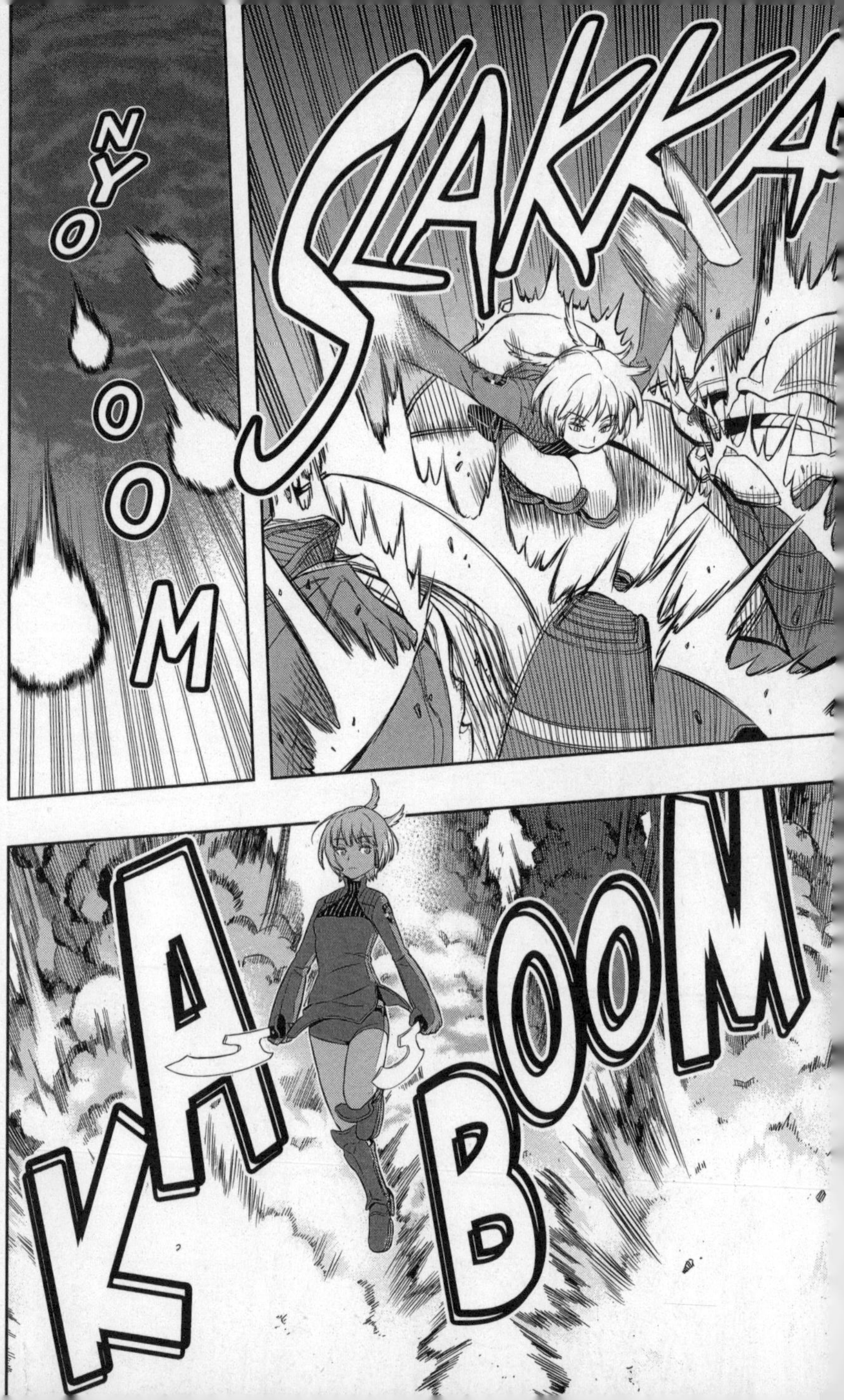
SLAKKA
NYOOOM
KABOOM

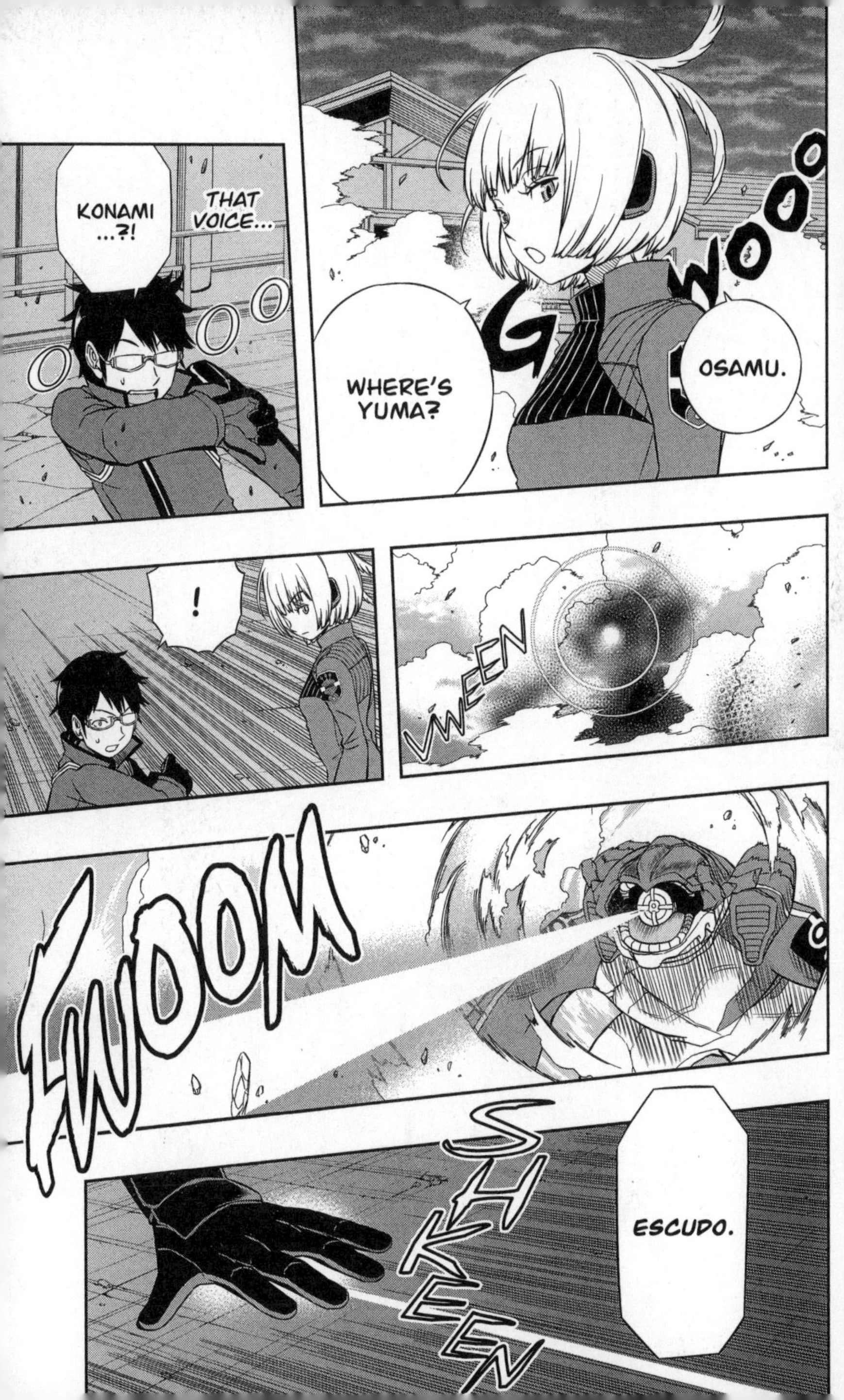
OSAMU.
GWOOO
WHERE'S YUMA?
THAT VOICE...
KONAMI ...?!
OOOO
VWEEN
!
FWOOM
ESCUDO.
SHKEEN

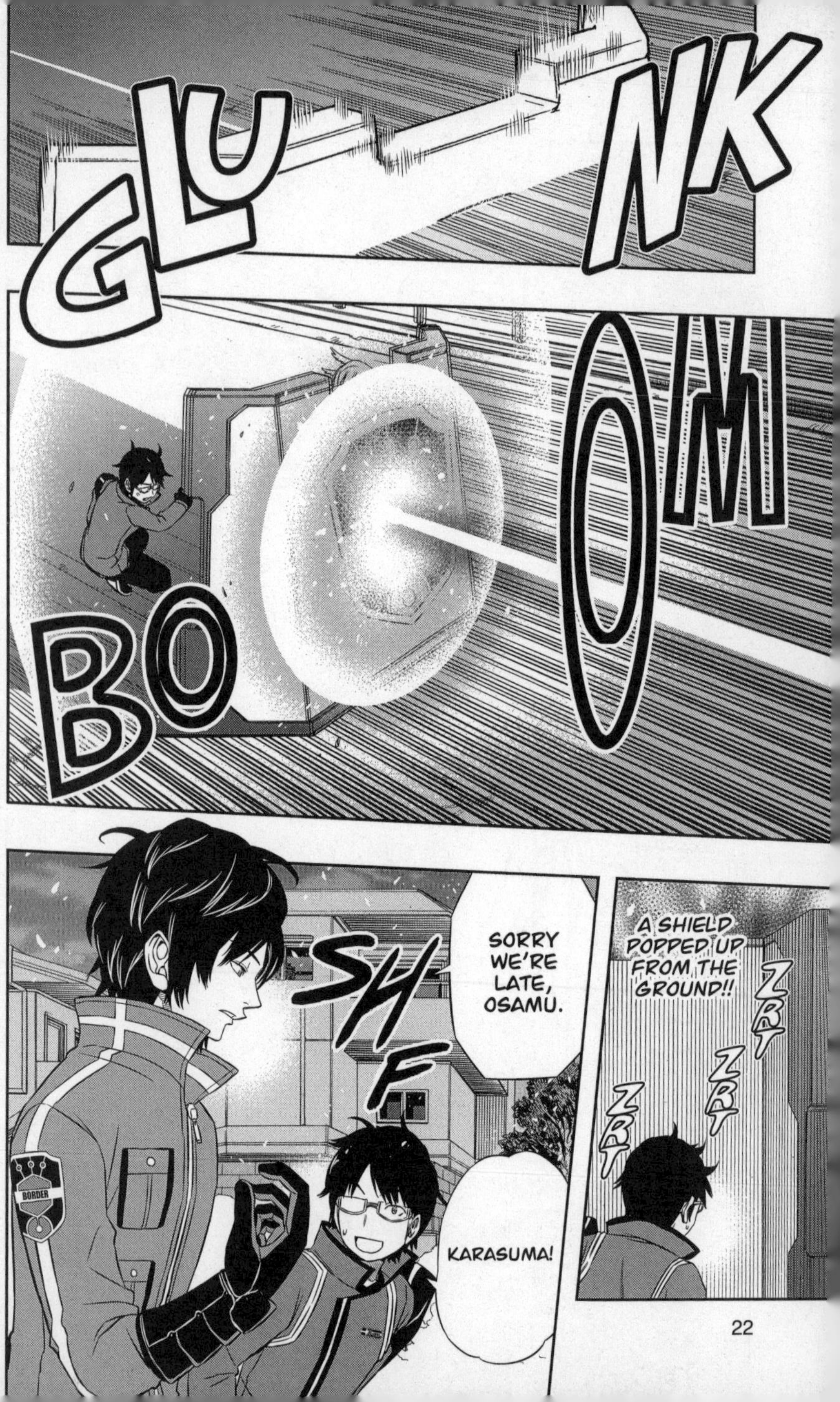
GLUNK
BOOM
A SHIELD POPPED UP FROM THE GROUND!!
ZRT
ZRT
ZRT
SHF
SORRY WE'RE LATE, OSAMU.
KARASUMA!
BORDER

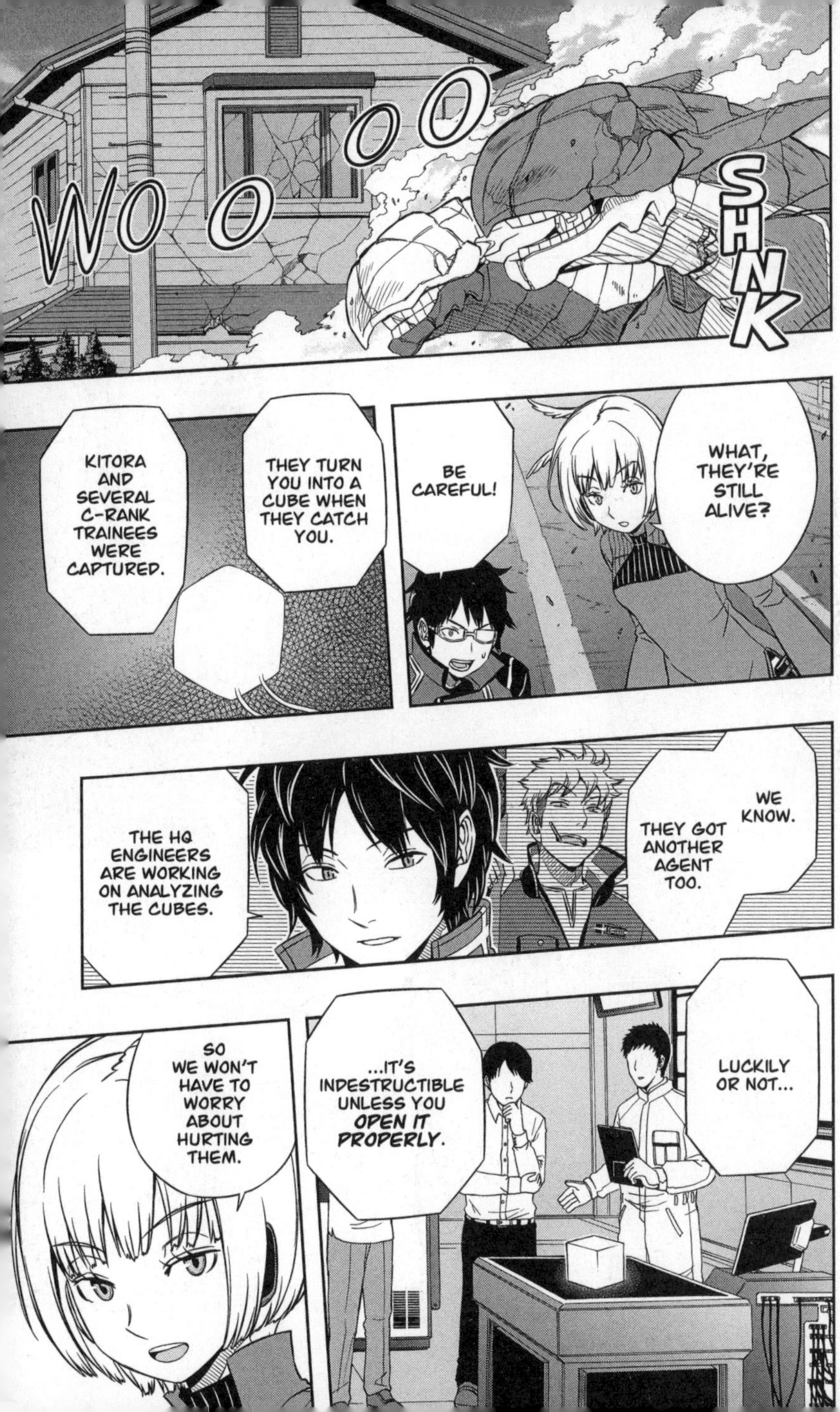
SHNK
WOOOOO
WHAT, THEY'RE STILL ALIVE?
BE CAREFUL!
THEY TURN YOU INTO A CUBE WHEN THEY CATCH YOU.
KITORA AND SEVERAL C-RANK TRAINEES WERE CAPTURED.
WE KNOW.
THEY GOT ANOTHER AGENT TOO.
THE HQ ENGINEERS ARE WORKING ON ANALYZING THE CUBES.
LUCKILY OR NOT...
...IT'S INDESTRUCTIBLE UNLESS YOU *OPEN IT PROPERLY*.
SO WE WON'T HAVE TO WORRY ABOUT HURTING THEM.

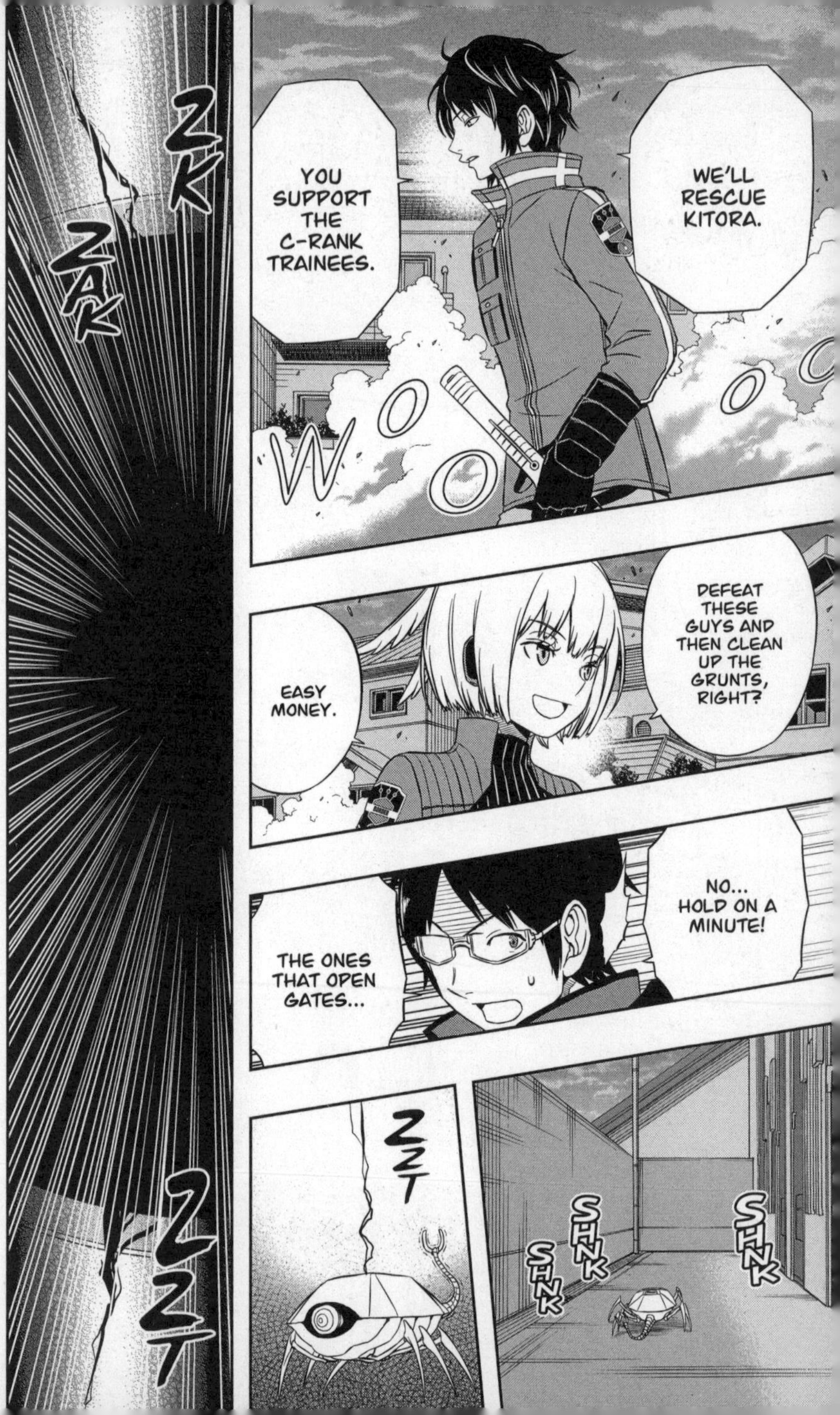
WE'LL RESCUE KITORA.
YOU SUPPORT THE C-RANK TRAINEES.
WOOOO
DEFEAT THESE GUYS AND THEN CLEAN UP THE GRUNTS, RIGHT?
EASY MONEY.
NO... HOLD ON A MINUTE!
THE ONES THAT OPEN GATES...
SHNK
SHNK
SHNK
ZZT
ZK
ZAK
ZZT

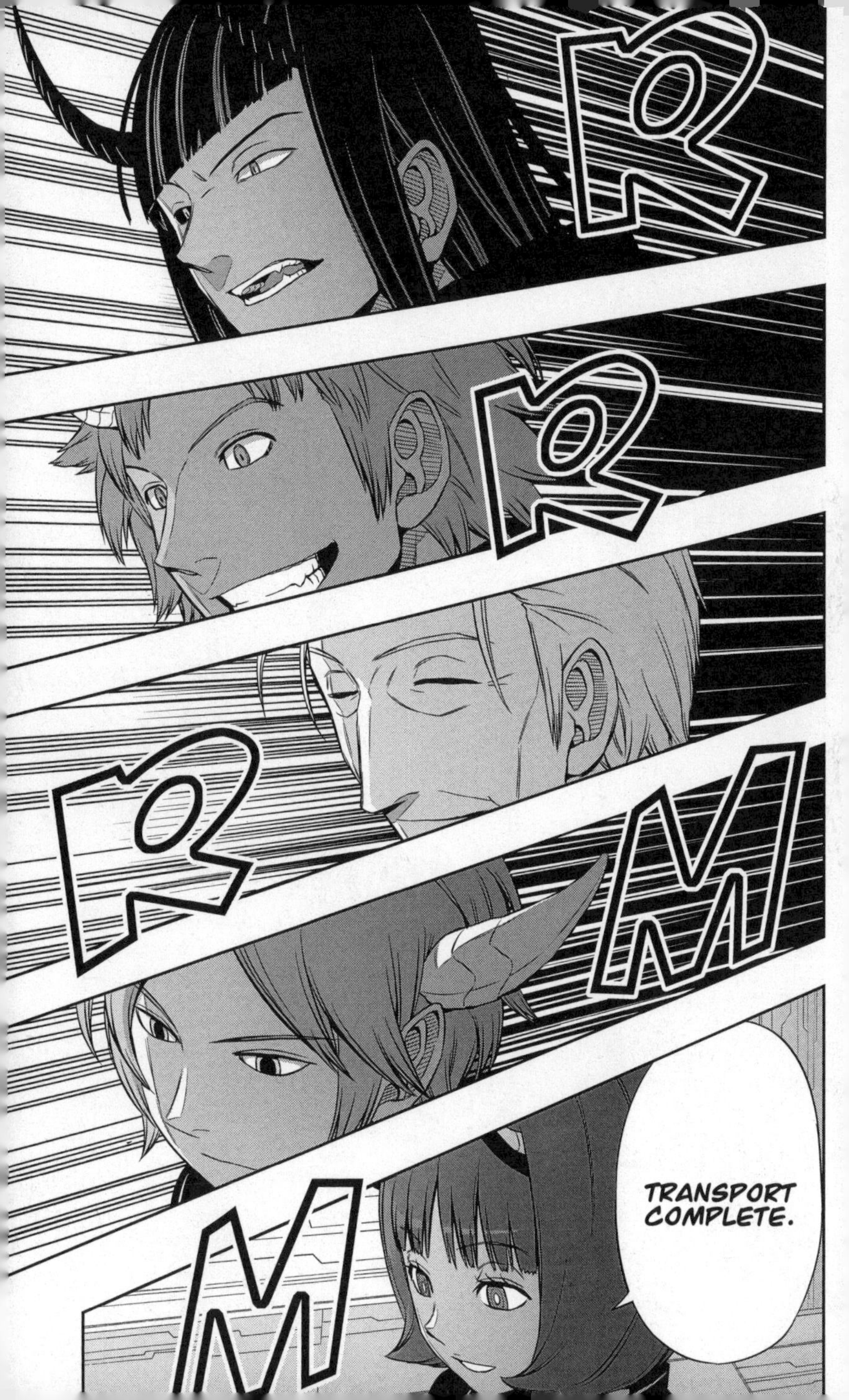
R
R
R
M
M
TRANSPORT COMPLETE.

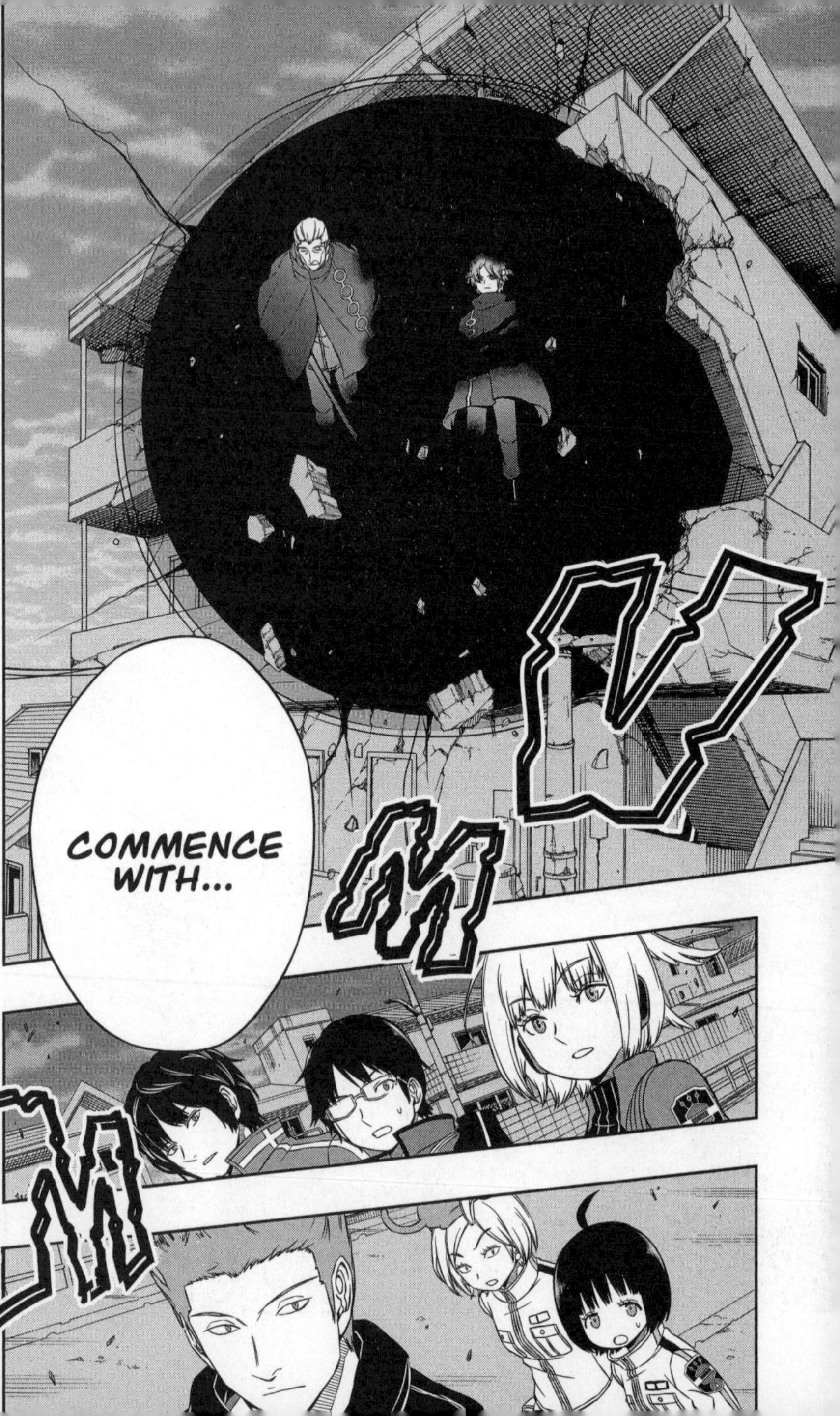
COMMENCE WITH...

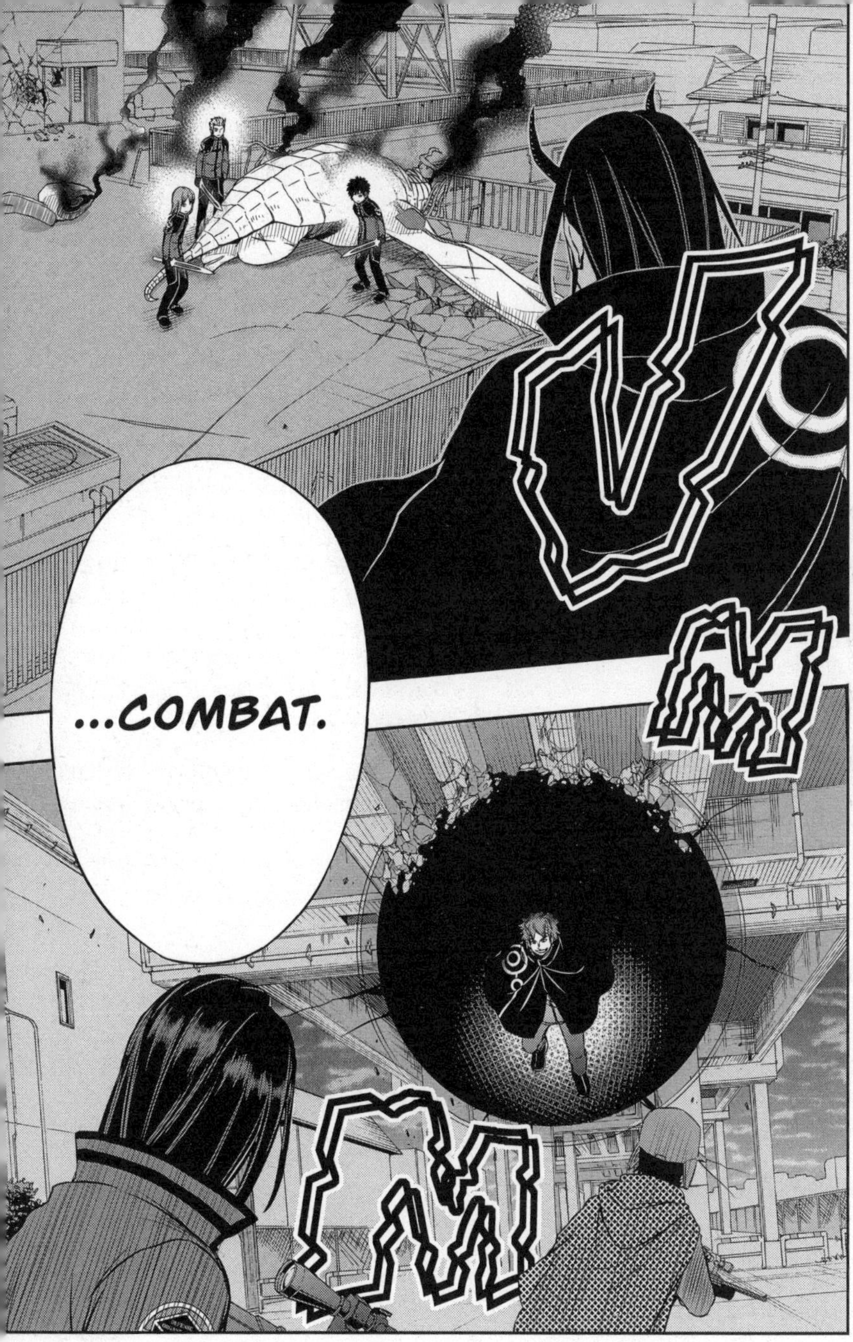
...COMBAT.

Q&A: Part 4

Questions curated by my editor.

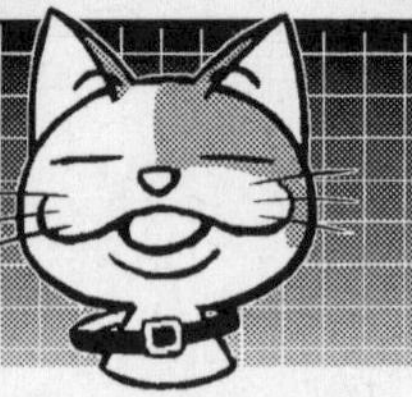

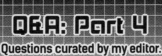

■How are Trion body uniform designs decided?

There are several basic designs, and each squad adds their own embellishments. The jersey style is popular because it doesn't intimidate civilians. Some suits, like Kazama Squad's, have functional additions.

■Is Trion capacity inherited?

Sometimes, but not necessarily. For example, Chika's parents don't have high Trion.

■Do Operators go on away missions?

According to Usami in volume 3, they do. Border has portable computers that operate on Trion, enabling them to support agents without a power supply.

■How many A and B-Rank squads are there?

There are currently eight A-Rank Squads and 20 B-Rank Squads, but they are always in flux from the Rank Wars.

■What does Reiji like to cook?

A dish of stir-fried vegetables with meat, meat and more meat. It's become a staple at Tamakoma.

■How do newly enlisted agents find mentors?

First, you watch matches or videos of people who are good and study up. When you get to a certain level of competence, talk to them directly or get someone to introduce you. Or you can challenge them in individual matches.

■Has anyone risen to A-Rank without mentors (besides the initial members)?

Several. Like Izumi, Kikuchihara and Yoneya. You can get better without a mentor if you have good rivals.

■When Tachikawa destroyed the Ilgar, did he teleport or jump from the roof?

He probably used an optional Trigger called a Grasshopper. Midorikawa uses it in this volume.

■Do A-Rank high schoolers all go to the same school?

There are two schools affiliated with Border (one regular and one college prep). Kodera, Narasaka, Usami, Utagawa and Kikuchihara go to the college prep school. Most of the others go to a regular school. Some, like Konami (and Kitora), go to a private girls school.

■Where is the physical body while the Trion body is activated?

Stored where the Trion body was, inside the Trigger holder.

Chapter 54 Aftokrator

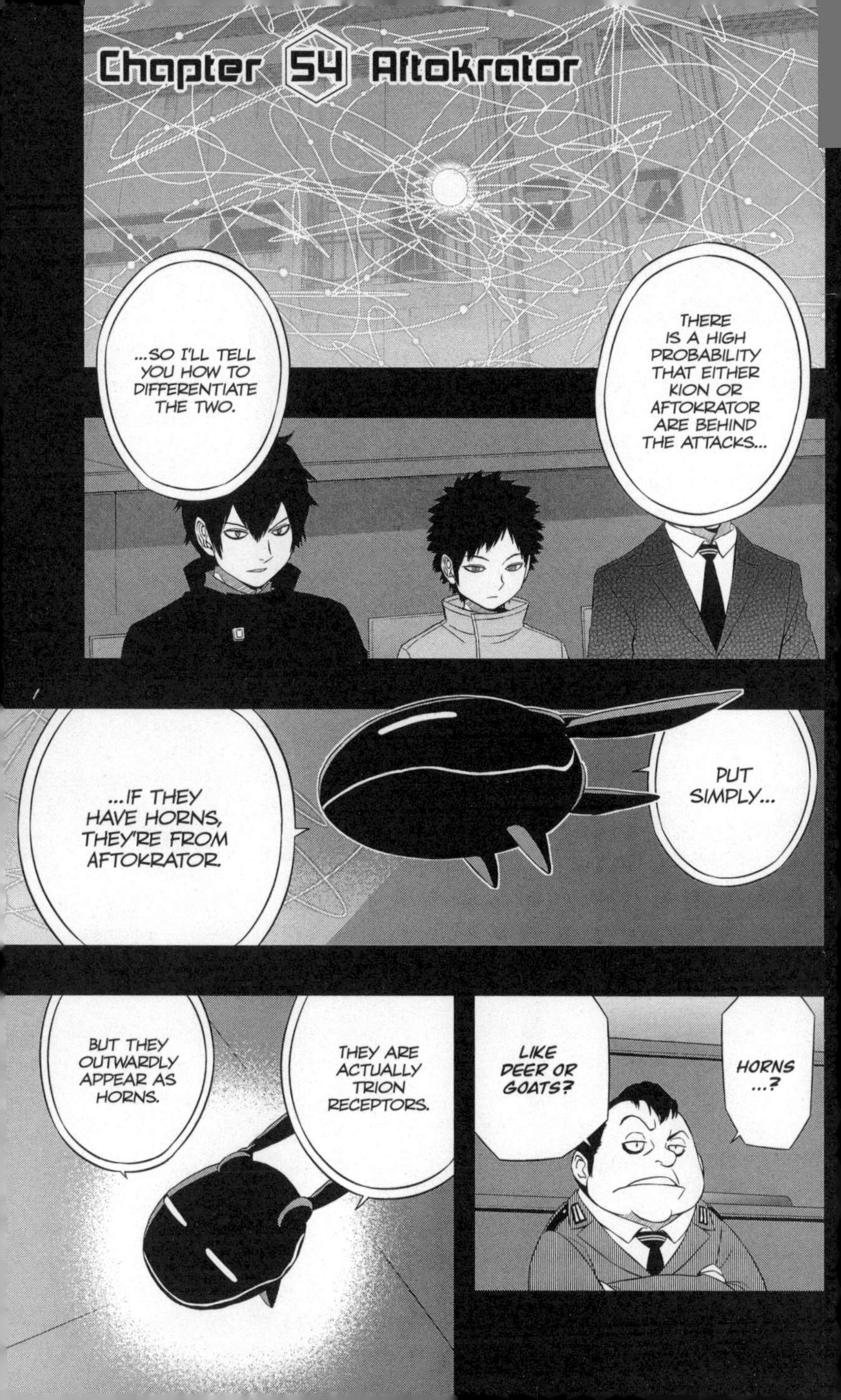

THERE IS A HIGH PROBABILITY THAT EITHER KION OR AFTOKRATOR ARE BEHIND THE ATTACKS...
...SO I'LL TELL YOU HOW TO DIFFERENTIATE THE TWO.
PUT SIMPLY...
...IF THEY HAVE HORNS, THEY'RE FROM AFTOKRATOR.
HORNS ...?
LIKE DEER OR GOATS?
THEY ARE ACTUALLY TRION RECEPTORS.
BUT THEY OUTWARDLY APPEAR AS HORNS.

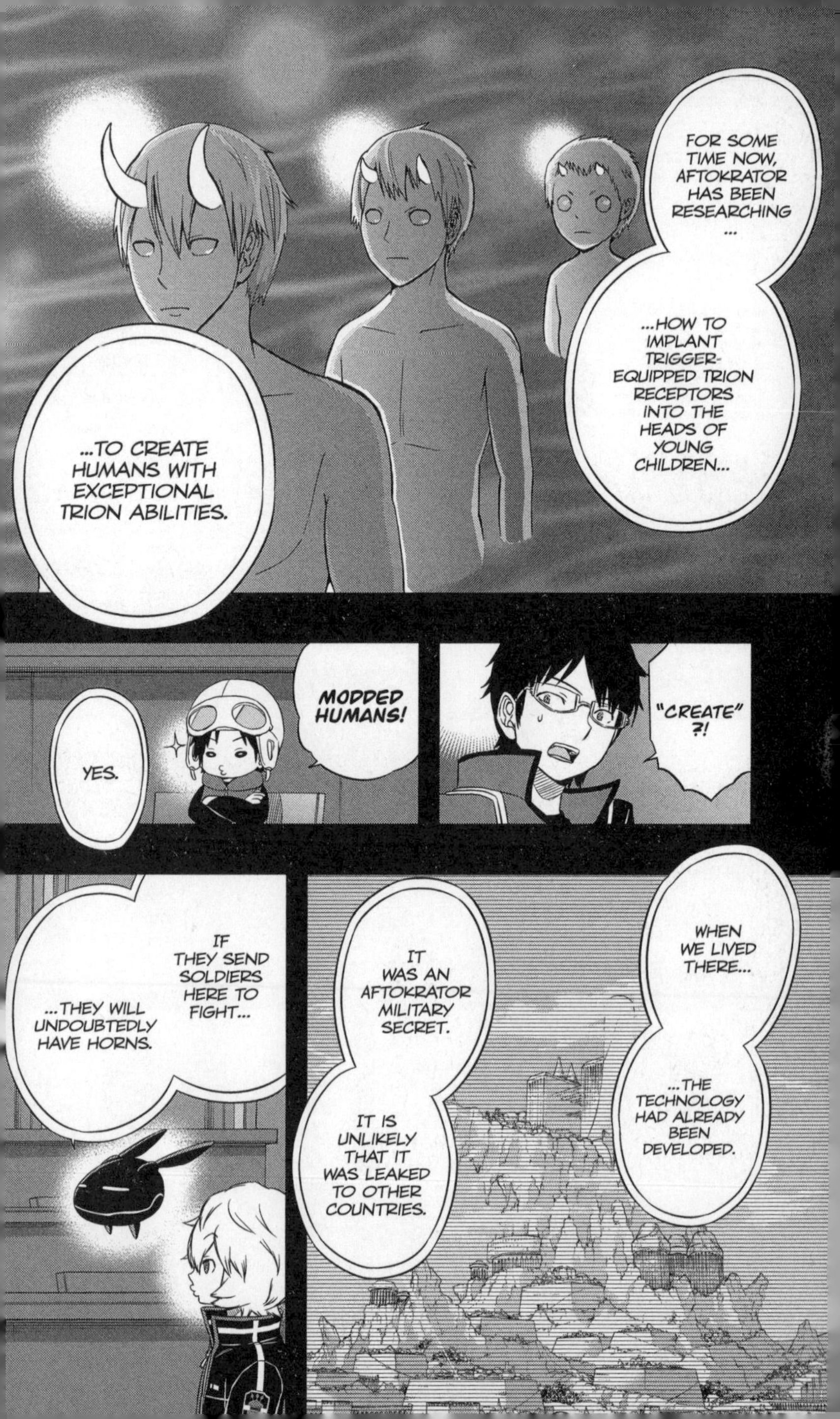
FOR SOME TIME NOW, AFTOKRATOR HAS BEEN RESEARCHING ...
...HOW TO IMPLANT TRIGGER-EQUIPPED TRION RECEPTORS INTO THE HEADS OF YOUNG CHILDREN...
...TO CREATE HUMANS WITH EXCEPTIONAL TRION ABILITIES.
"CREATE" ?!
MODDED HUMANS!
YES.
WHEN WE LIVED THERE...
...THE TECHNOLOGY HAD ALREADY BEEN DEVELOPED.
IT WAS AN AFTOKRATOR MILITARY SECRET.
IT IS UNLIKELY THAT IT WAS LEAKED TO OTHER COUNTRIES.
IF THEY SEND SOLDIERS HERE TO FIGHT...
...THEY WILL UNDOUBTEDLY HAVE HORNS.

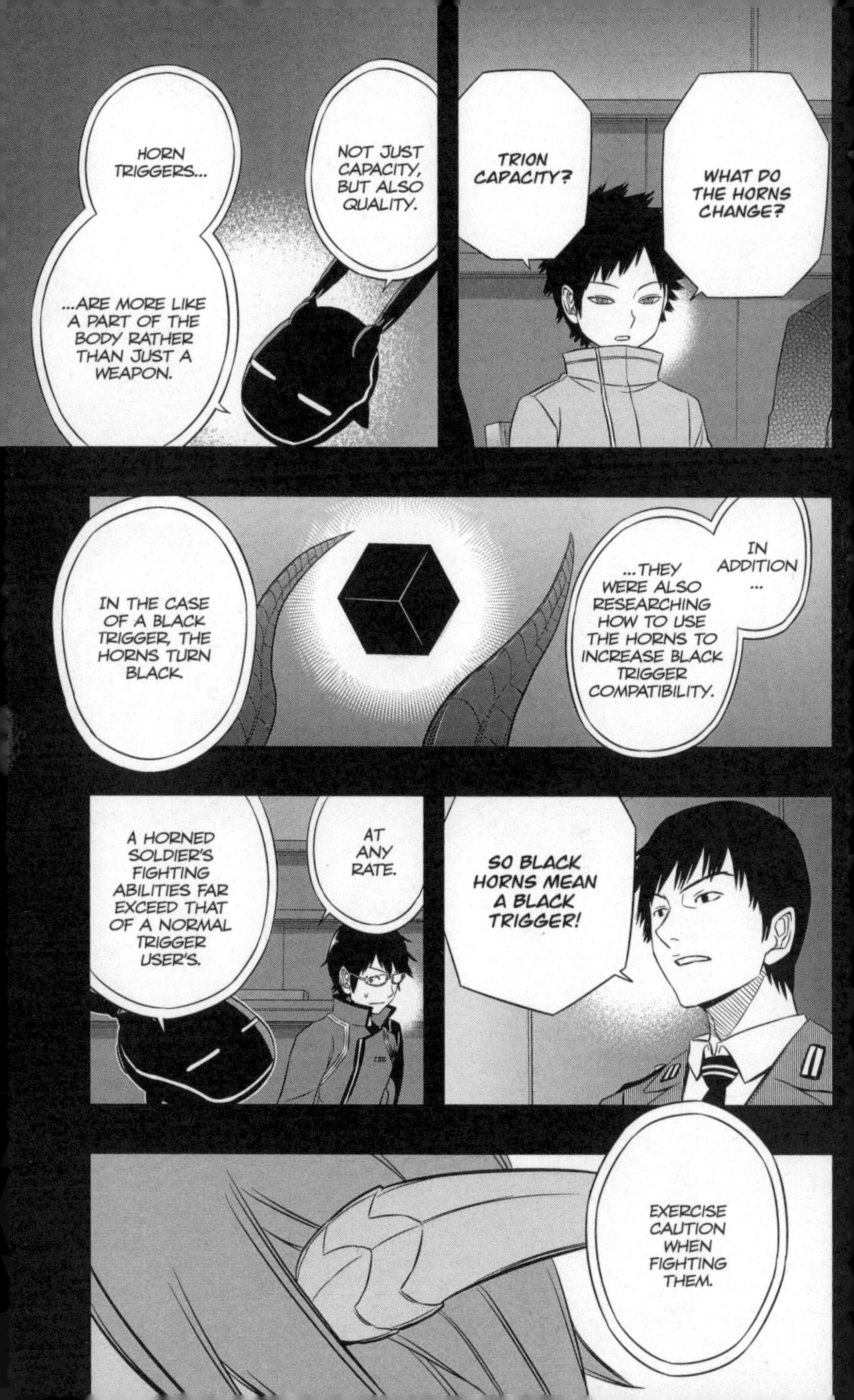
WHAT DO THE HORNS CHANGE?
TRION CAPACITY?
NOT JUST CAPACITY, BUT ALSO QUALITY.
HORN TRIGGERS...
...ARE MORE LIKE A PART OF THE BODY RATHER THAN JUST A WEAPON.
IN ADDITION...
...THEY WERE ALSO RESEARCHING HOW TO USE THE HORNS TO INCREASE BLACK TRIGGER COMPATIBILITY.
IN THE CASE OF A BLACK TRIGGER, THE HORNS TURN BLACK.
SO BLACK HORNS MEAN A BLACK TRIGGER!
AT ANY RATE.
A HORNED SOLDIER'S FIGHTING ABILITIES FAR EXCEED THAT OF A NORMAL TRIGGER USER'S.
EXERCISE CAUTION WHEN FIGHTING THEM.

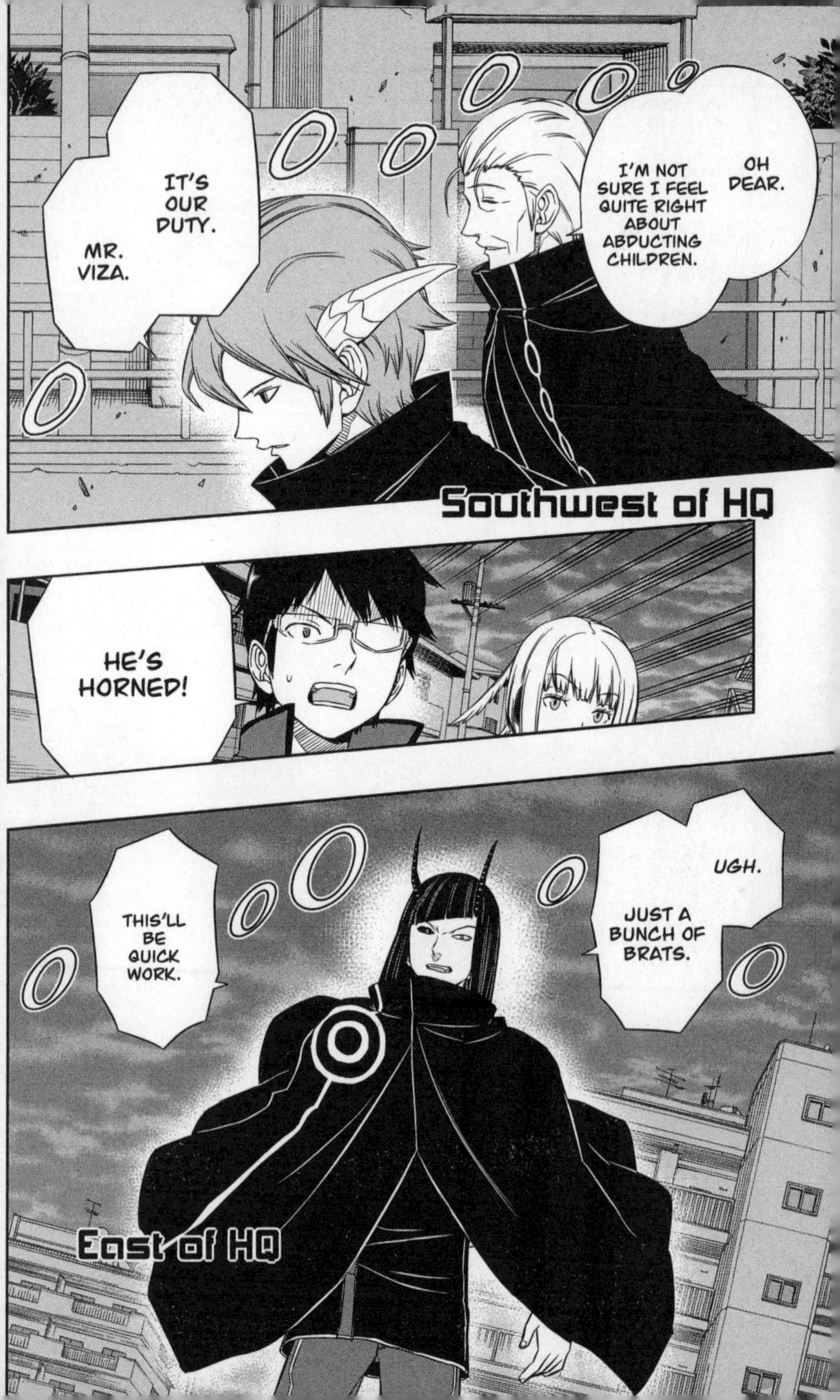
OH DEAR.
I'M NOT SURE I FEEL QUITE RIGHT ABOUT ABDUCTING CHILDREN.
IT'S OUR DUTY.
MR. VIZA.
Southwest of HQ
HE'S HORNED!
UGH.
JUST A BUNCH OF BRATS.
THIS'LL BE QUICK WORK.
East of HQ

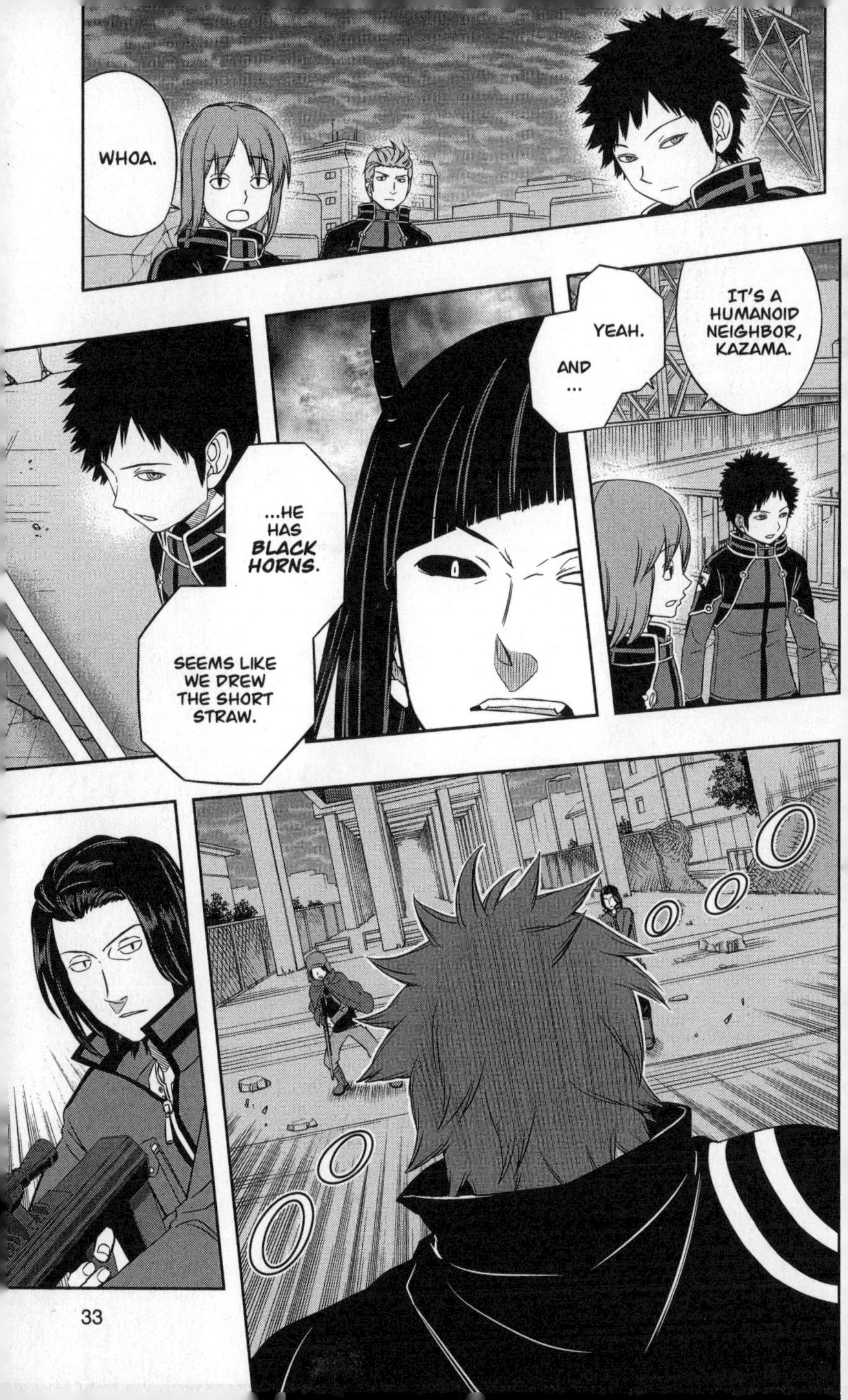
WHOA.
IT'S A HUMANOID NEIGHBOR, KAZAMA.
YEAH.
AND ...
...HE HAS BLACK HORNS.
SEEMS LIKE WE DREW THE SHORT STRAW.

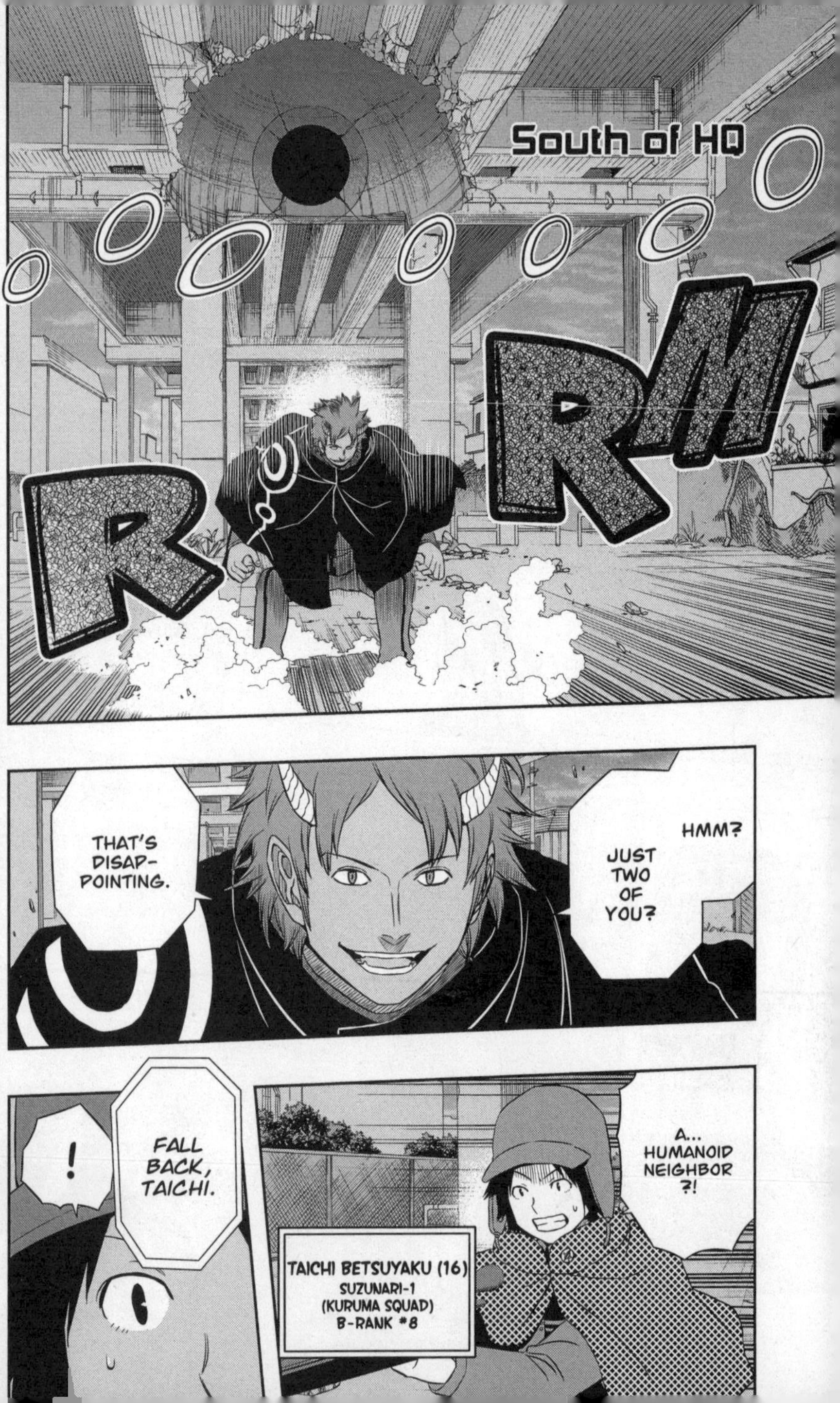
South of HQ
ROOOOOOORM
HMM?
JUST TWO OF YOU?
THAT'S DISAP-POINTING.
A... HUMANOID NEIGHBOR?!
TAICHI BETSUYAKU (16)
SUZUNARI-1
(KURUMA SQUAD)
B-RANK #8
FALL BACK, TAICHI.
!

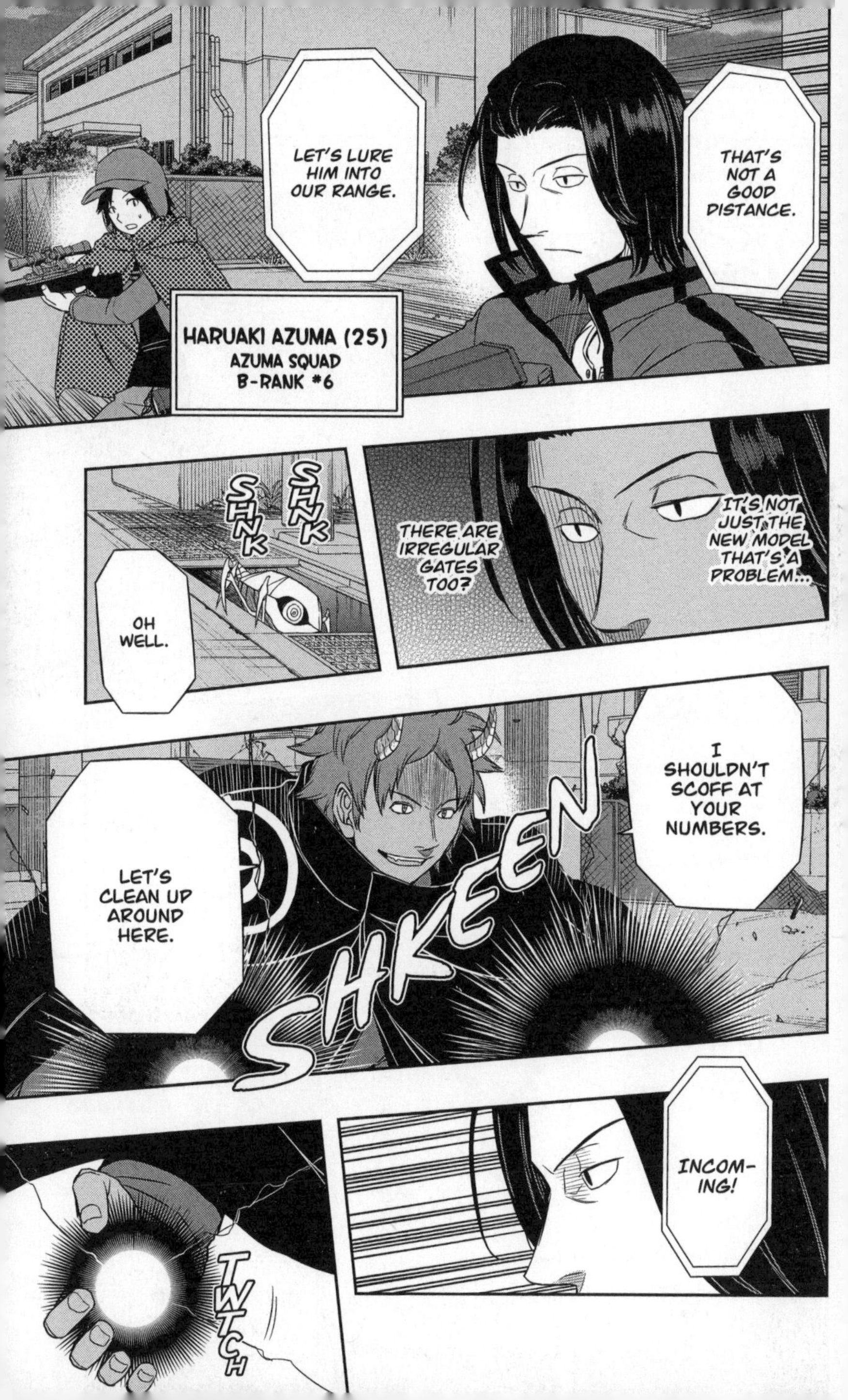
THAT'S NOT A GOOD DISTANCE.
LET'S LURE HIM INTO OUR RANGE.
HARUAKI AZUMA (25)
AZUMA SQUAD
B-RANK #6
IT'S NOT JUST THE NEW MODEL THAT'S A PROBLEM...
THERE ARE IRREGULAR GATES TOO?
SHNK
SHNK
OH WELL.
I SHOULDN'T SCOFF AT YOUR NUMBERS.
SHKEEN
LET'S CLEAN UP AROUND HERE.
INCOM-ING!
TWTCH

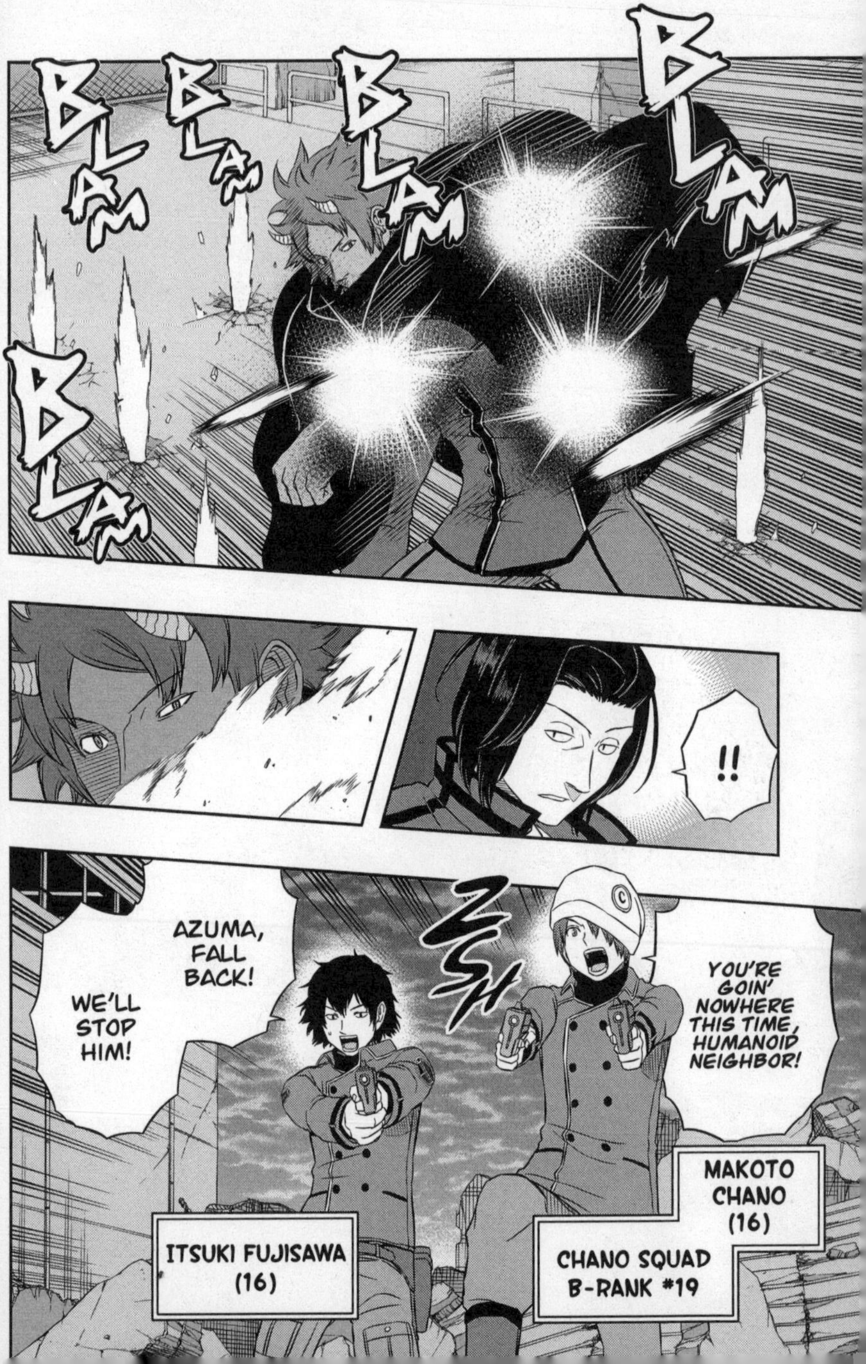
BLAM
BLAM
BLAM
BLAM
!!
YOU'RE GOIN' NOWHERE THIS TIME, HUMANOID NEIGHBOR!
ZSH
AZUMA, FALL BACK!
WE'LL STOP HIM!
MAKOTO CHANO (16)
CHANO SQUAD B-RANK #19
ITSUKI FUJISAWA (16)

READ THIS WAY

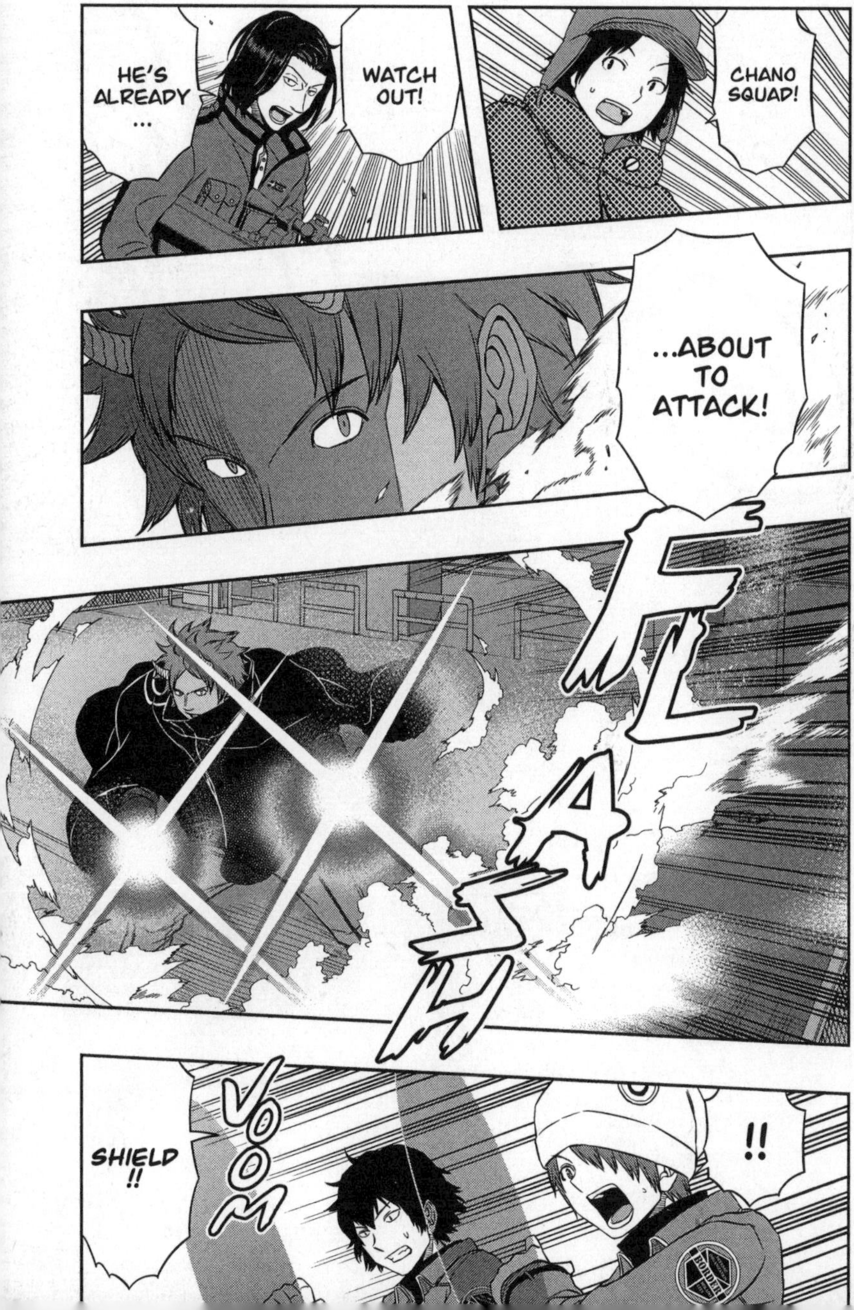
CHANO SQUAD!
WATCH OUT!
HE'S ALREADY ...
...ABOUT TO ATTACK!
FLASH
!!
VOOM
SHIELD !!

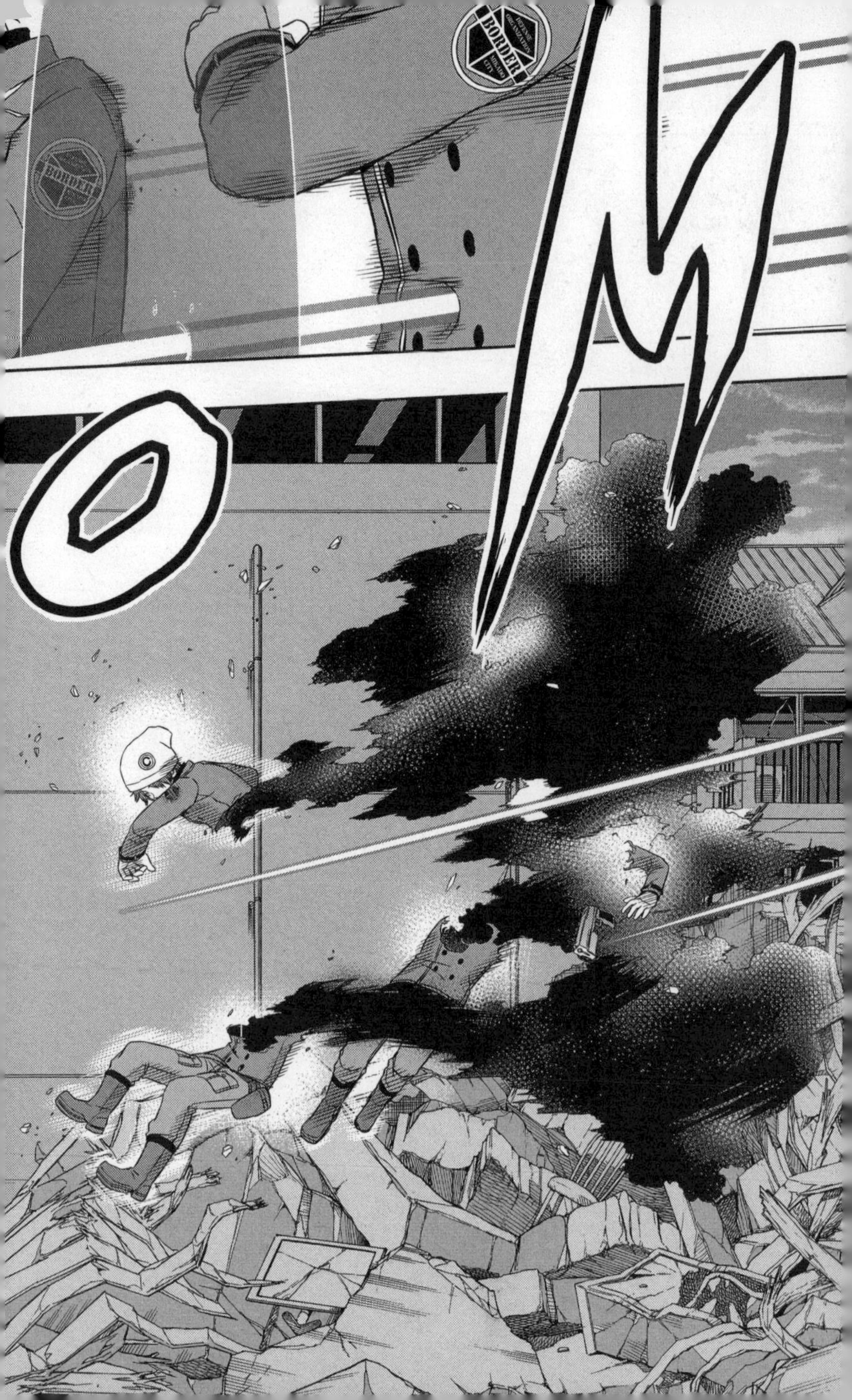
OM
BORDER

READ THIS WAY

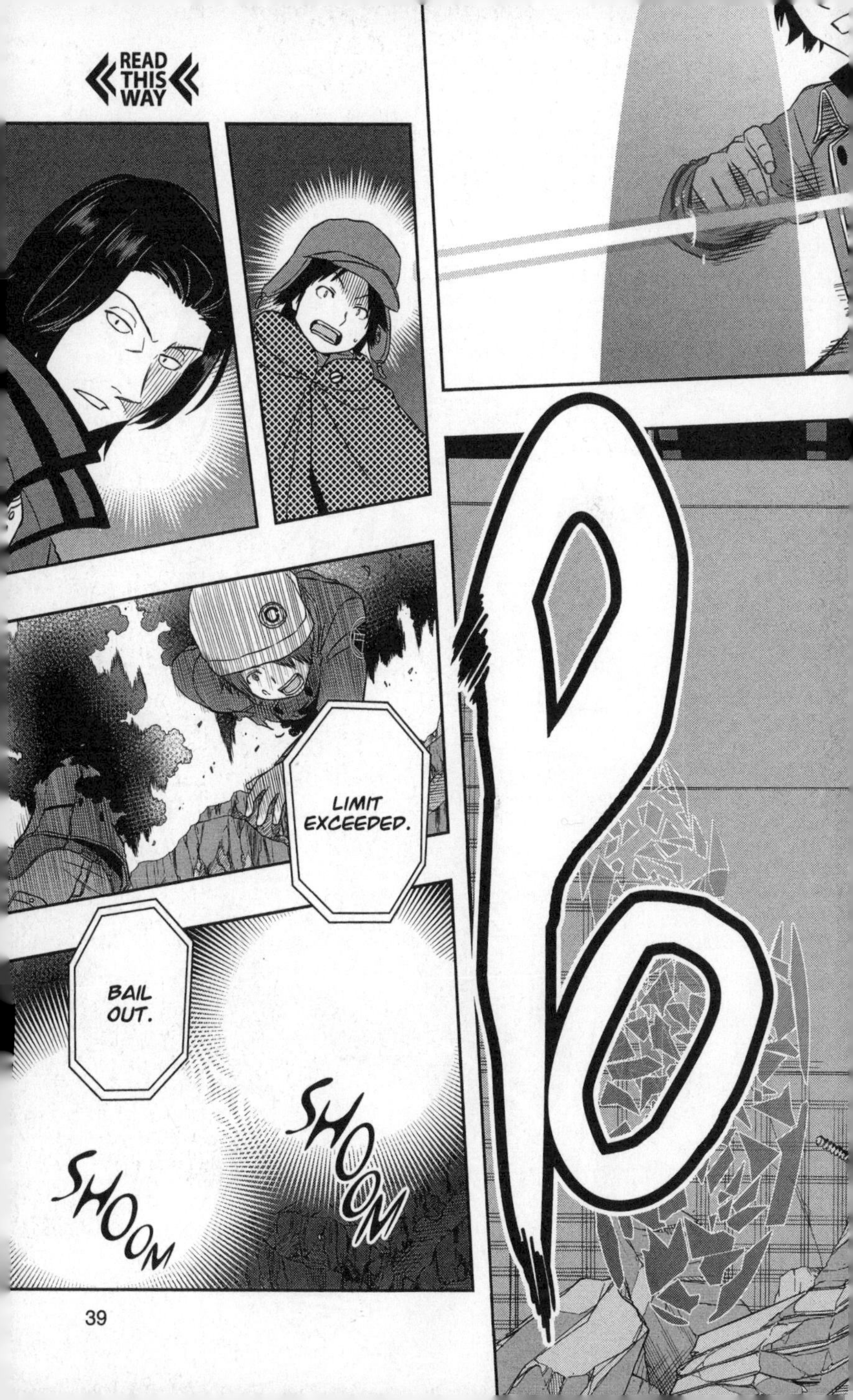
LIMIT EXCEEDED.
BAIL OUT.
SHOOM
SHOOM

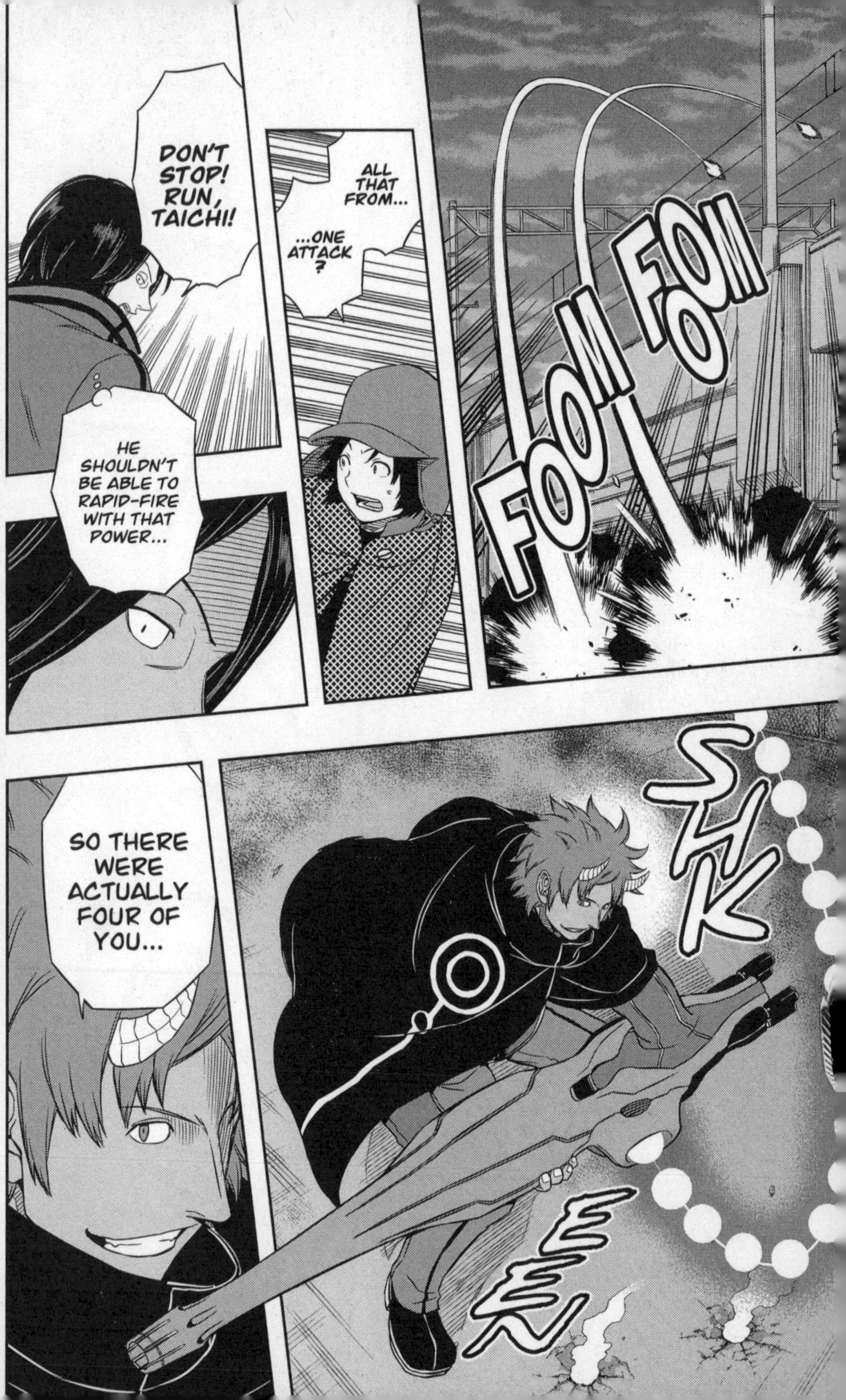

FOOM FOOM
ALL THAT FROM...
...ONE ATTACK?
DON'T STOP! RUN, TAICHI!
HE SHOULDN'T BE ABLE TO RAPID-FIRE WITH THAT POWER...
SHK
EEEN
SO THERE WERE ACTUALLY FOUR OF YOU...

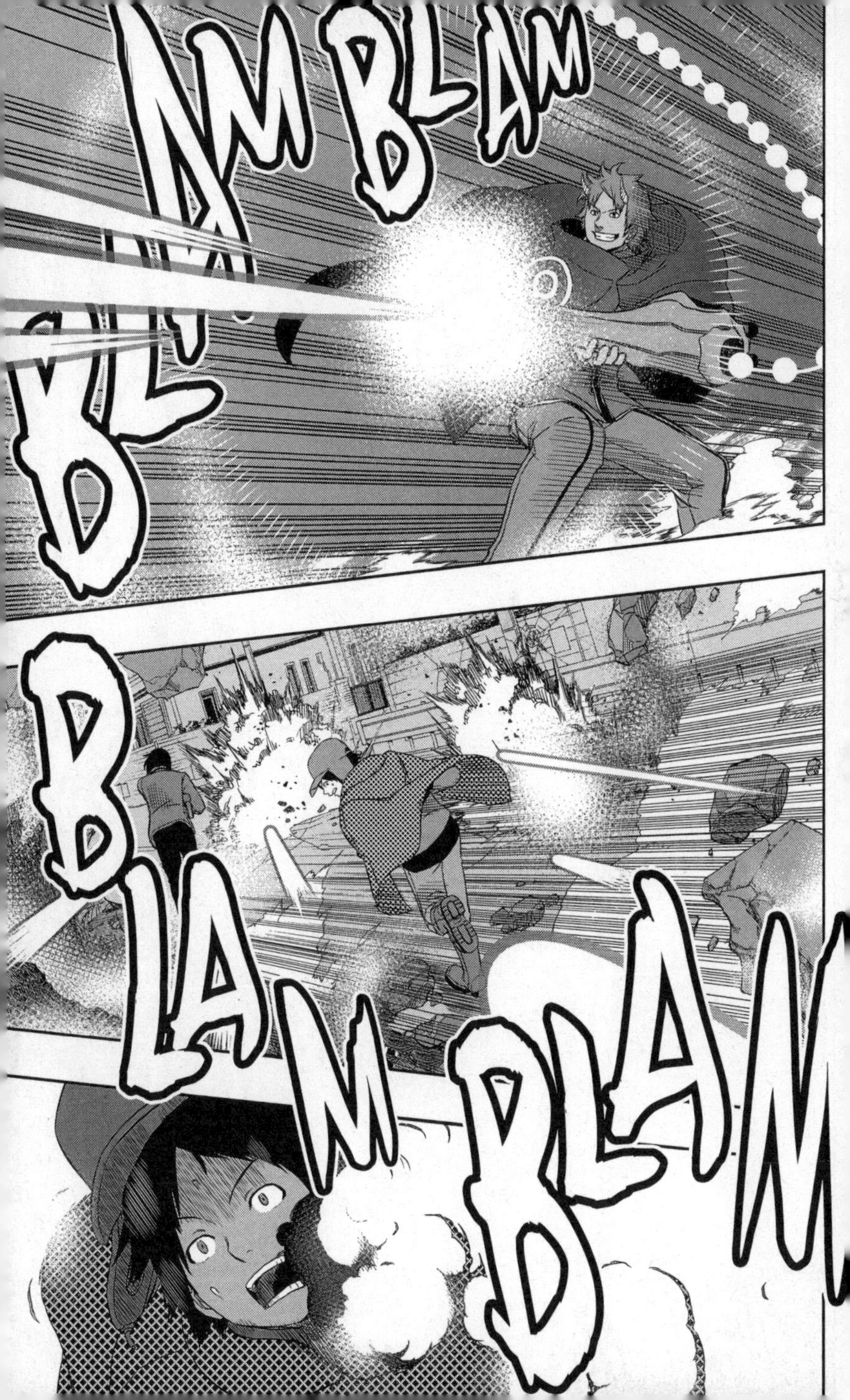
BLAM BLAM
BLAM
BLAM

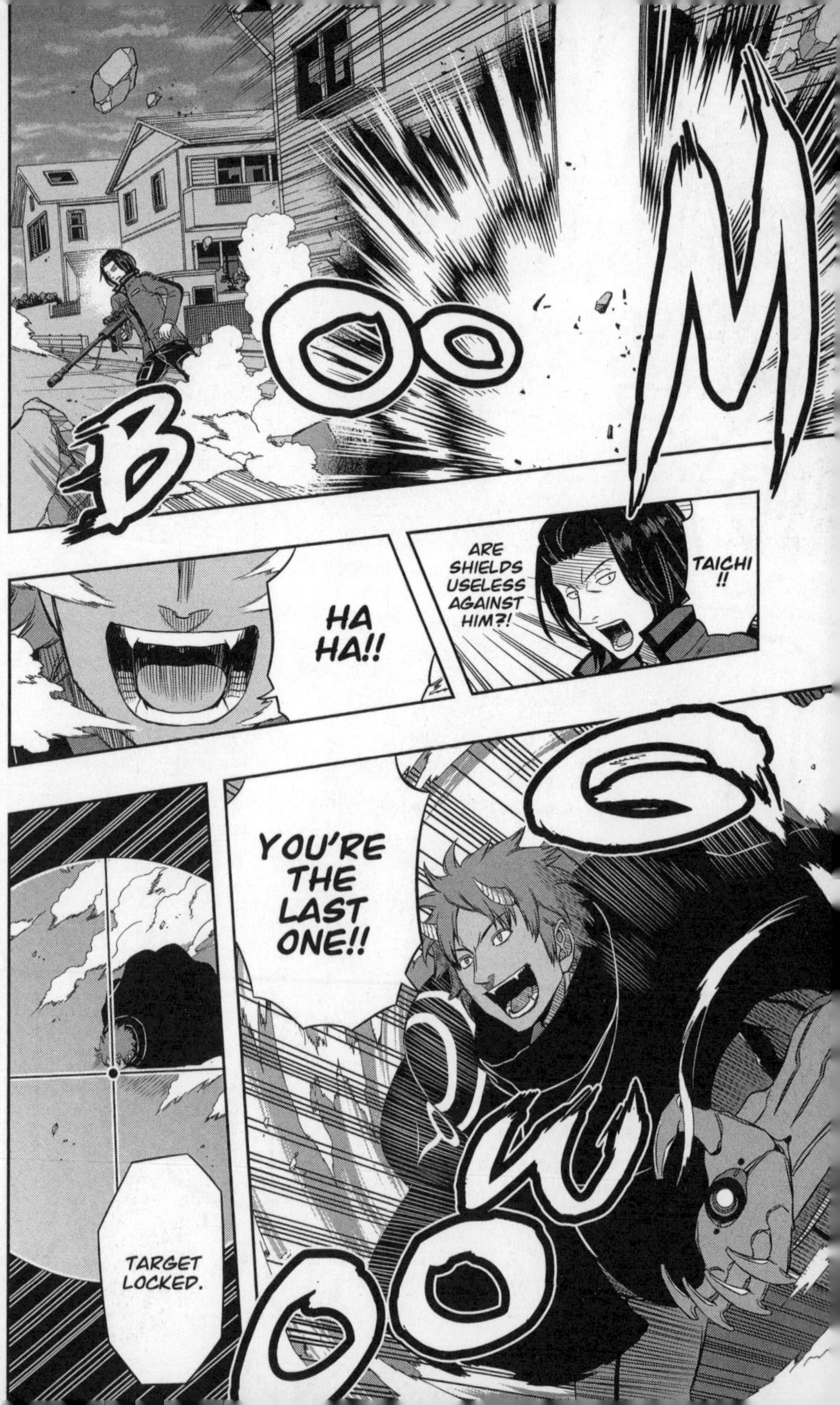
BOOM
TAICHI!!
ARE SHIELDS USELESS AGAINST HIM?!
HA HA!!
GWOO
YOU'RE THE LAST ONE!!
TARGET LOCKED.

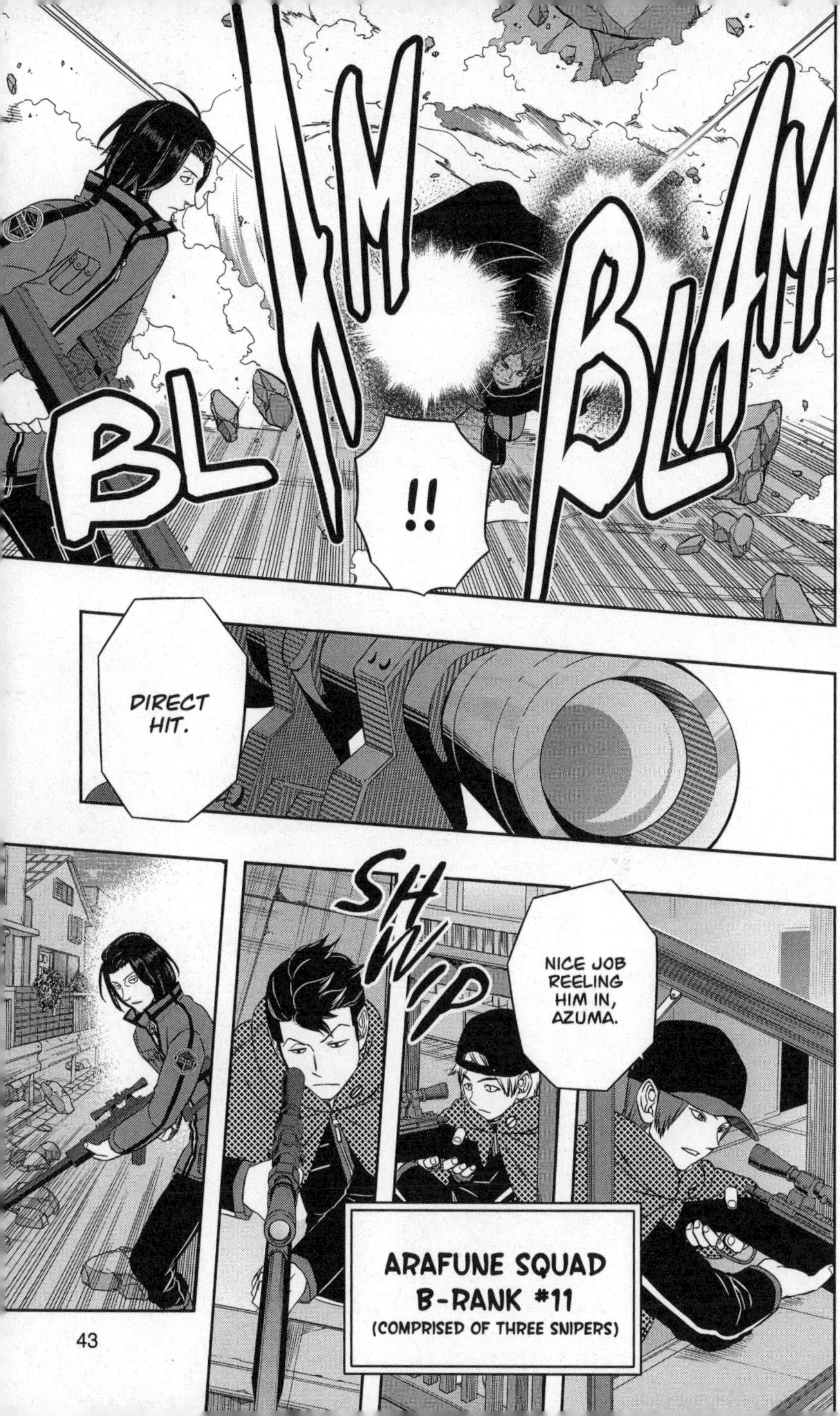
BLAM
BLAM
!!
DIRECT HIT.
SHWIP
NICE JOB REELING HIM IN, AZUMA.
ARAFUNE SQUAD
B-RANK #11
(COMPRISED OF THREE SNIPERS)

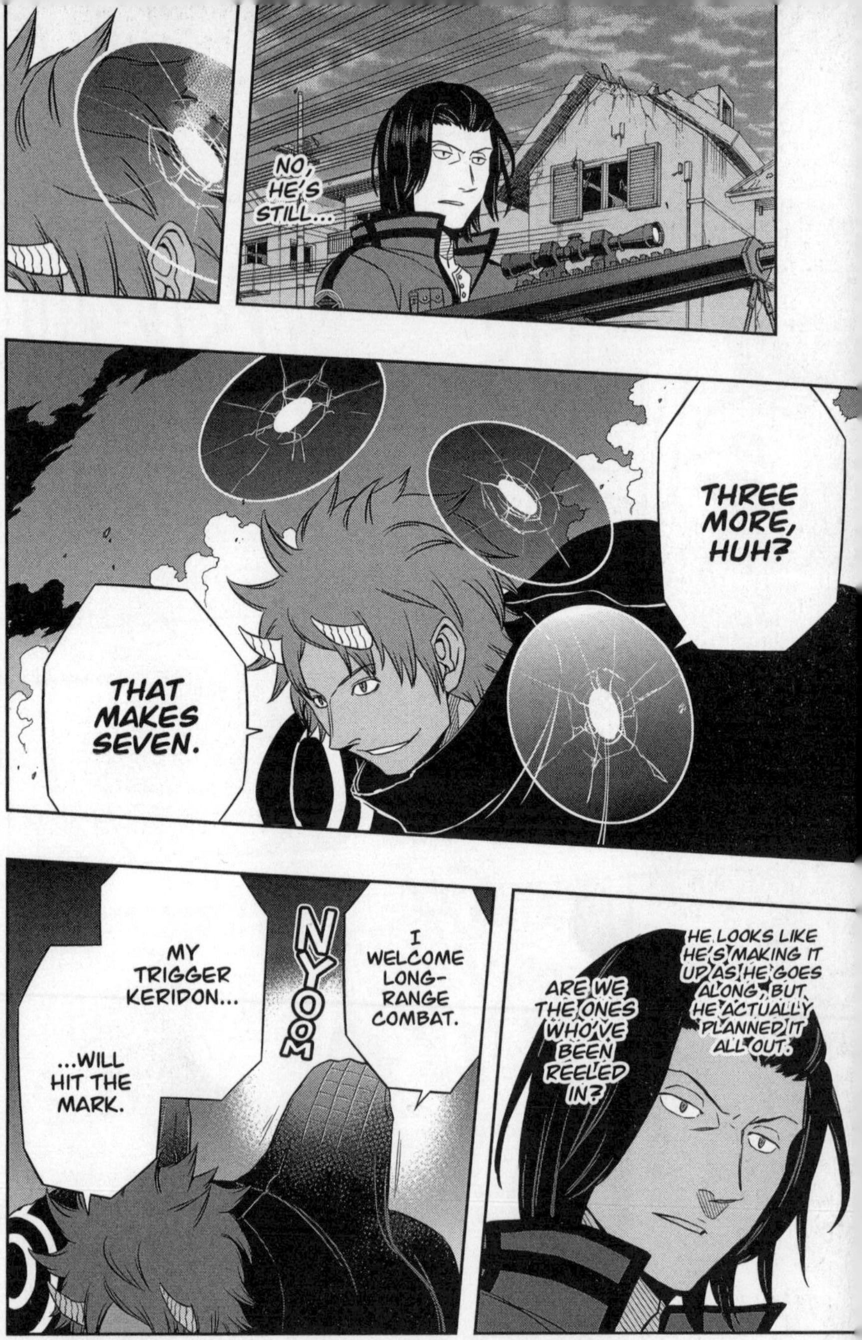
NO, HE'S STILL...
THREE MORE, HUH?
THAT MAKES SEVEN.
HE LOOKS LIKE HE'S MAKING IT UP AS HE GOES ALONG, BUT HE ACTUALLY PLANNED IT ALL OUT.
ARE WE THE ONES WHO'VE BEEN REELED IN?
I WELCOME LONG-RANGE COMBAT.
NYOOM
MY TRIGGER KERIDON...
...WILL HIT THE MARK.

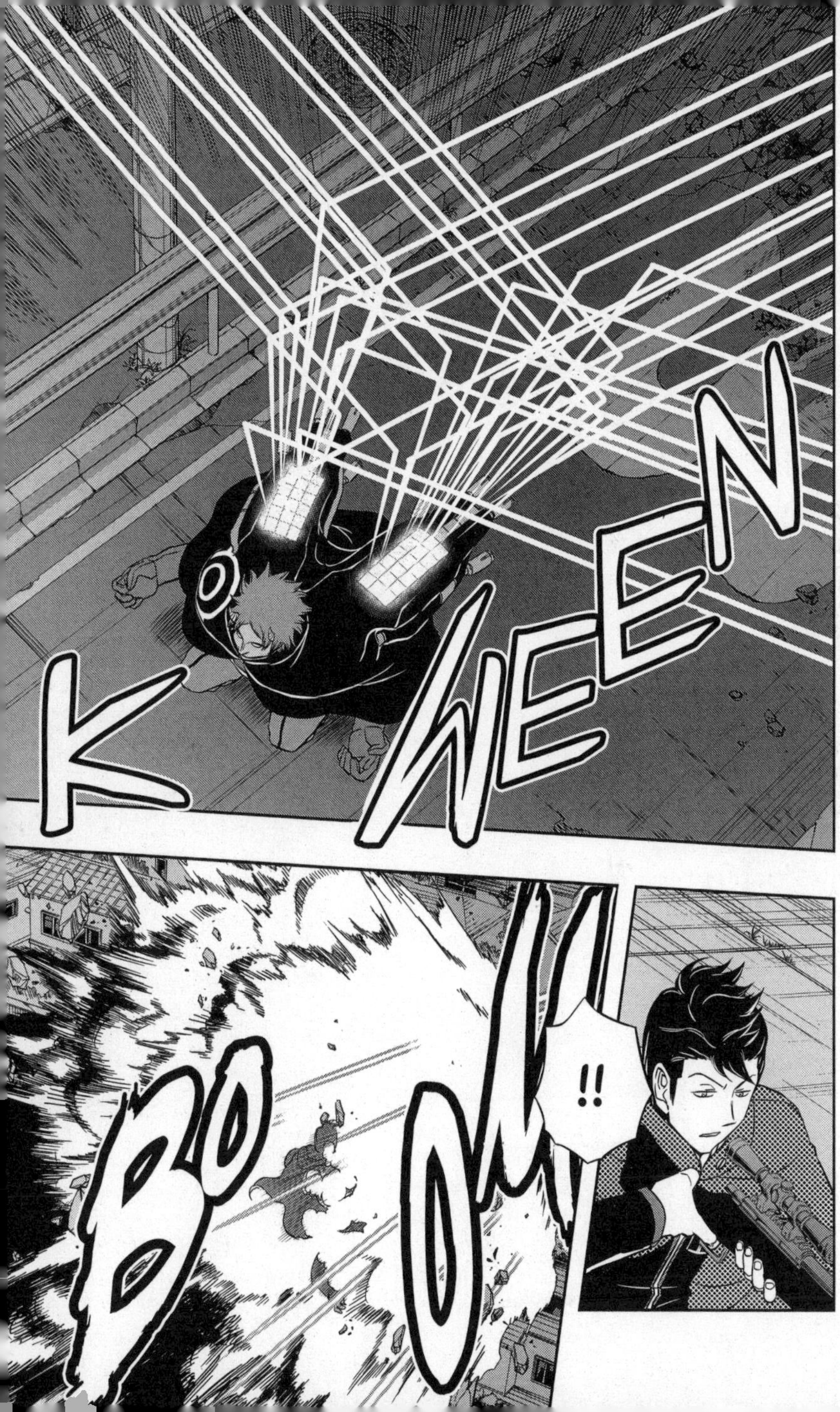
KWEEN
!!
BOOM

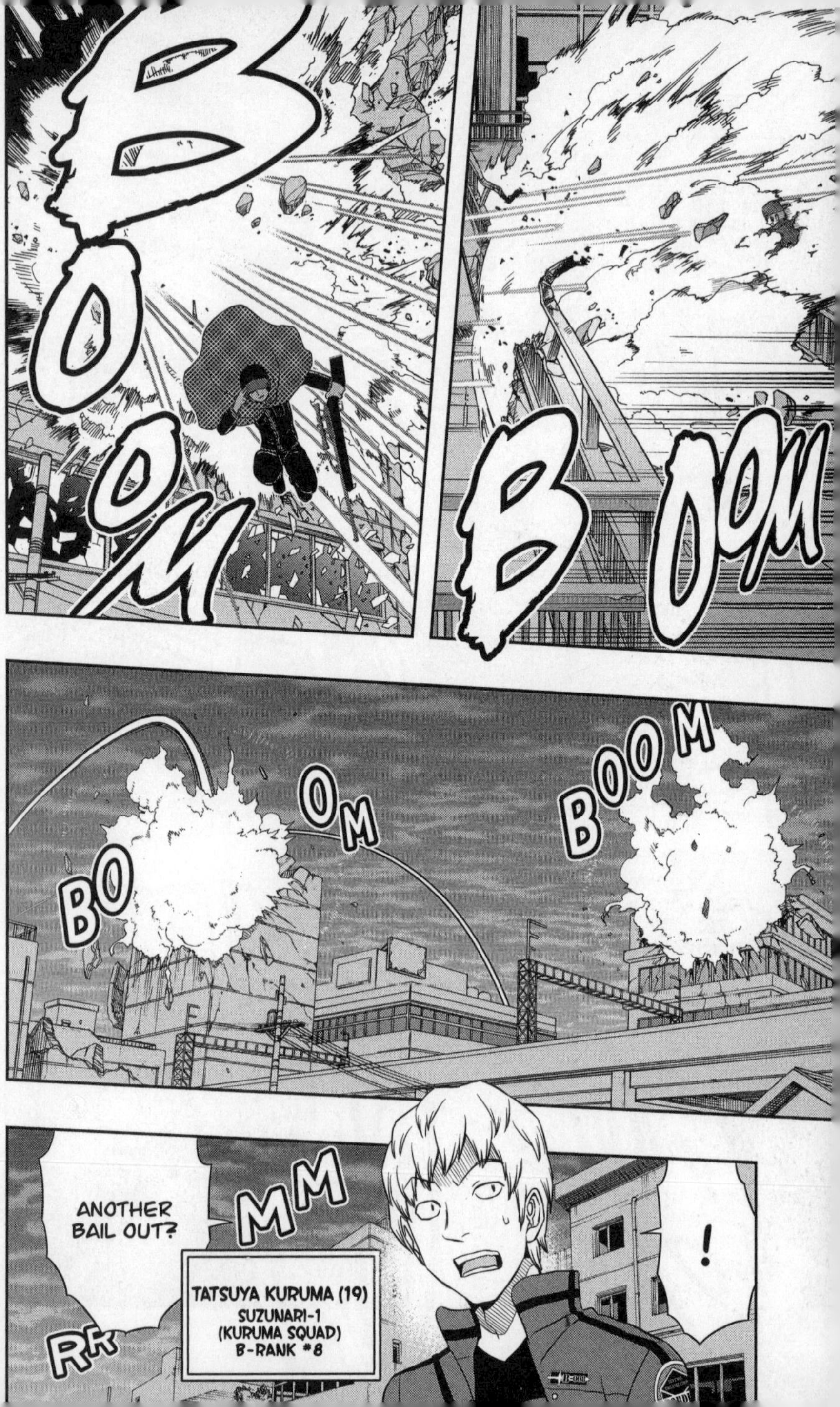
BOOM
BOOM
BOOM
BOOM
!
TATSUYA KURUMA (19)
SUZUNARI-1
(KURUMA SQUAD)
B-RANK #8
ANOTHER BAIL OUT?
MM
RR

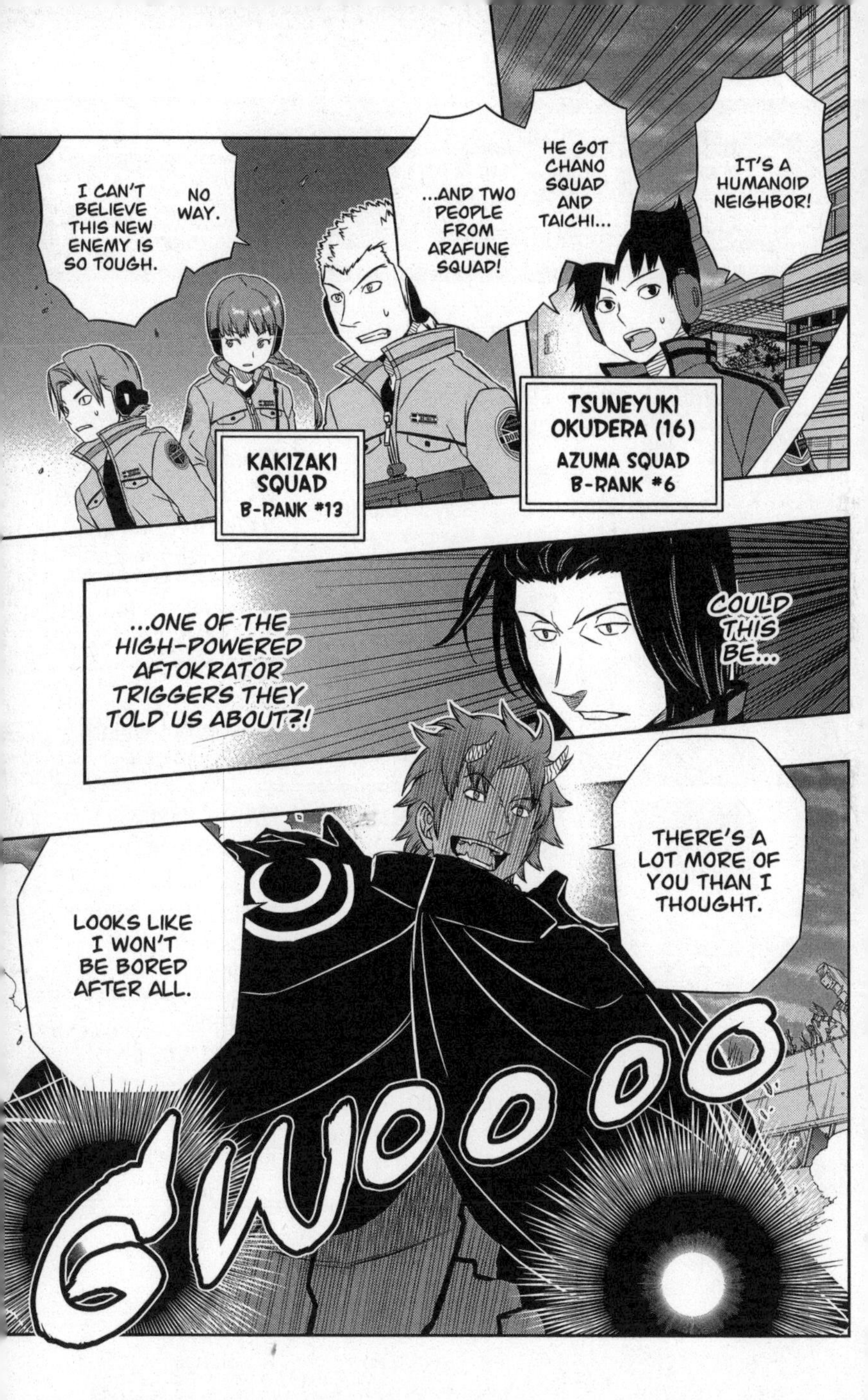
IT'S A HUMANOID NEIGHBOR!
HE GOT CHANO SQUAD AND TAICHI...
...AND TWO PEOPLE FROM ARAFUNE SQUAD!
NO WAY.
I CAN'T BELIEVE THIS NEW ENEMY IS SO TOUGH.
TSUNEYUKI OKUDERA (16) AZUMA SQUAD B-RANK #6
KAKIZAKI SQUAD B-RANK #13
COULD THIS BE...
...ONE OF THE HIGH-POWERED AFTOKRATOR TRIGGERS THEY TOLD US ABOUT?!
THERE'S A LOT MORE OF YOU THAN I THOUGHT.
LOOKS LIKE I WON'T BE BORED AFTER ALL.
GWOOOOO

Arafune Squad

B-011

Border HQ B-Rank #11

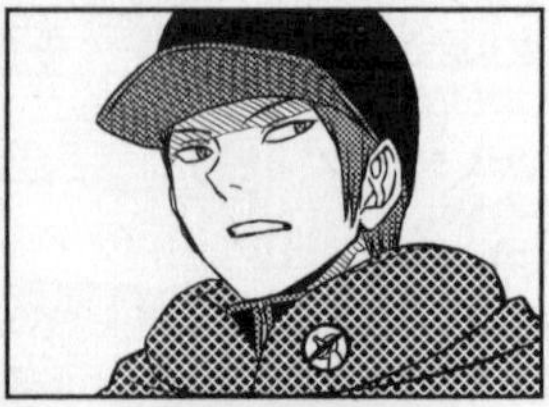

Tetsuji Arafune
Captain, Sniper

■18 years old (high school student)
■Born Sept. 9

■Lupus, Blood type B
■Height: 5'9"
■Likes: Okonomiyaki, chilled tofu, action movies, tea

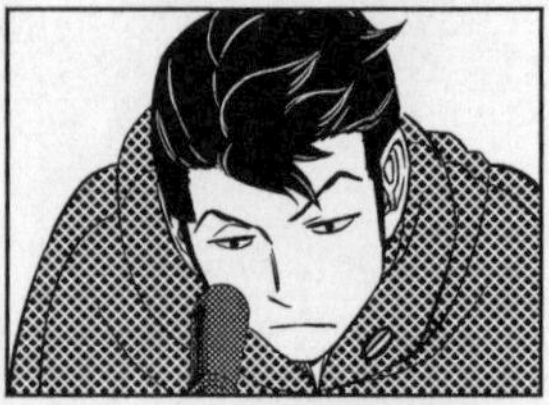

Atsushi Hokari
Sniper

■18 years old (high school student)
■Born June 15

■Lepus, Blood type O
■Height: 5'11"
■Likes: Chicken, raw veggies, weight training, festivals

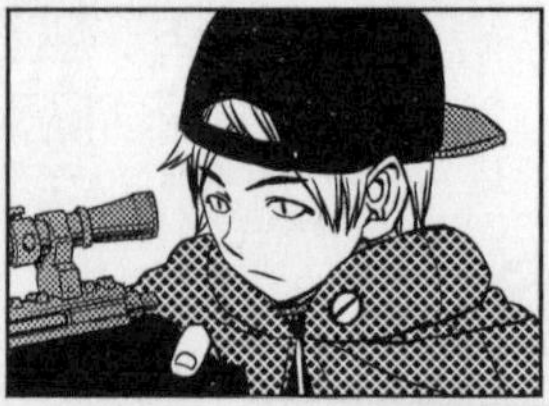

Yoshito Hanzaki
Sniper

■16 years old (high school student)
■Born Feb. 10

■Amphibious, Blood type O
■Height: 5'3"
■Likes: Omelet rice, ice cream, naps, games

Rin Kagami
Operator

■18 years old (high school student)
■Born Sept. 19

■Lupus, Blood type B
■Height: 5'3"
■Likes: Caramel, water, drawing, sculpting

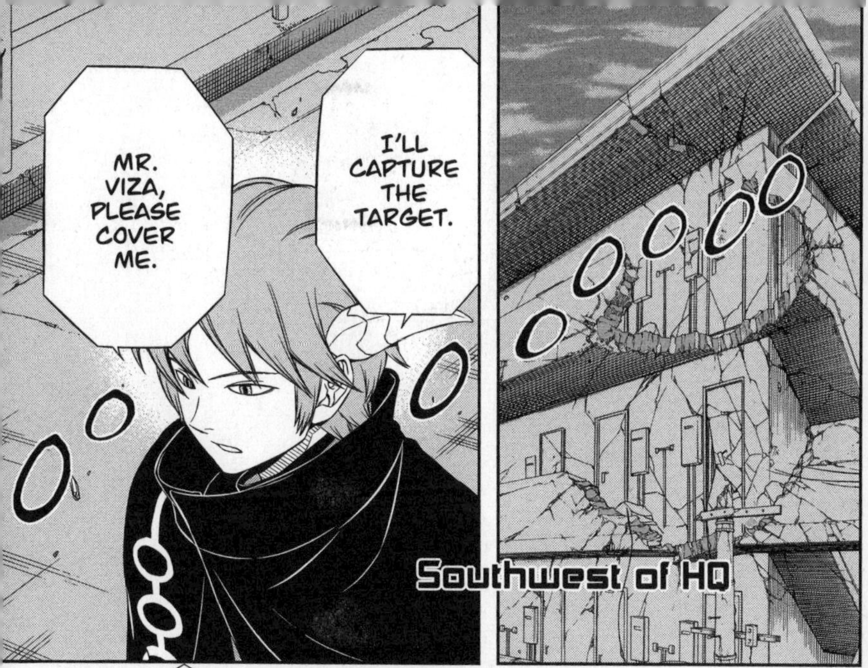
Southwest of HQ
I'LL CAPTURE THE TARGET.
MR. VIZA, PLEASE COVER ME.

Chapter 55 Tamakoma-1: Part 2

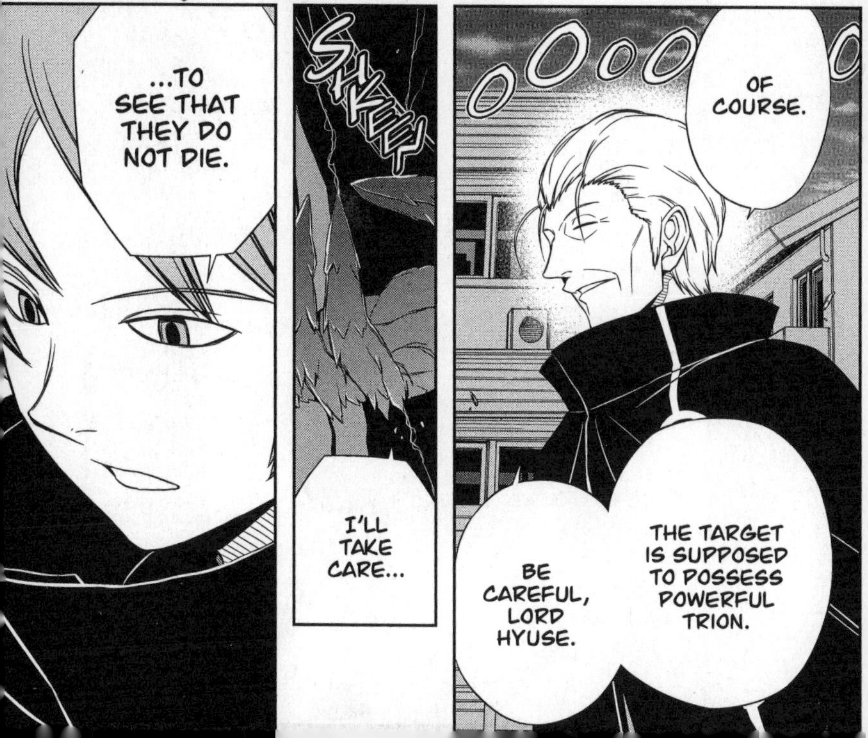
OF COURSE.
THE TARGET IS SUPPOSED TO POSSESS POWERFUL TRION.
BE CAREFUL, LORD HYUSE.
I'LL TAKE CARE...
...TO SEE THAT THEY DO NOT DIE.

Chapter 55 Tamakoma Squad-1: Part 2

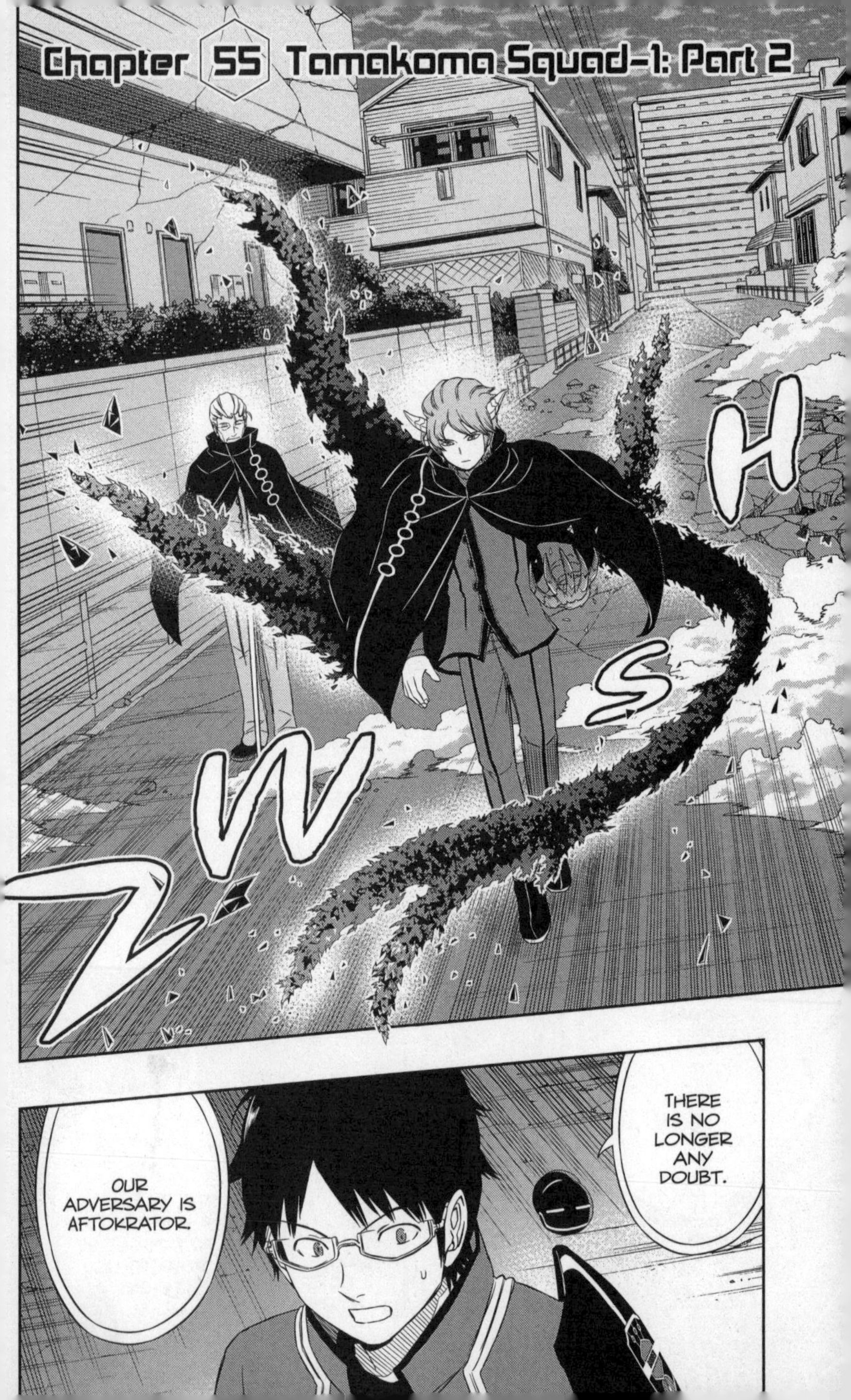
ZWSH
THERE IS NO LONGER ANY DOUBT.
OUR ADVERSARY IS AFTOKRATOR.

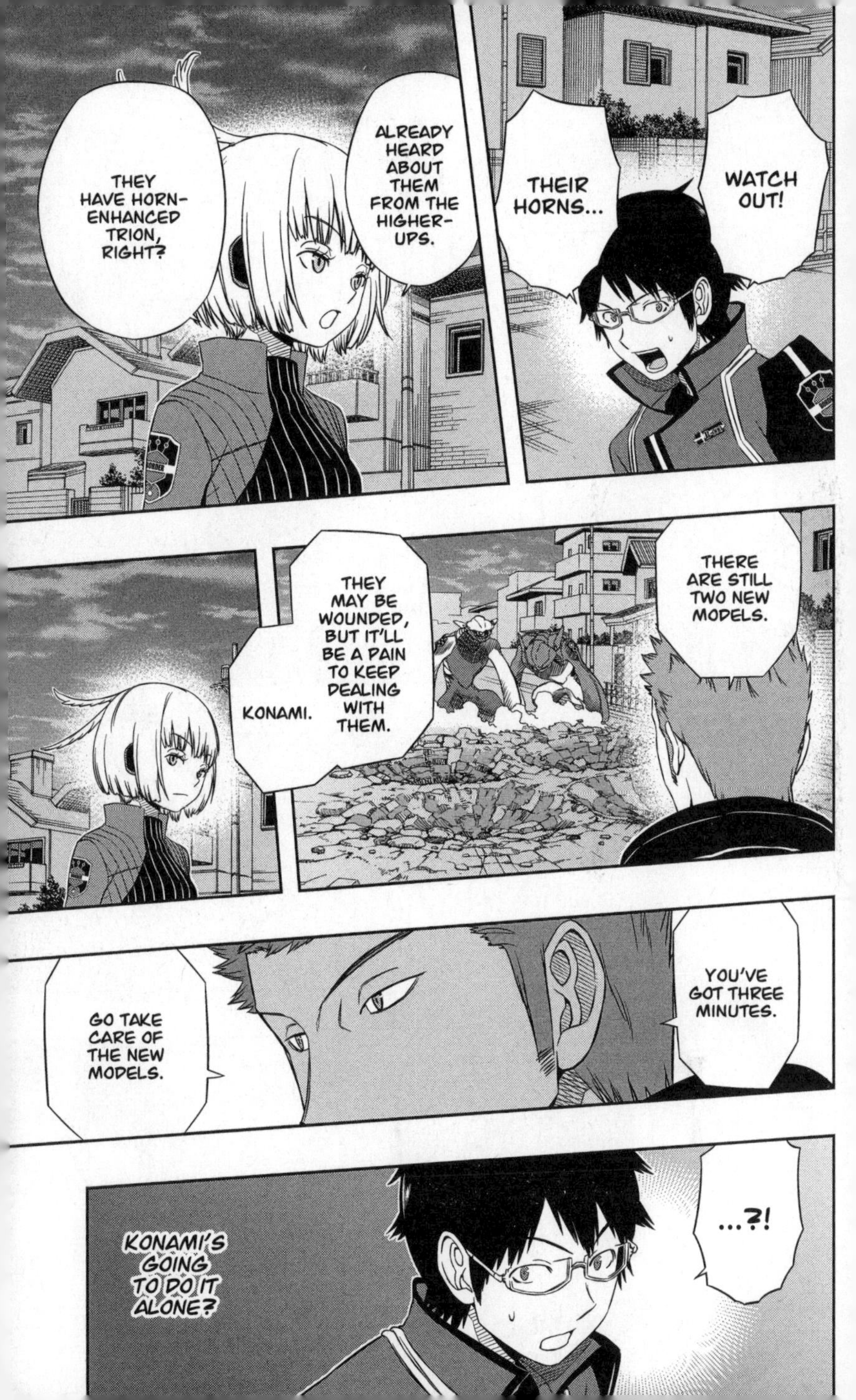
WATCH OUT!
THEIR HORNS...
ALREADY HEARD ABOUT THEM FROM THE HIGHER-UPS.
THEY HAVE HORN-ENHANCED TRION, RIGHT?
THERE ARE STILL TWO NEW MODELS.
THEY MAY BE WOUNDED, BUT IT'LL BE A PAIN TO KEEP DEALING WITH THEM.
KONAMI.
YOU'VE GOT THREE MINUTES.
GO TAKE CARE OF THE NEW MODELS.
...?!
KONAMI'S GOING TO DO IT ALONE?

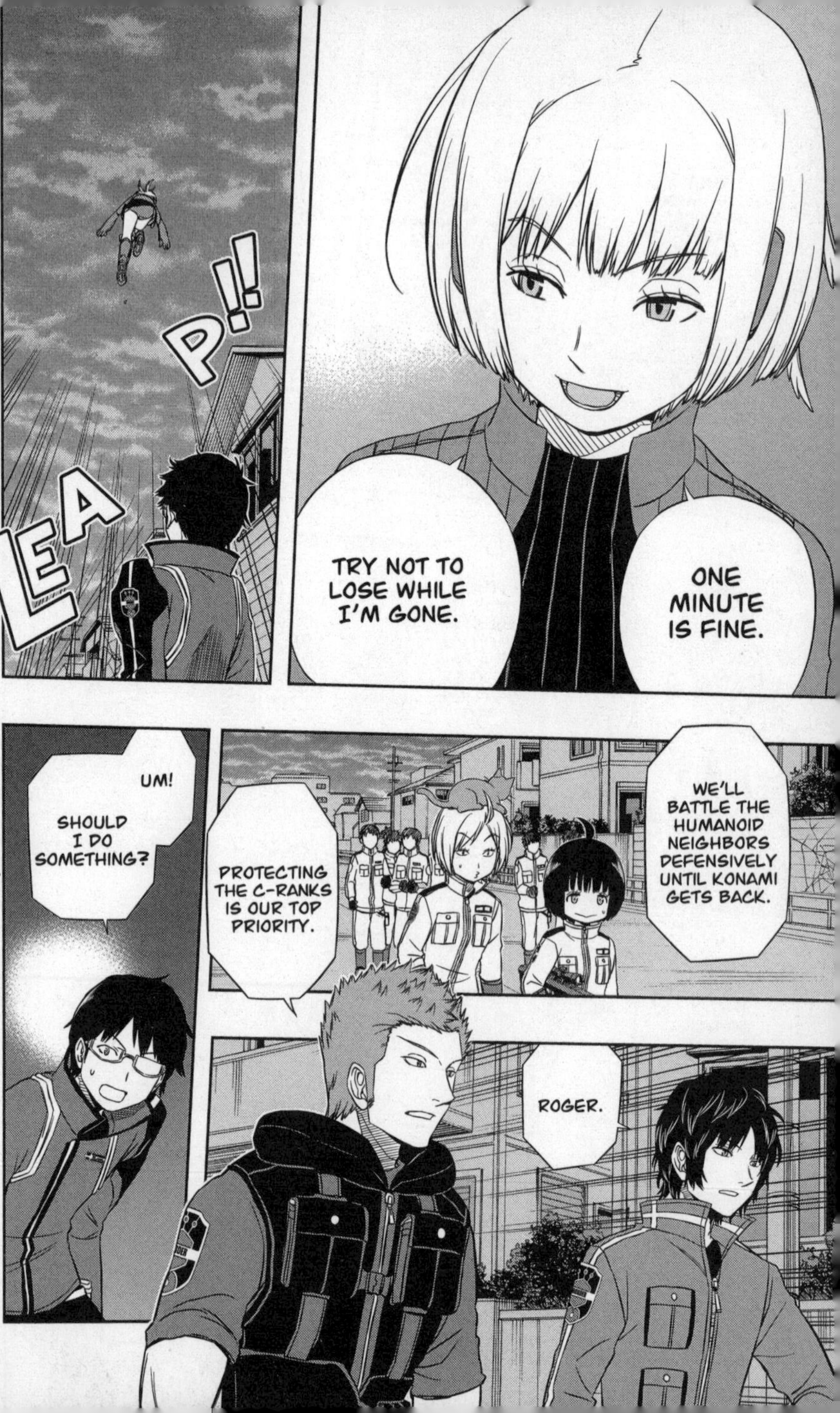
ONE MINUTE IS FINE.
TRY NOT TO LOSE WHILE I'M GONE.
LEAP!!
WE'LL BATTLE THE HUMANOID NEIGHBORS DEFENSIVELY UNTIL KONAMI GETS BACK.
PROTECTING THE C-RANKS IS OUR TOP PRIORITY.
ROGER.
UM!
SHOULD I DO SOMETHING?

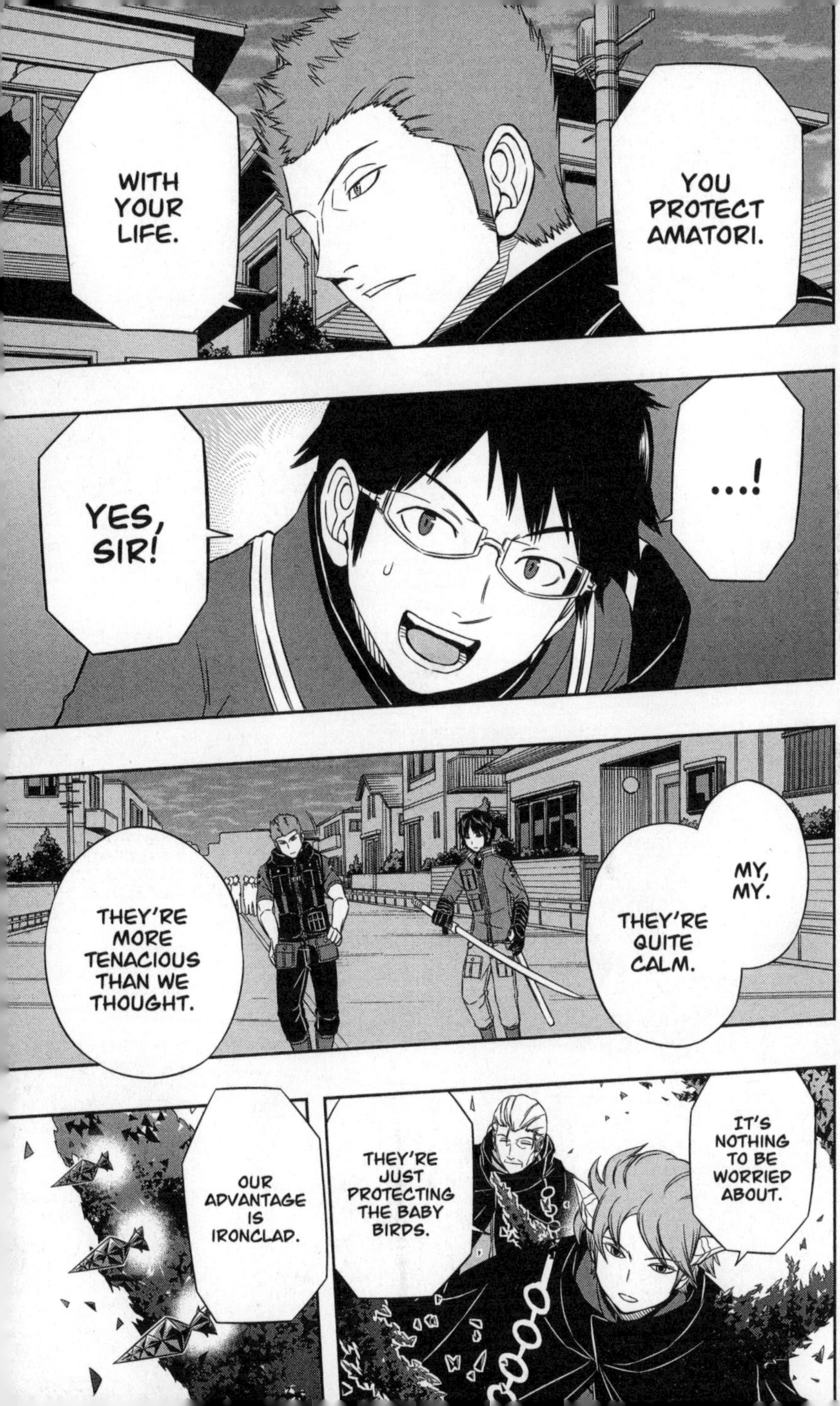
YOU PROTECT AMATORI.
WITH YOUR LIFE.
...!
YES, SIR!
MY, MY.
THEY'RE QUITE CALM.
THEY'RE MORE TENACIOUS THAN WE THOUGHT.
IT'S NOTHING TO BE WORRIED ABOUT.
THEY'RE JUST PROTECTING THE BABY BIRDS.
OUR ADVANTAGE IS IRONCLAD.

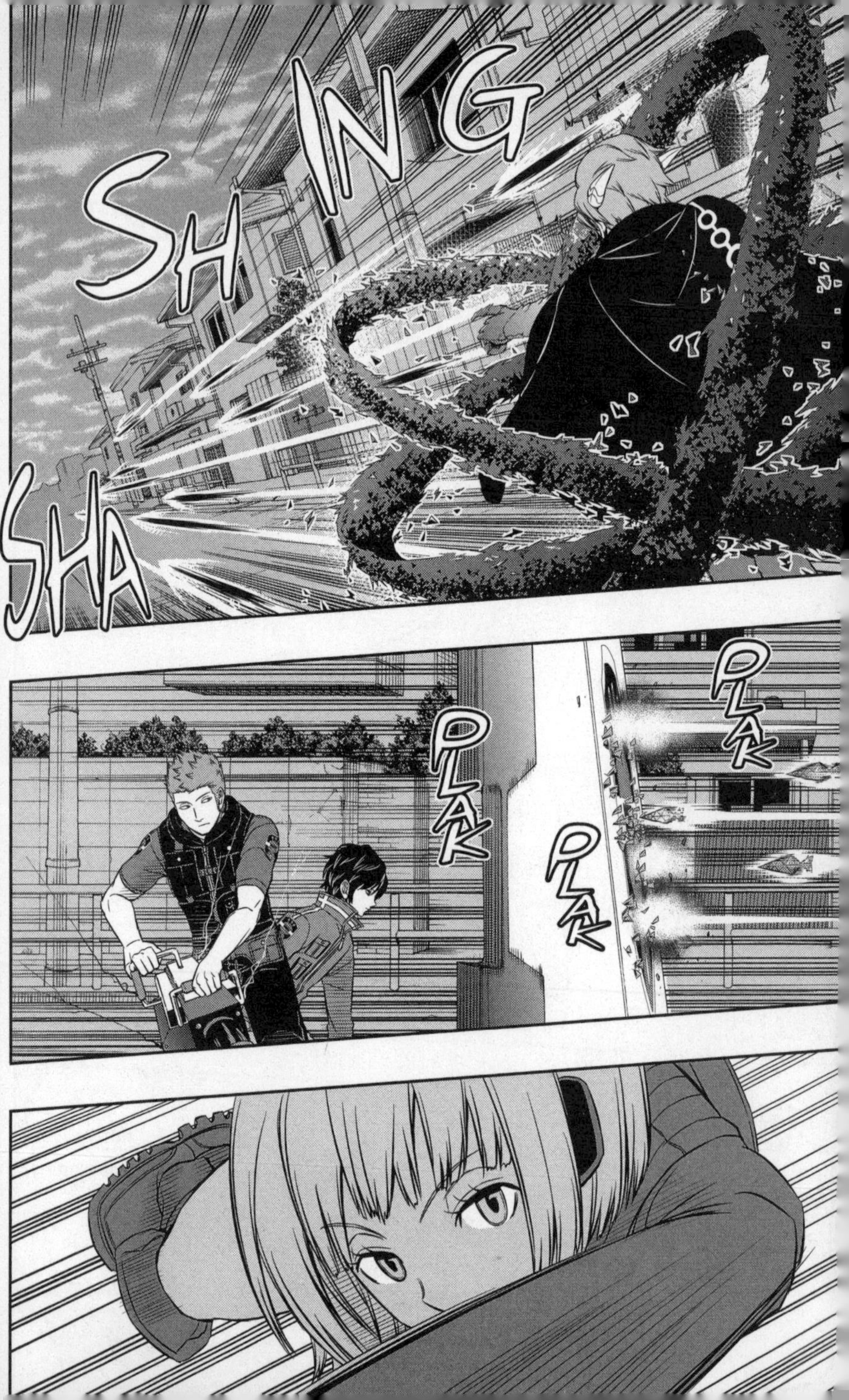
SHING
SHA
PLAK
PLAK
PLAK

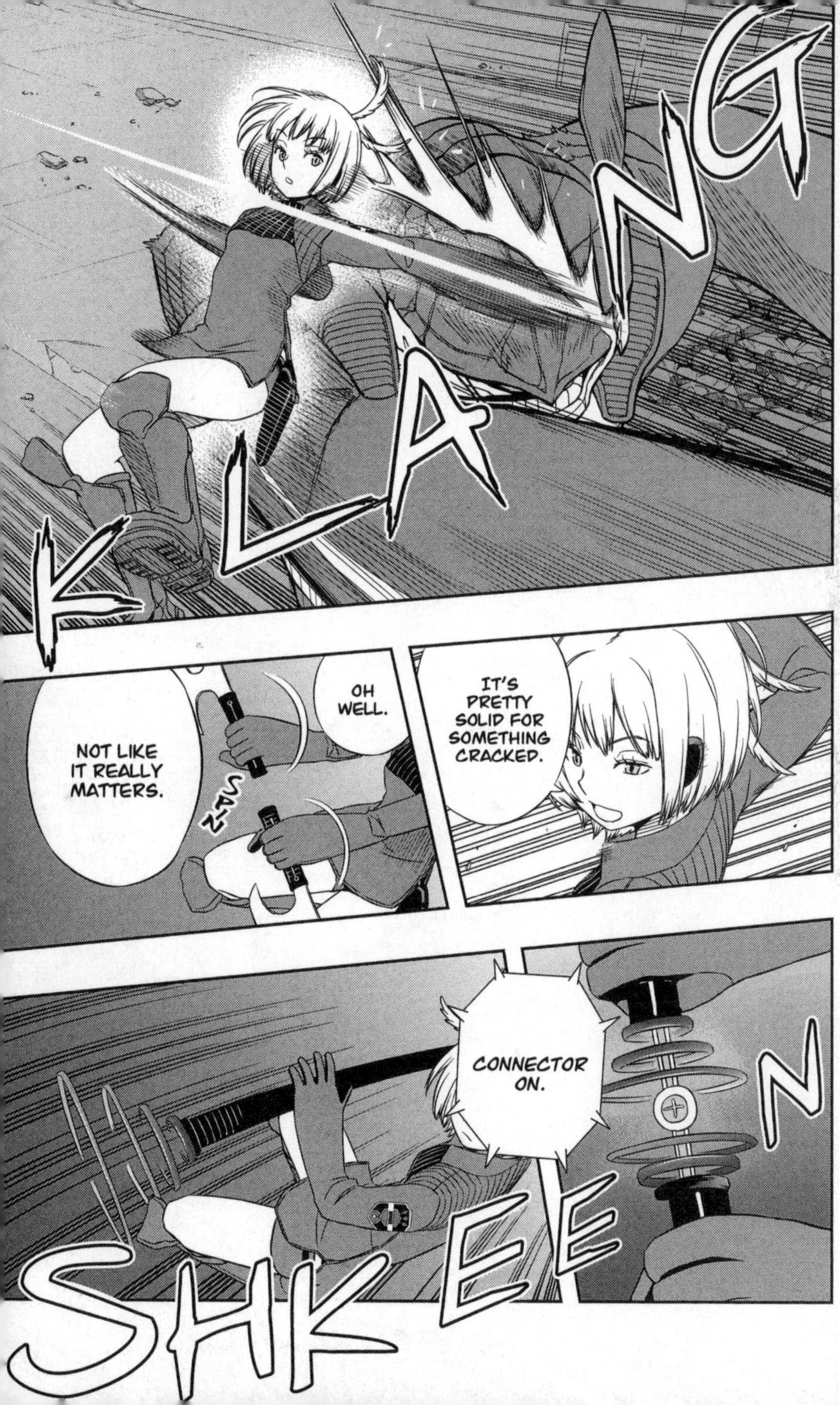
KLANG
IT'S PRETTY SOLID FOR SOMETHING CRACKED.
OH WELL.
NOT LIKE IT REALLY MATTERS.
SPIN
CONNECTOR ON.
SHKEEN

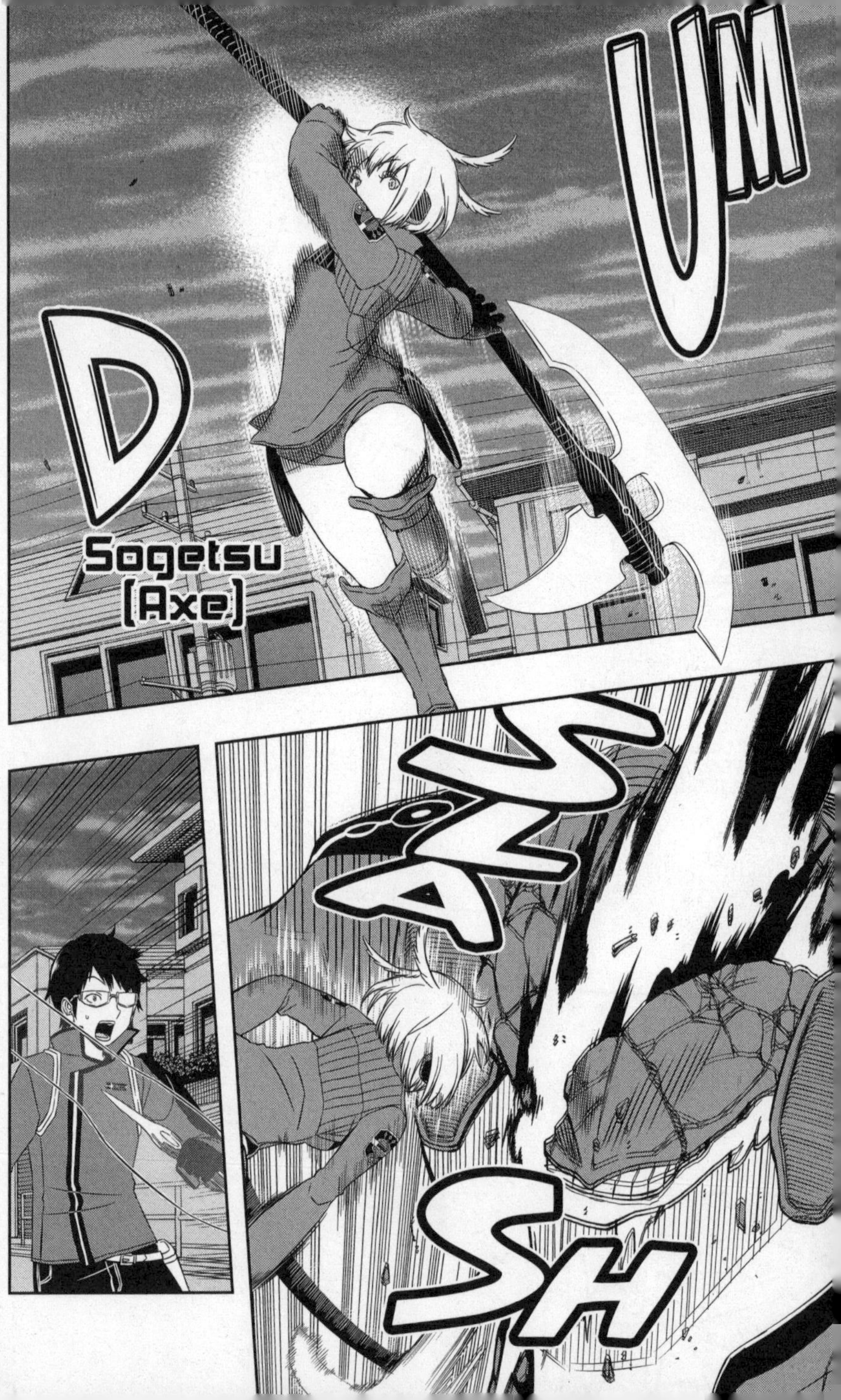
DUM
Sogetsu
[Axe]
SWASH

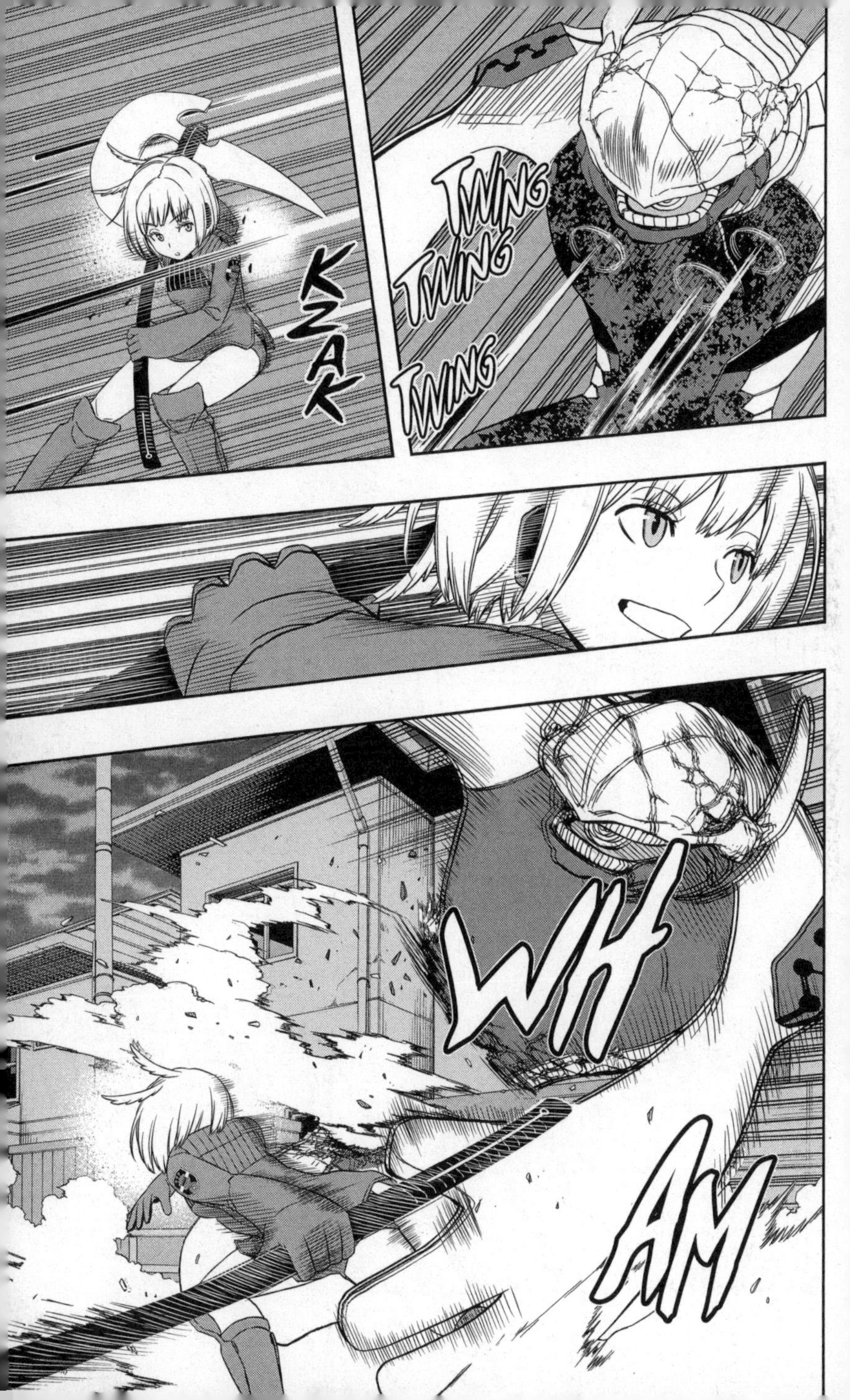
TWING
TWING
TWING
KZAK
WHAM

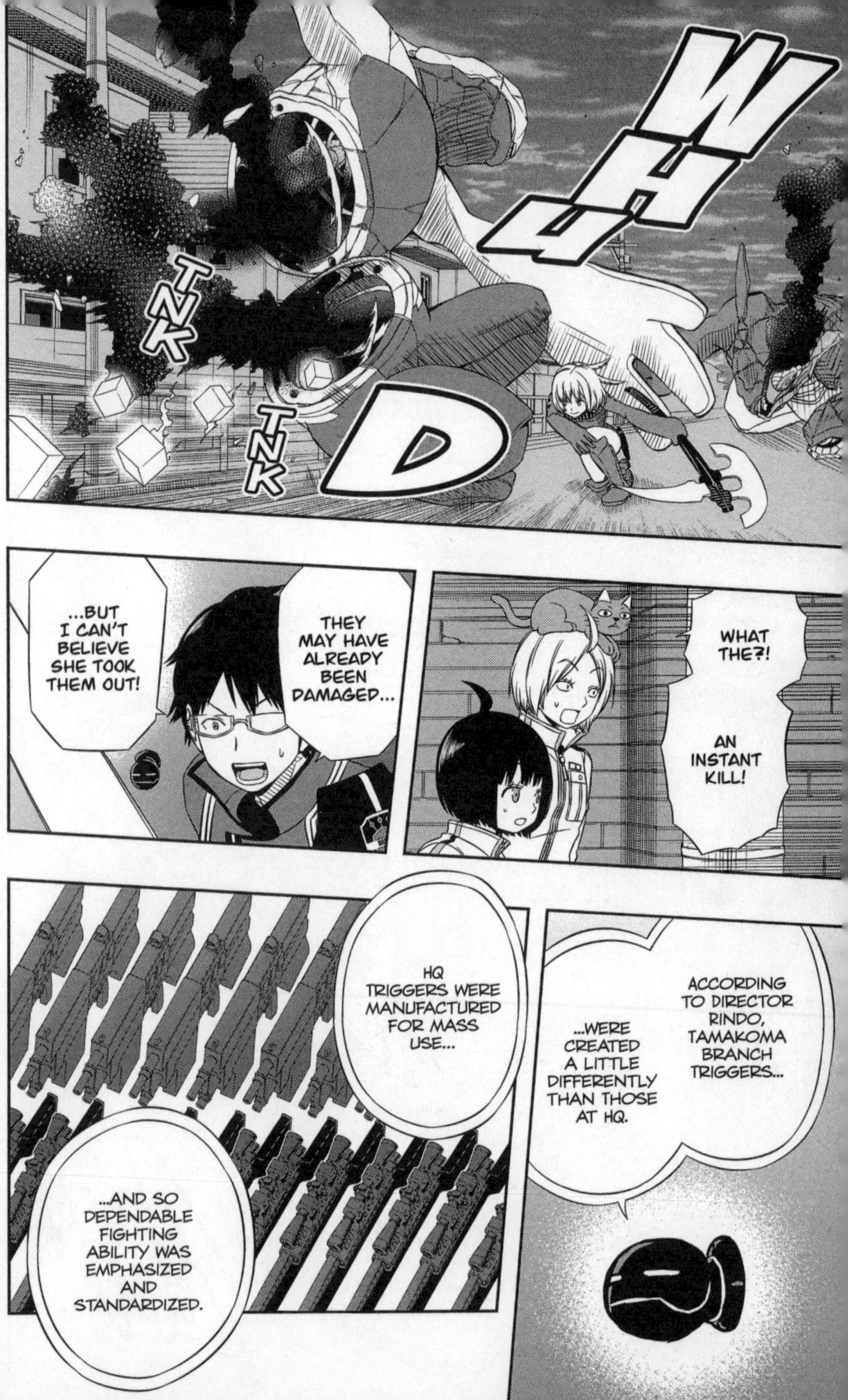
WHUD
TNK
TNK
WHAT THE?!
AN INSTANT KILL!
THEY MAY HAVE ALREADY BEEN DAMAGED...
...BUT I CAN'T BELIEVE SHE TOOK THEM OUT!
ACCORDING TO DIRECTOR RINDO, TAMAKOMA BRANCH TRIGGERS...
...WERE CREATED A LITTLE DIFFERENTLY THAN THOSE AT HQ.
HQ TRIGGERS WERE MANUFACTURED FOR MASS USE...
...AND SO DEPENDABLE FIGHTING ABILITY WAS EMPHASIZED AND STANDARDIZED.

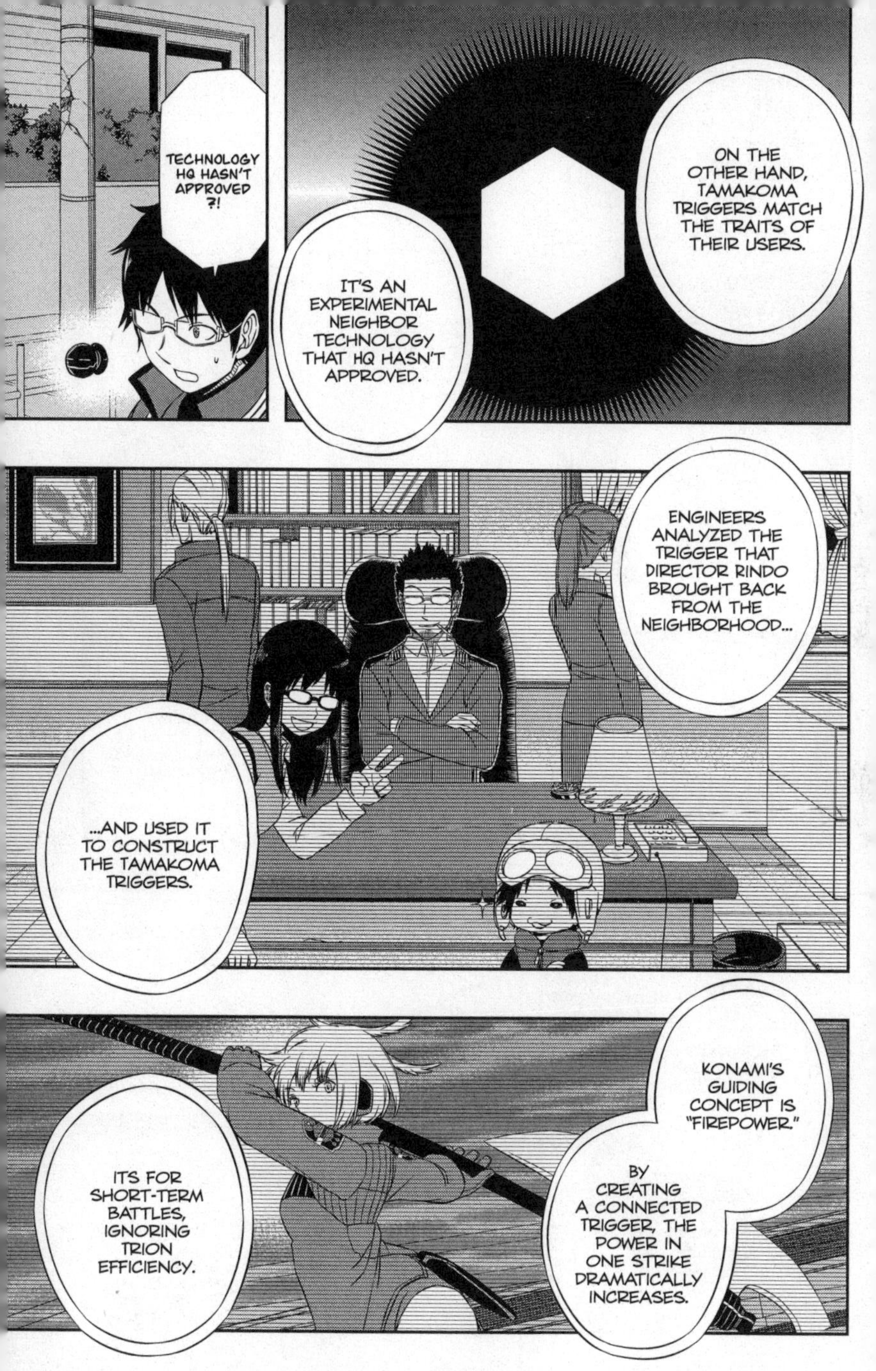
ON THE OTHER HAND, TAMAKOMA TRIGGERS MATCH THE TRAITS OF THEIR USERS.
IT'S AN EXPERIMENTAL NEIGHBOR TECHNOLOGY THAT HQ HASN'T APPROVED.
TECHNOLOGY HQ HASN'T APPROVED ?!
ENGINEERS ANALYZED THE TRIGGER THAT DIRECTOR RINDO BROUGHT BACK FROM THE NEIGHBORHOOD...
...AND USED IT TO CONSTRUCT THE TAMAKOMA TRIGGERS.
KONAMI'S GUIDING CONCEPT IS "FIREPOWER."
BY CREATING A CONNECTED TRIGGER, THE POWER IN ONE STRIKE DRAMATICALLY INCREASES.
ITS FOR SHORT-TERM BATTLES, IGNORING TRION EFFICIENCY.

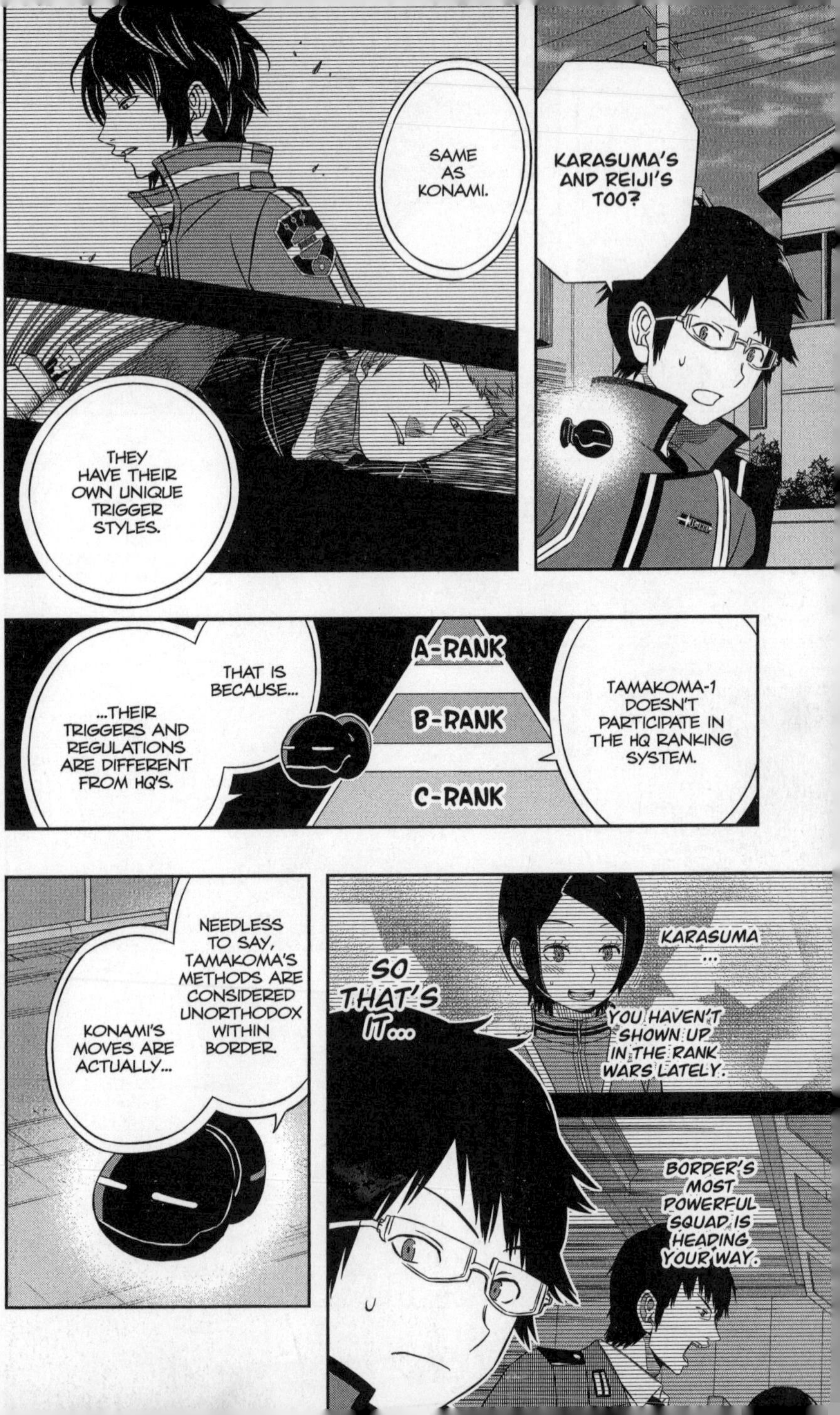
KARASUMA'S AND REIJI'S TOO?
SAME AS KONAMI.
THEY HAVE THEIR OWN UNIQUE TRIGGER STYLES.
TAMAKOMA-1 DOESN'T PARTICIPATE IN THE HQ RANKING SYSTEM.
A-RANK
B-RANK
C-RANK
THAT IS BECAUSE...
...THEIR TRIGGERS AND REGULATIONS ARE DIFFERENT FROM HQ'S.
KARASUMA...
YOU HAVEN'T SHOWN UP IN THE RANK WARS LATELY.
SO THAT'S IT...
BORDER'S MOST POWERFUL SQUAD IS HEADING YOUR WAY.
NEEDLESS TO SAY, TAMAKOMA'S METHODS ARE CONSIDERED UNORTHODOX WITHIN BORDER.
KONAMI'S MOVES ARE ACTUALLY...

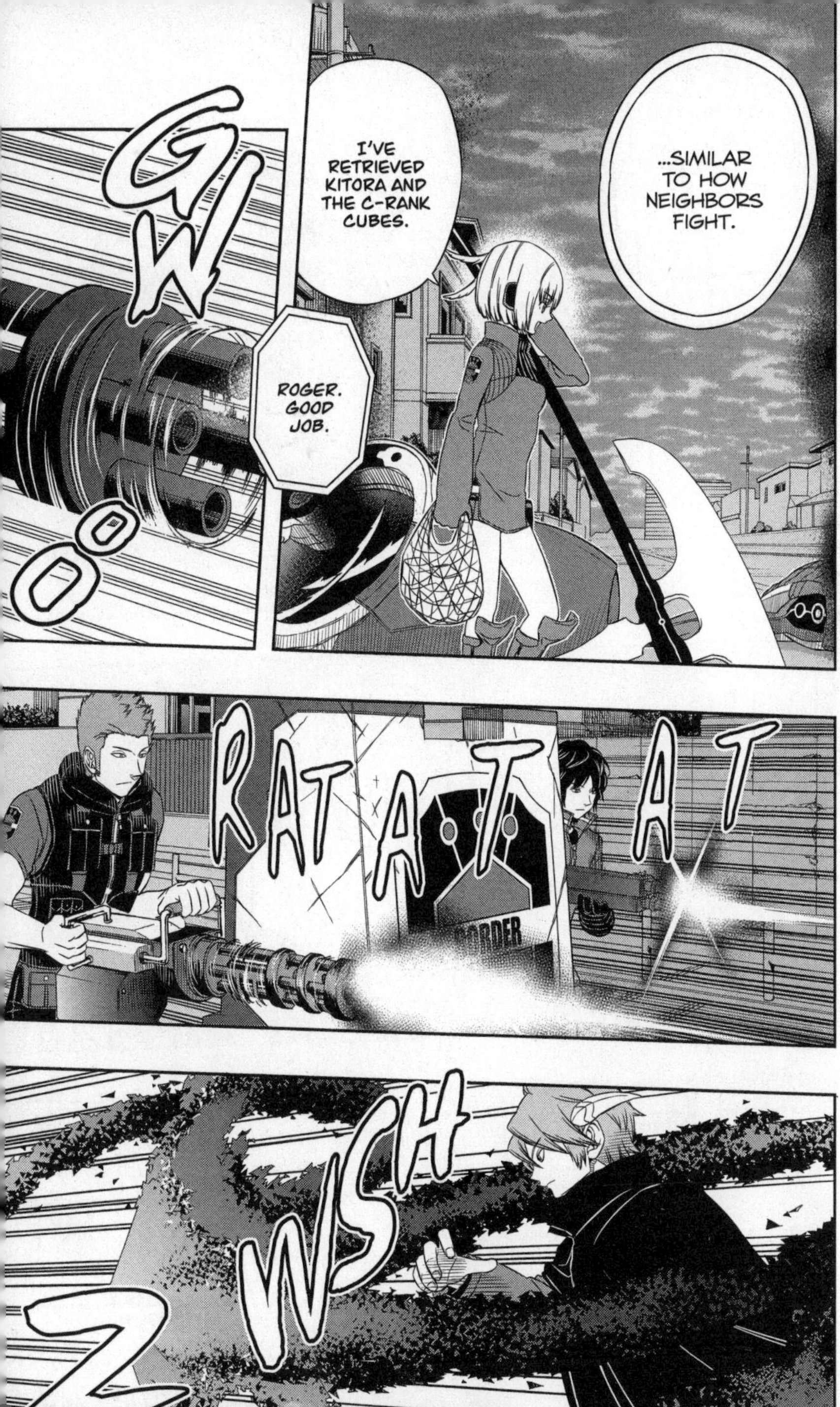
...SIMILAR TO HOW NEIGHBORS FIGHT.
I'VE RETRIEVED KITORA AND THE C-RANK CUBES.
ROGER. GOOD JOB.
GWOOO
RAT-A-TAT
ZWSH

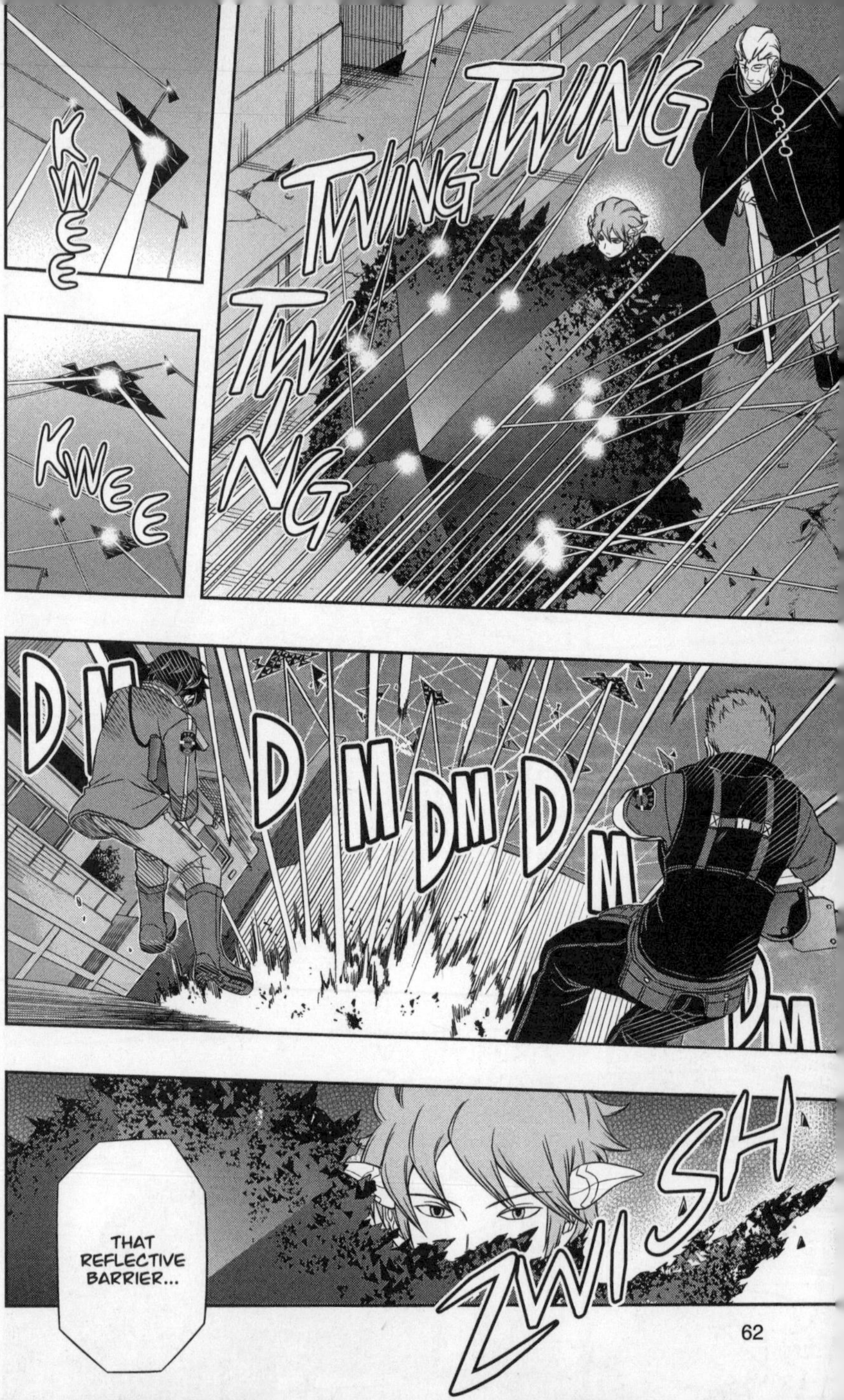
TWING TWING
TWING
KWEE
KWEE
DM
D M
DM
D M
DM
ZWISH
THAT REFLECTIVE BARRIER...

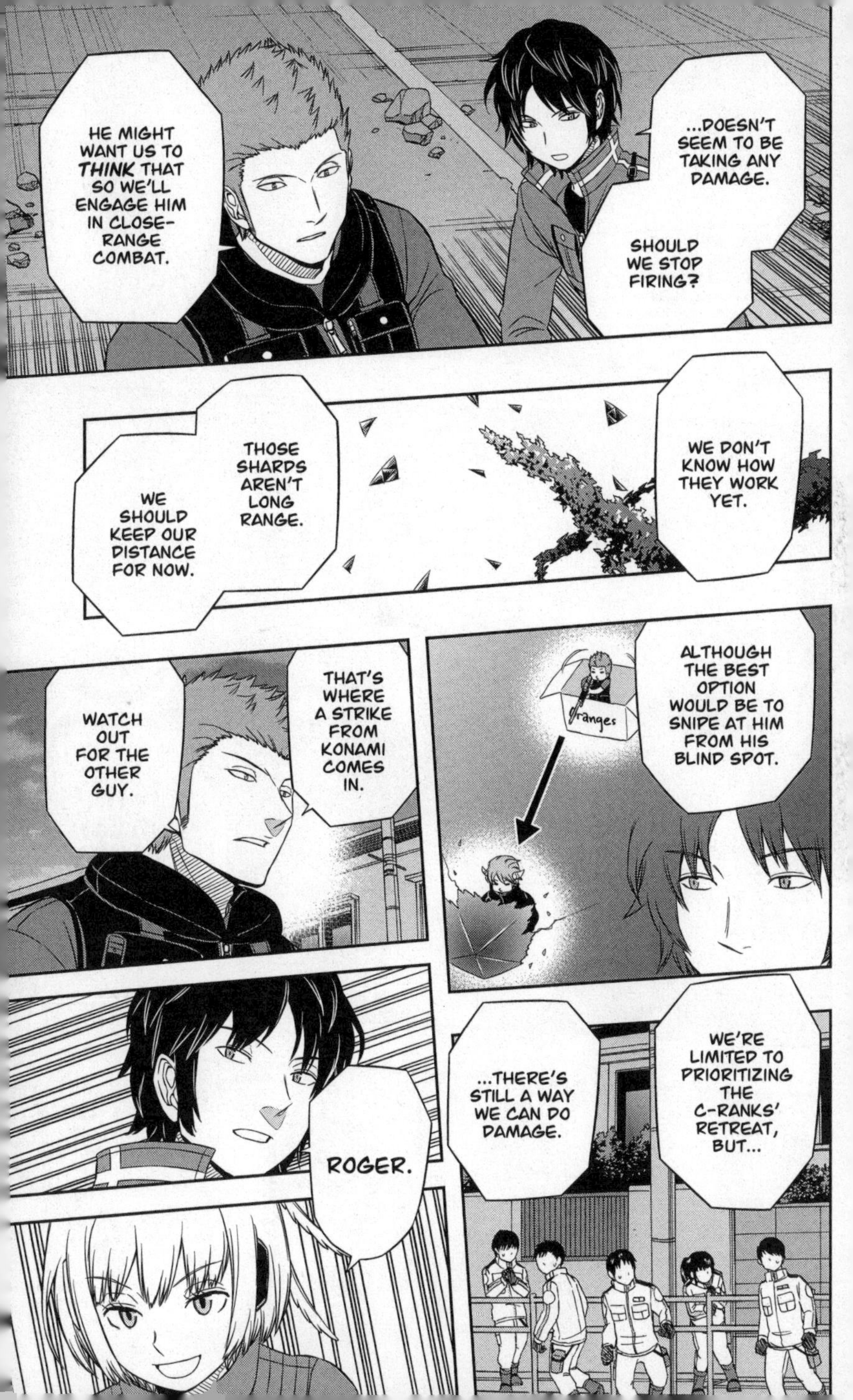
...DOESN'T SEEM TO BE TAKING ANY DAMAGE.
SHOULD WE STOP FIRING?
HE MIGHT WANT US TO *THINK* THAT SO WE'LL ENGAGE HIM IN CLOSE-RANGE COMBAT.
WE DON'T KNOW HOW THEY WORK YET.
THOSE SHARDS AREN'T LONG RANGE.
WE SHOULD KEEP OUR DISTANCE FOR NOW.
ALTHOUGH THE BEST OPTION WOULD BE TO SNIPE AT HIM FROM HIS BLIND SPOT.
Oranges
THAT'S WHERE A STRIKE FROM KONAMI COMES IN.
WATCH OUT FOR THE OTHER GUY.
WE'RE LIMITED TO PRIORITIZING THE C-RANKS' RETREAT, BUT...
...THERE'S STILL A WAY WE CAN DO DAMAGE.
ROGER.

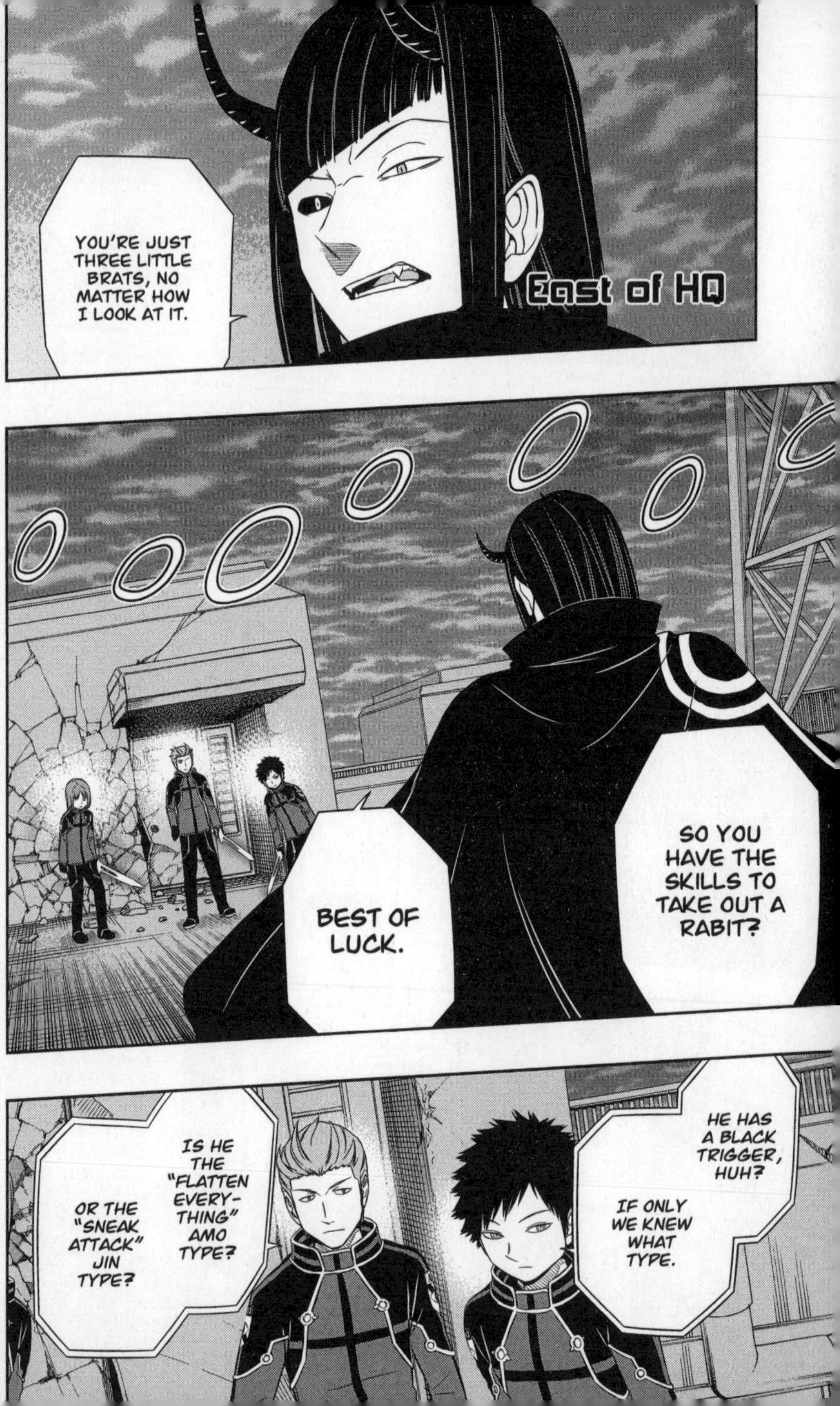
East of HQ
YOU'RE JUST THREE LITTLE BRATS, NO MATTER HOW I LOOK AT IT.
SO YOU HAVE THE SKILLS TO TAKE OUT A RABIT?
BEST OF LUCK.
HE HAS A BLACK TRIGGER, HUH?
IF ONLY WE KNEW WHAT TYPE.
IS HE THE "FLATTEN EVERYTHING" AMO TYPE?
OR THE "SNEAK ATTACK" JIN TYPE?

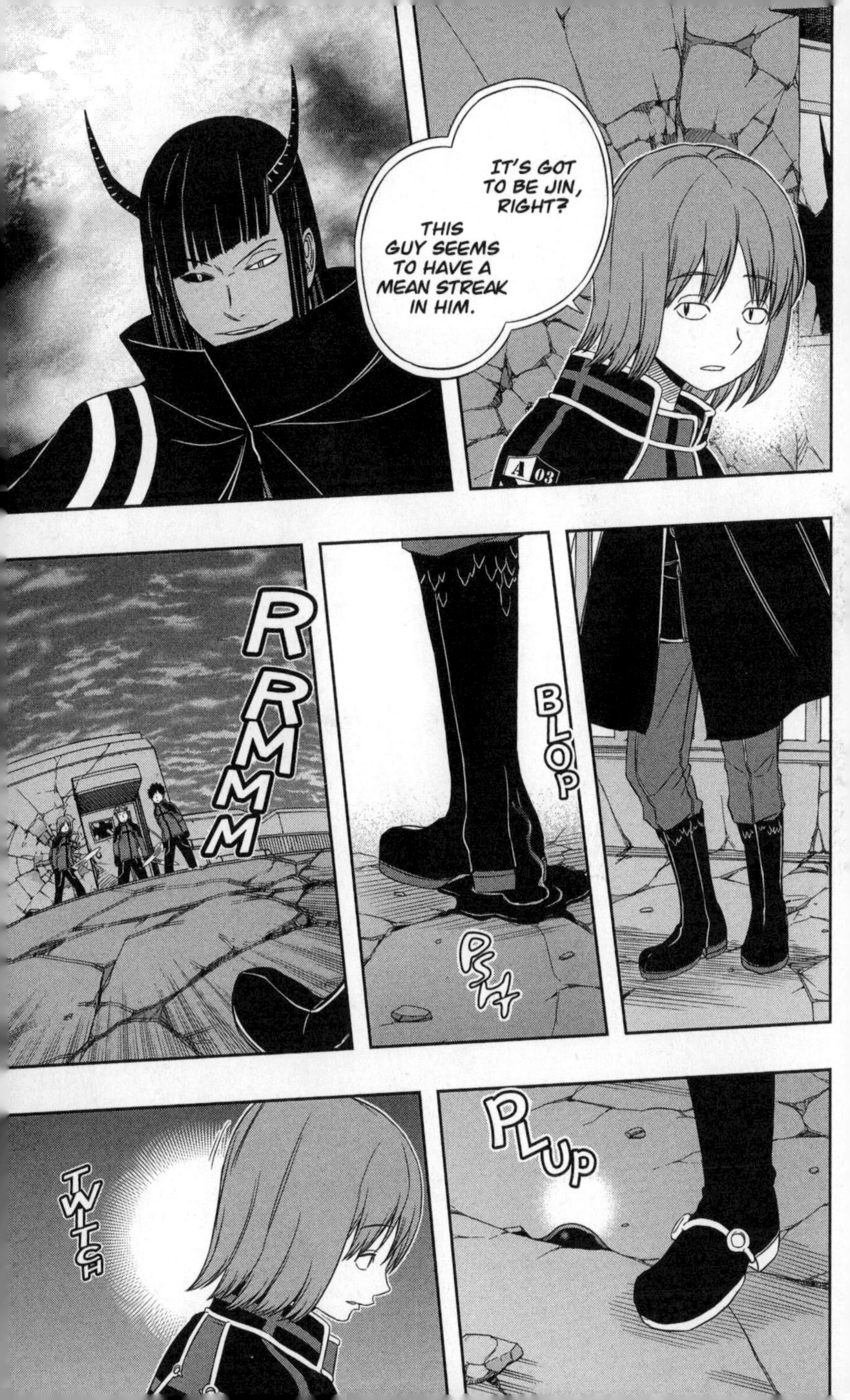

IT'S GOT TO BE JIN, RIGHT?
THIS GUY SEEMS TO HAVE A MEAN STREAK IN HIM.
BLOP
PSHT
RRMMMM
PLUP
TWITCH

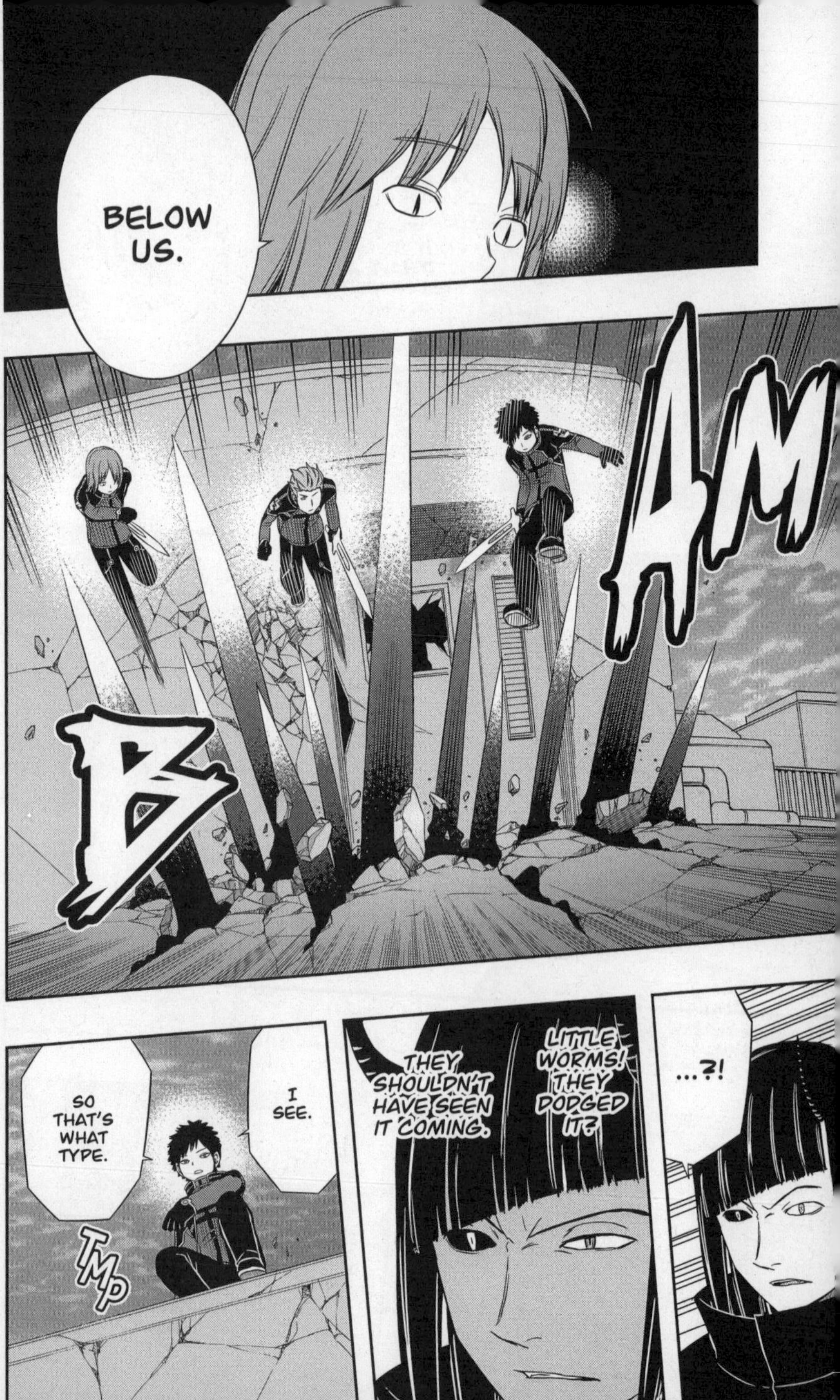
BELOW US.
BAM
...?!
LITTLE WORMS! THEY DODGED IT?
THEY SHOULDN'T HAVE SEEN IT COMING.
I SEE.
SO THAT'S WHAT TYPE.
TMP

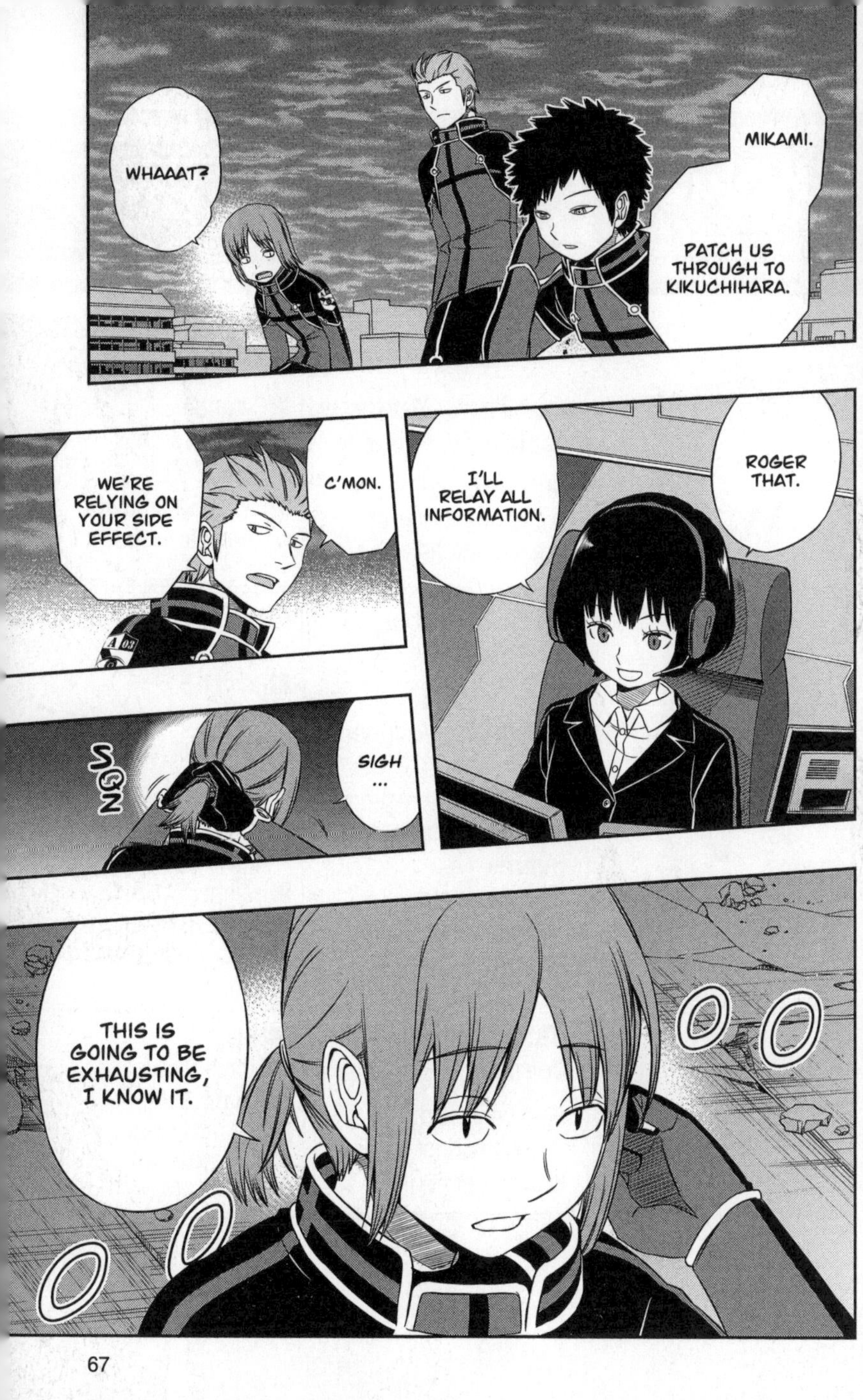
MIKAMI.
PATCH US THROUGH TO KIKUCHIHARA.
WHAAAT?
ROGER THAT.
I'LL RELAY ALL INFORMATION.
C'MON.
WE'RE RELYING ON YOUR SIDE EFFECT.
SIGH ...
THIS IS GOING TO BE EXHAUSTING, I KNOW IT.

Kakizaki Squad
Border HQ B-Rank #13

B-013

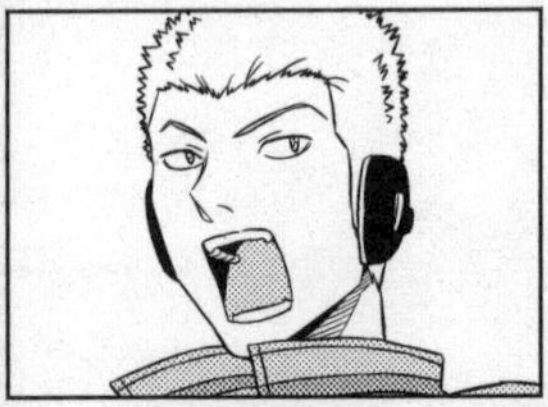

Kuniharu Kakizaki
Captain, All-Rounder

■19 years old (college student)
■Born Nov. 25

■Cetacea, Blood type A
■Height: 5'10"
■Likes: Beef bowl, watermelon, sports

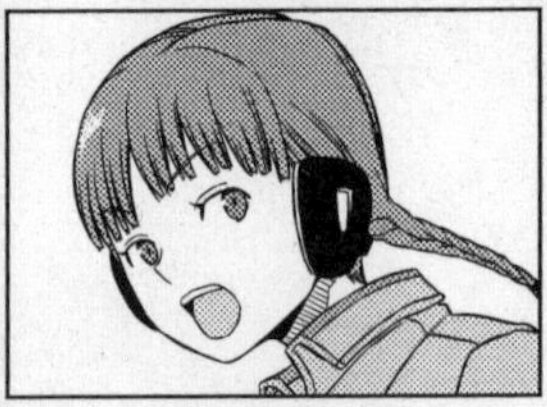

Fumika Teruya
All-Rounder

■16 years old (high school student)
■Born July 21

■Gladius, Blood type O
■Height: 5'2"
■Likes: Flan, noodles, piano, dogs

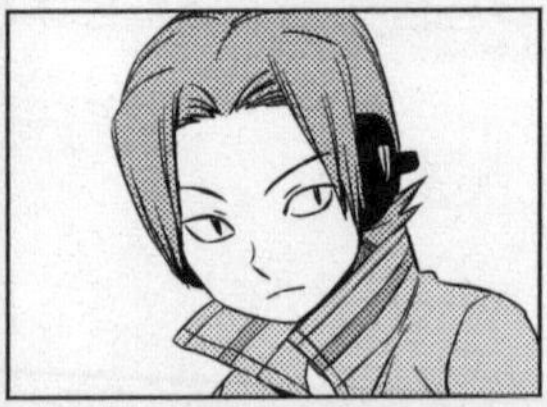

Kotaro Tomoe
Gunner

■14 years old (middle school student)
■Born Dec. 2

■Cetacea, Blood type B
■Height: 5'1"
■Likes: Hashed meat and rice, watermelon, manga

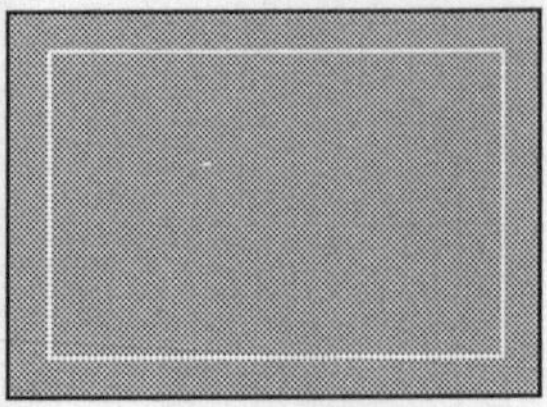

Madoka Ui
Operator

■16 years old (high school student)
■Born April 26

■Felis, Blood type B
■Height: 5'2"
■Likes: Tempura, chilled noodles, manga, cats

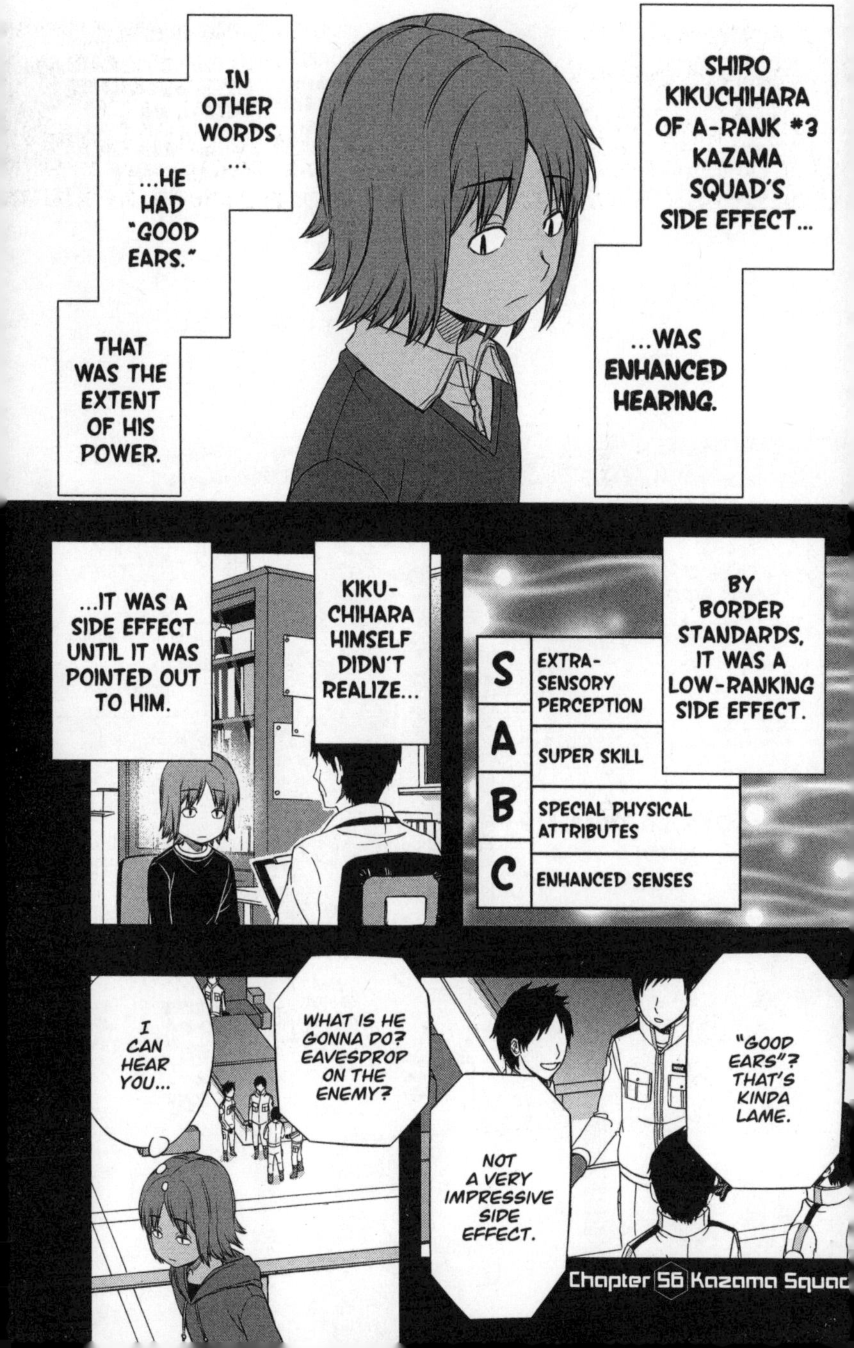
SHIRO KIKUCHIHARA OF A-RANK #3 KAZAMA SQUAD'S SIDE EFFECT...
...WAS ENHANCED HEARING.
IN OTHER WORDS ...
...HE HAD "GOOD EARS."
THAT WAS THE EXTENT OF HIS POWER.
BY BORDER STANDARDS, IT WAS A LOW-RANKING SIDE EFFECT.
S EXTRA-SENSORY PERCEPTION
A SUPER SKILL
B SPECIAL PHYSICAL ATTRIBUTES
C ENHANCED SENSES
KIKU-CHIHARA HIMSELF DIDN'T REALIZE...
...IT WAS A SIDE EFFECT UNTIL IT WAS POINTED OUT TO HIM.
"GOOD EARS"? THAT'S KINDA LAME.
NOT A VERY IMPRESSIVE SIDE EFFECT.
WHAT IS HE GONNA DO? EAVESDROP ON THE ENEMY?
I CAN HEAR YOU...
Chapter 56 Kazama Squad

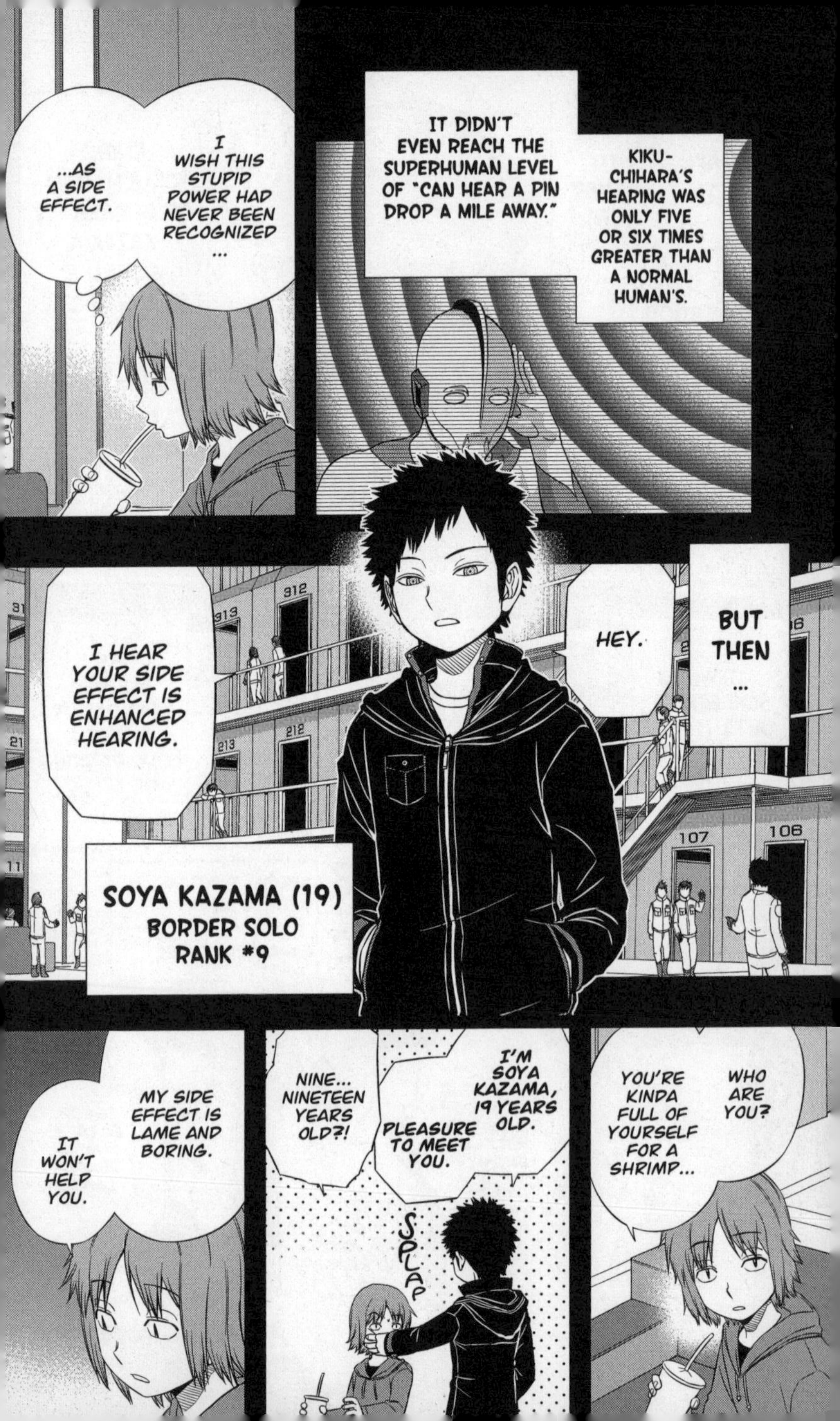
KIKU-CHIHARA'S HEARING WAS ONLY FIVE OR SIX TIMES GREATER THAN A NORMAL HUMAN'S.
IT DIDN'T EVEN REACH THE SUPERHUMAN LEVEL OF "CAN HEAR A PIN DROP A MILE AWAY."
I WISH THIS STUPID POWER HAD NEVER BEEN RECOGNIZED...
...AS A SIDE EFFECT.
BUT THEN...
HEY.
I HEAR YOUR SIDE EFFECT IS ENHANCED HEARING.
SOYA KAZAMA (19) BORDER SOLO RANK #9
WHO ARE YOU?
YOU'RE KINDA FULL OF YOURSELF FOR A SHRIMP...
I'M SOYA KAZAMA, 19 YEARS OLD.
PLEASURE TO MEET YOU.
NINE... NINETEEN YEARS OLD?!
SPLAP
MY SIDE EFFECT IS LAME AND BORING.
IT WON'T HELP YOU.

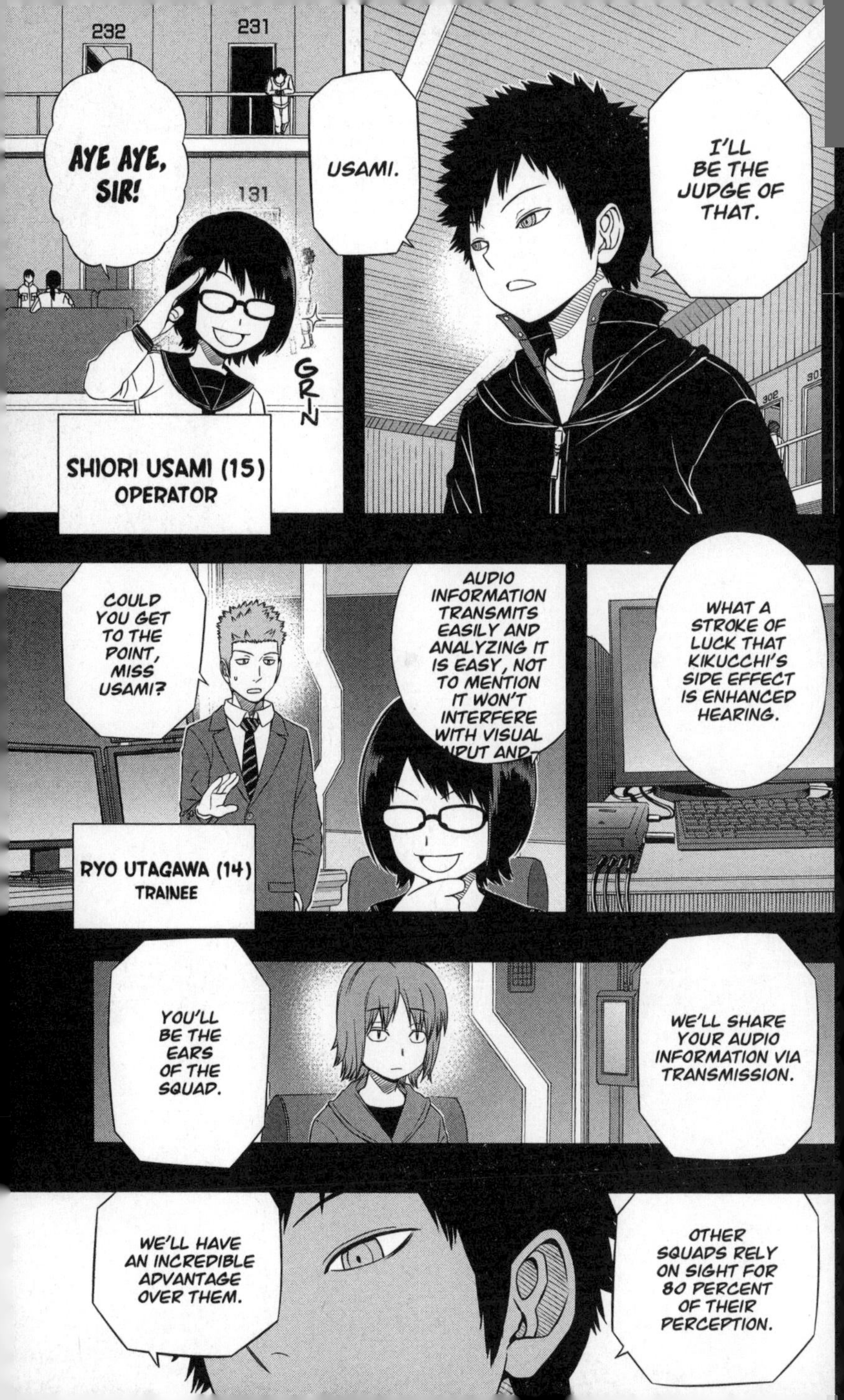
I'LL BE THE JUDGE OF THAT.
USAMI.
AYE AYE, SIR!
GRIN
SHIORI USAMI (15) OPERATOR
WHAT A STROKE OF LUCK THAT KIKUCCHI'S SIDE EFFECT IS ENHANCED HEARING.
AUDIO INFORMATION TRANSMITS EASILY AND ANALYZING IT IS EASY, NOT TO MENTION IT WON'T INTERFERE WITH VISUAL INPUT AND—
COULD YOU GET TO THE POINT, MISS USAMI?
RYO UTAGAWA (14) TRAINEE
WE'LL SHARE YOUR AUDIO INFORMATION VIA TRANSMISSION.
YOU'LL BE THE EARS OF THE SQUAD.
OTHER SQUADS RELY ON SIGHT FOR 80 PERCENT OF THEIR PERCEPTION.
WE'LL HAVE AN INCREDIBLE ADVANTAGE OVER THEM.

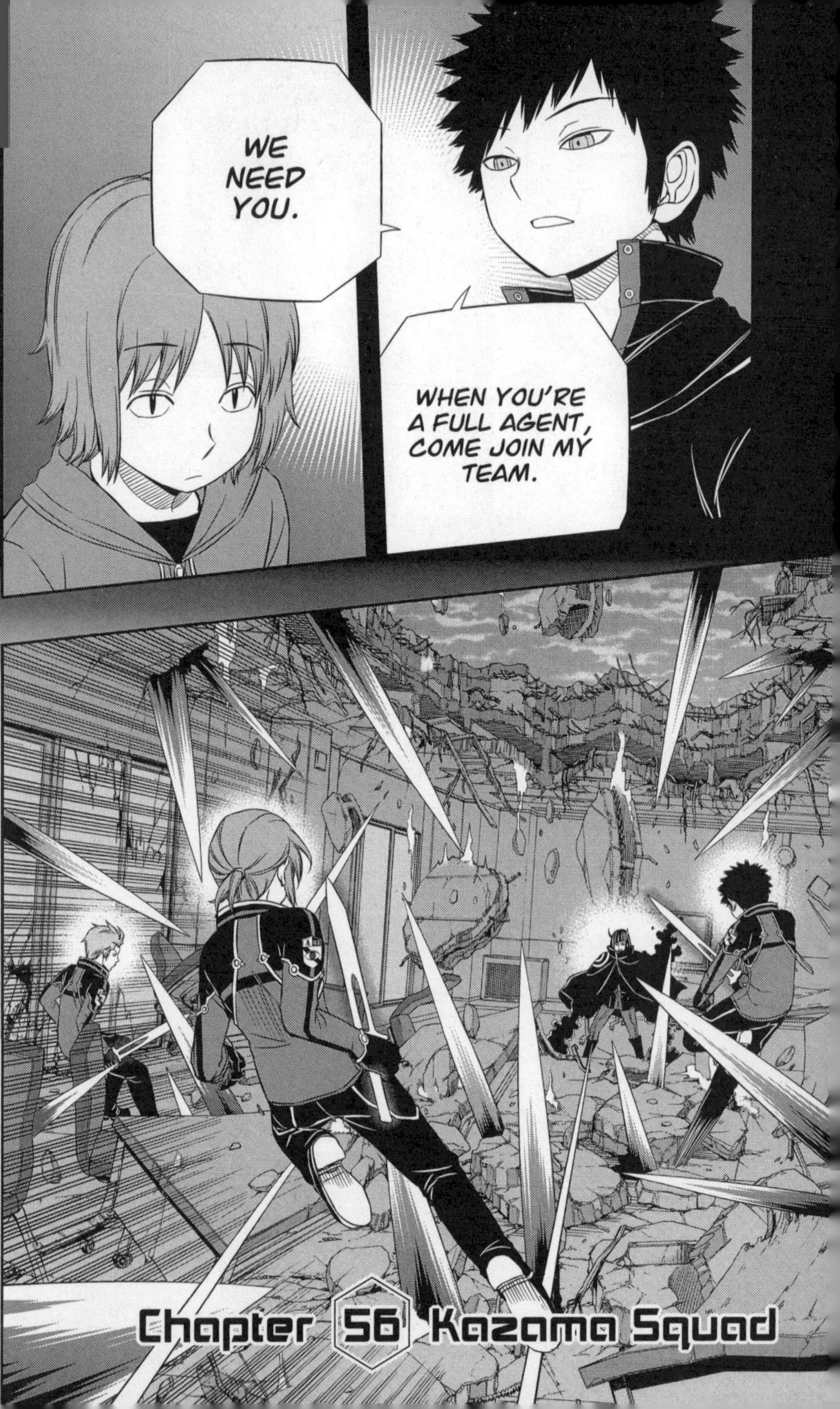
WHEN YOU'RE A FULL AGENT, COME JOIN MY TEAM.
WE NEED YOU.
Chapter 56 Kazama Squad

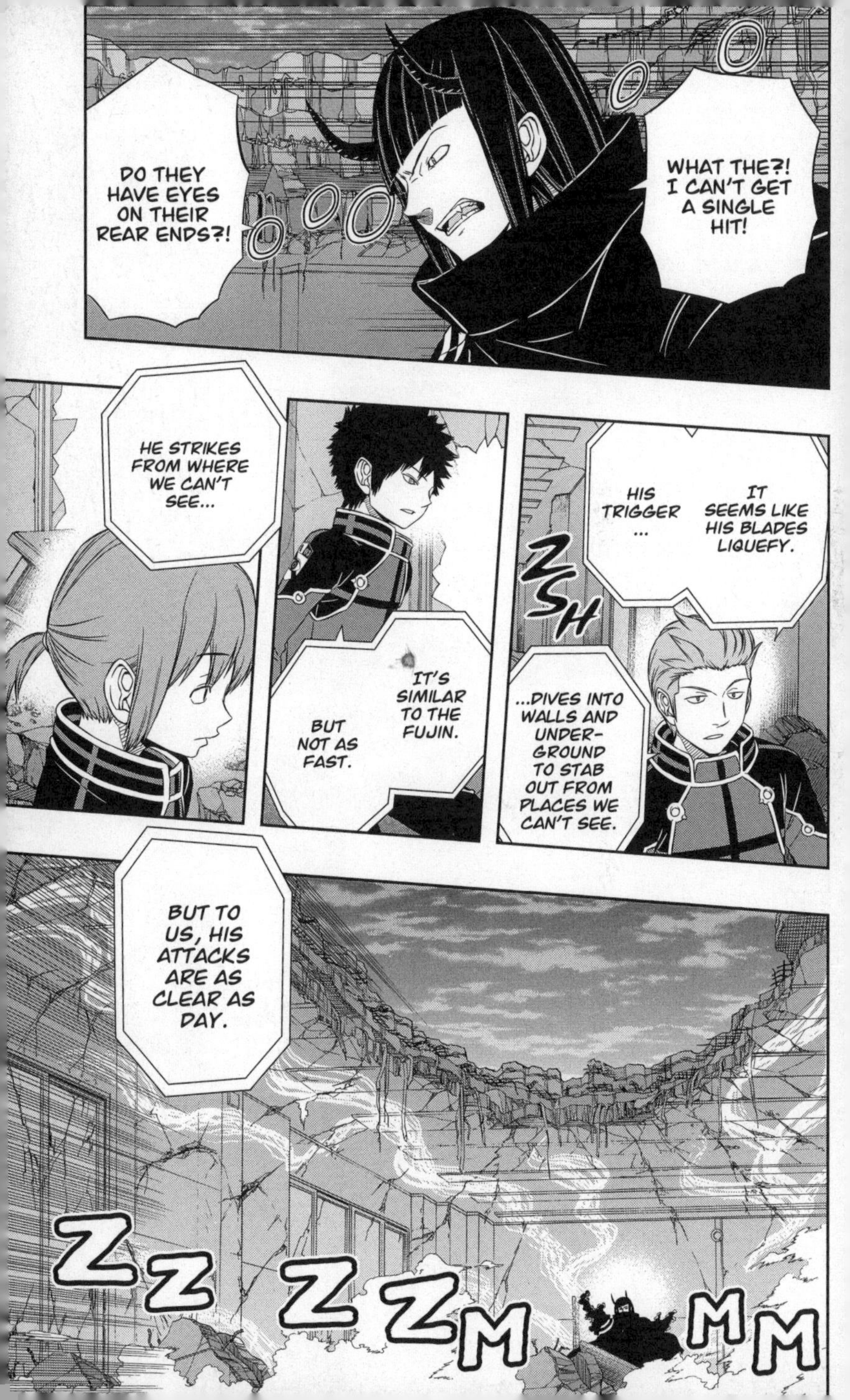
WHAT THE?! I CAN'T GET A SINGLE HIT!
DO THEY HAVE EYES ON THEIR REAR ENDS?!
IT SEEMS LIKE HIS BLADES LIQUEFY.
HIS TRIGGER...
ZSH
...DIVES INTO WALLS AND UNDER-GROUND TO STAB OUT FROM PLACES WE CAN'T SEE.
IT'S SIMILAR TO THE FUJIN.
BUT NOT AS FAST.
HE STRIKES FROM WHERE WE CAN'T SEE...
BUT TO US, HIS ATTACKS ARE AS CLEAR AS DAY.
ZZZZMMM

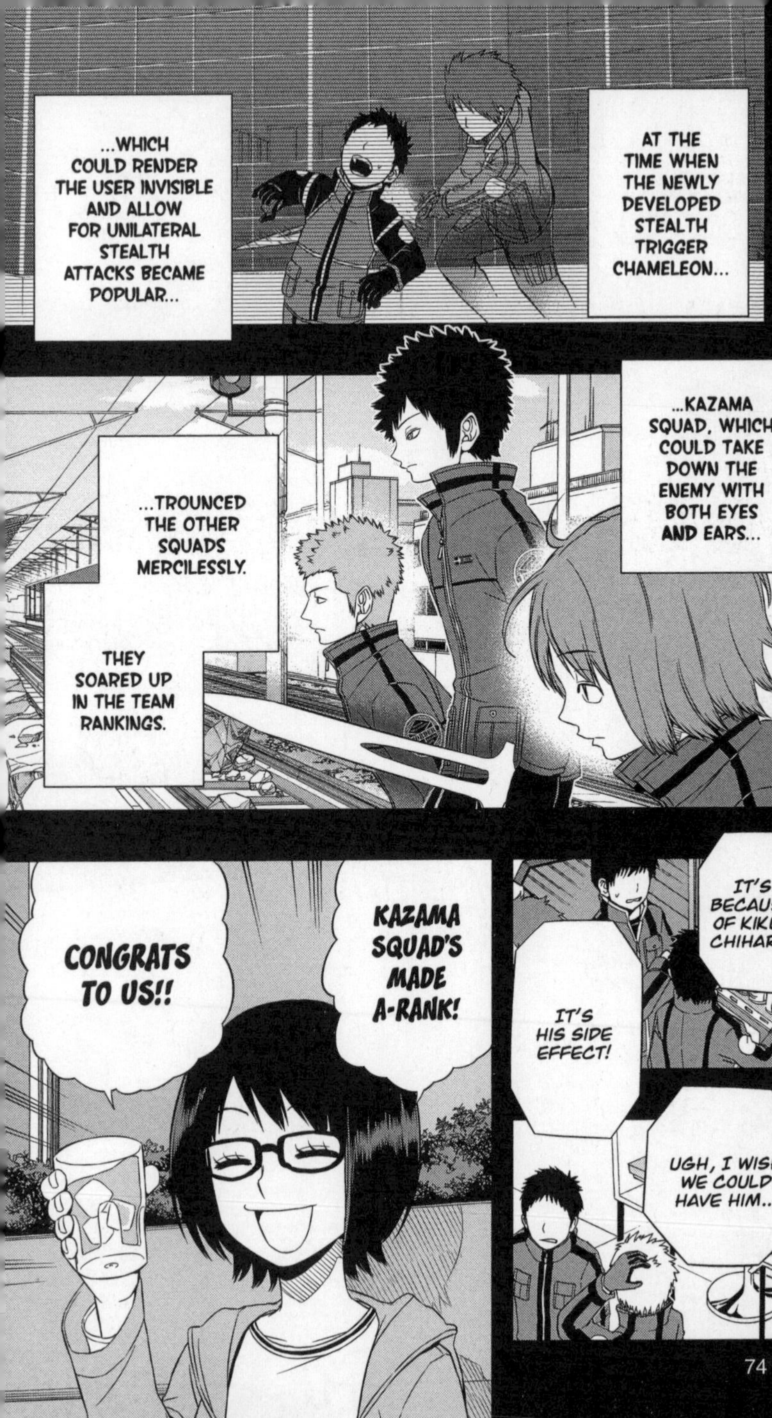
AT THE TIME WHEN THE NEWLY DEVELOPED STEALTH TRIGGER CHAMELEON...
...WHICH COULD RENDER THE USER INVISIBLE AND ALLOW FOR UNILATERAL STEALTH ATTACKS BECAME POPULAR...
...KAZAMA SQUAD, WHICH COULD TAKE DOWN THE ENEMY WITH BOTH EYES AND EARS...
...TROUNCED THE OTHER SQUADS MERCILESSLY.
THEY SOARED UP IN THE TEAM RANKINGS.
IT'S BECAUSE OF KIKU-CHIHARA!
IT'S HIS SIDE EFFECT!
UGH, I WISH WE COULD HAVE HIM...
KAZAMA SQUAD'S MADE A-RANK!
CONGRATS TO US!!

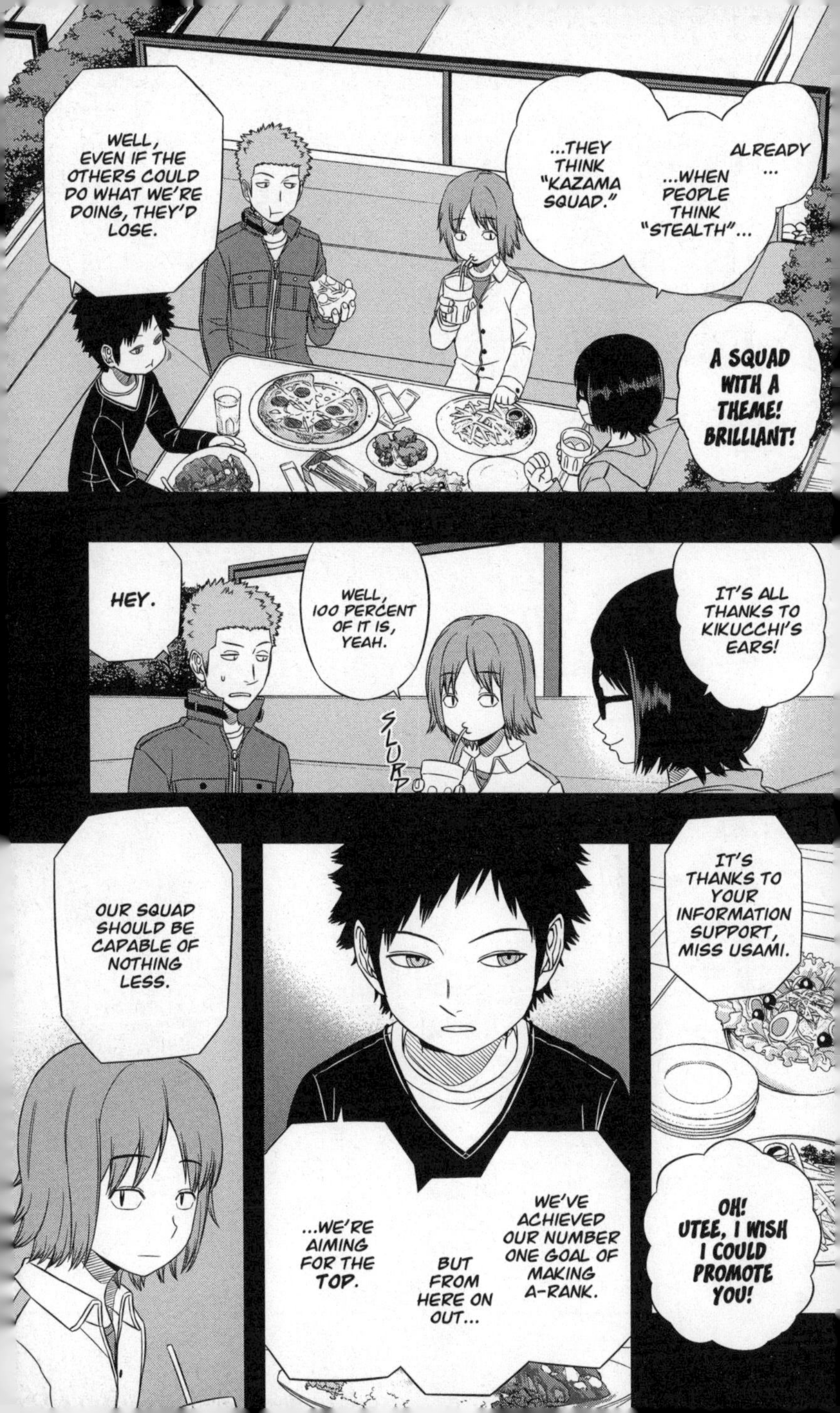
ALREADY ...
...WHEN PEOPLE THINK "STEALTH"...
...THEY THINK "KAZAMA SQUAD."
A SQUAD WITH A THEME! BRILLIANT!
WELL, EVEN IF THE OTHERS COULD DO WHAT WE'RE DOING, THEY'D LOSE.
IT'S ALL THANKS TO KIKUCCHI'S EARS!
WELL, 100 PERCENT OF IT IS, YEAH.
SLURP
HEY.
IT'S THANKS TO YOUR INFORMATION SUPPORT, MISS USAMI.
OH! UTEE, I WISH I COULD PROMOTE YOU!
WE'VE ACHIEVED OUR NUMBER ONE GOAL OF MAKING A-RANK.
BUT FROM HERE ON OUT...
...WE'RE AIMING FOR THE TOP.
OUR SQUAD SHOULD BE CAPABLE OF NOTHING LESS.

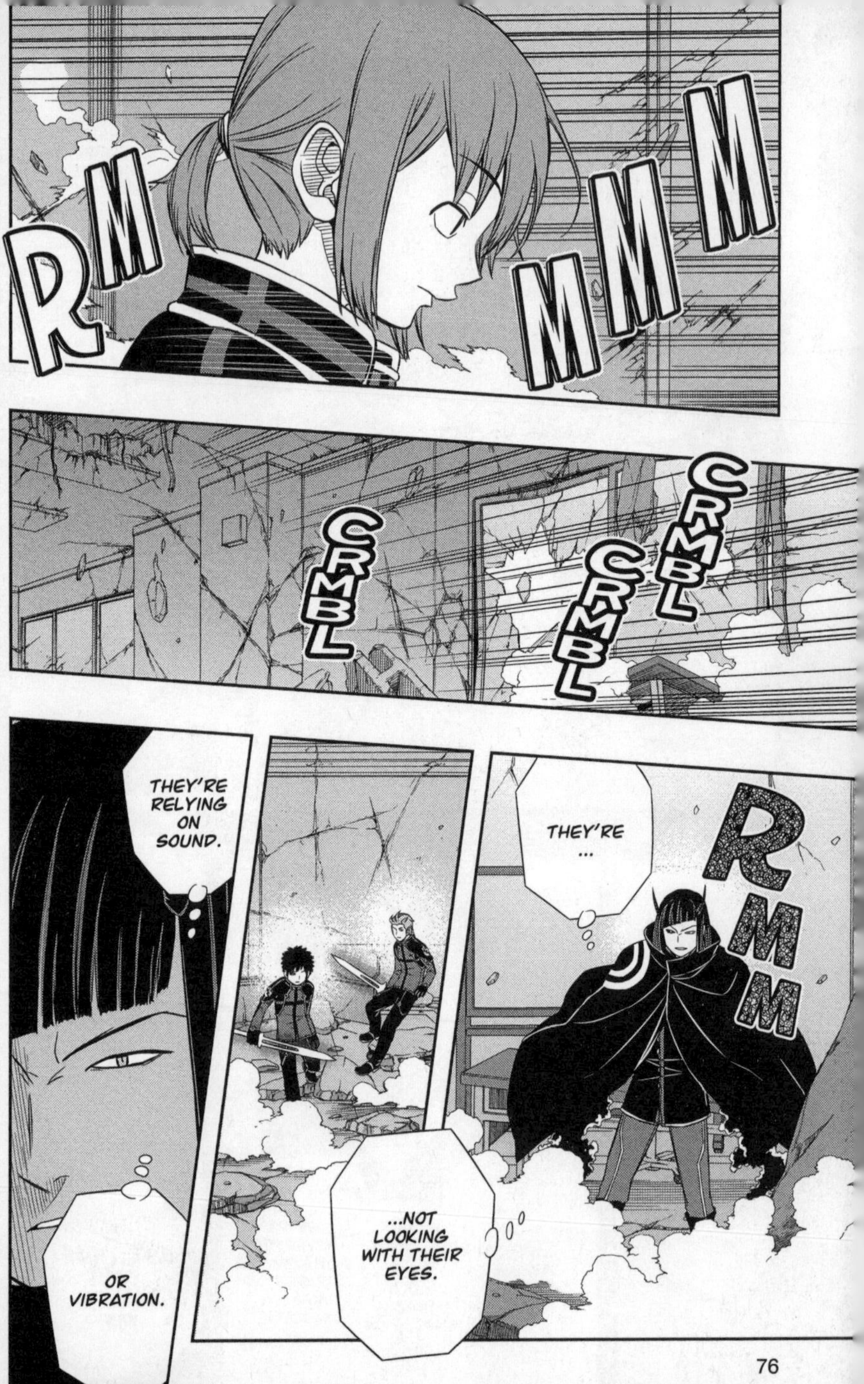
RMMMMM
CRMBL
CRMBL
CRMBL
THEY'RE ...
RMM
...NOT LOOKING WITH THEIR EYES.
THEY'RE RELYING ON SOUND.
OR VIBRATION.

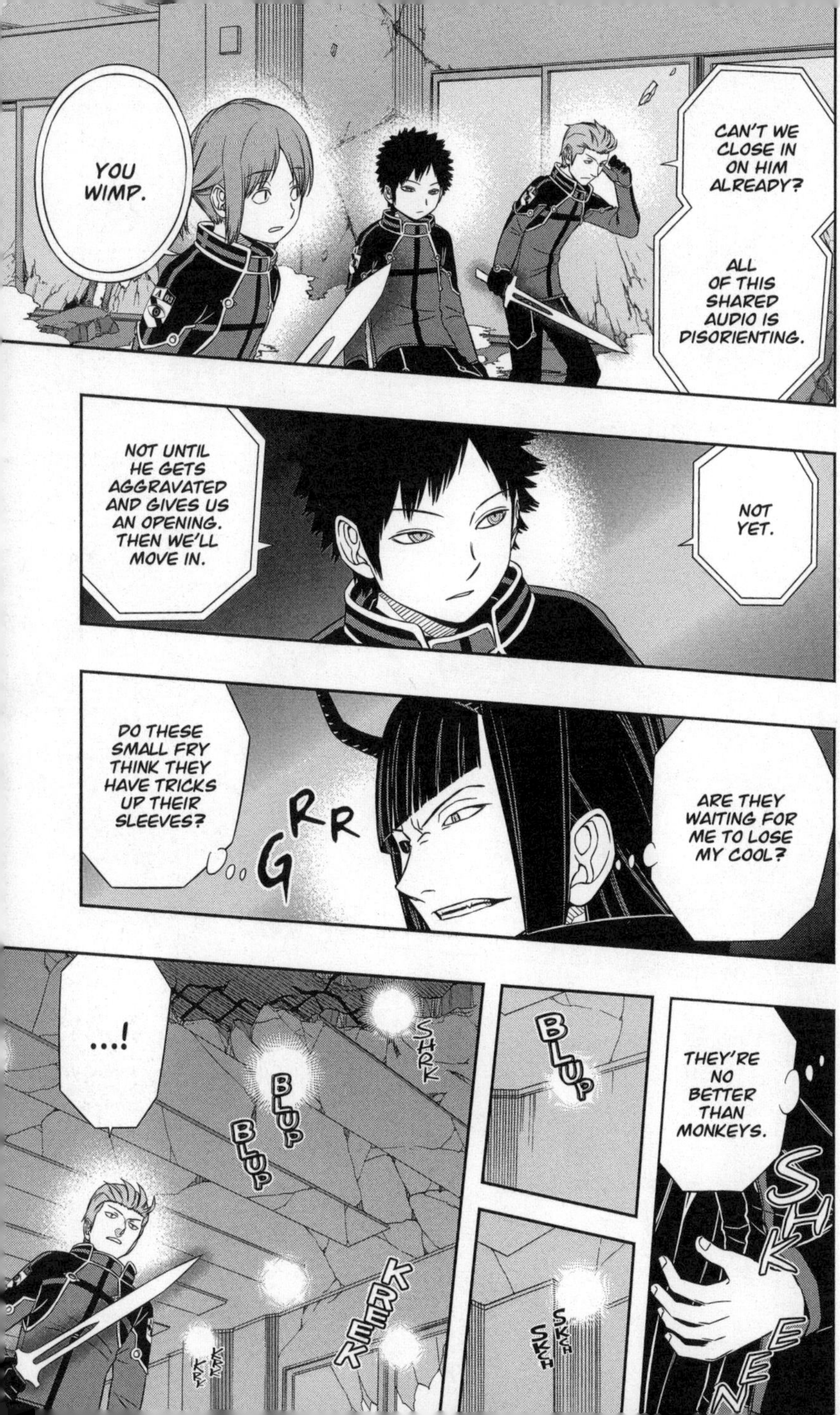
CAN'T WE CLOSE IN ON HIM ALREADY?
ALL OF THIS SHARED AUDIO IS DISORIENTING.
YOU WIMP.
NOT YET.
NOT UNTIL HE GETS AGGRAVATED AND GIVES US AN OPENING. THEN WE'LL MOVE IN.
ARE THEY WAITING FOR ME TO LOSE MY COOL?
GRR
DO THESE SMALL FRY THINK THEY HAVE TRICKS UP THEIR SLEEVES?
THEY'RE NO BETTER THAN MONKEYS.
SHKEEEN
BLUP
SKCH SKCH
...!
SHRK
BLUP
BLUP
KREK
KRK KRK

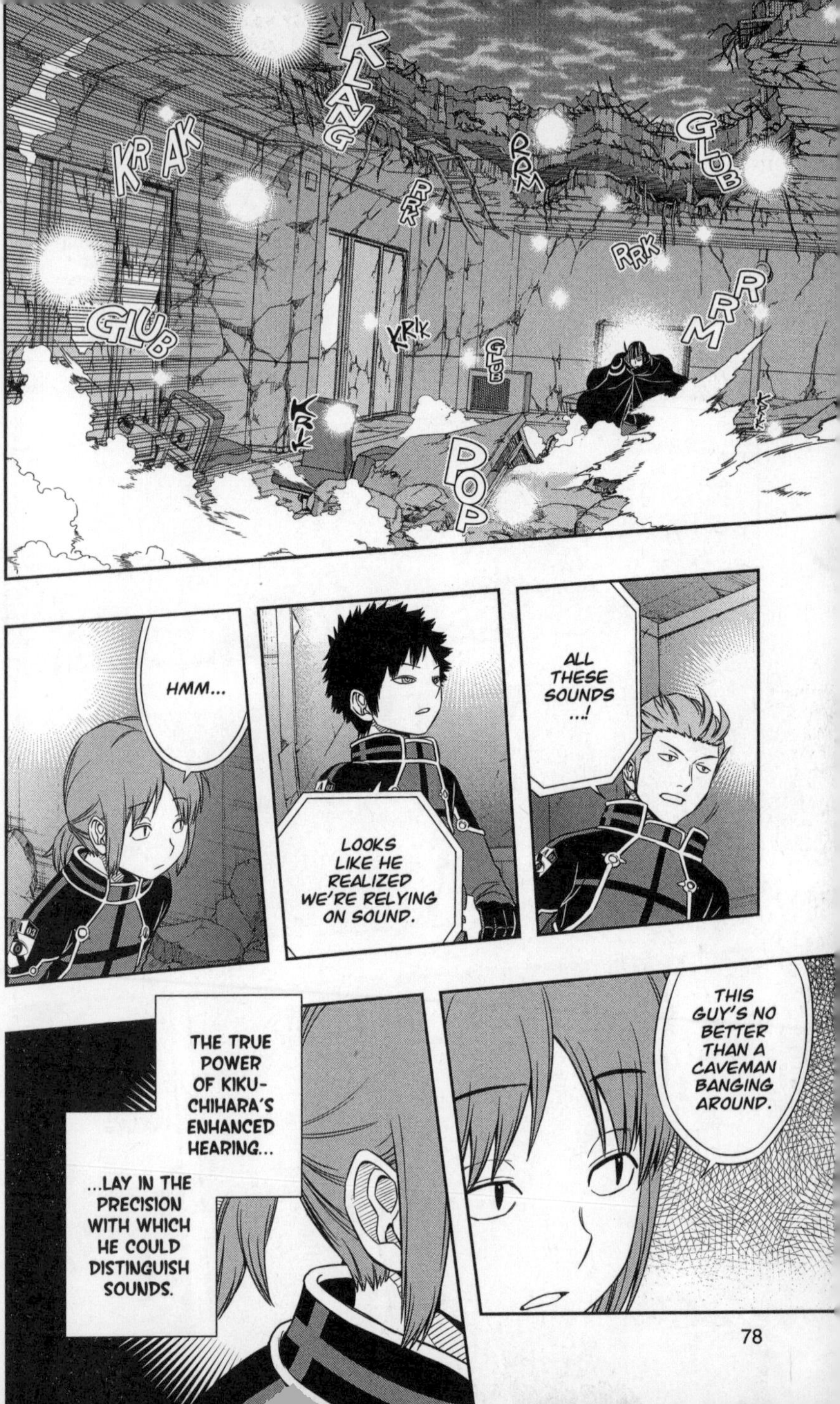
GLUB
RRRM
RRK
RRM
KLANG
RRK
KRAK
GLUB
KRIK
GLUB
KRK
KRK
POP
ALL THESE SOUNDS...!
LOOKS LIKE HE REALIZED WE'RE RELYING ON SOUND.
HMM...
THIS GUY'S NO BETTER THAN A CAVEMAN BANGING AROUND.
THE TRUE POWER OF KIKU-CHIHARA'S ENHANCED HEARING...
...LAY IN THE PRECISION WITH WHICH HE COULD DISTINGUISH SOUNDS.

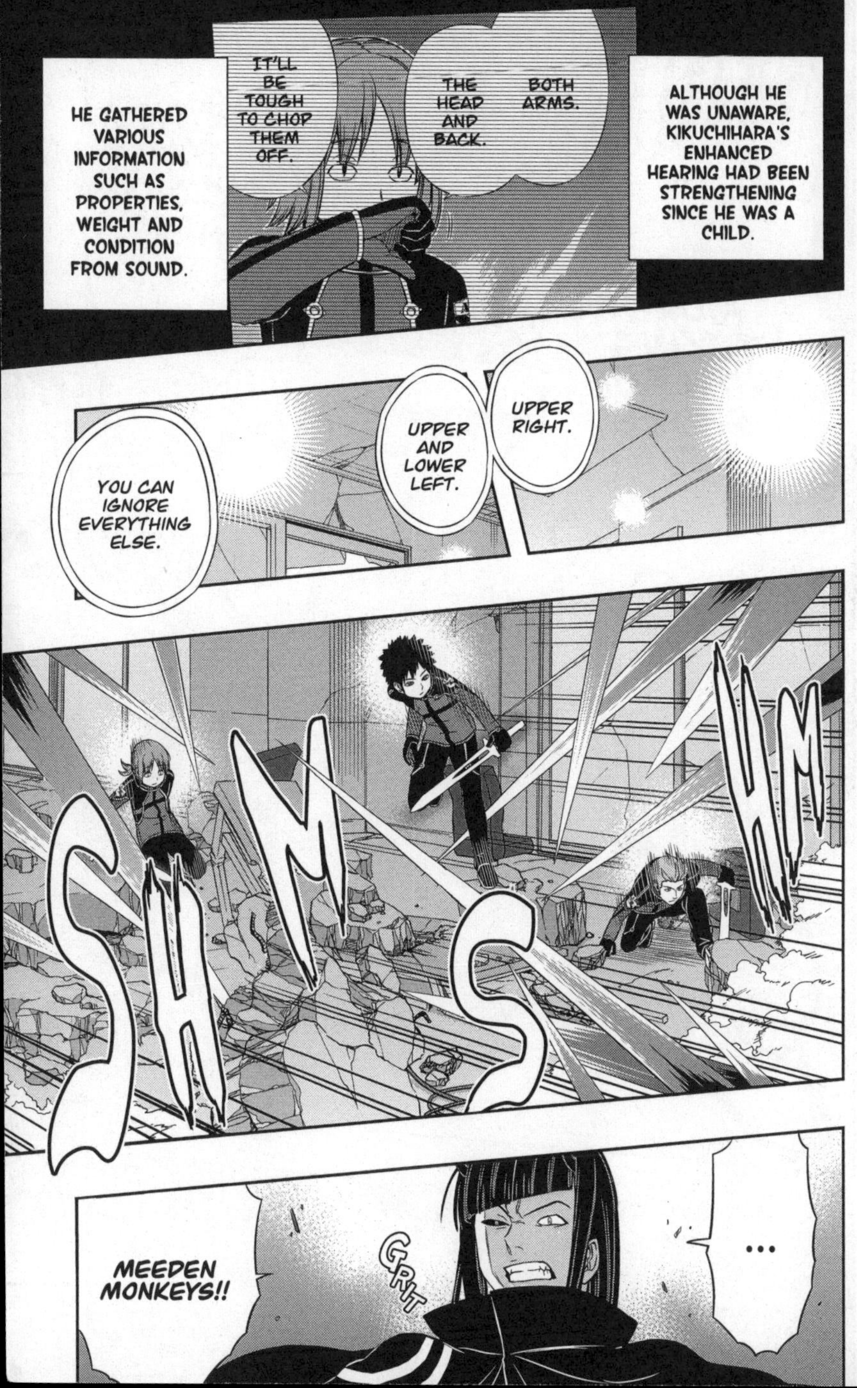
ALTHOUGH HE WAS UNAWARE, KIKUCHIHARA'S ENHANCED HEARING HAD BEEN STRENGTHENING SINCE HE WAS A CHILD.
BOTH ARMS.
THE HEAD AND BACK.
IT'LL BE TOUGH TO CHOP THEM OFF.
HE GATHERED VARIOUS INFORMATION SUCH AS PROPERTIES, WEIGHT AND CONDITION FROM SOUND.
UPPER RIGHT.
UPPER AND LOWER LEFT.
YOU CAN IGNORE EVERYTHING ELSE.
SHM
SHM
...
GRIT
MEEDEN MONKEYS!!

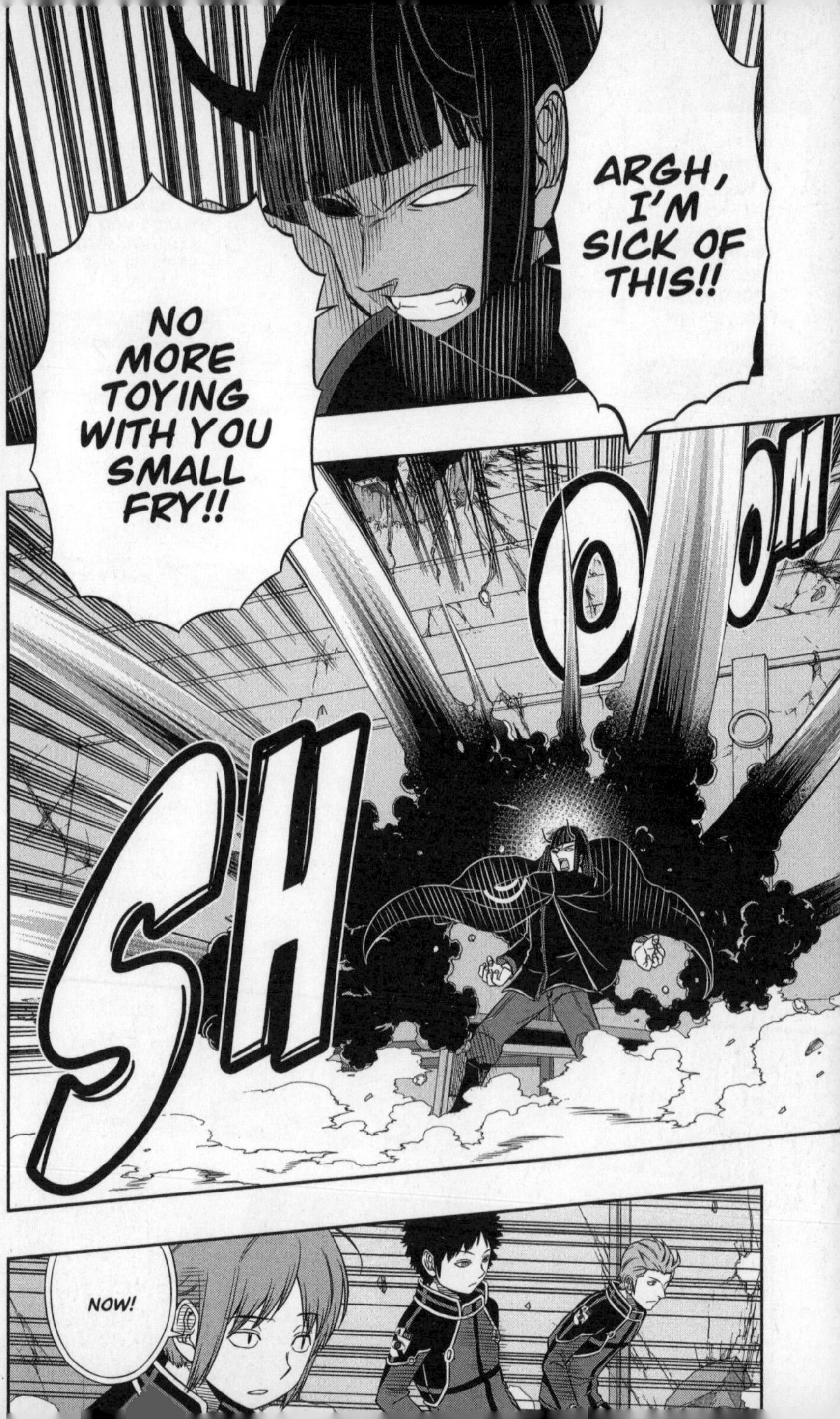
ARGH, I'M SICK OF THIS!!
NO MORE TOYING WITH YOU SMALL FRY!!
SHOOM
NOW!

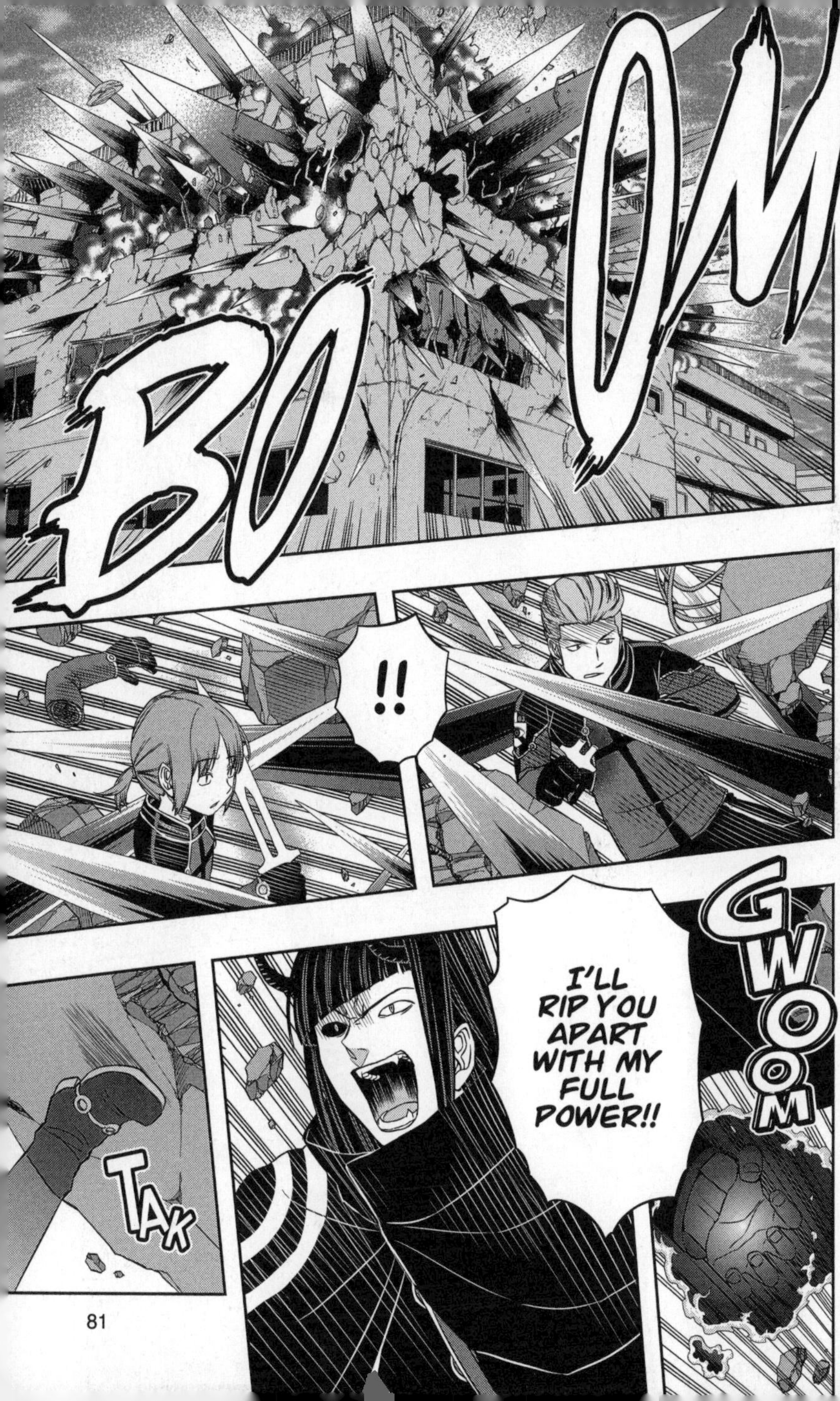
BOOM
!!
GWOOM
I'LL RIP YOU APART WITH MY FULL POWER!!
TAK

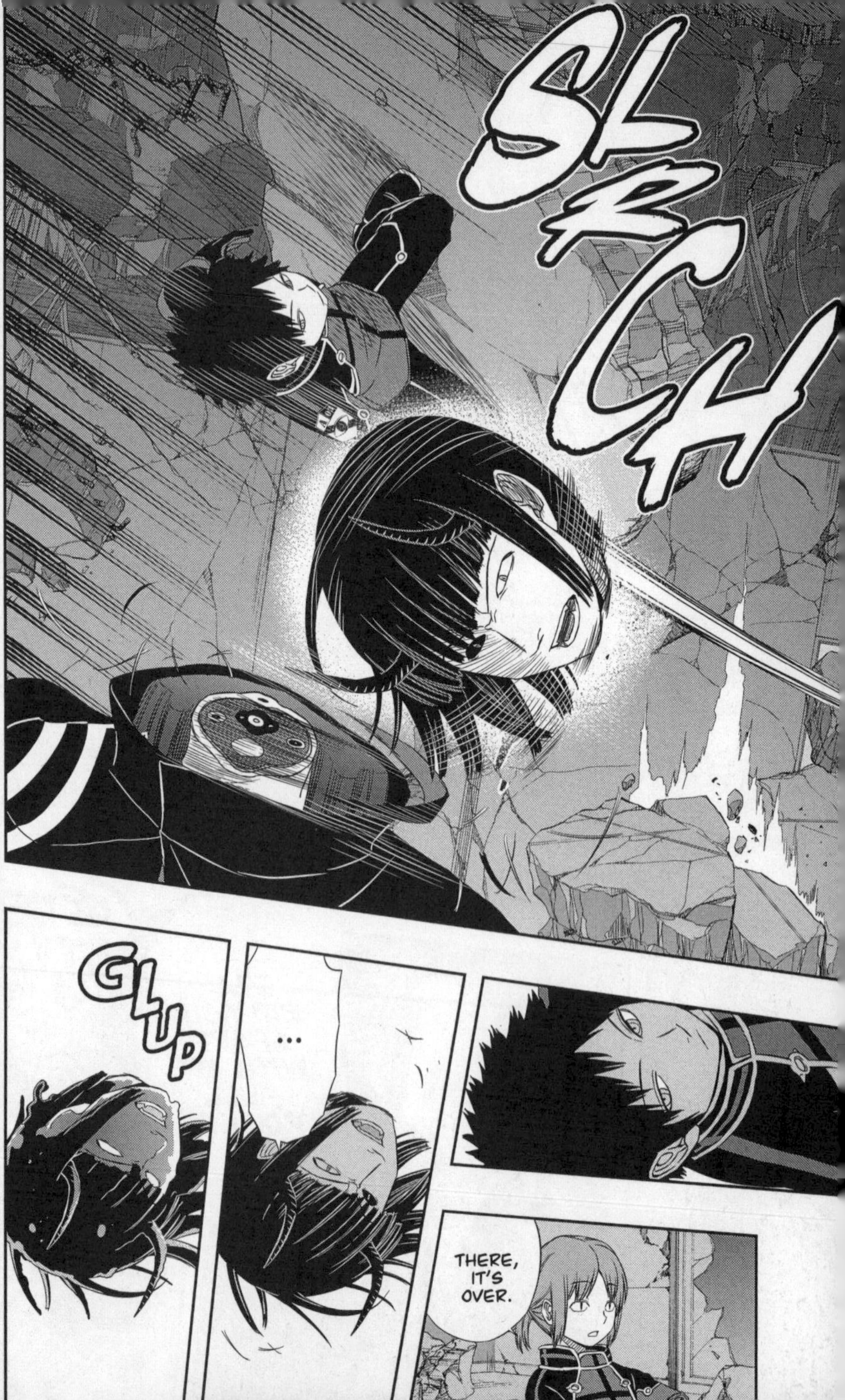
SLRCH
THERE, IT'S OVER.
...
GLUP

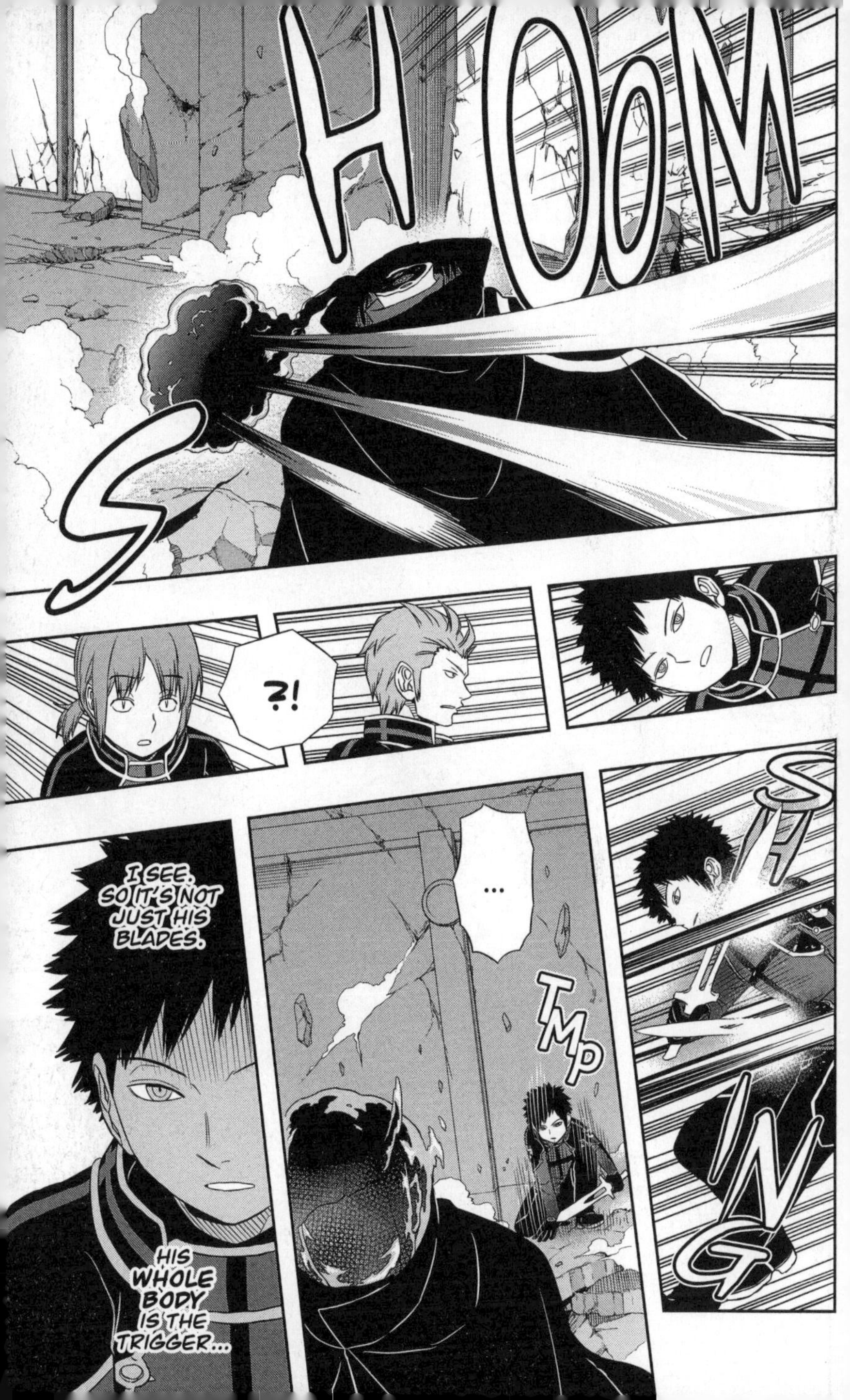
HOOM
S
?!
SHING
...
TMP
I SEE. SO IT'S NOT JUST HIS BLADES.
HIS WHOLE BODY IS THE TRIGGER...

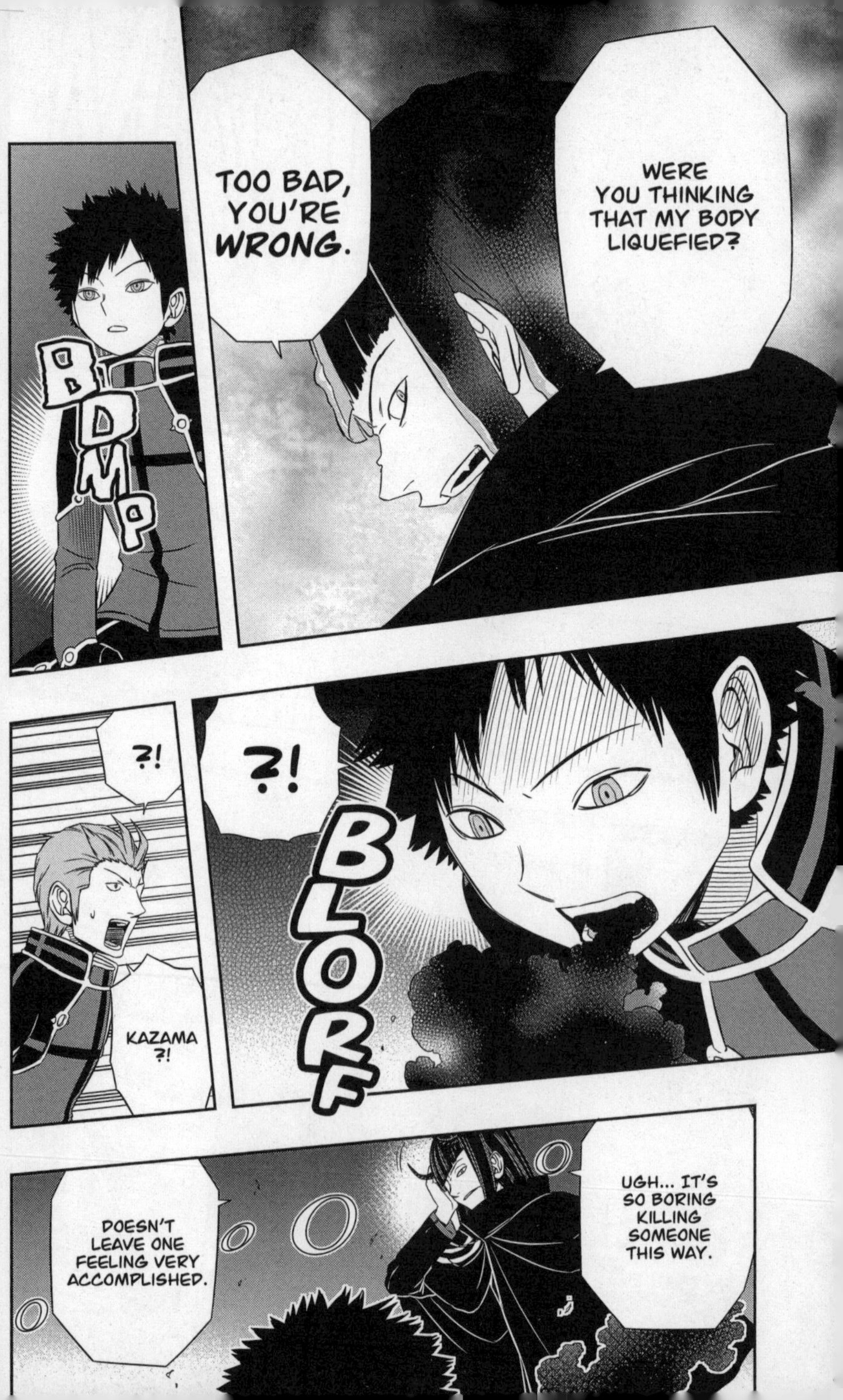
WERE YOU THINKING THAT MY BODY LIQUEFIED?
TOO BAD, YOU'RE WRONG.
BDMP
?!
BLORF
?!
KAZAMA ?!
UGH... IT'S SO BORING KILLING SOMEONE THIS WAY.
DOESN'T LEAVE ONE FEELING VERY ACCOMPLISHED.

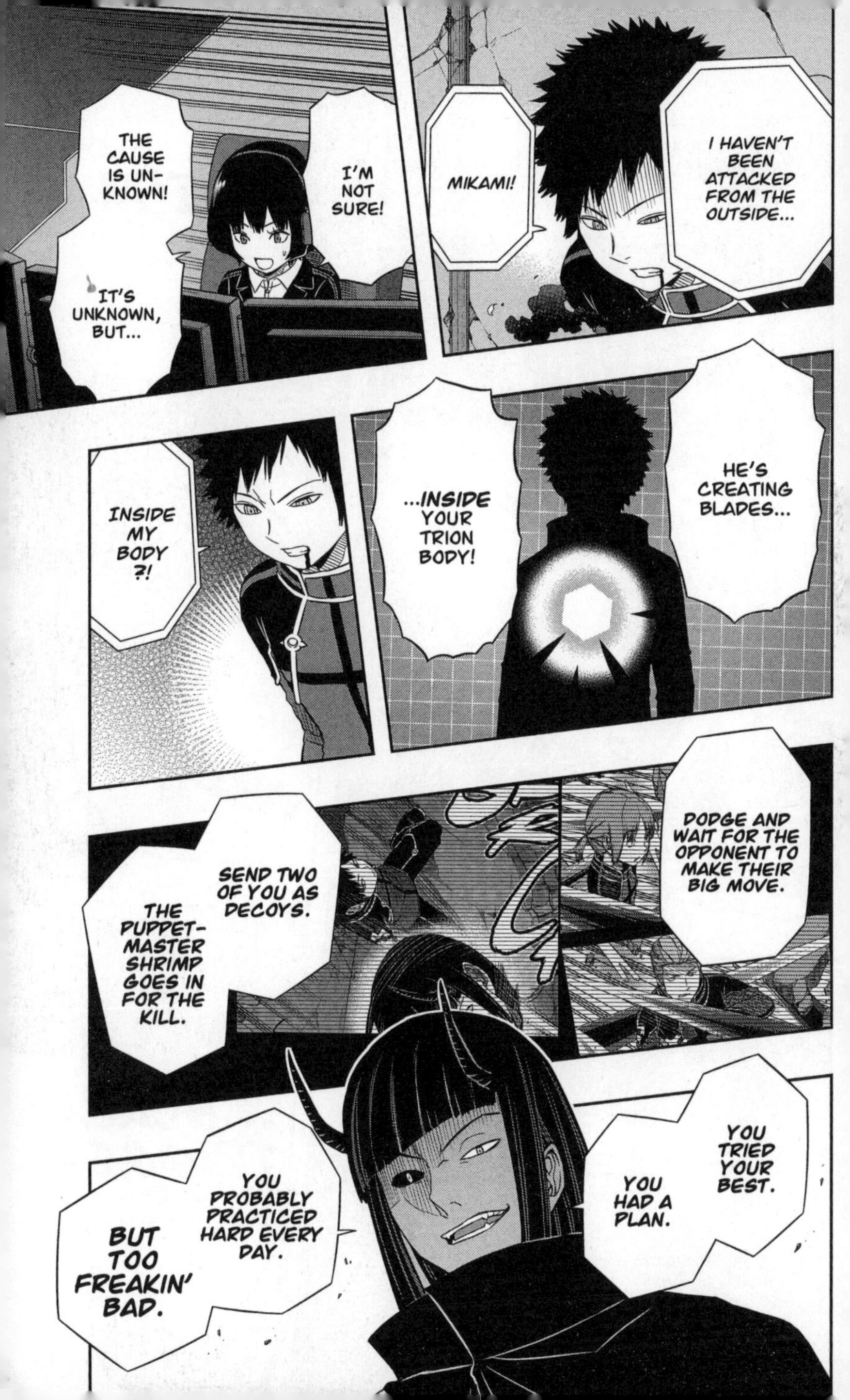
I HAVEN'T BEEN ATTACKED FROM THE OUTSIDE...
MIKAMI!
I'M NOT SURE!
THE CAUSE IS UN-KNOWN!
IT'S UNKNOWN, BUT...
HE'S CREATING BLADES...
...INSIDE YOUR TRION BODY!
INSIDE MY BODY ?!
DODGE AND WAIT FOR THE OPPONENT TO MAKE THEIR BIG MOVE.
SEND TWO OF YOU AS DECOYS.
THE PUPPET-MASTER SHRIMP GOES IN FOR THE KILL.
YOU TRIED YOUR BEST.
YOU HAD A PLAN.
YOU PROBABLY PRACTICED HARD EVERY DAY.
BUT TOO FREAKIN' BAD.

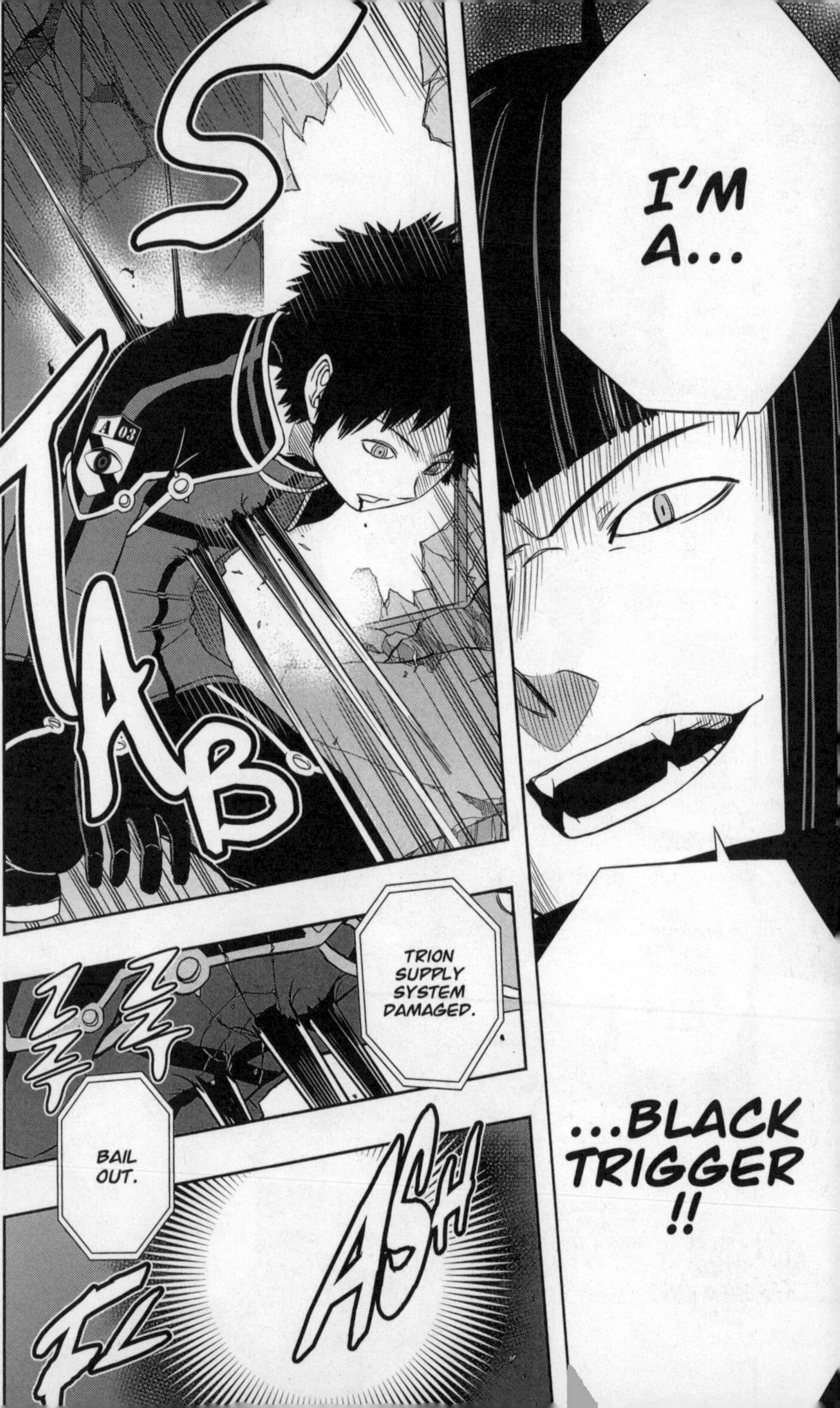
I'M A...
...BLACK TRIGGER!!
STAB
TRION SUPPLY SYSTEM DAMAGED.
BAIL OUT.
FLASH

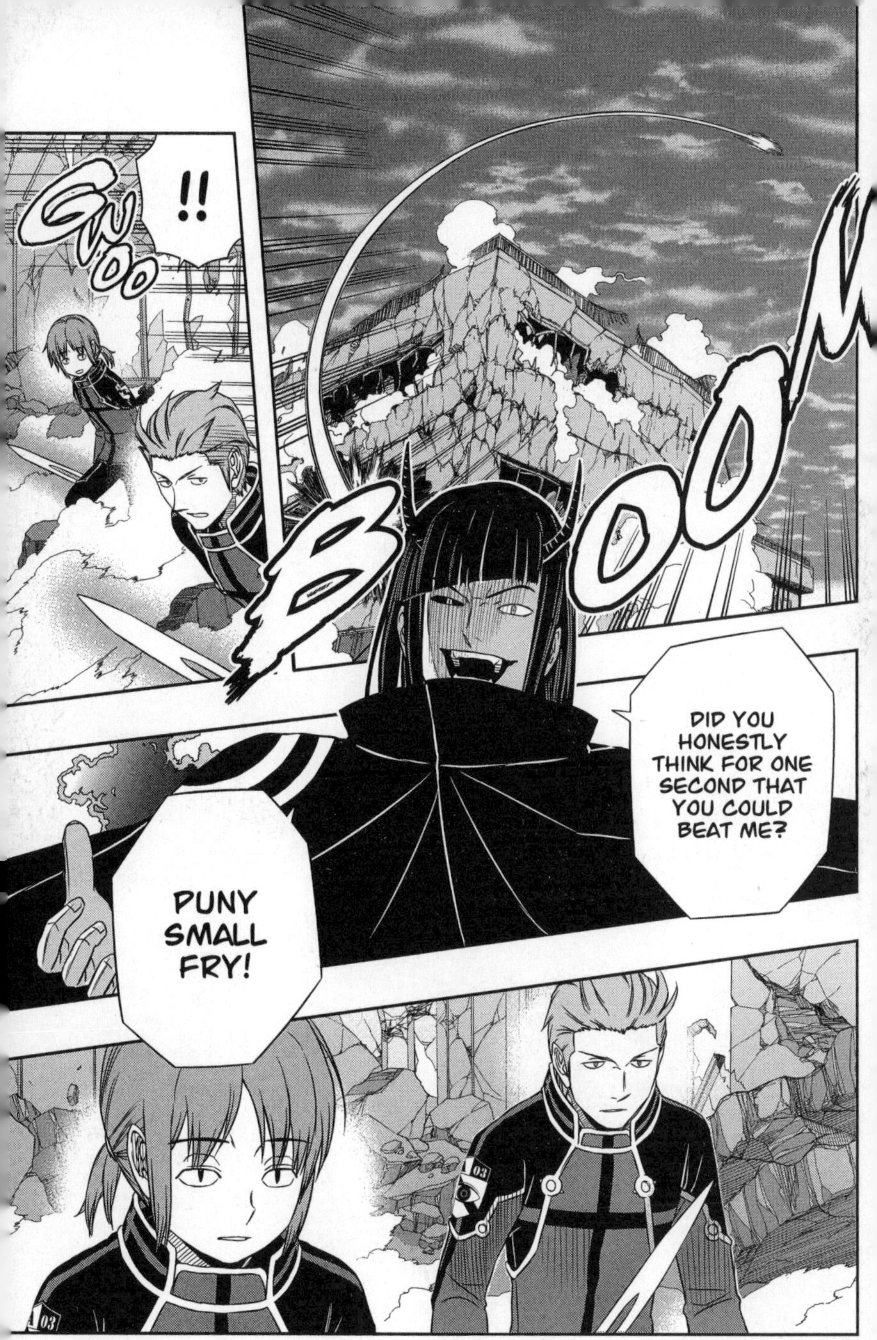
BOOOM
!!
GWOO
DID YOU HONESTLY THINK FOR ONE SECOND THAT YOU COULD BEAT ME?
PUNY SMALL FRY!

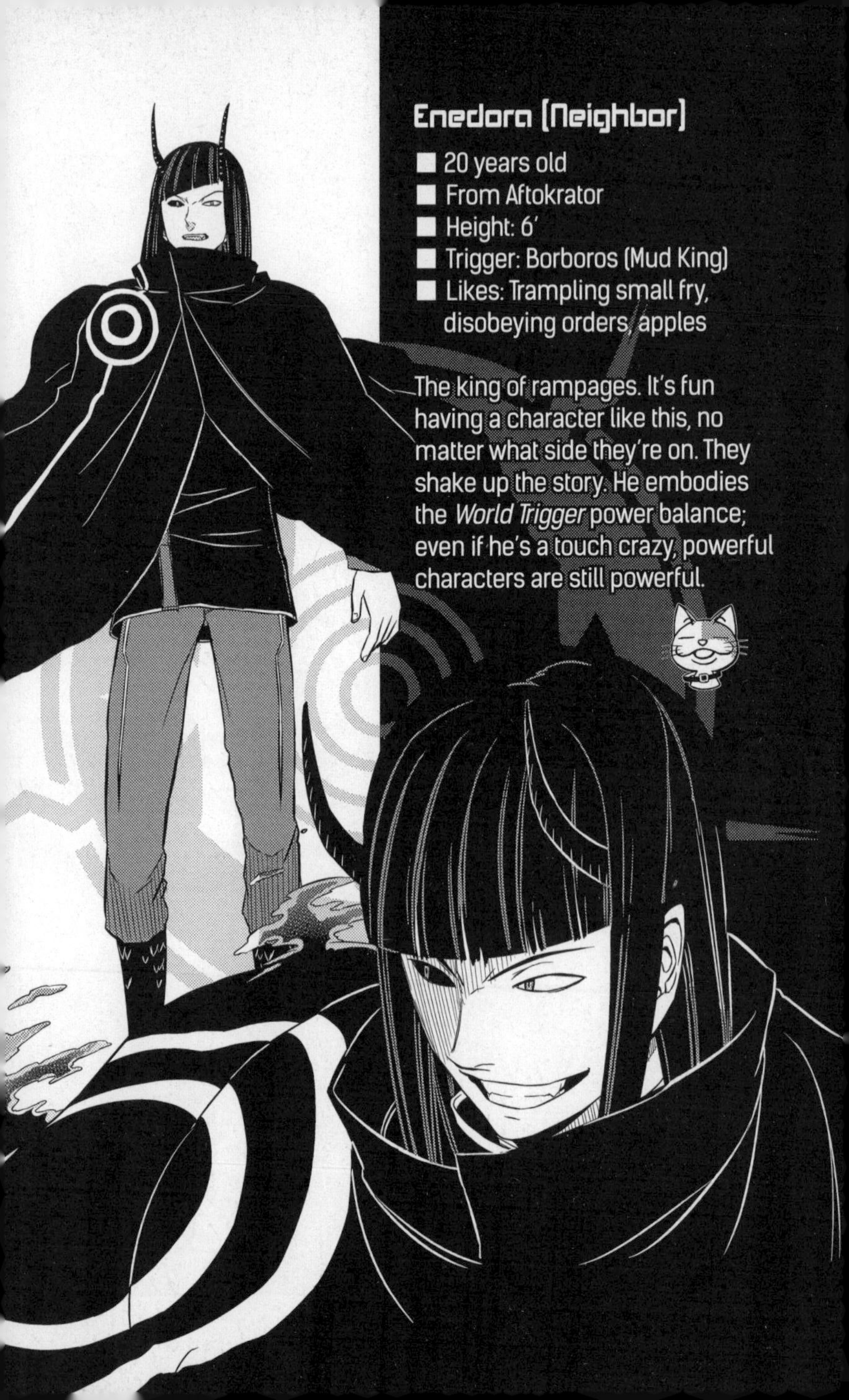

Enedora [Neighbor]

- 20 years old
- From Aftokrator
- Height: 6'
- Trigger: Borboros (Mud King)
- Likes: Trampling small fry, disobeying orders, apples

The king of rampages. It's fun having a character like this, no matter what side they're on. They shake up the story. He embodies the *World Trigger* power balance; even if he's a touch crazy, powerful characters are still powerful.

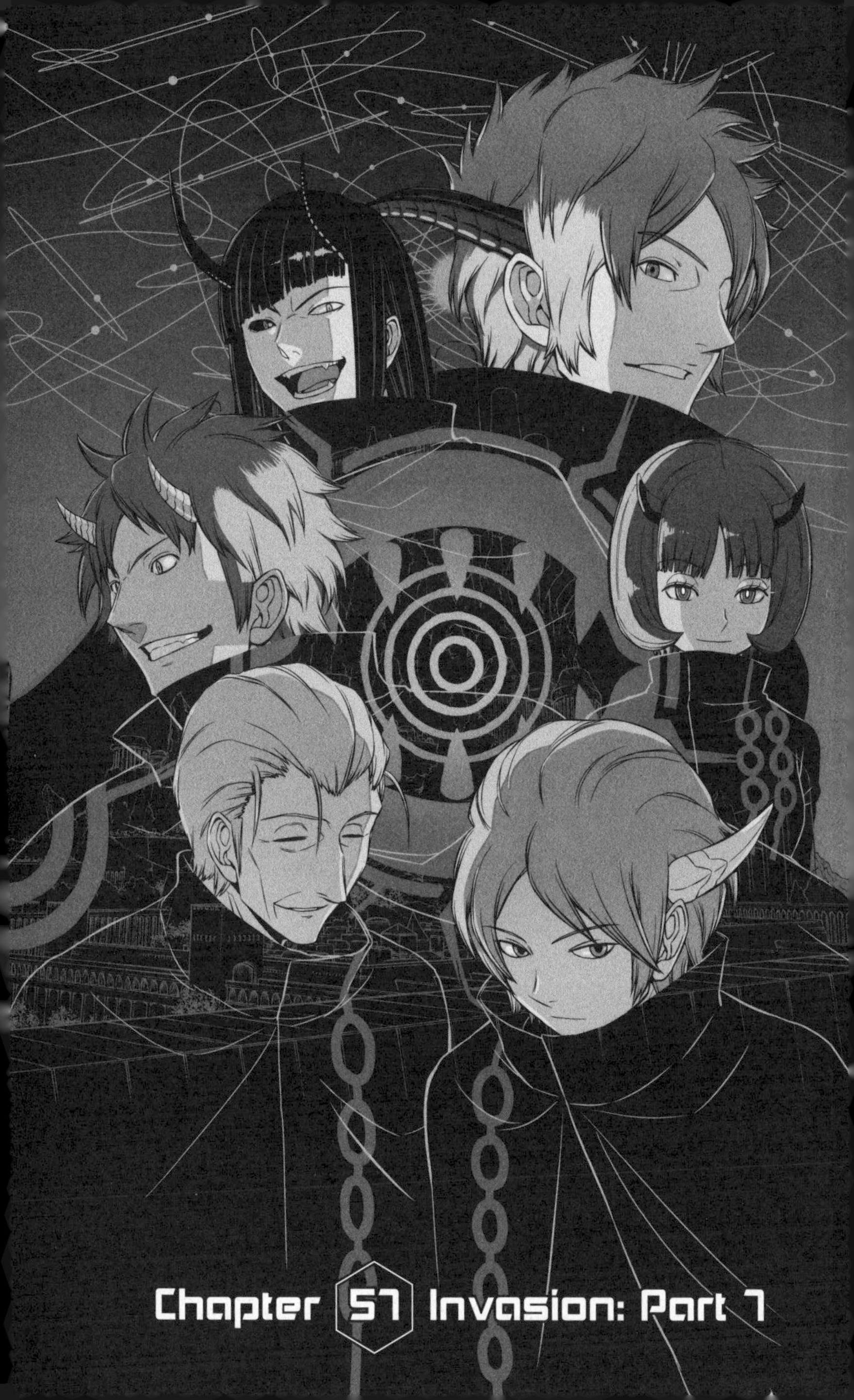

Chapter 51 Invasion: Part 1

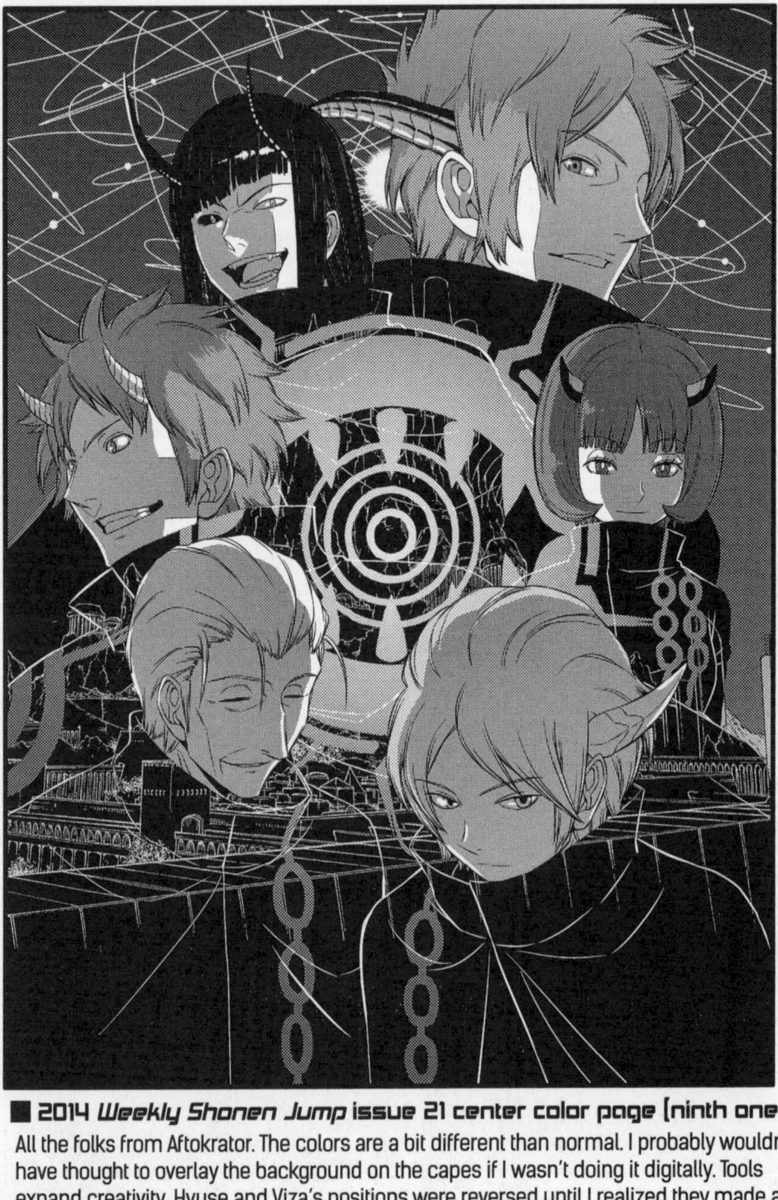

■ 2014 *Weekly Shonen Jump* issue 21 center color page [ninth one]

All the folks from Aftokrator. The colors are a bit different than normal. I probably wouldn't have thought to overlay the background on the capes if I wasn't doing it digitally. Tools expand creativity. Hyuse and Viza's positions were reversed until I realized they made a "choo-choo train" composition.

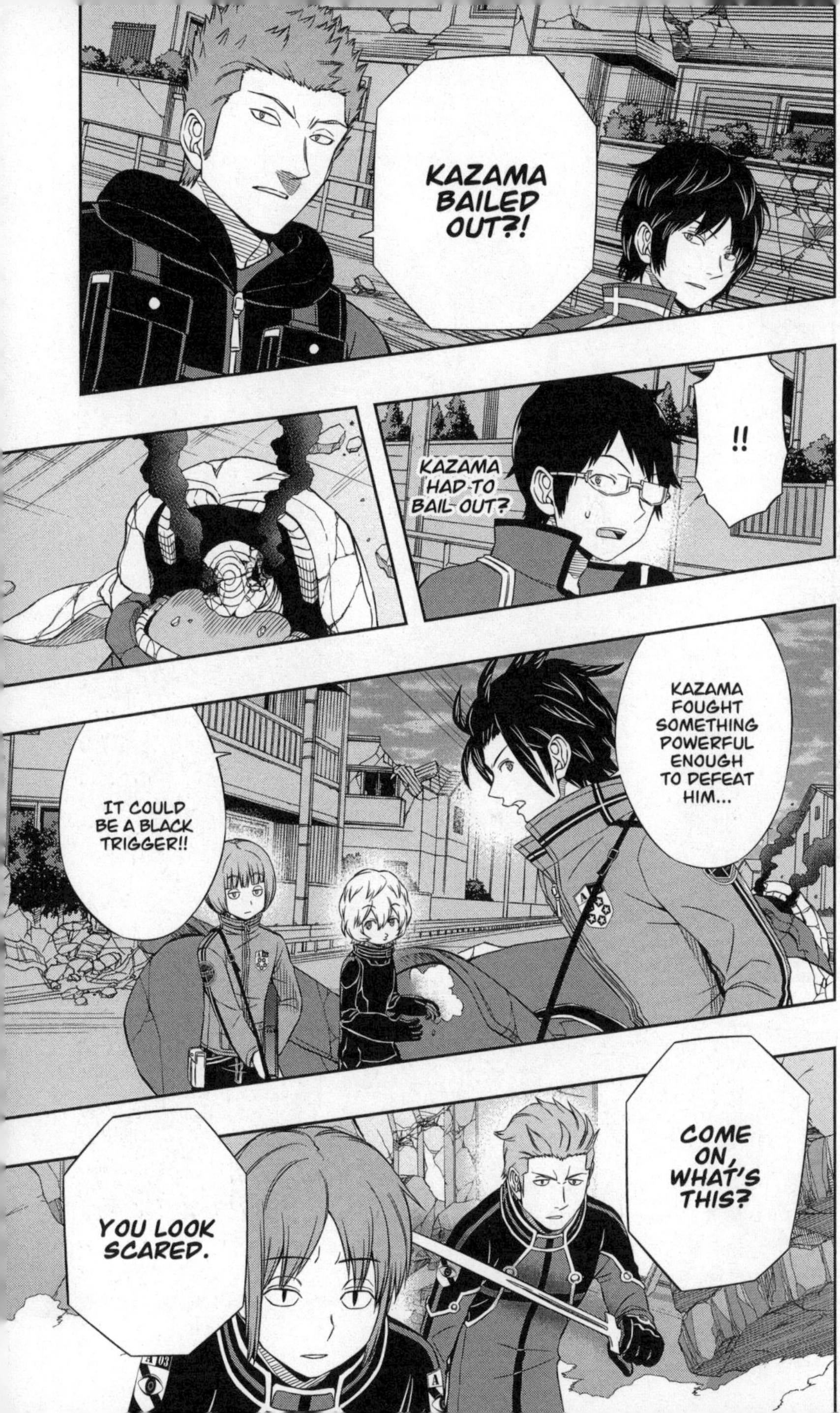
KAZAMA BAILED OUT?!
!!
KAZAMA HAD TO BAIL OUT?
KAZAMA FOUGHT SOMETHING POWERFUL ENOUGH TO DEFEAT HIM...
IT COULD BE A BLACK TRIGGER!!
COME ON, WHAT'S THIS?
YOU LOOK SCARED.

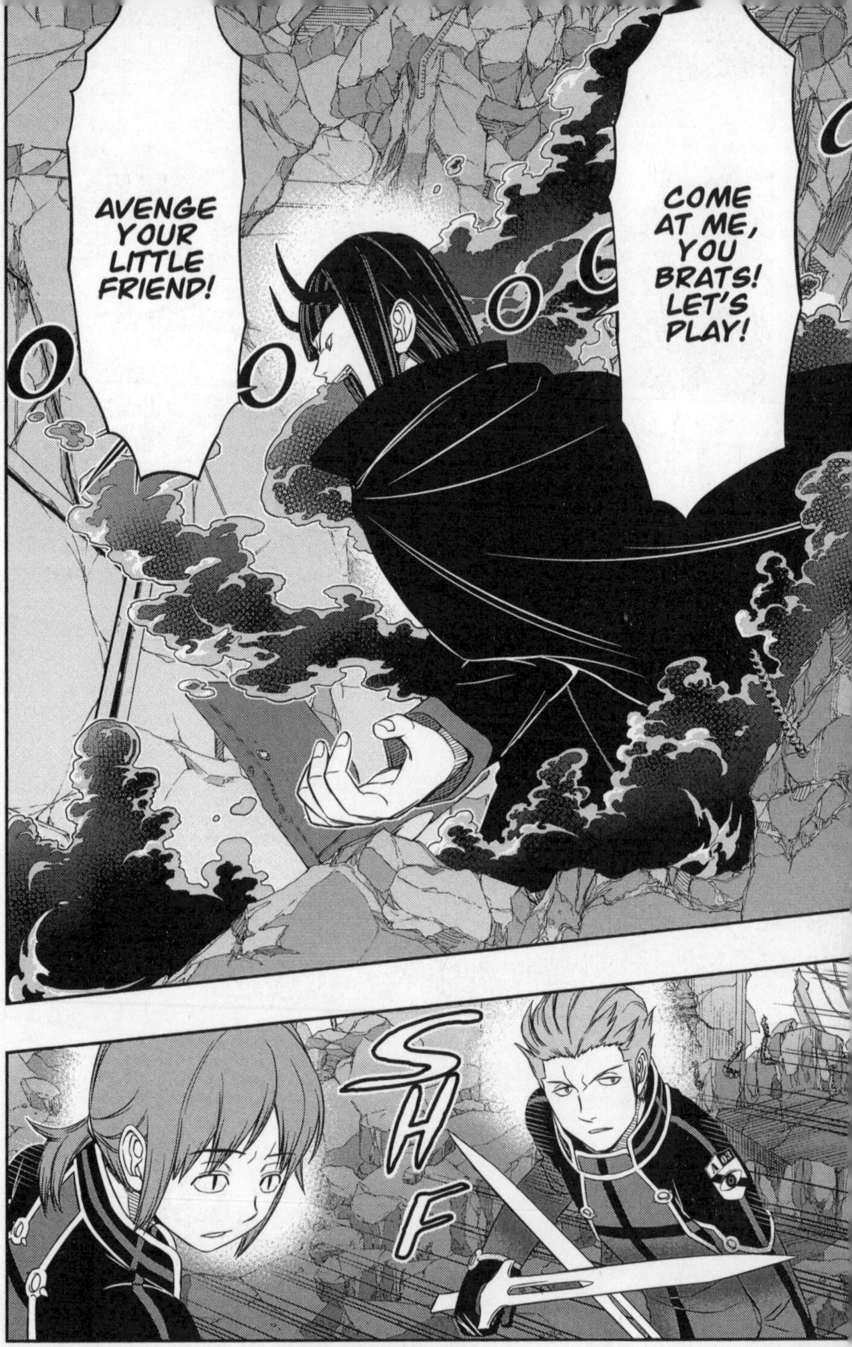
COME AT ME, YOU BRATS! LET'S PLAY!
AVENGE YOUR LITTLE FRIEND!
SHF

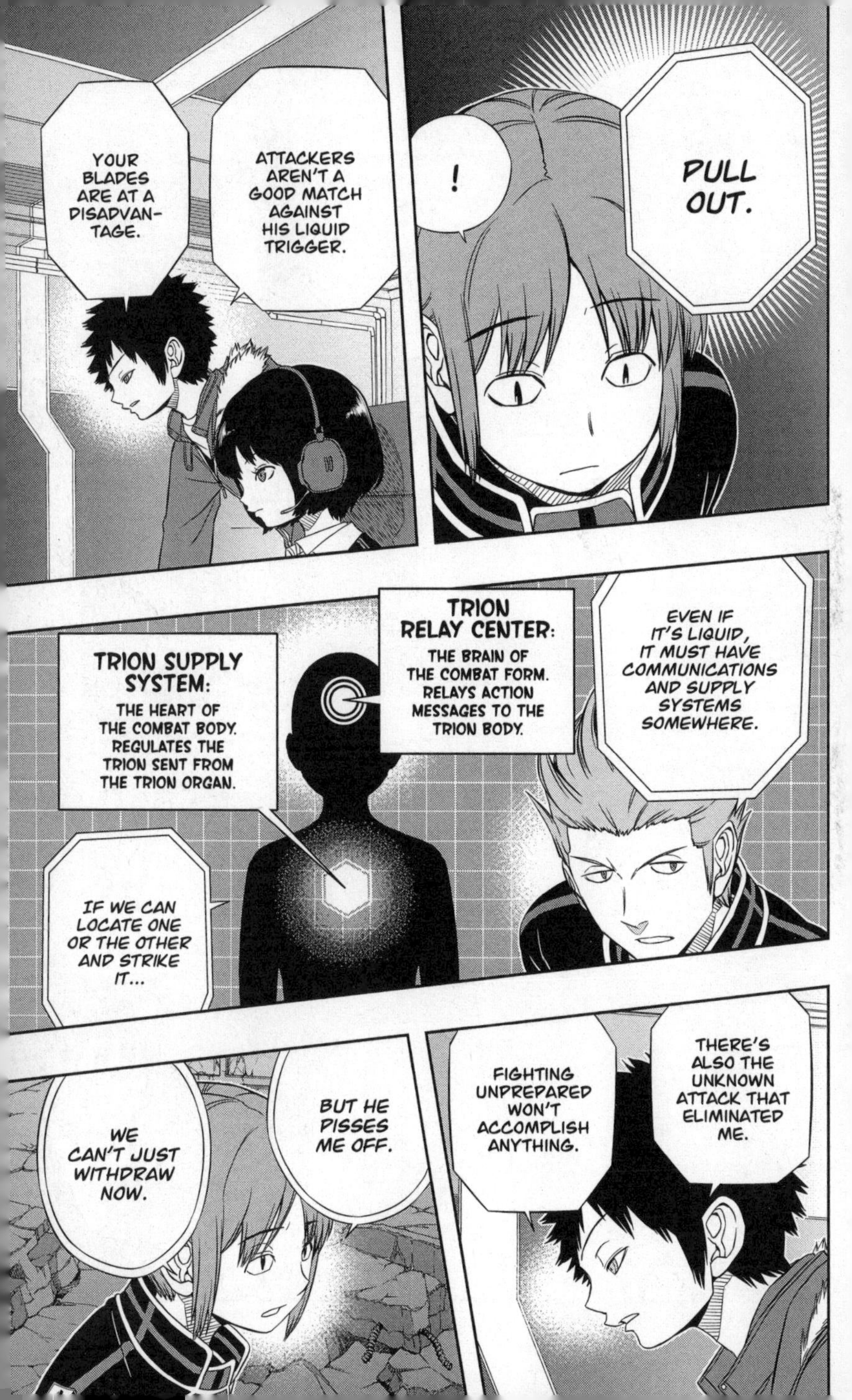
PULL OUT.
!
ATTACKERS AREN'T A GOOD MATCH AGAINST HIS LIQUID TRIGGER.
YOUR BLADES ARE AT A DISADVANTAGE.
EVEN IF IT'S LIQUID, IT MUST HAVE COMMUNICATIONS AND SUPPLY SYSTEMS SOMEWHERE.
TRION RELAY CENTER: THE BRAIN OF THE COMBAT FORM. RELAYS ACTION MESSAGES TO THE TRION BODY.
TRION SUPPLY SYSTEM: THE HEART OF THE COMBAT BODY. REGULATES THE TRION SENT FROM THE TRION ORGAN.
IF WE CAN LOCATE ONE OR THE OTHER AND STRIKE IT...
THERE'S ALSO THE UNKNOWN ATTACK THAT ELIMINATED ME.
FIGHTING UNPREPARED WON'T ACCOMPLISH ANYTHING.
BUT HE PISSES ME OFF.
WE CAN'T JUST WITHDRAW NOW.

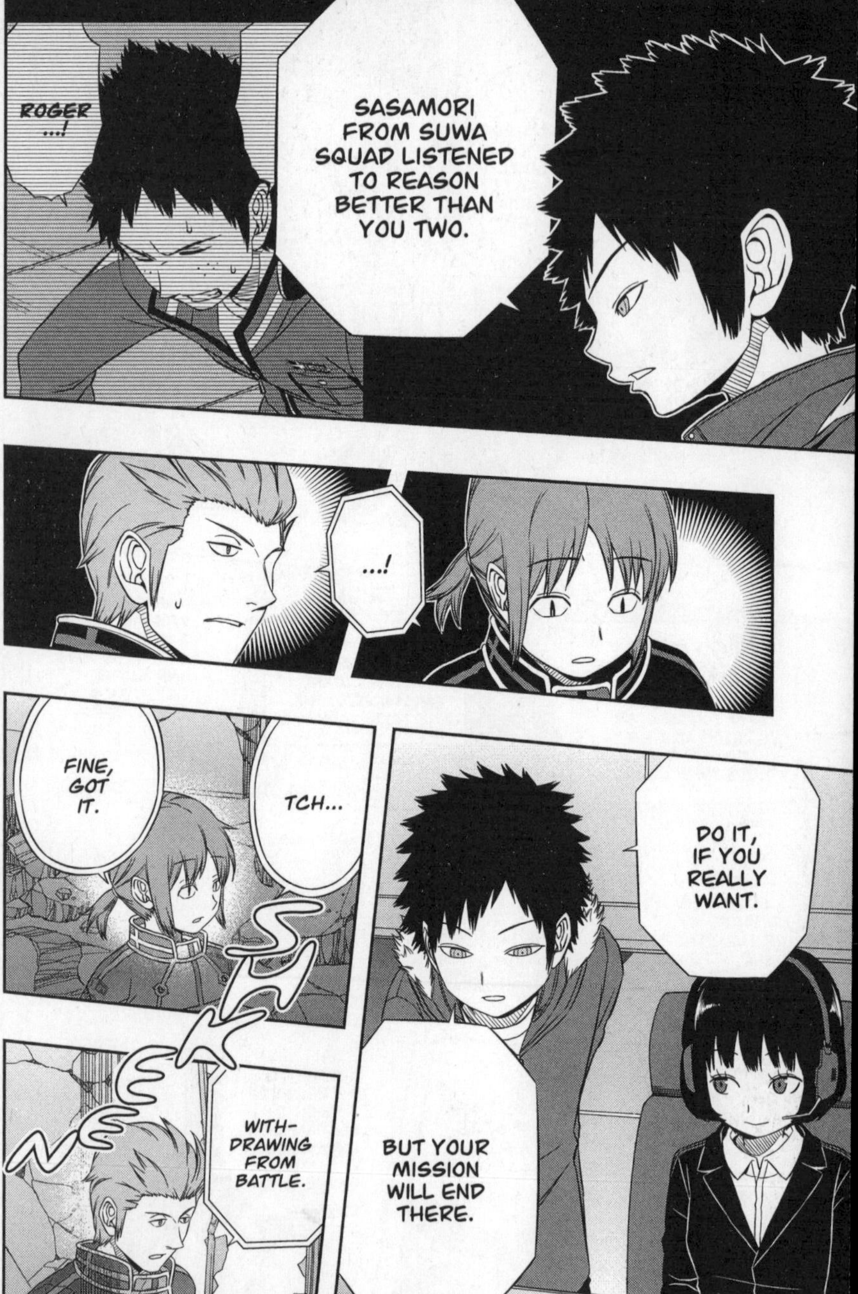
SASAMORI FROM SUWA SQUAD LISTENED TO REASON BETTER THAN YOU TWO.
ROGER ...!
...!
DO IT, IF YOU REALLY WANT.
BUT YOUR MISSION WILL END THERE.
TCH...
FINE, GOT IT.
WITH-DRAWING FROM BATTLE.

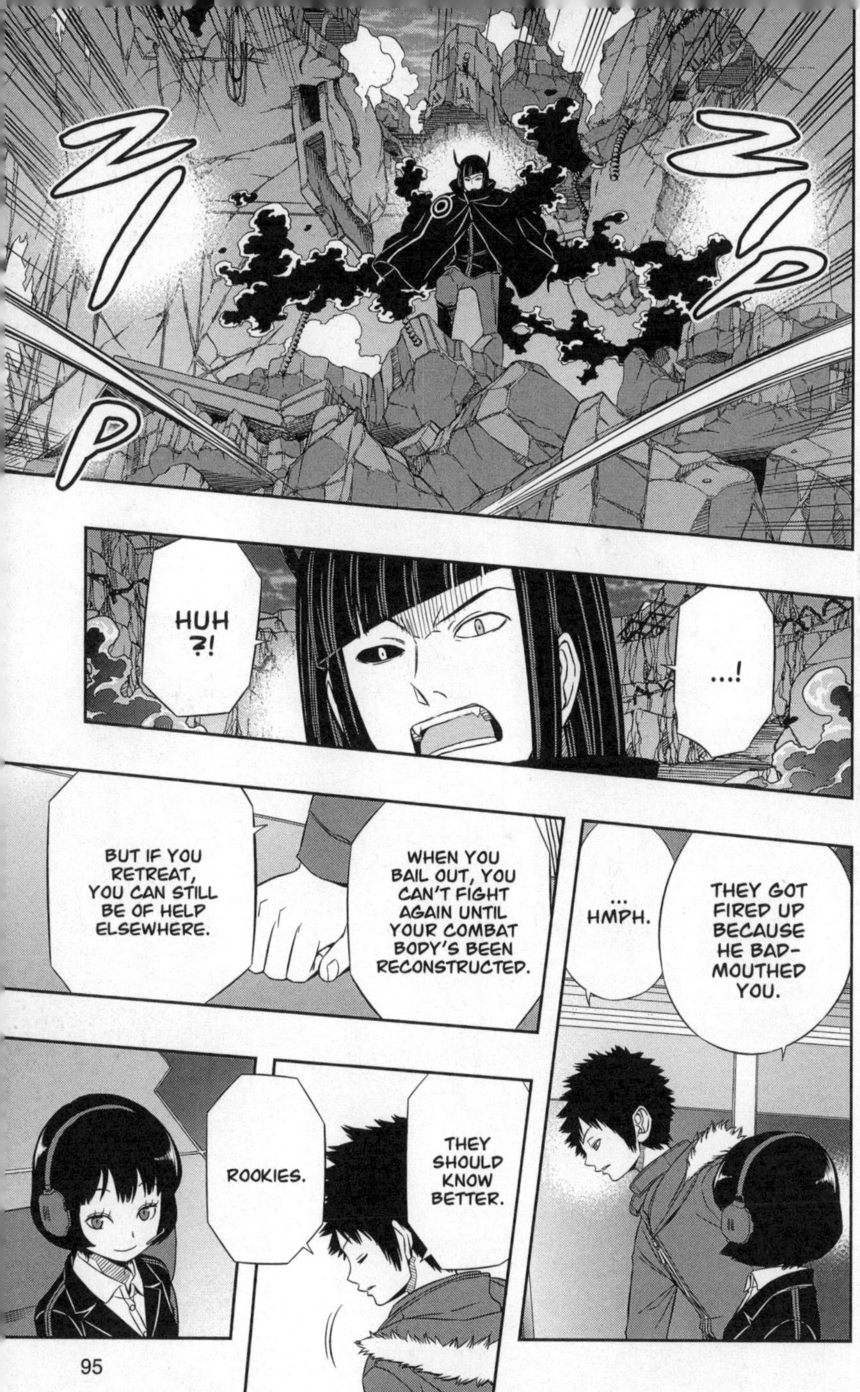
ZIP
ZIP
...!
HUH ?!
THEY GOT FIRED UP BECAUSE HE BAD-MOUTHED YOU.
... HMPH.
WHEN YOU BAIL OUT, YOU CAN'T FIGHT AGAIN UNTIL YOUR COMBAT BODY'S BEEN RECONSTRUCTED.
BUT IF YOU RETREAT, YOU CAN STILL BE OF HELP ELSEWHERE.
THEY SHOULD KNOW BETTER.
ROOKIES.

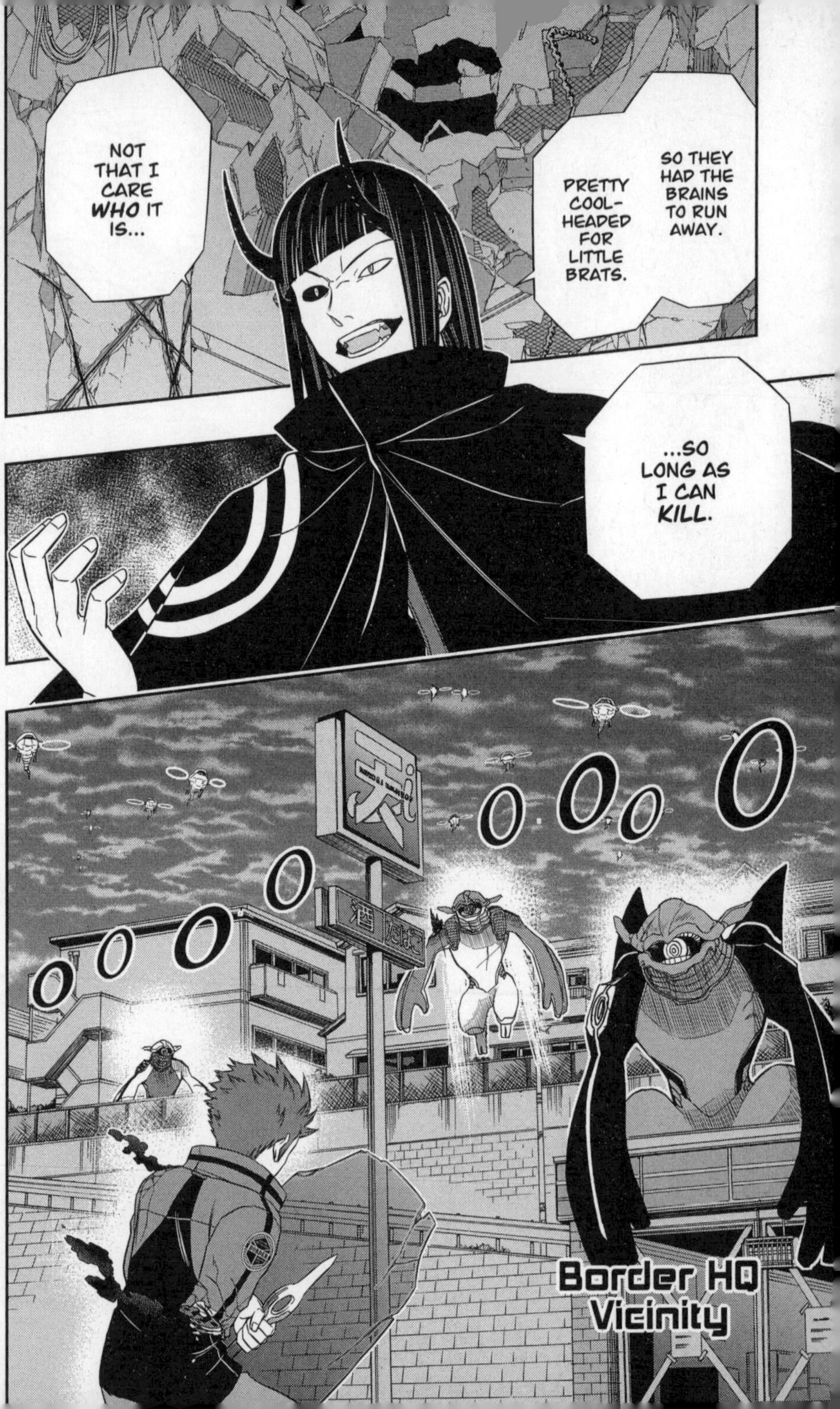

SO THEY HAD THE BRAINS TO RUN AWAY.
PRETTY COOL-HEADED FOR LITTLE BRATS.
NOT THAT I CARE WHO IT IS...
...SO LONG AS I CAN KILL.
Border HQ Vicinity

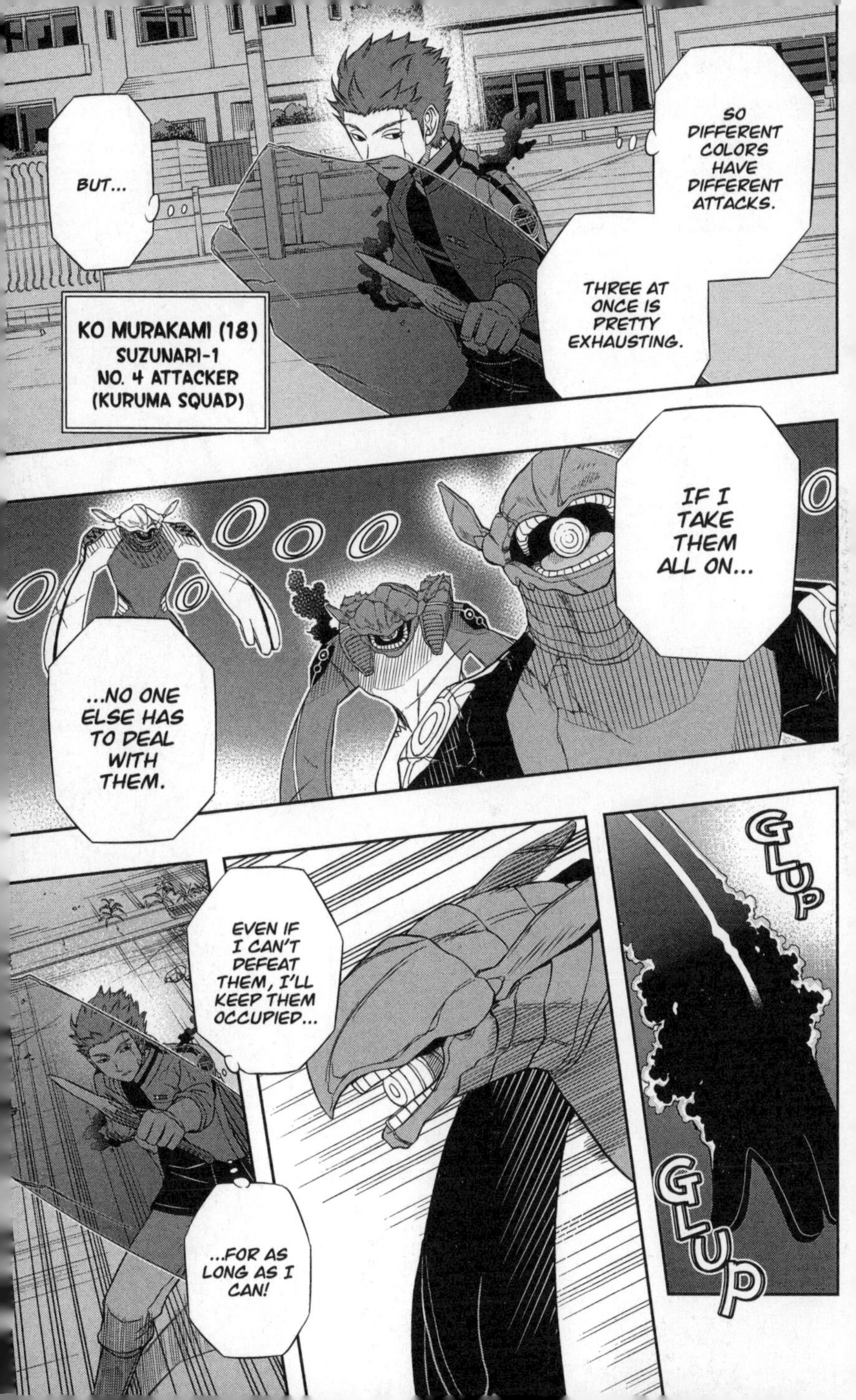
SO DIFFERENT COLORS HAVE DIFFERENT ATTACKS.
THREE AT ONCE IS PRETTY EXHAUSTING.
BUT...
KO MURAKAMI (18)
SUZUNARI-1
NO. 4 ATTACKER
(KURUMA SQUAD)
IF I TAKE THEM ALL ON...
...NO ONE ELSE HAS TO DEAL WITH THEM.
GLUP
GLUP
EVEN IF I CAN'T DEFEAT THEM, I'LL KEEP THEM OCCUPIED...
...FOR AS LONG AS I CAN!

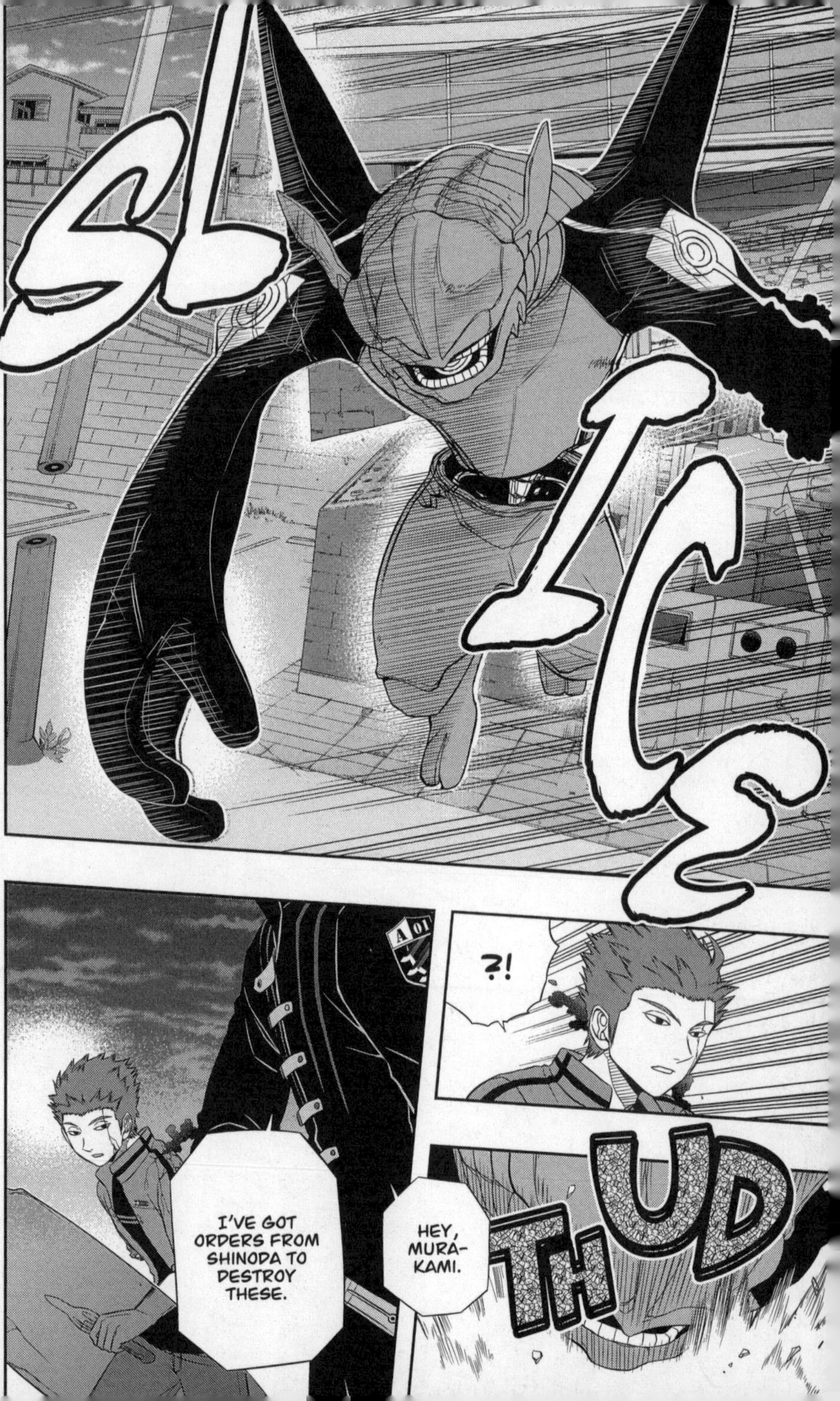
SLICE
?!
THUD
HEY, MURA-KAMI.
I'VE GOT ORDERS FROM SHINODA TO DESTROY THESE.

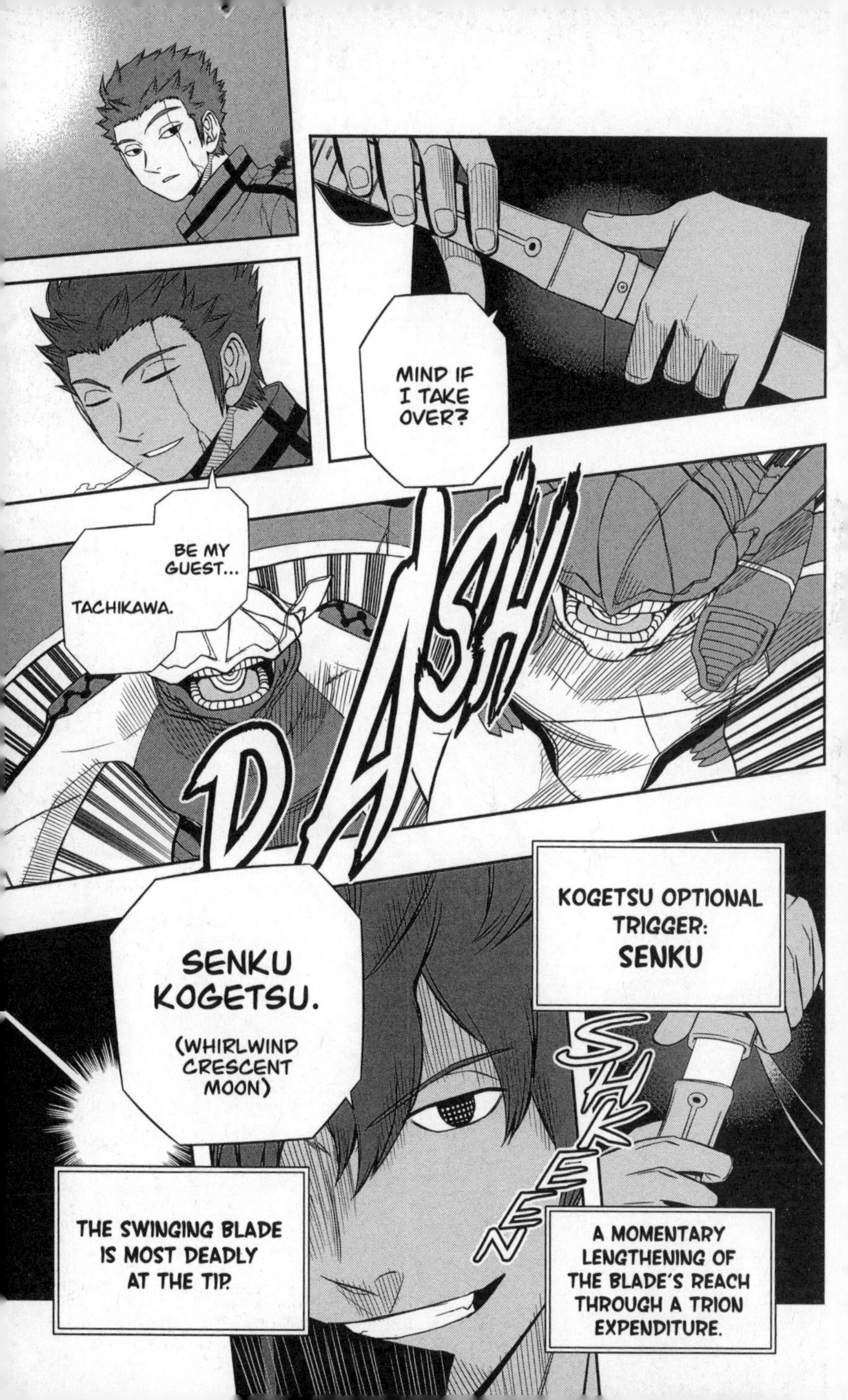
MIND IF I TAKE OVER?
BE MY GUEST... TACHIKAWA.
DASH
KOGETSU OPTIONAL TRIGGER: SENKU
SENKU KOGETSU. (WHIRLWIND CRESCENT MOON)
SHKEEEN
A MOMENTARY LENGTHENING OF THE BLADE'S REACH THROUGH A TRION EXPENDITURE.
THE SWINGING BLADE IS MOST DEADLY AT THE TIP.

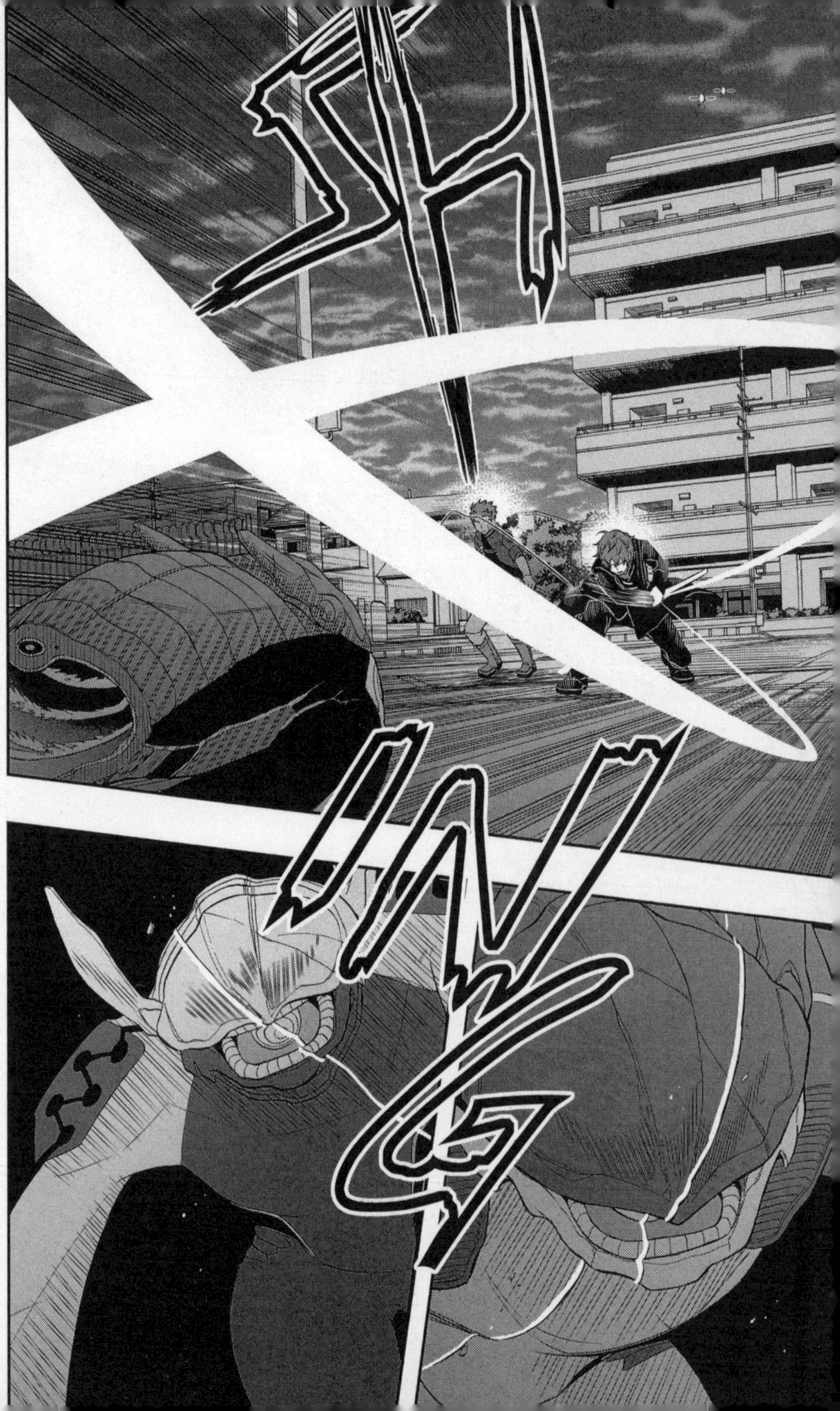

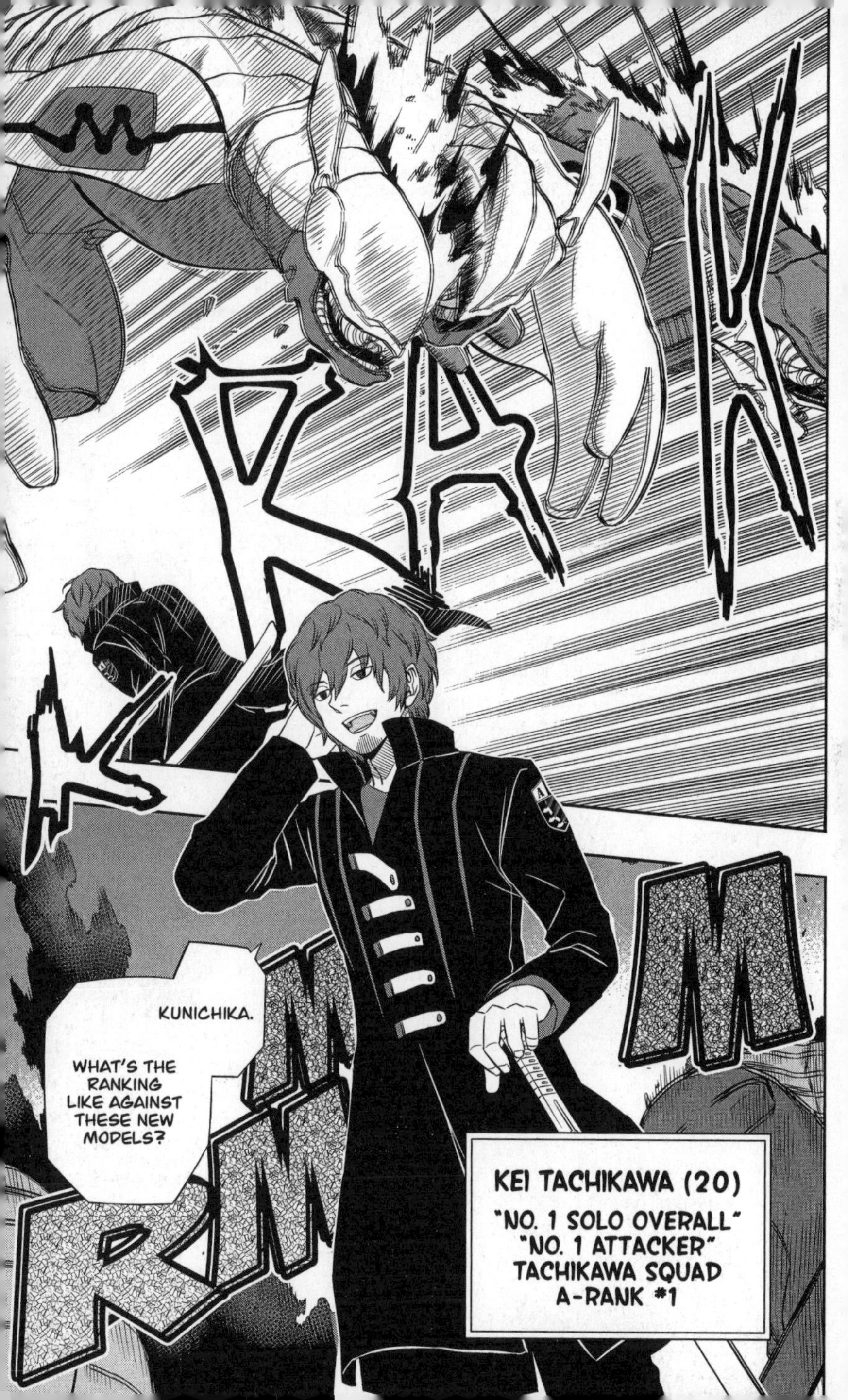
KUNICHIKA.
WHAT'S THE RANKING LIKE AGAINST THESE NEW MODELS?
KEI TACHIKAWA (20)
"NO. 1 SOLO OVERALL"
"NO. 1 ATTACKER"
TACHIKAWA SQUAD
A-RANK #1

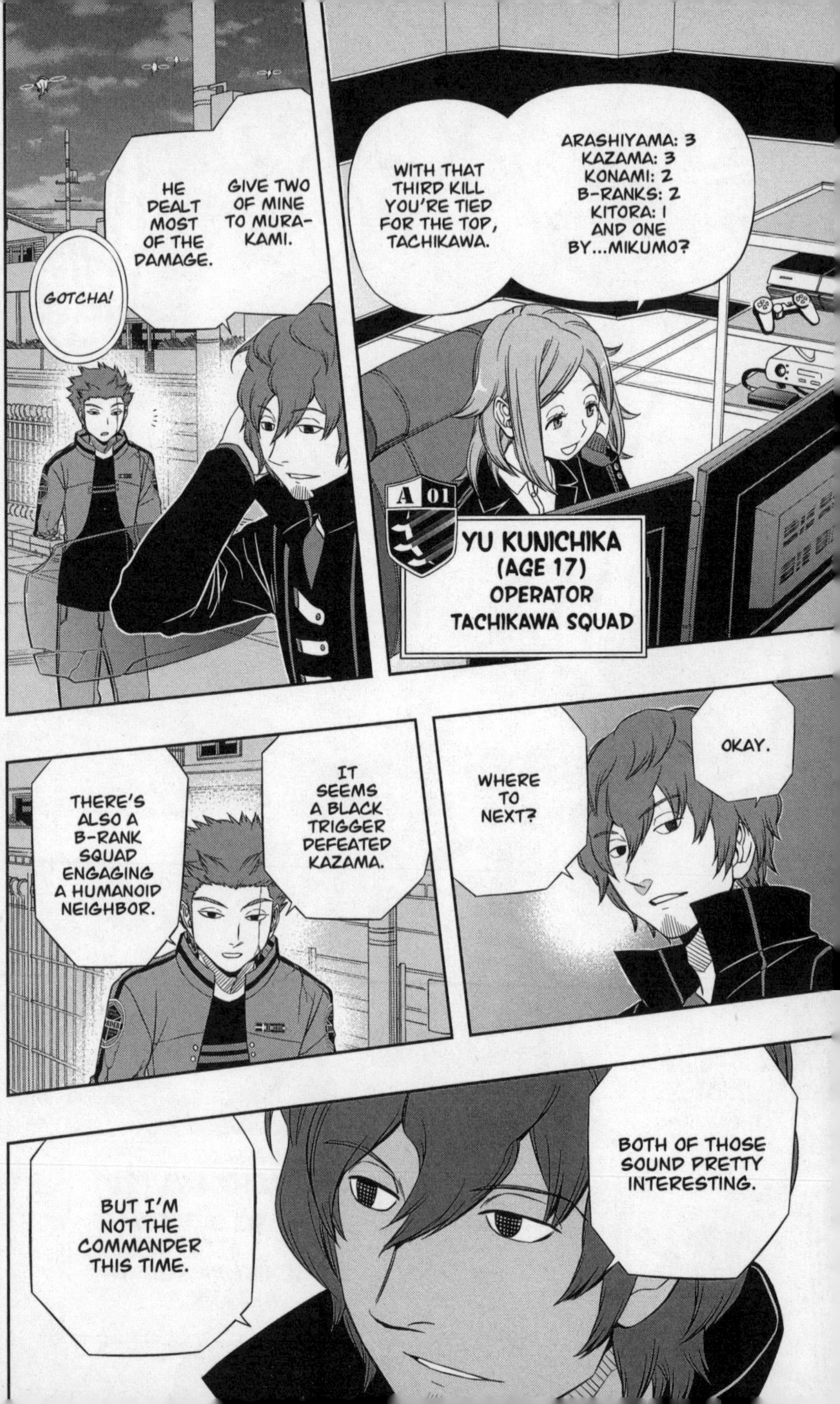
ARASHIYAMA: 3 KAZAMA: 3 KONAMI: 2 B-RANKS: 2 KITORA: 1 AND ONE BY...MIKUMO?
WITH THAT THIRD KILL YOU'RE TIED FOR THE TOP, TACHIKAWA.
YU KUNICHIKA (AGE 17) OPERATOR TACHIKAWA SQUAD
A 01
GIVE TWO OF MINE TO MURA-KAMI.
HE DEALT MOST OF THE DAMAGE.
GOTCHA!
OKAY.
WHERE TO NEXT?
IT SEEMS A BLACK TRIGGER DEFEATED KAZAMA.
THERE'S ALSO A B-RANK SQUAD ENGAGING A HUMANOID NEIGHBOR.
BOTH OF THOSE SOUND PRETTY INTERESTING.
BUT I'M NOT THE COMMANDER THIS TIME.

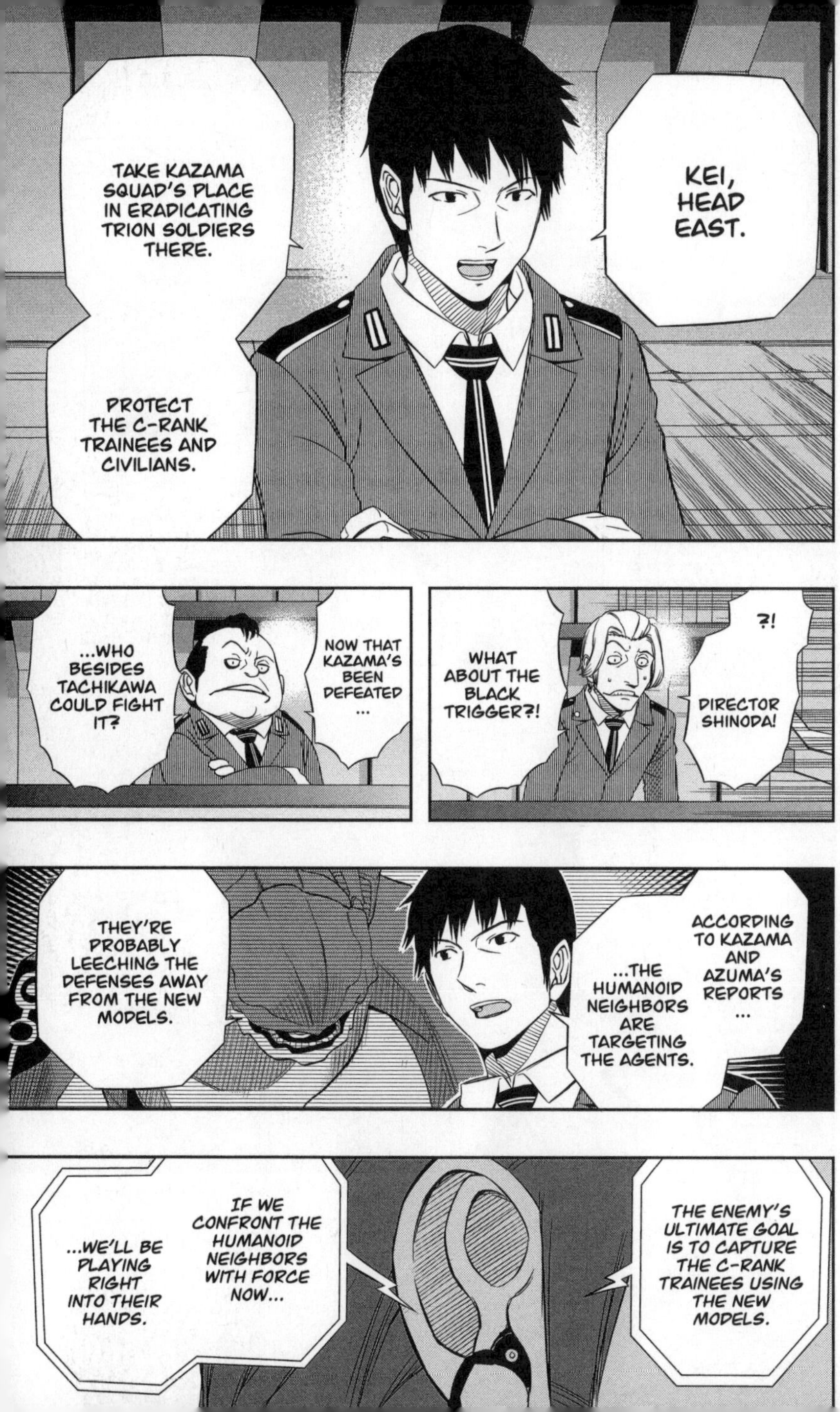
KEI, HEAD EAST.
TAKE KAZAMA SQUAD'S PLACE IN ERADICATING TRION SOLDIERS THERE.
PROTECT THE C-RANK TRAINEES AND CIVILIANS.
?!
DIRECTOR SHINODA!
WHAT ABOUT THE BLACK TRIGGER?!
NOW THAT KAZAMA'S BEEN DEFEATED...
...WHO BESIDES TACHIKAWA COULD FIGHT IT?
ACCORDING TO KAZAMA AND AZUMA'S REPORTS...
...THE HUMANOID NEIGHBORS ARE TARGETING THE AGENTS.
THEY'RE PROBABLY LEECHING THE DEFENSES AWAY FROM THE NEW MODELS.
THE ENEMY'S ULTIMATE GOAL IS TO CAPTURE THE C-RANK TRAINEES USING THE NEW MODELS.
IF WE CONFRONT THE HUMANOID NEIGHBORS WITH FORCE NOW...
...WE'LL BE PLAYING RIGHT INTO THEIR HANDS.

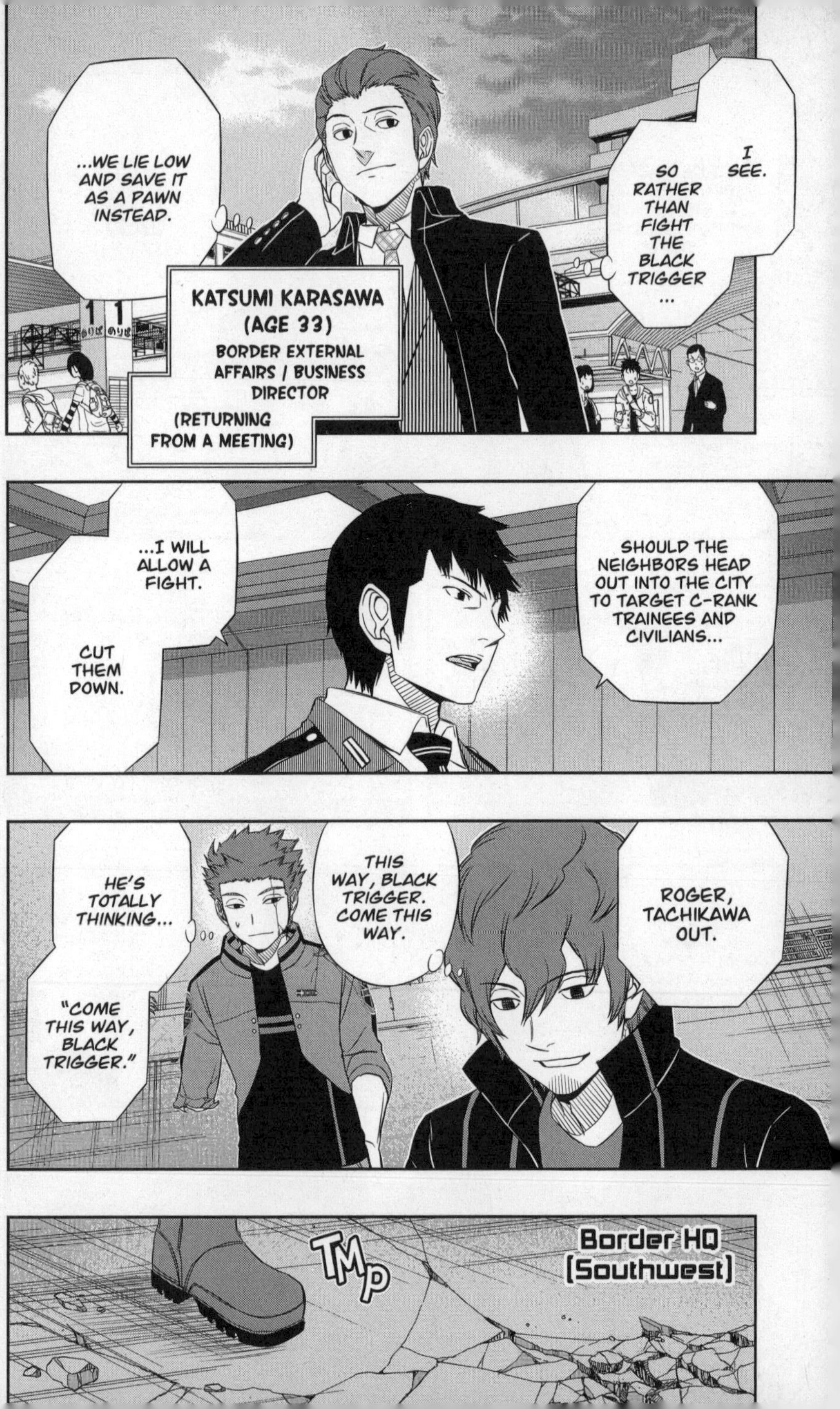
I SEE.
SO RATHER THAN FIGHT THE BLACK TRIGGER ...
...WE LIE LOW AND SAVE IT AS A PAWN INSTEAD.
KATSUMI KARASAWA (AGE 33)
BORDER EXTERNAL AFFAIRS / BUSINESS DIRECTOR
(RETURNING FROM A MEETING)
SHOULD THE NEIGHBORS HEAD OUT INTO THE CITY TO TARGET C-RANK TRAINEES AND CIVILIANS...
...I WILL ALLOW A FIGHT.
CUT THEM DOWN.
ROGER, TACHIKAWA OUT.
THIS WAY, BLACK TRIGGER. COME THIS WAY.
HE'S TOTALLY THINKING...
"COME THIS WAY, BLACK TRIGGER."
Border HQ [Southwest]
TMP

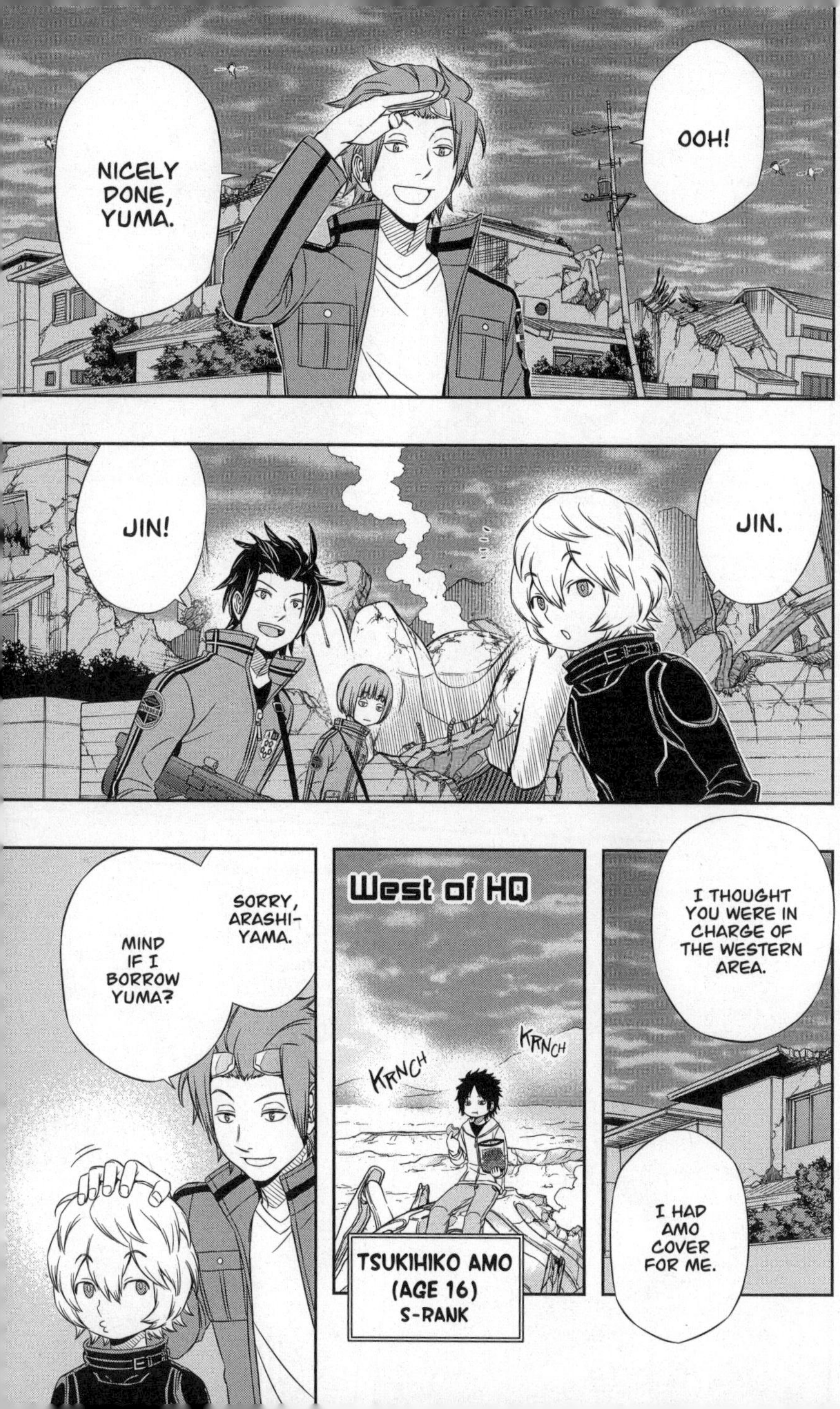
OOH!
NICELY DONE, YUMA.
JIN.
JIN!
I THOUGHT YOU WERE IN CHARGE OF THE WESTERN AREA.
I HAD AMO COVER FOR ME.
West of HQ
KRNCH
KRNCH
TSUKIHIKO AMO (AGE 16) S-RANK
SORRY, ARASHI-YAMA.
MIND IF I BORROW YUMA?

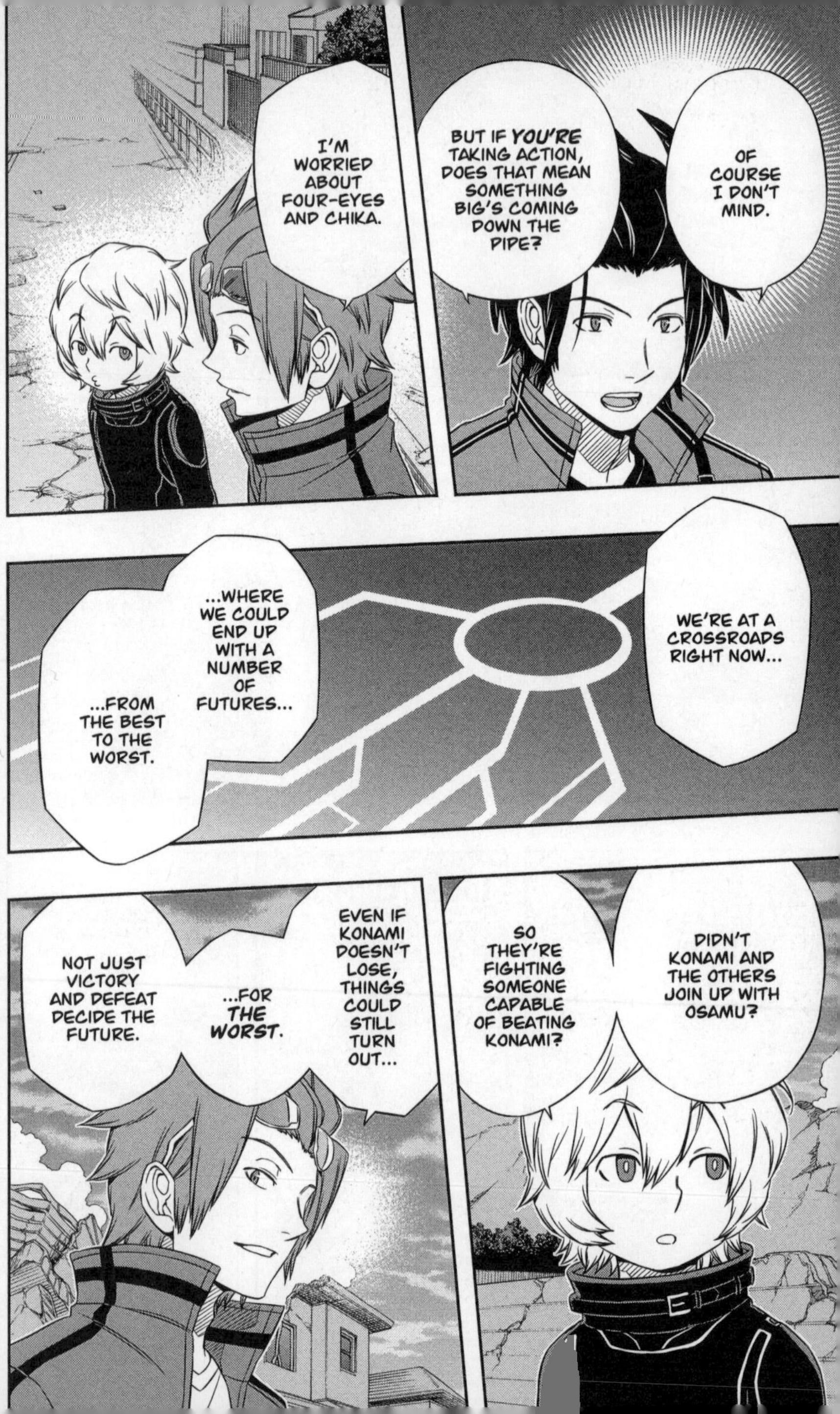
OF COURSE I DON'T MIND.
BUT IF *YOU'RE* TAKING ACTION, DOES THAT MEAN SOMETHING BIG'S COMING DOWN THE PIPE?
I'M WORRIED ABOUT FOUR-EYES AND CHIKA.
WE'RE AT A CROSSROADS RIGHT NOW...
...WHERE WE COULD END UP WITH A NUMBER OF FUTURES...
...FROM THE BEST TO THE WORST.
DIDN'T KONAMI AND THE OTHERS JOIN UP WITH OSAMU?
SO THEY'RE FIGHTING SOMEONE CAPABLE OF BEATING KONAMI?
EVEN IF KONAMI DOESN'T LOSE, THINGS COULD STILL TURN OUT...
...FOR *THE WORST*.
NOT JUST VICTORY AND DEFEAT DECIDE THE FUTURE.

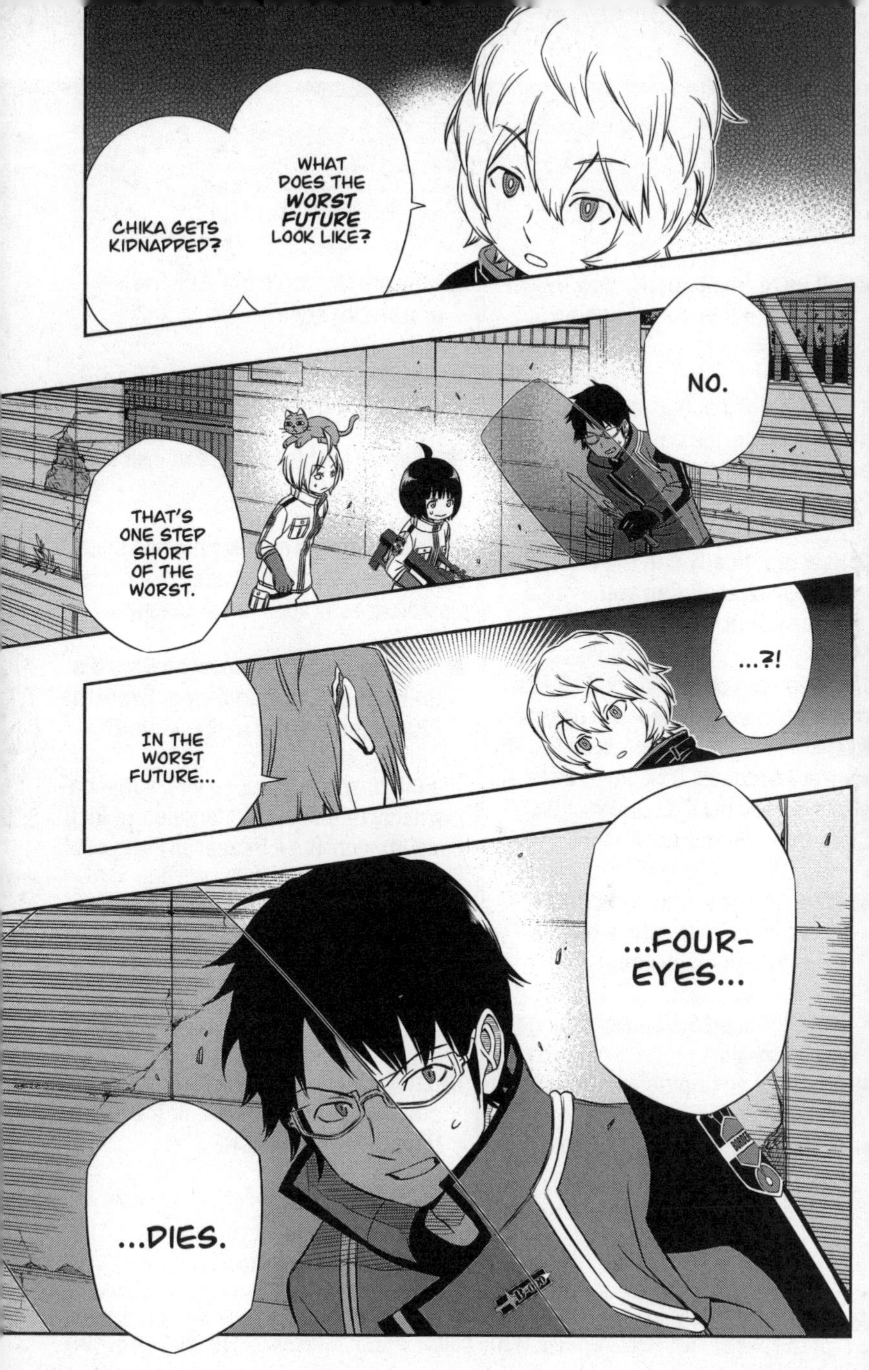
WHAT DOES THE WORST FUTURE LOOK LIKE?
CHIKA GETS KIDNAPPED?
NO.
THAT'S ONE STEP SHORT OF THE WORST.
...?!
IN THE WORST FUTURE...
...FOUR-EYES...
...DIES.

Q&A: Part 5

I can't answer some of these questions yet.

■ Tell us more about the gun Trigger (a shotgun?) Suwa was using in chapter 45.

It's a shotgun that blasts a bunch of largish bullets. You can adjust the angle of the blast to some extent. Pro: high firepower. Con: slow reload.

■ How drastically can the Scorpion change shape? Can you wrap it around your whole body?

The shape can change a good bit. How much it can expand depends on your Trion levels, but the wider it is spread, the weaker it becomes. It would be as fragile as glass if you put it around your body. Chika might be able to pull it off.

■ Tell us more wacky anecdotes about Tachikawa, who's bad at everything non-combat.

- He pronounced the English "danger" like "dang-ah."
- He thought an unplugged computer was broken.
- He picked out the dried fruit from granola and threw the rest away.

■ Why are Osamu's glasses frames under-rim style?

He picked it up from his father (who's still alive, by the way).

■ When do people start to call their seniors "Mr./Mrs./Miss"?

People older than high school and college start to get called "Mr./Mrs./Miss." So when Osamu doesn't add "Mr." to Kazama...

■ The round parts of Kazama Squad's uniform react when they activate the Chameleon. What're they doing?

The uniform is embedded with a mechanism that reduces the Chameleon's Trion consumption. But it increases the cost of the combat body.

■ Is Utagawa an Attacker or All-Rounder?

The first editions of the graphic novels (in Japan) have it wrong. He's an All-Rounder.

■ Can you not put away the Kogetsu only while it's selected, or the whole time the Trigger is on?

Once the Kogetsu is selected, it is always out. It disappears in the art sometimes, but that's just me forgetting to draw it.

■ I sometimes answer questions I get in my fan mail on my official Twitter feed. My editor cracks a creepy smile when I get more followers. **World Trigger official Twitter account: @W_Trigger_off**

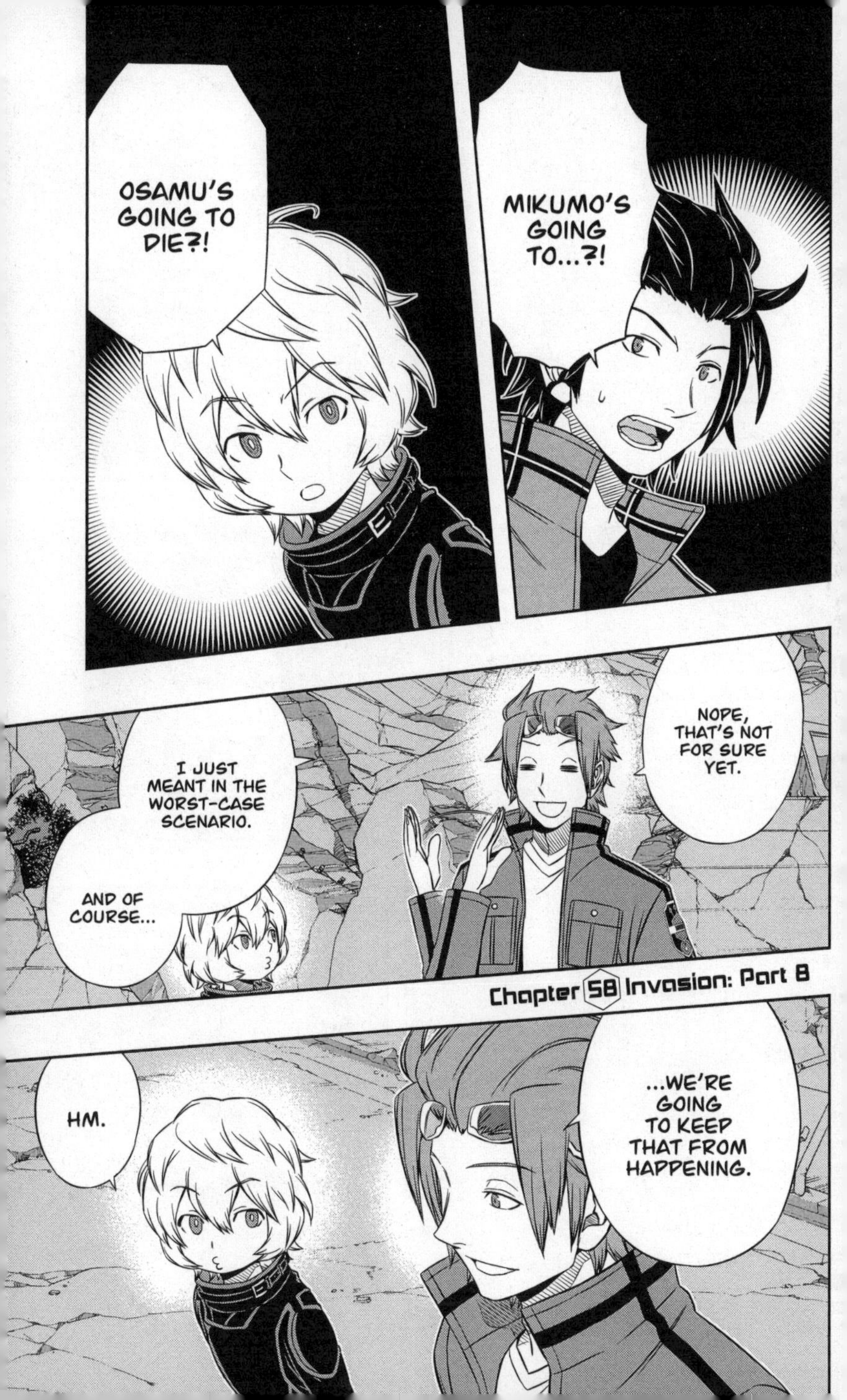
MIKUMO'S GOING TO...?!
OSAMU'S GOING TO DIE?!
NOPE, THAT'S NOT FOR SURE YET.
I JUST MEANT IN THE WORST-CASE SCENARIO.
AND OF COURSE...
Chapter 58 Invasion: Part 8
...WE'RE GOING TO KEEP THAT FROM HAPPENING.
HM.

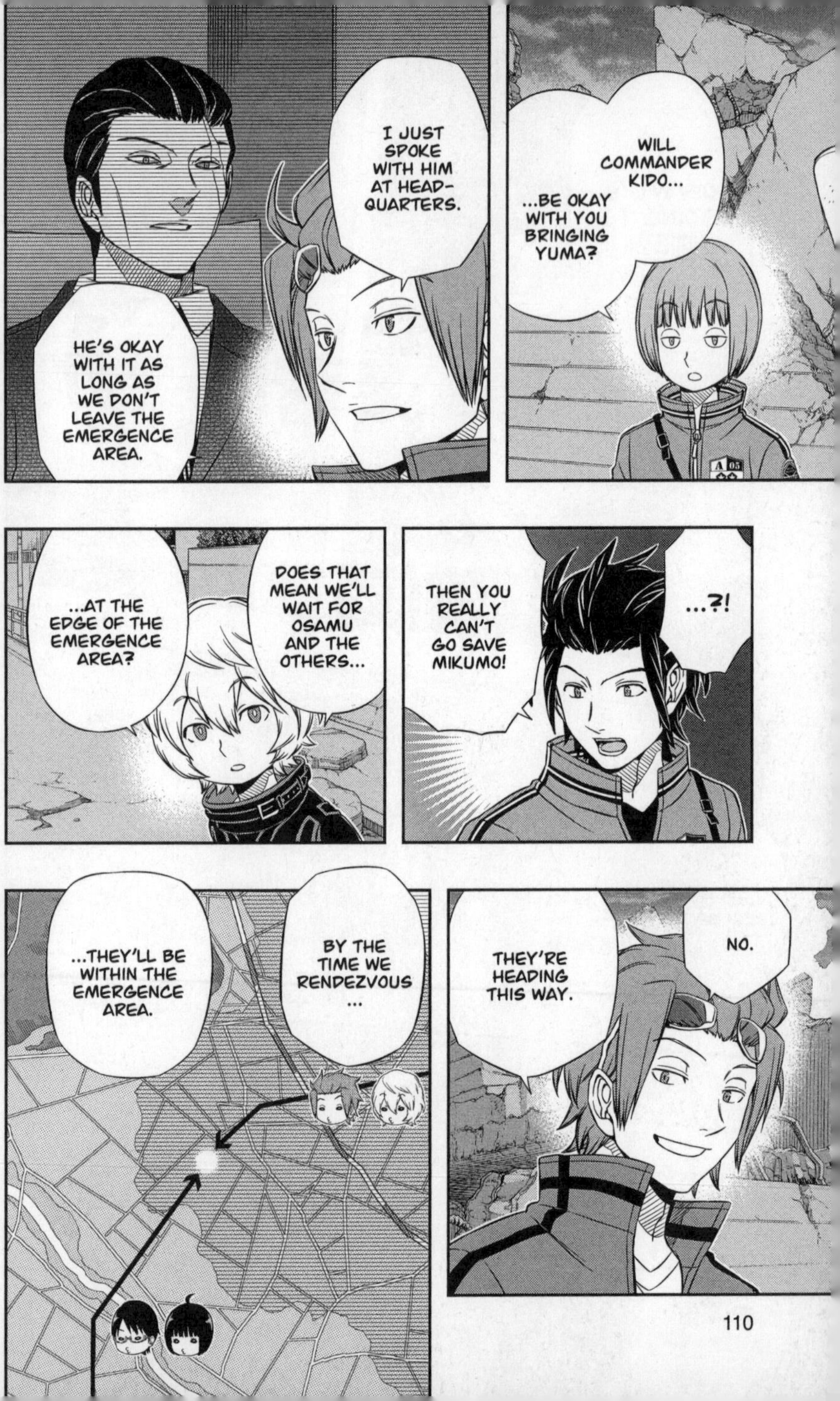
WILL COMMANDER KIDO...
...BE OKAY WITH YOU BRINGING YUMA?
I JUST SPOKE WITH HIM AT HEAD-QUARTERS.
HE'S OKAY WITH IT AS LONG AS WE DON'T LEAVE THE EMERGENCE AREA.
...?!
THEN YOU REALLY CAN'T GO SAVE MIKUMO!
DOES THAT MEAN WE'LL WAIT FOR OSAMU AND THE OTHERS...
...AT THE EDGE OF THE EMERGENCE AREA?
NO.
THEY'RE HEADING THIS WAY.
BY THE TIME WE RENDEZVOUS...
...THEY'LL BE WITHIN THE EMERGENCE AREA.

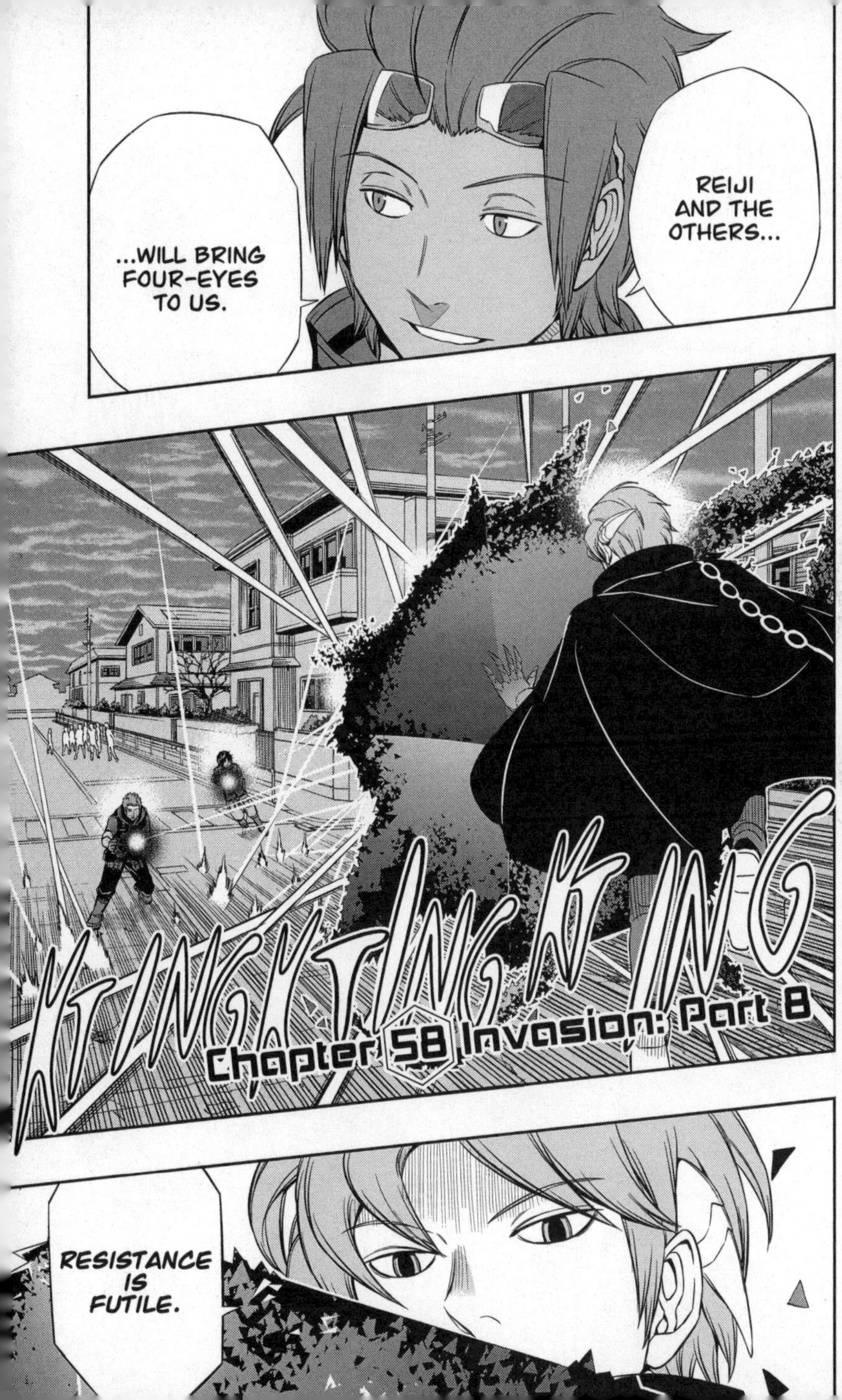
REIJI AND THE OTHERS...
...WILL BRING FOUR-EYES TO US.
KLING KLING KLING
Chapter 58 Invasion: Part 8
RESISTANCE IS FUTILE.

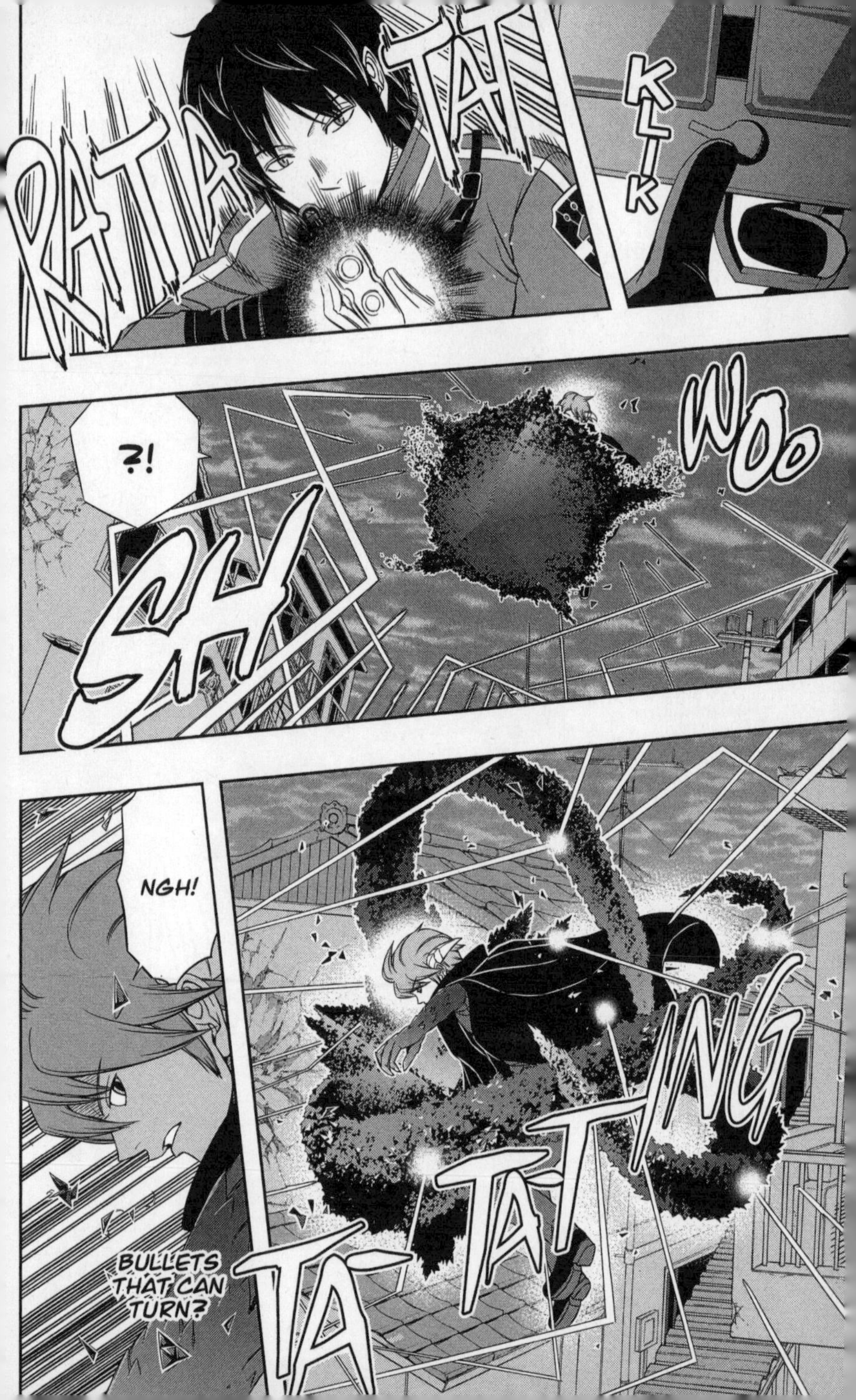

KLIK
RATTA TAT
WOO
?!
SH
TA TATING
NGH!
BULLETS THAT CAN TURN?

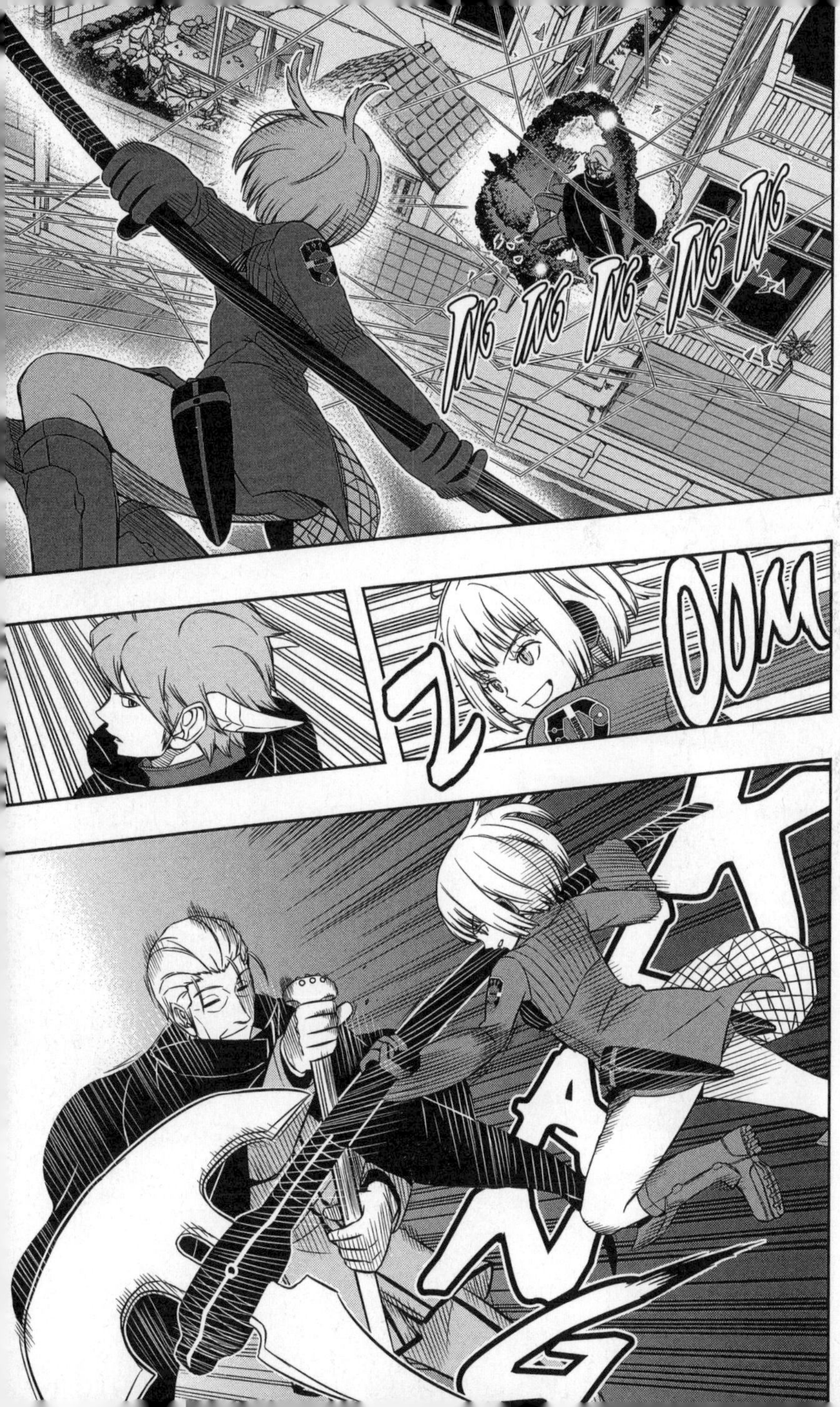
TING TING TING TING TING
ZOOM

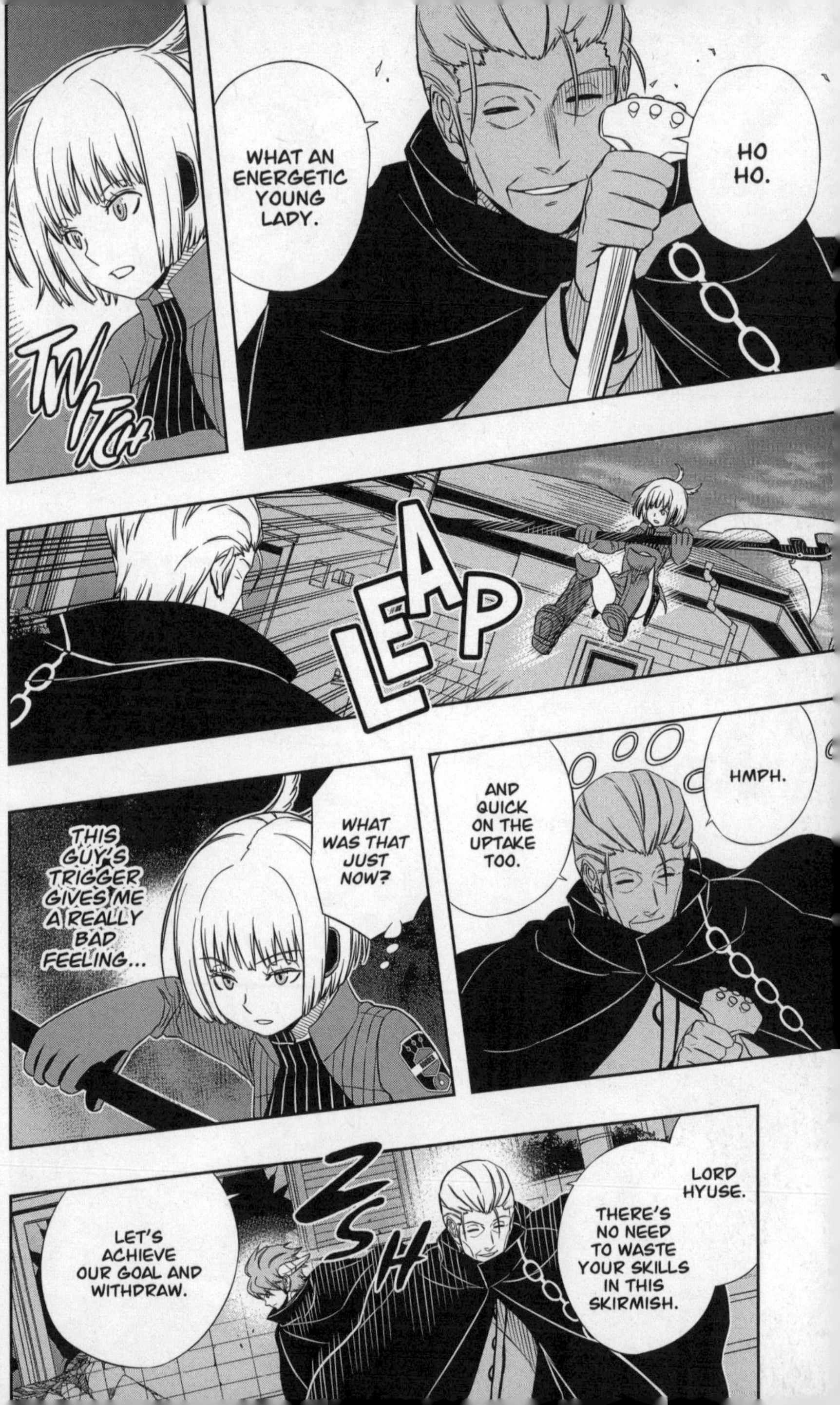
HO HO.
WHAT AN ENERGETIC YOUNG LADY.
TWITCH
LEAP
HMPH.
AND QUICK ON THE UPTAKE TOO.
WHAT WAS THAT JUST NOW?
THIS GUY'S TRIGGER GIVES ME A REALLY BAD FEELING...
LORD HYUSE.
THERE'S NO NEED TO WASTE YOUR SKILLS IN THIS SKIRMISH.
ZSH
LET'S ACHIEVE OUR GOAL AND WITHDRAW.

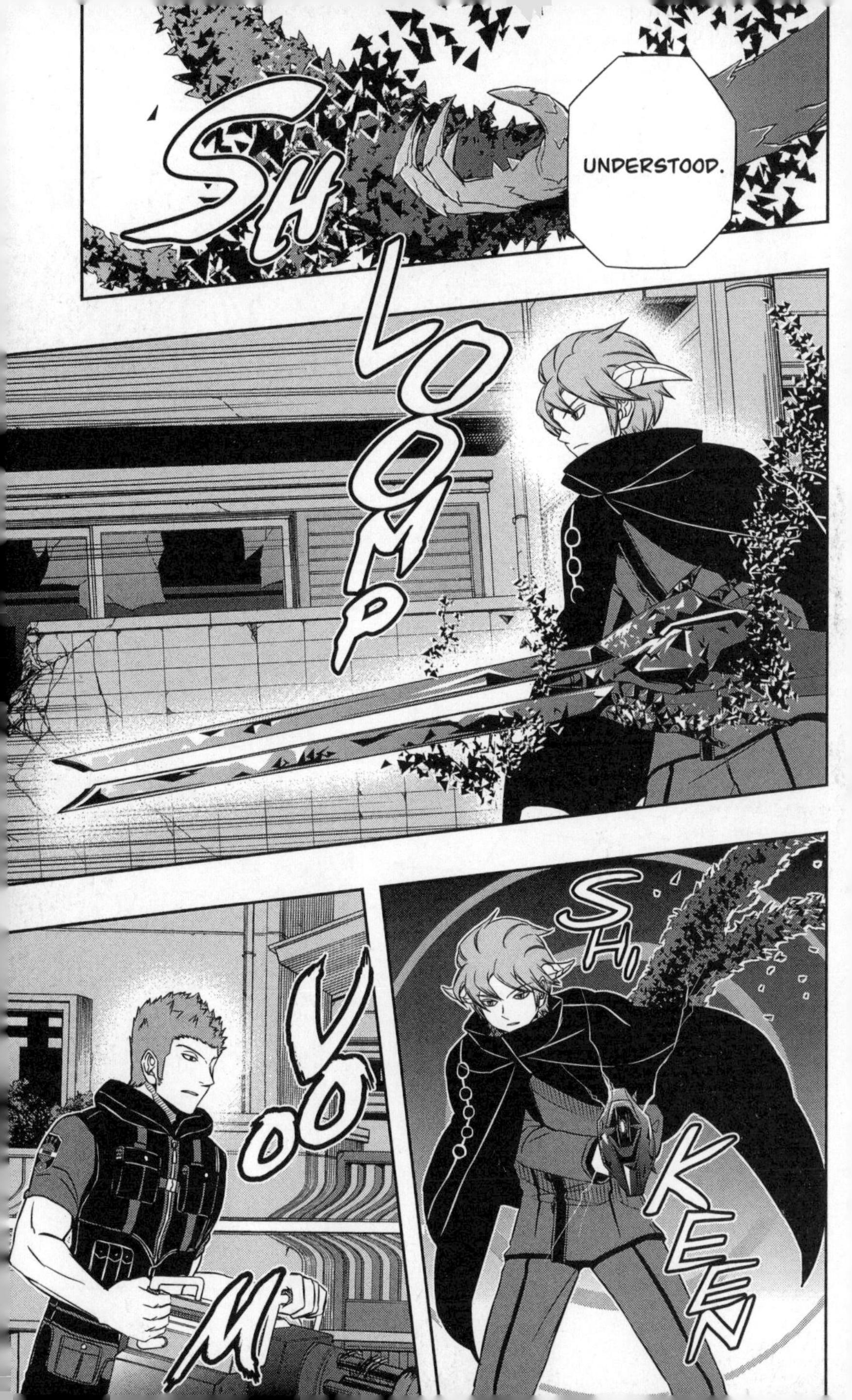
UNDERSTOOD.
SHLOOMP
SHIKEEN
VOOM

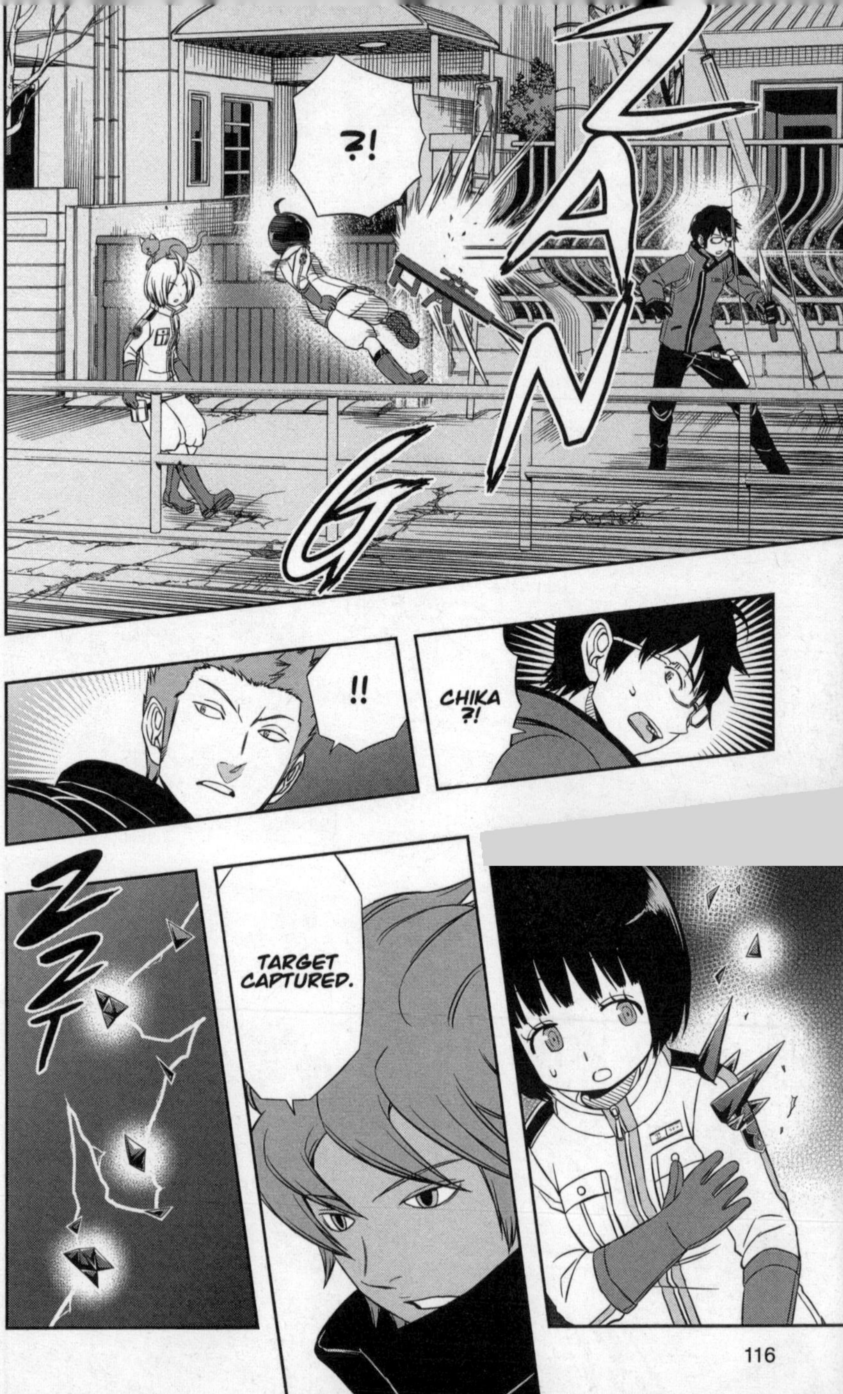
?!
ZANG
CHIKA ?!
!!
TARGET CAPTURED.
ZZZT

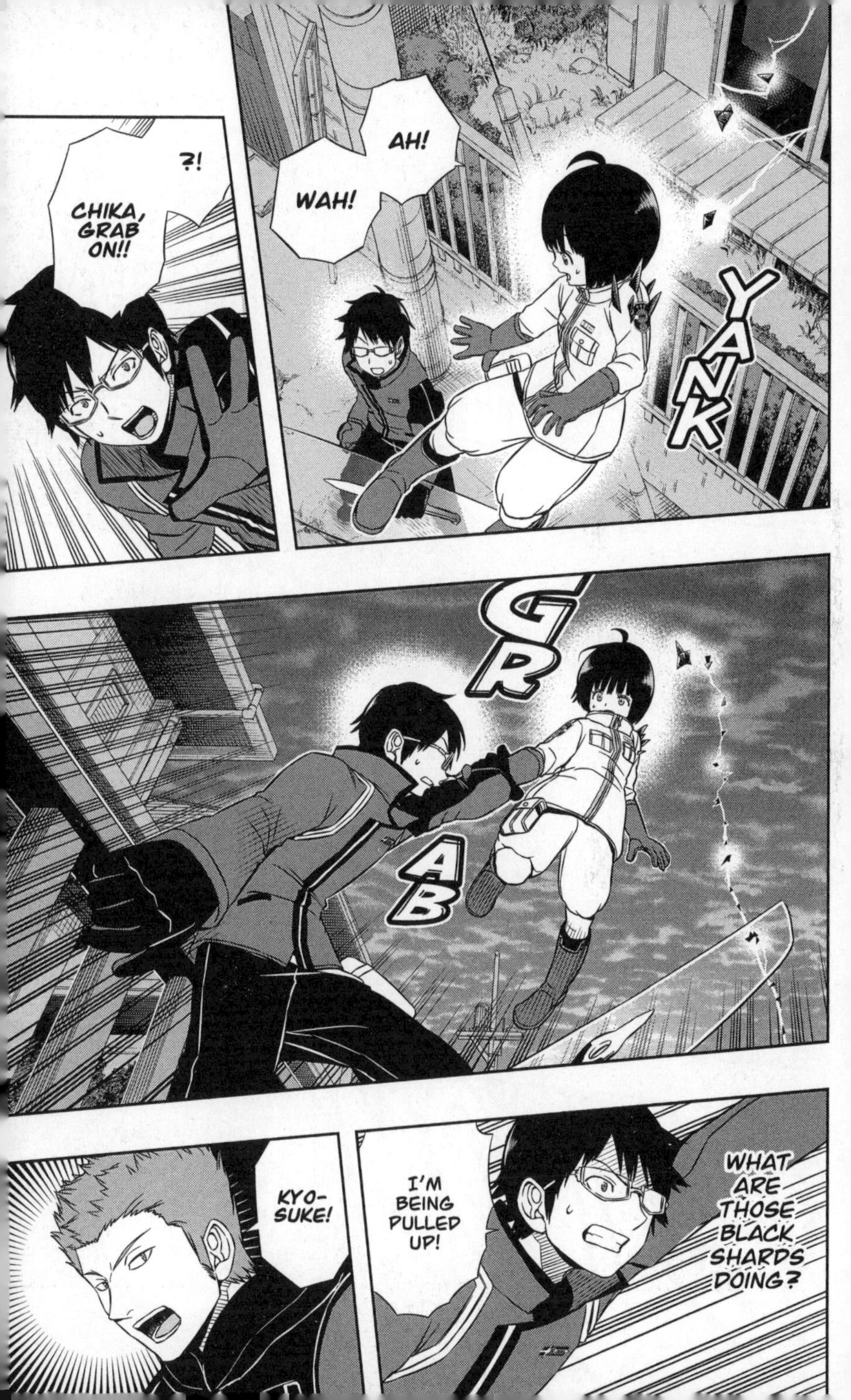
AH!
WAH!
YANK
?!
CHIKA, GRAB ON!!
GRAB
WHAT ARE THOSE BLACK SHARDS DOING?
I'M BEING PULLED UP!
KYO-SUKE!

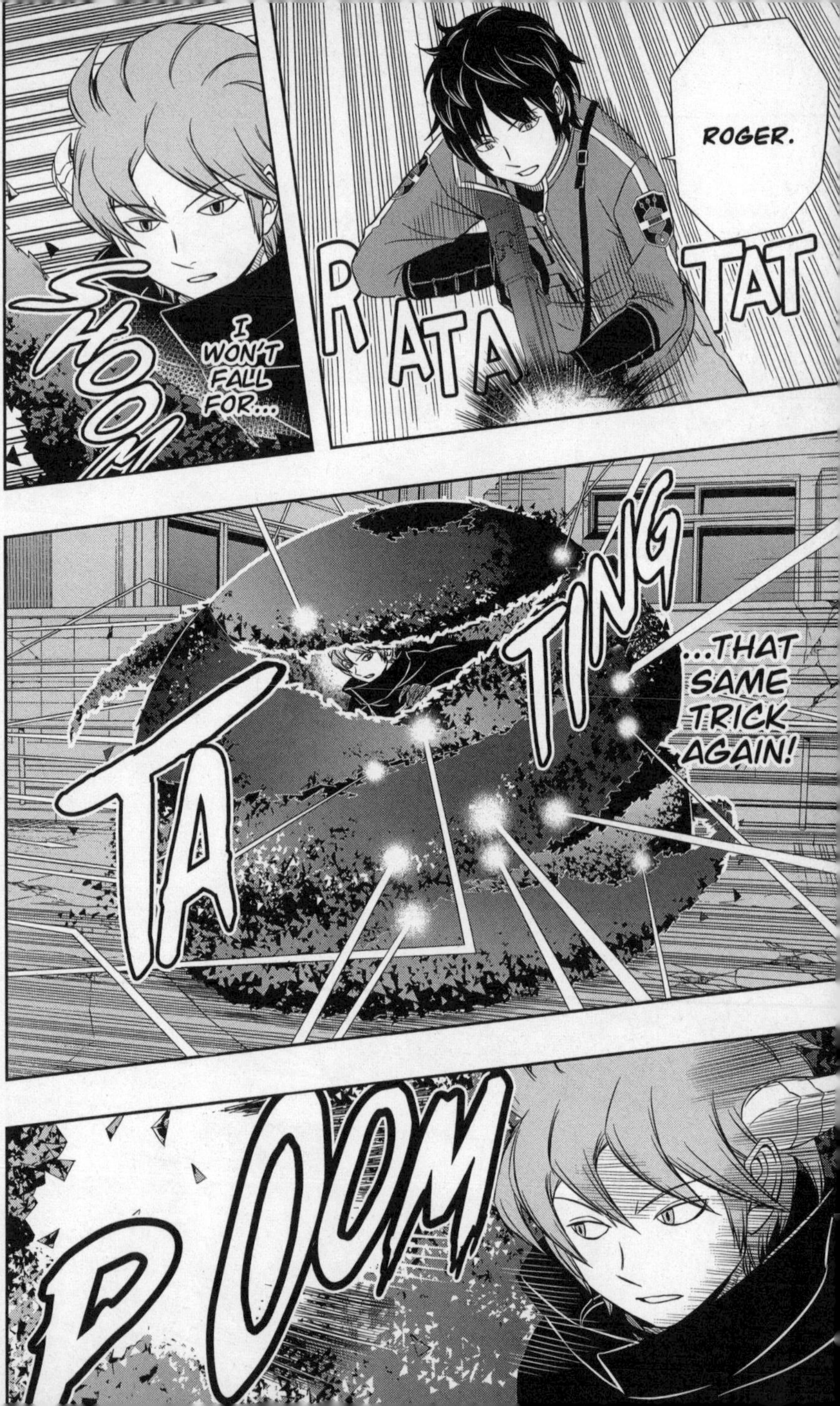
ROGER.
RATATAT
SHOOM
I WON'T FALL FOR...
TA TING
...THAT SAME TRICK AGAIN!
DOOM

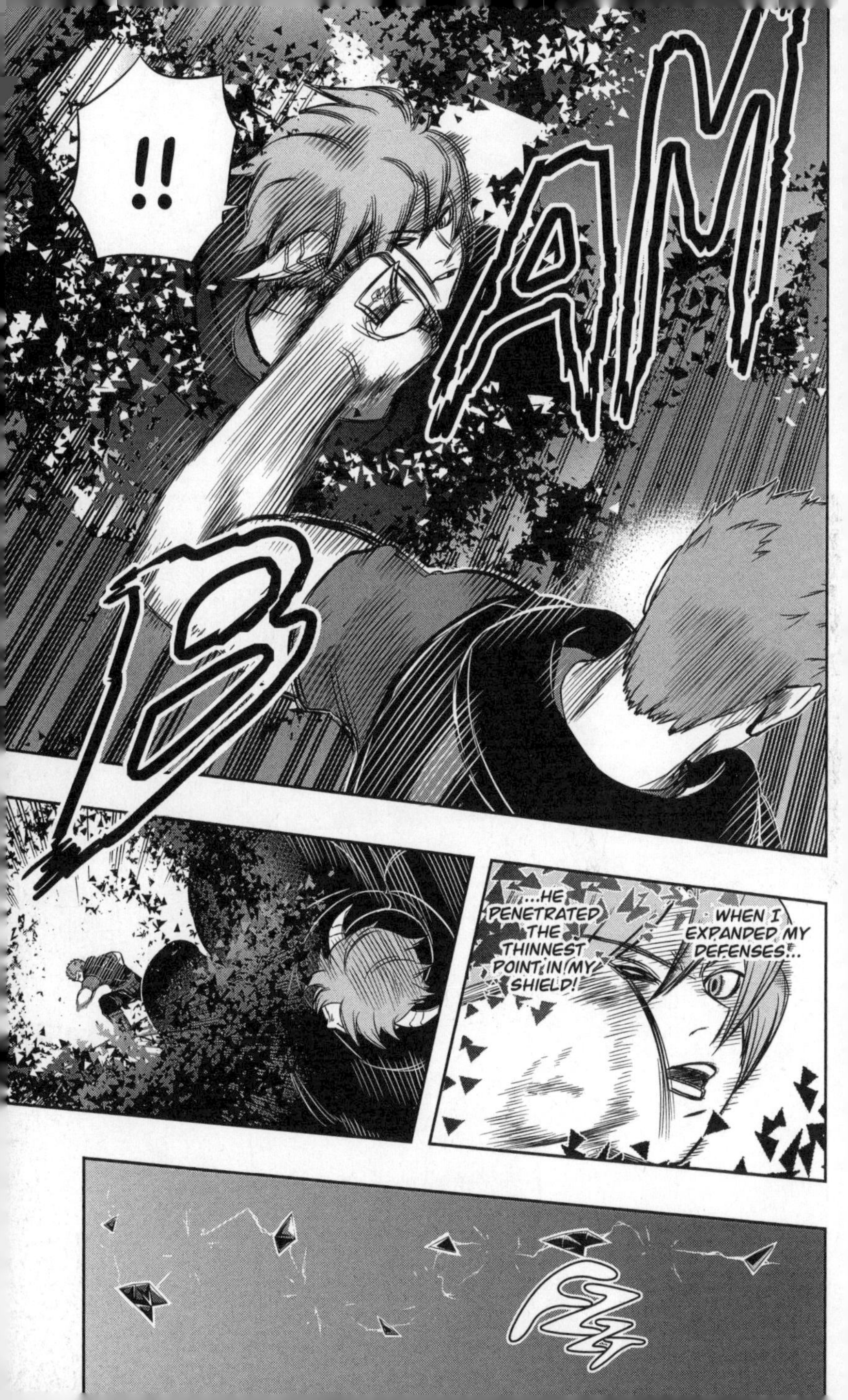
!!
BAM
WHEN I EXPANDED MY DEFENSES...
...HE PENETRATED THE THINNEST POINT IN MY SHIELD!
FZZT

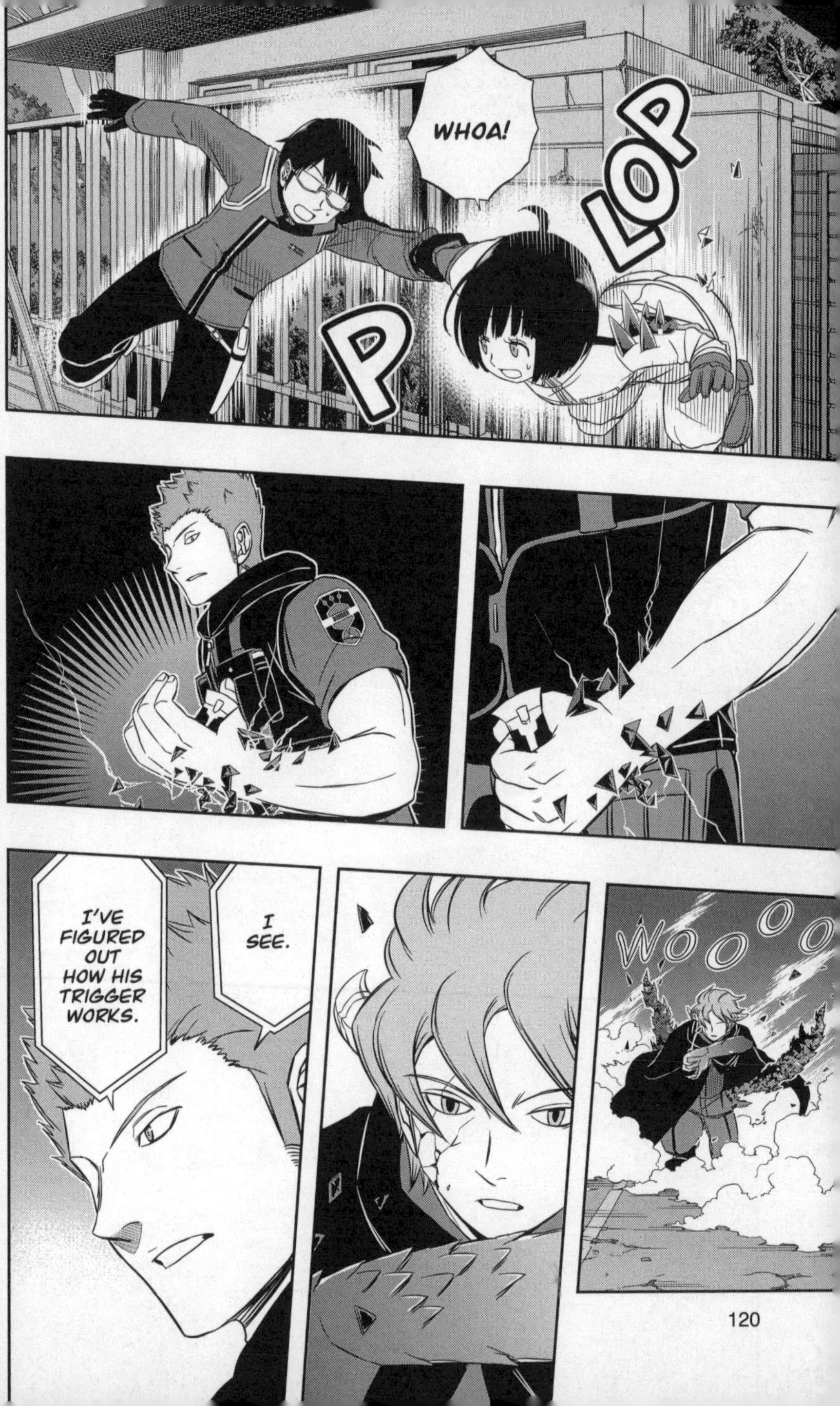
WHOA!
PLOP
WOOOO
I SEE.
I'VE FIGURED OUT HOW HIS TRIGGER WORKS.

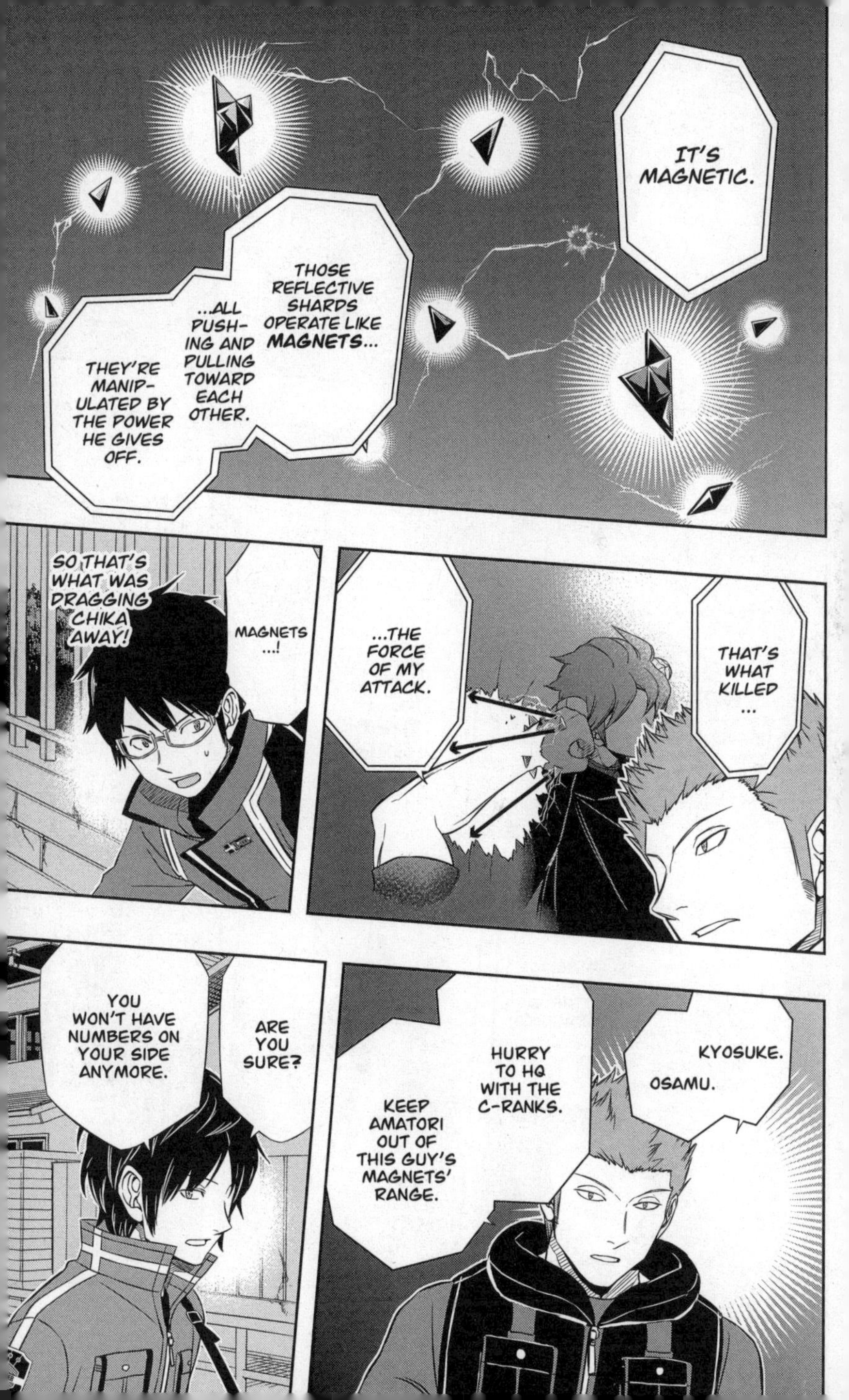
IT'S MAGNETIC.
THOSE REFLECTIVE SHARDS OPERATE LIKE MAGNETS...
...ALL PUSHING AND PULLING TOWARD EACH OTHER.
THEY'RE MANIPULATED BY THE POWER HE GIVES OFF.
THAT'S WHAT KILLED ...
...THE FORCE OF MY ATTACK.
MAGNETS ...!
SO THAT'S WHAT WAS DRAGGING CHIKA AWAY!
KYOSUKE.
OSAMU.
HURRY TO HQ WITH THE C-RANKS.
KEEP AMATORI OUT OF THIS GUY'S MAGNETS' RANGE.
ARE YOU SURE?
YOU WON'T HAVE NUMBERS ON YOUR SIDE ANYMORE.

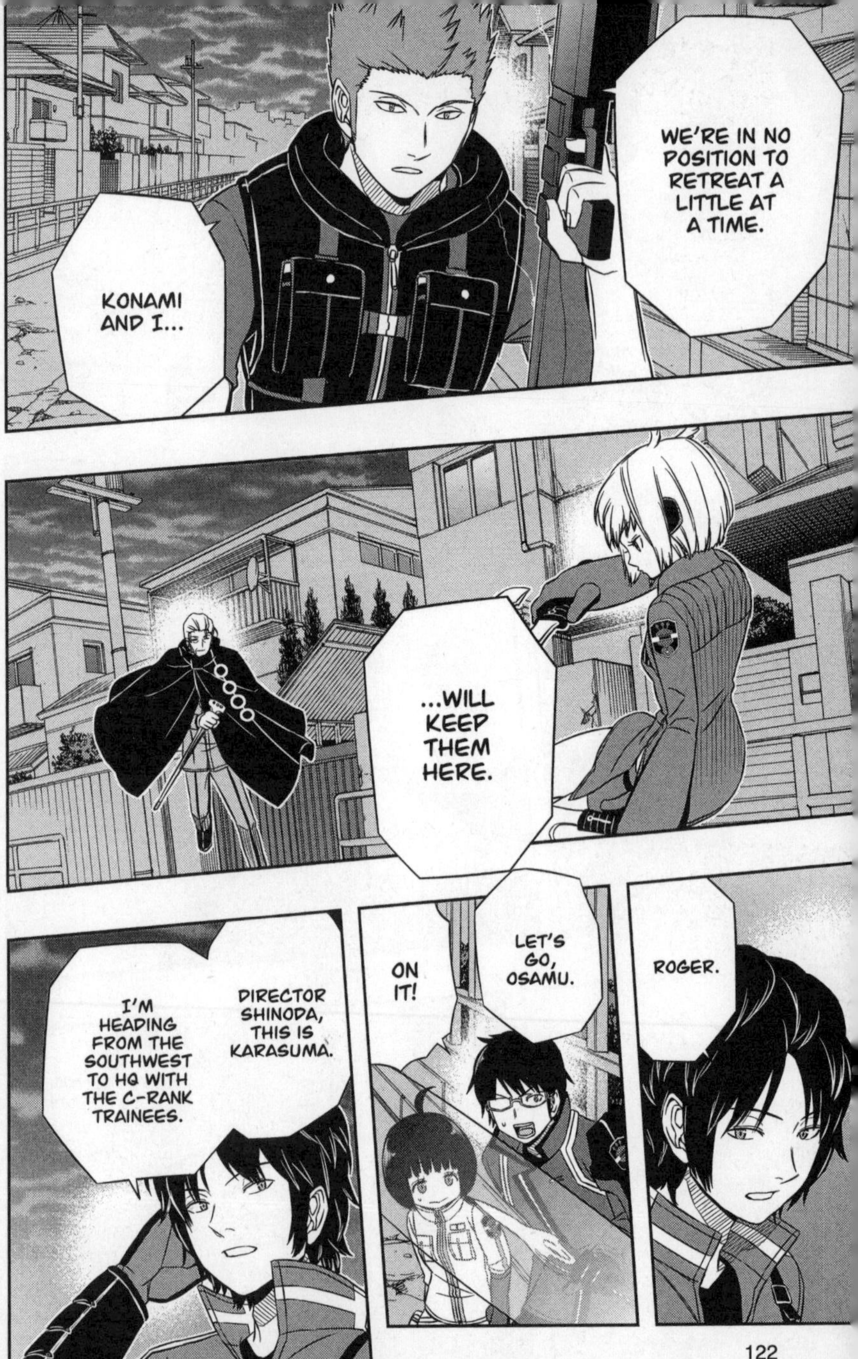
WE'RE IN NO POSITION TO RETREAT A LITTLE AT A TIME.
KONAMI AND I...
...WILL KEEP THEM HERE.
ROGER.
LET'S GO, OSAMU.
ON IT!
DIRECTOR SHINODA, THIS IS KARASUMA.
I'M HEADING FROM THE SOUTHWEST TO HQ WITH THE C-RANK TRAINEES.

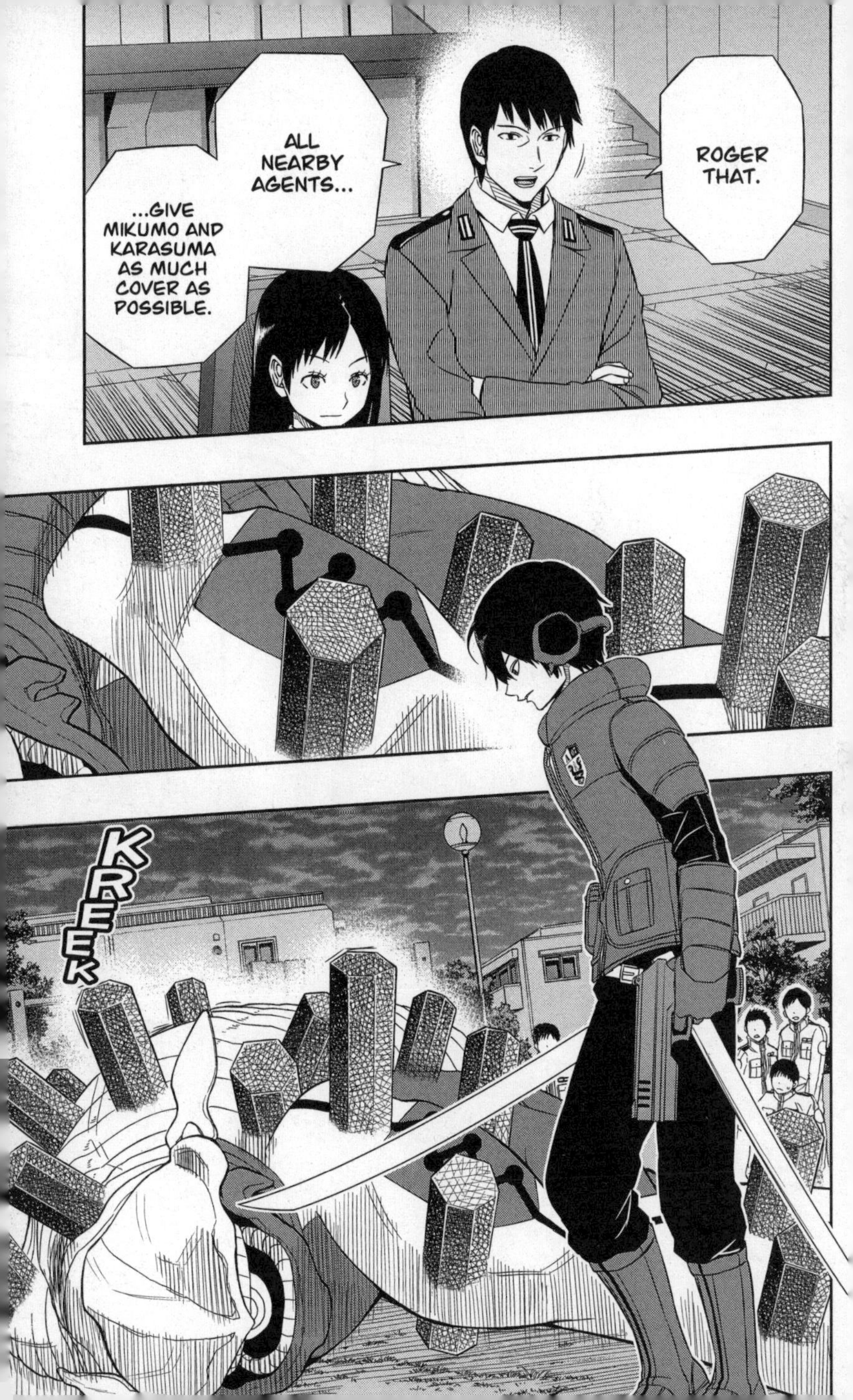
ROGER THAT.
ALL NEARBY AGENTS...
...GIVE MIKUMO AND KARASUMA AS MUCH COVER AS POSSIBLE.
KREEK

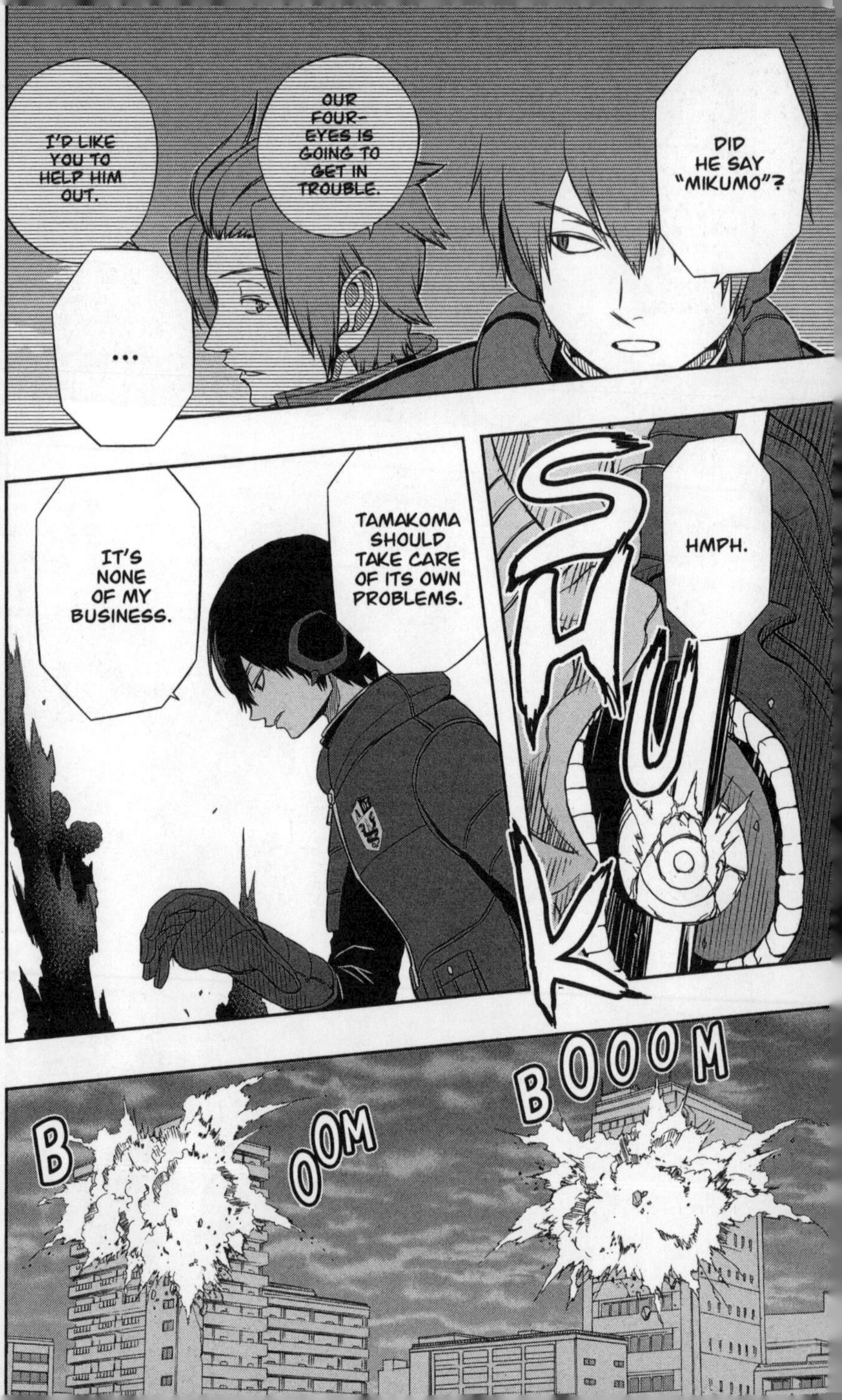
DID HE SAY "MIKUMO"?
OUR FOUR-EYES IS GOING TO GET IN TROUBLE.
I'D LIKE YOU TO HELP HIM OUT.
...
HMPH.
SHUK
TAMAKOMA SHOULD TAKE CARE OF ITS OWN PROBLEMS.
IT'S NONE OF MY BUSINESS.
BOOOM
BOOM

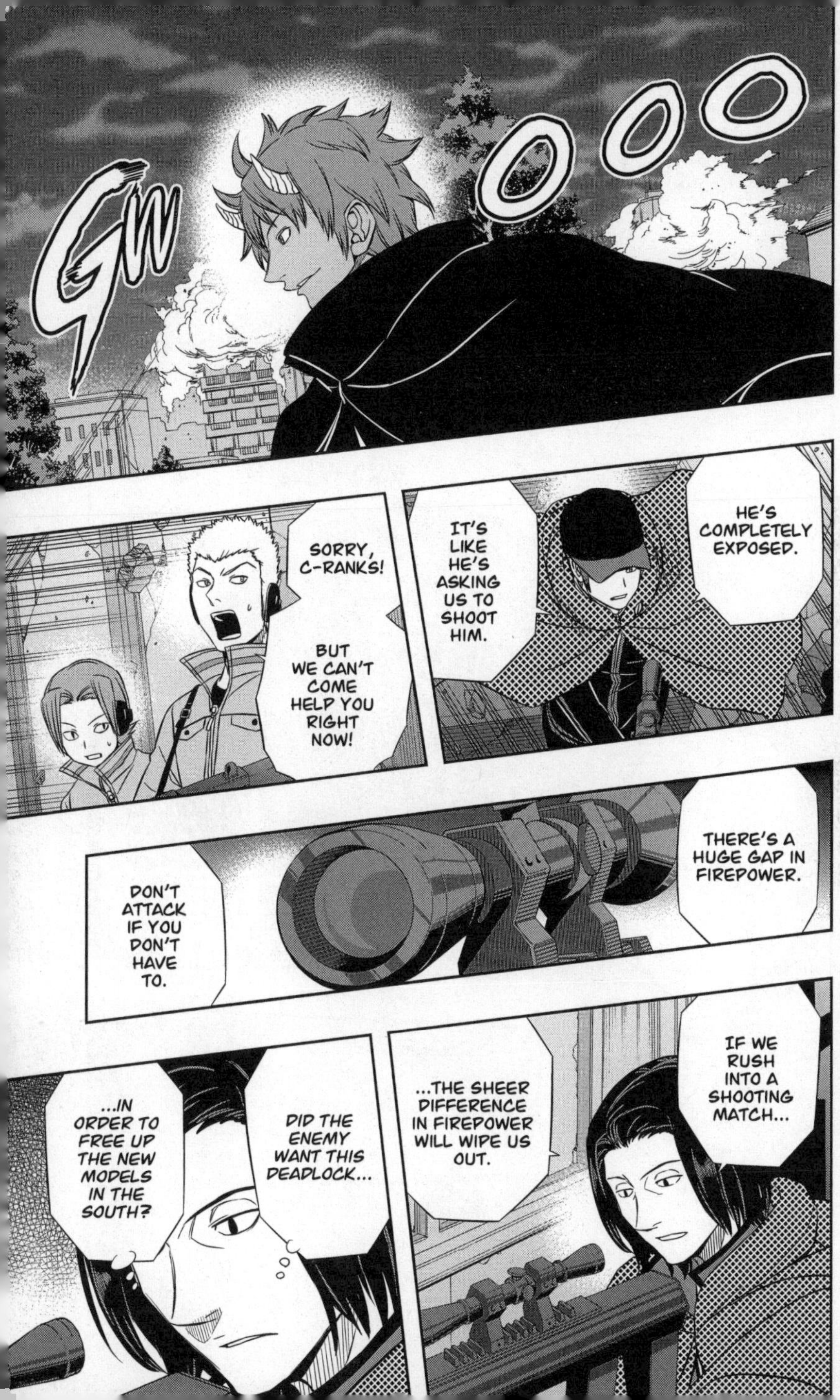
GWOOOO
HE'S COMPLETELY EXPOSED.
IT'S LIKE HE'S ASKING US TO SHOOT HIM.
SORRY, C-RANKS!
BUT WE CAN'T COME HELP YOU RIGHT NOW!
THERE'S A HUGE GAP IN FIREPOWER.
DON'T ATTACK IF YOU DON'T HAVE TO.
IF WE RUSH INTO A SHOOTING MATCH...
...THE SHEER DIFFERENCE IN FIREPOWER WILL WIPE US OUT.
DID THE ENEMY WANT THIS DEADLOCK...
...IN ORDER TO FREE UP THE NEW MODELS IN THE SOUTH?

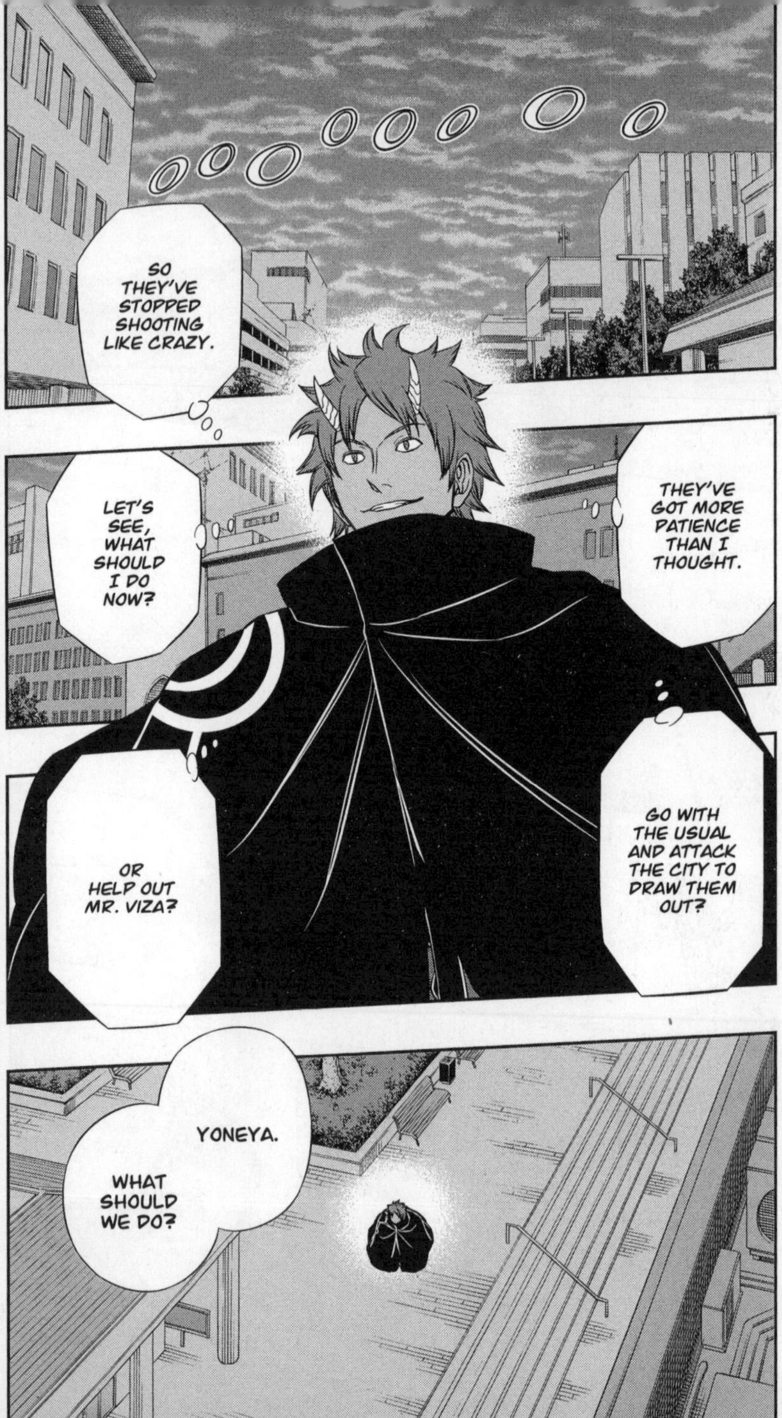
SO THEY'VE STOPPED SHOOTING LIKE CRAZY.
THEY'VE GOT MORE PATIENCE THAN I THOUGHT.
LET'S SEE, WHAT SHOULD I DO NOW?
GO WITH THE USUAL AND ATTACK THE CITY TO DRAW THEM OUT?
OR HELP OUT MR. VIZA?
YONEYA.
WHAT SHOULD WE DO?

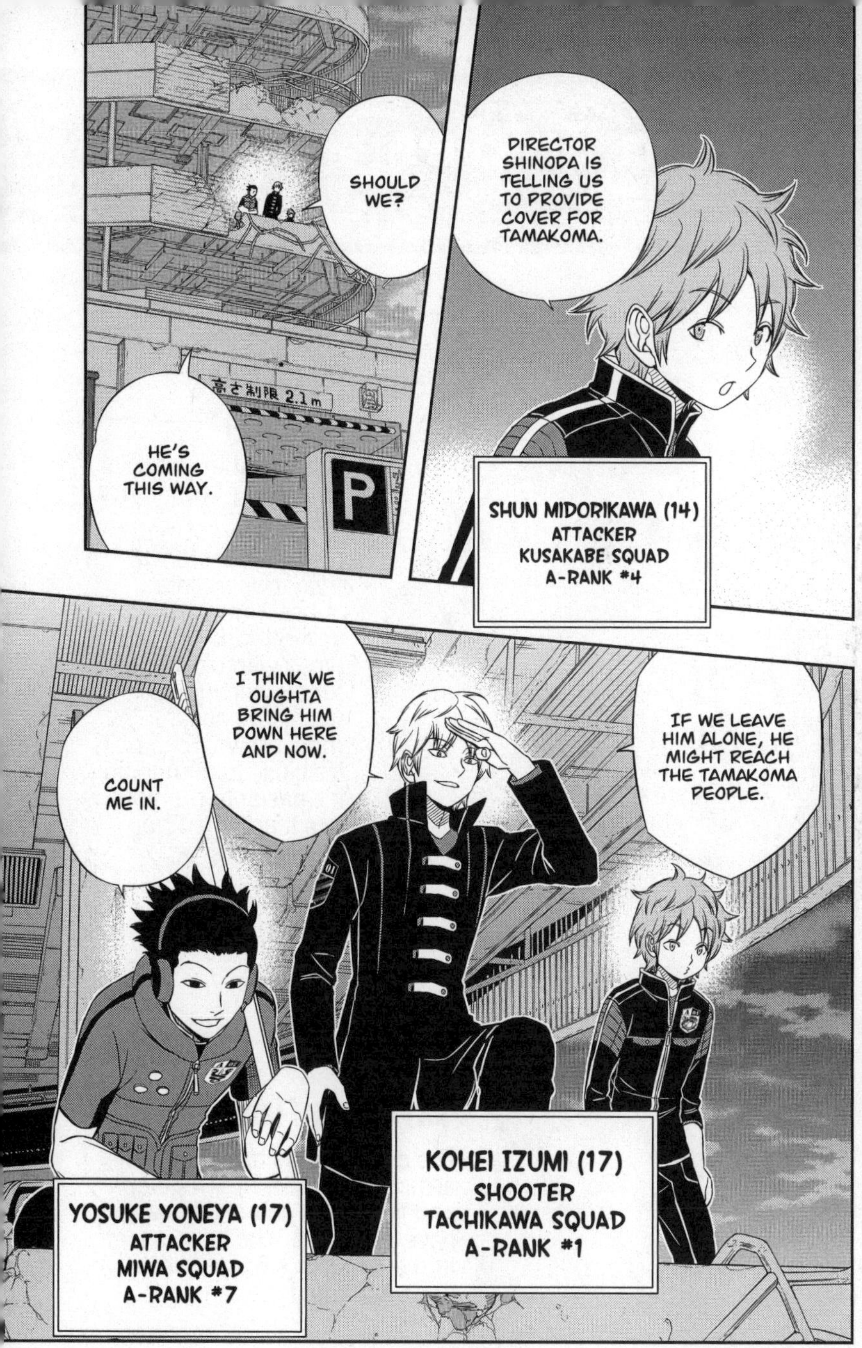
DIRECTOR SHINODA IS TELLING US TO PROVIDE COVER FOR TAMAKOMA.
SHUN MIDORIKAWA (14) ATTACKER KUSAKABE SQUAD A-RANK #4
SHOULD WE?
高さ制限 2.1m
P
HE'S COMING THIS WAY.
IF WE LEAVE HIM ALONE, HE MIGHT REACH THE TAMAKOMA PEOPLE.
I THINK WE OUGHTA BRING HIM DOWN HERE AND NOW.
COUNT ME IN.
KOHEI IZUMI (17) SHOOTER TACHIKAWA SQUAD A-RANK #1
YOSUKE YONEYA (17) ATTACKER MIWA SQUAD A-RANK #7

Trion Soldier
Neighbor Minion

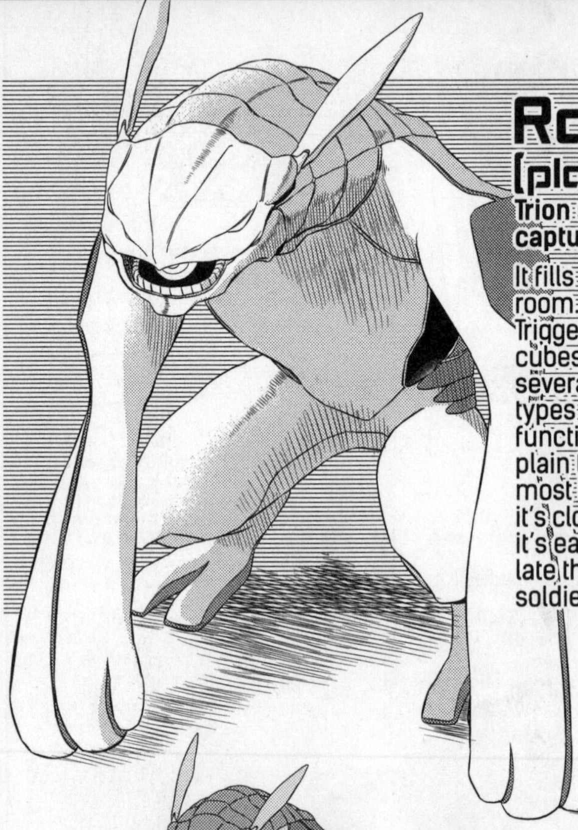

Rabit
[plain]

Trion soldier used for capturing Trion users.

It fills up a 7x7 meter room. It transforms Trigger users into cubes. There are several modded types with different functions, but the plain type has the most brawn. Since it's close to humanoid, it's easier to manipulate than other Trion soldiers.

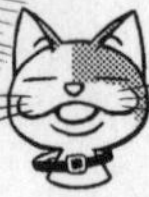

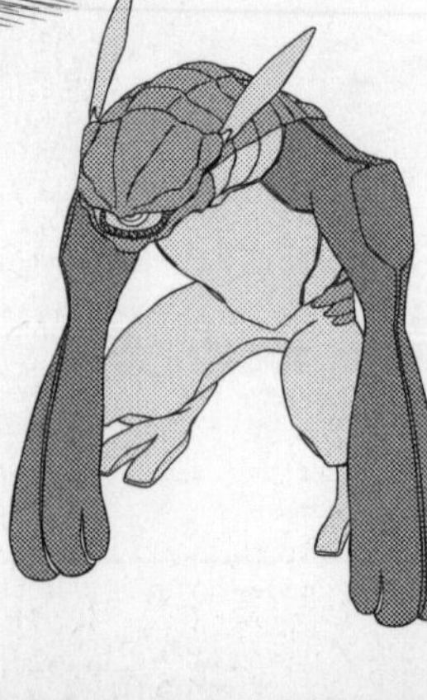

■Rabit Armor

The darker areas have thicker armor. Only Konami's Sogetsu and Tachikawa's Senku Kogetsu have penetrated the head so far, and only Yuma's Boost Penta has penetrated the arms.

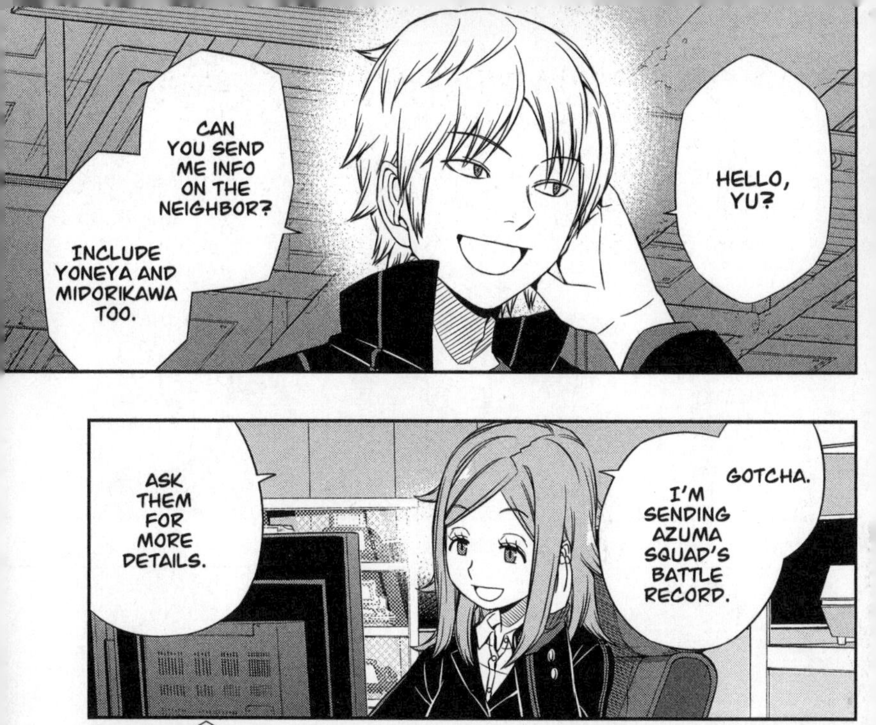
HELLO, YU?
CAN YOU SEND ME INFO ON THE NEIGHBOR?
INCLUDE YONEYA AND MIDORIKAWA TOO.
GOTCHA.
I'M SENDING AZUMA SQUAD'S BATTLE RECORD.
ASK THEM FOR MORE DETAILS.

Chapter 59 Invasion: Part 9

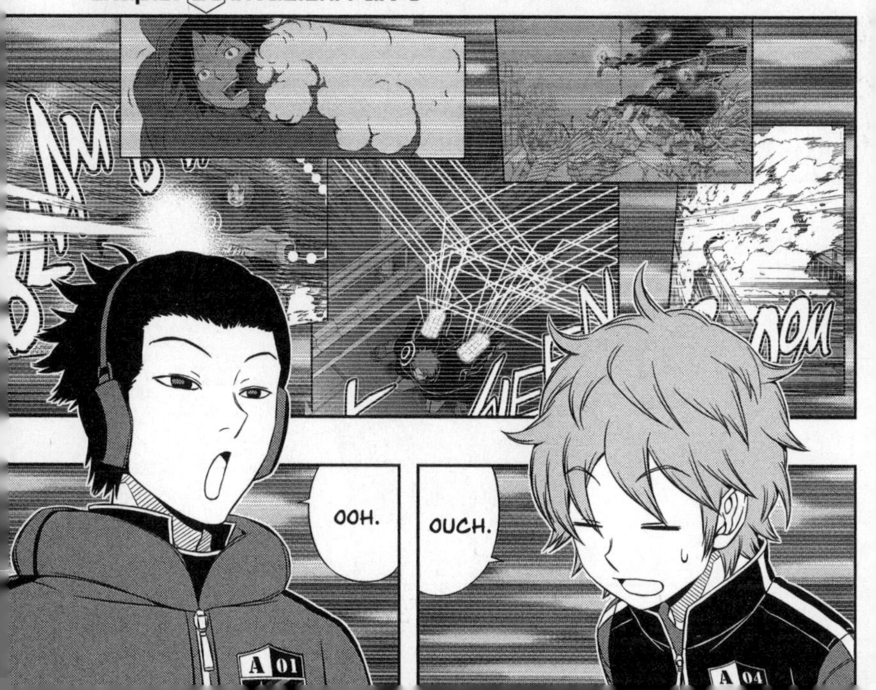
OUCH.
OOH.

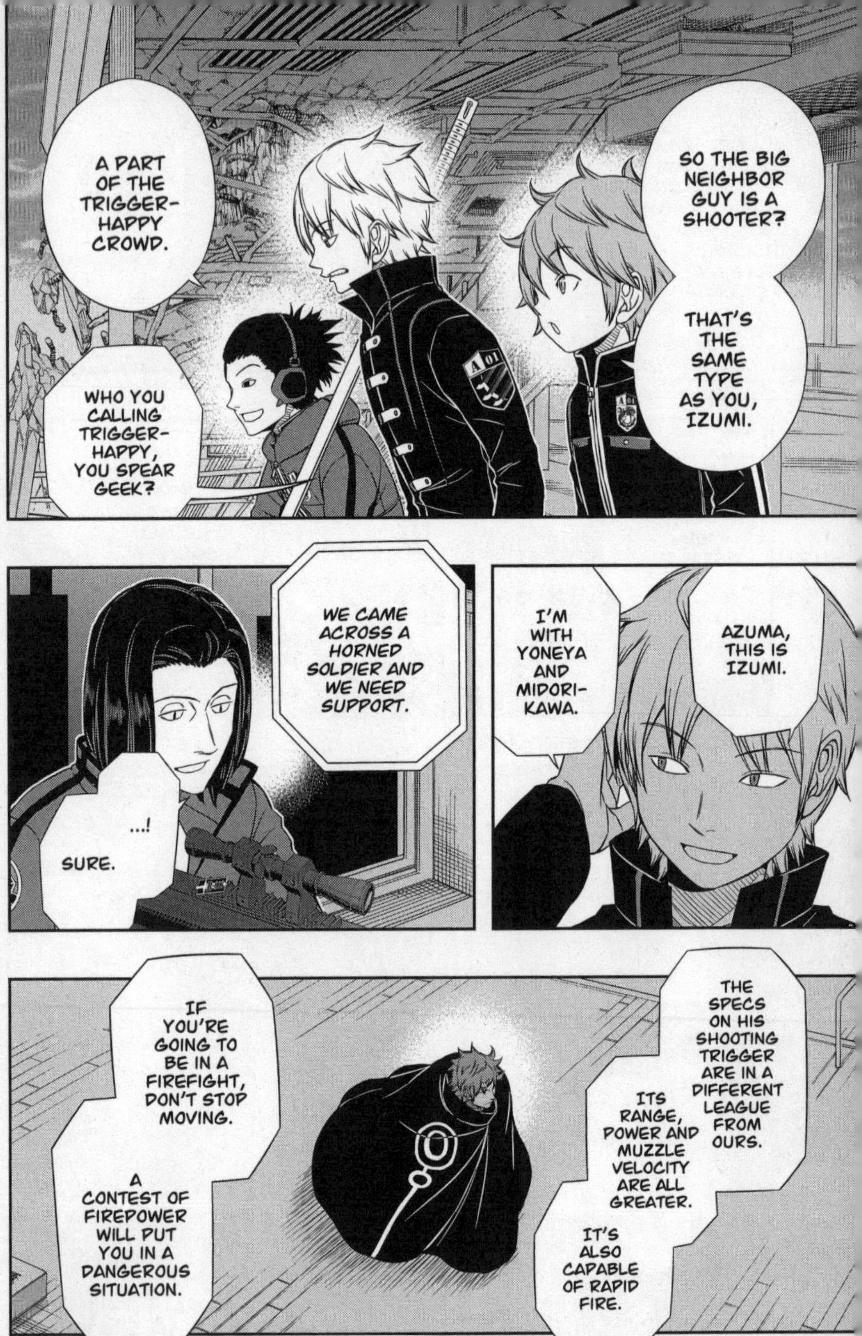

SO THE BIG NEIGHBOR GUY IS A SHOOTER?
THAT'S THE SAME TYPE AS YOU, IZUMI.
A PART OF THE TRIGGER-HAPPY CROWD.
WHO YOU CALLING TRIGGER-HAPPY, YOU SPEAR GEEK?
AZUMA, THIS IS IZUMI.
I'M WITH YONEYA AND MIDORIKAWA.
WE CAME ACROSS A HORNED SOLDIER AND WE NEED SUPPORT.
...!
SURE.
THE SPECS ON HIS SHOOTING TRIGGER ARE IN A DIFFERENT LEAGUE FROM OURS.
ITS RANGE, POWER AND MUZZLE VELOCITY ARE ALL GREATER.
IT'S ALSO CAPABLE OF RAPID FIRE.
IF YOU'RE GOING TO BE IN A FIREFIGHT, DON'T STOP MOVING.
A CONTEST OF FIREPOWER WILL PUT YOU IN A DANGEROUS SITUATION.

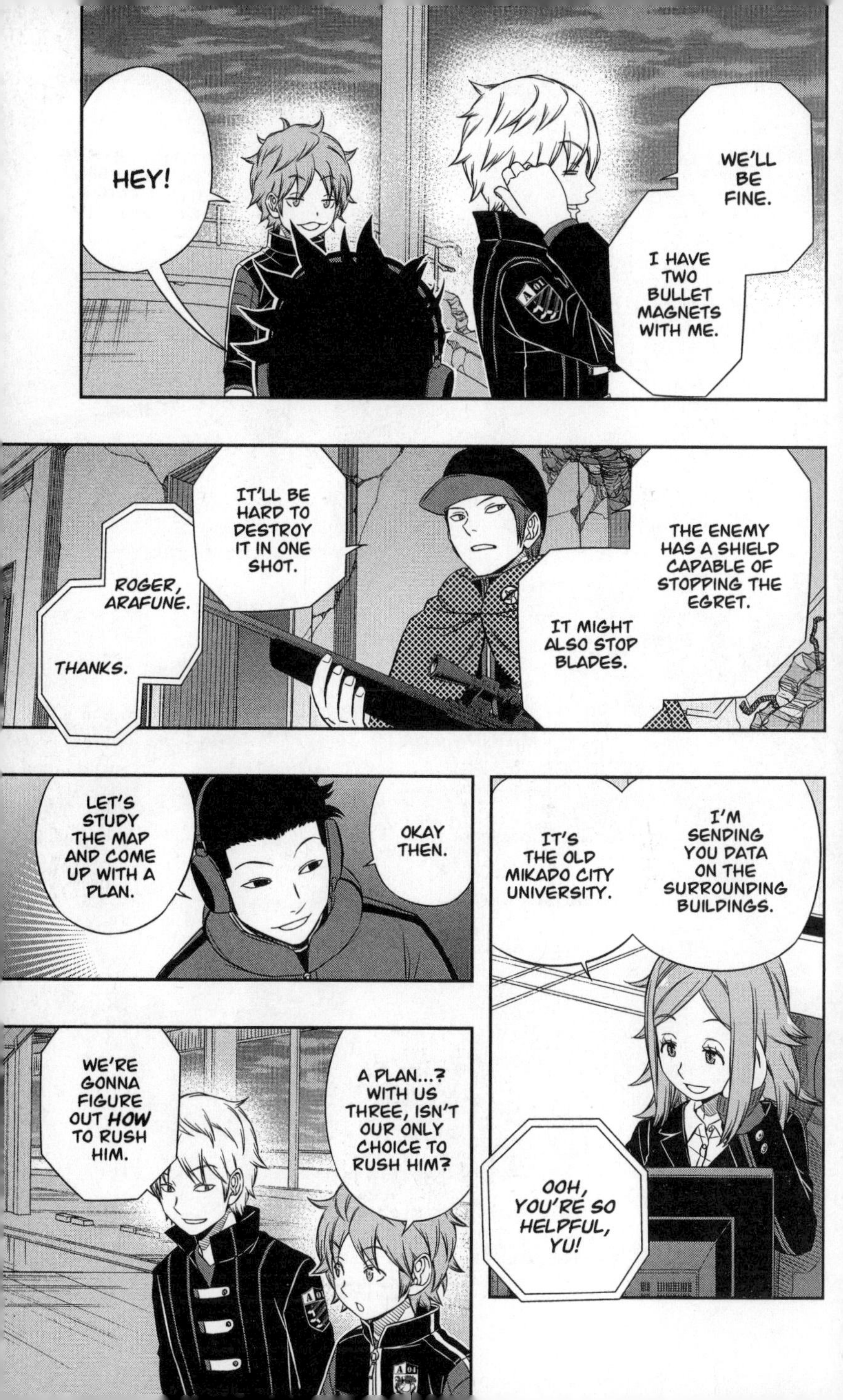
WE'LL BE FINE.
I HAVE TWO BULLET MAGNETS WITH ME.
HEY!
THE ENEMY HAS A SHIELD CAPABLE OF STOPPING THE EGRET.
IT MIGHT ALSO STOP BLADES.
IT'LL BE HARD TO DESTROY IT IN ONE SHOT.
ROGER, ARAFUNE.
THANKS.
I'M SENDING YOU DATA ON THE SURROUNDING BUILDINGS.
IT'S THE OLD MIKADO CITY UNIVERSITY.
OOH, YOU'RE SO HELPFUL, YU!
OKAY THEN.
LET'S STUDY THE MAP AND COME UP WITH A PLAN.
A PLAN...? WITH US THREE, ISN'T OUR ONLY CHOICE TO RUSH HIM?
WE'RE GONNA FIGURE OUT HOW TO RUSH HIM.

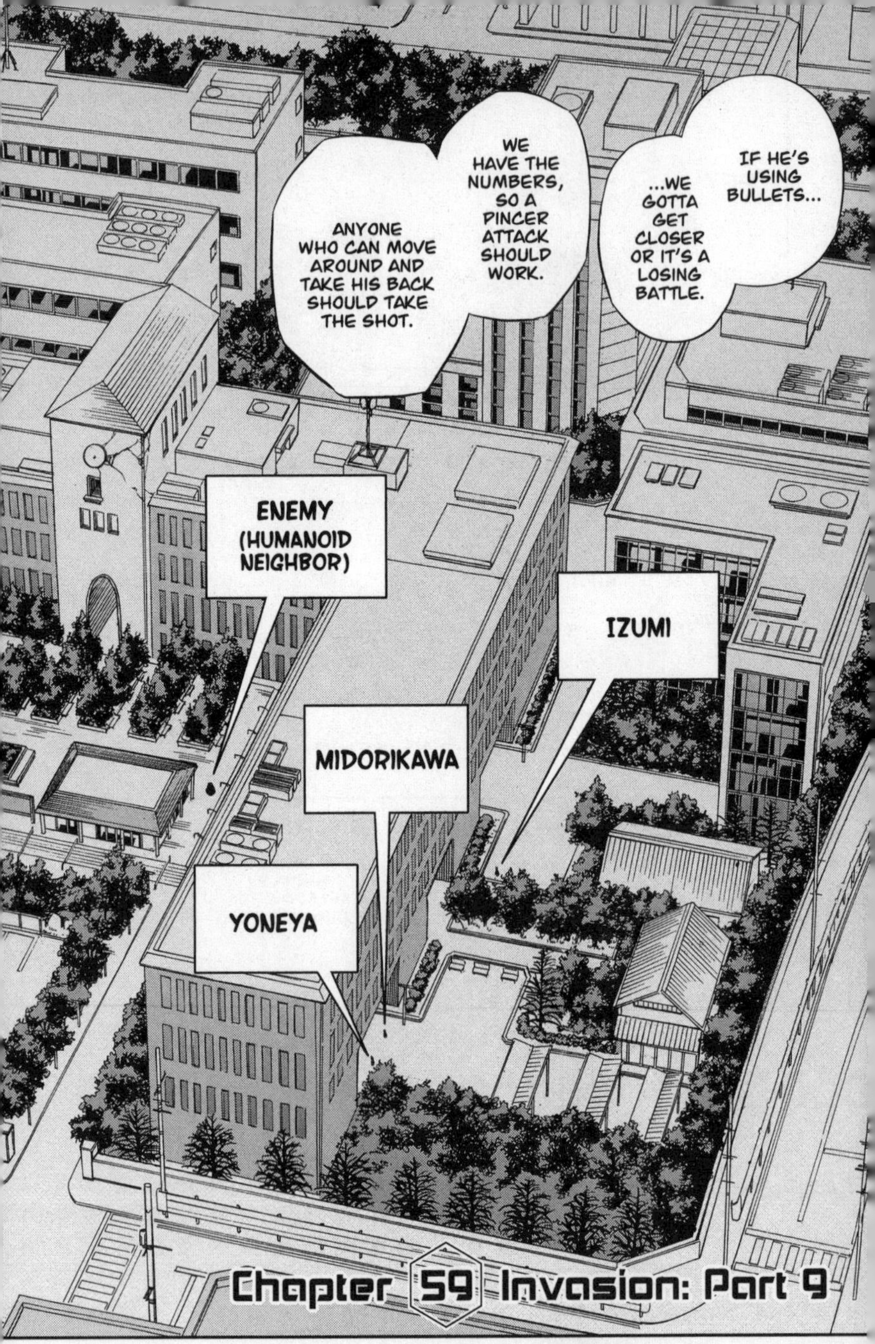
IF HE'S USING BULLETS...
...WE GOTTA GET CLOSER OR IT'S A LOSING BATTLE.
WE HAVE THE NUMBERS, SO A PINCER ATTACK SHOULD WORK.
ANYONE WHO CAN MOVE AROUND AND TAKE HIS BACK SHOULD TAKE THE SHOT.
ENEMY (HUMANOID NEIGHBOR)
IZUMI
MIDORIKAWA
YONEYA
Chapter 59 Invasion: Part 9

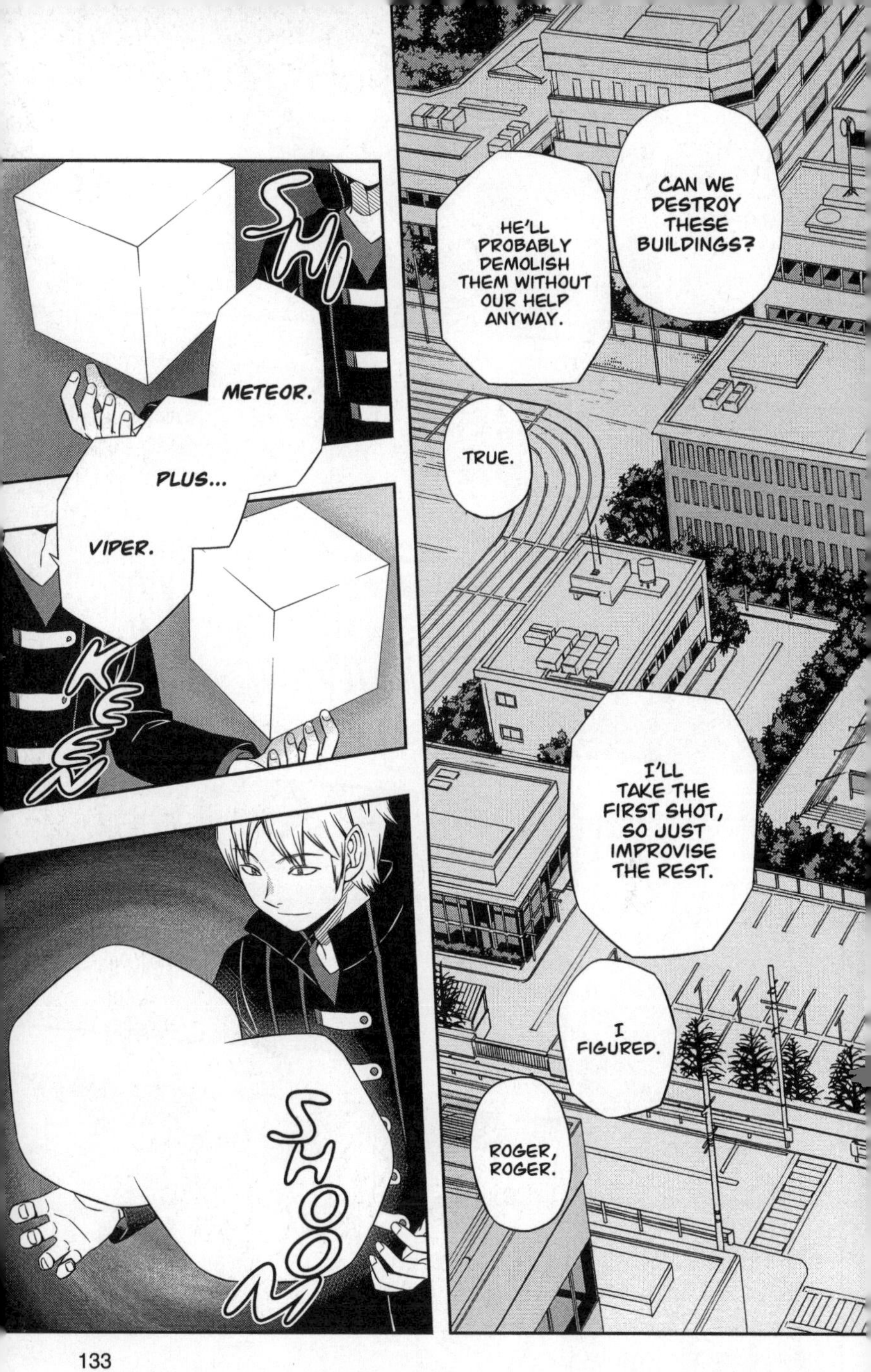
CAN WE DESTROY THESE BUILDINGS?
HE'LL PROBABLY DEMOLISH THEM WITHOUT OUR HELP ANYWAY.
TRUE.
I'LL TAKE THE FIRST SHOT, SO JUST IMPROVISE THE REST.
I FIGURED.
ROGER, ROGER.
SHI
METEOR.
PLUS...
VIPER.
KEEEN
SHOOM

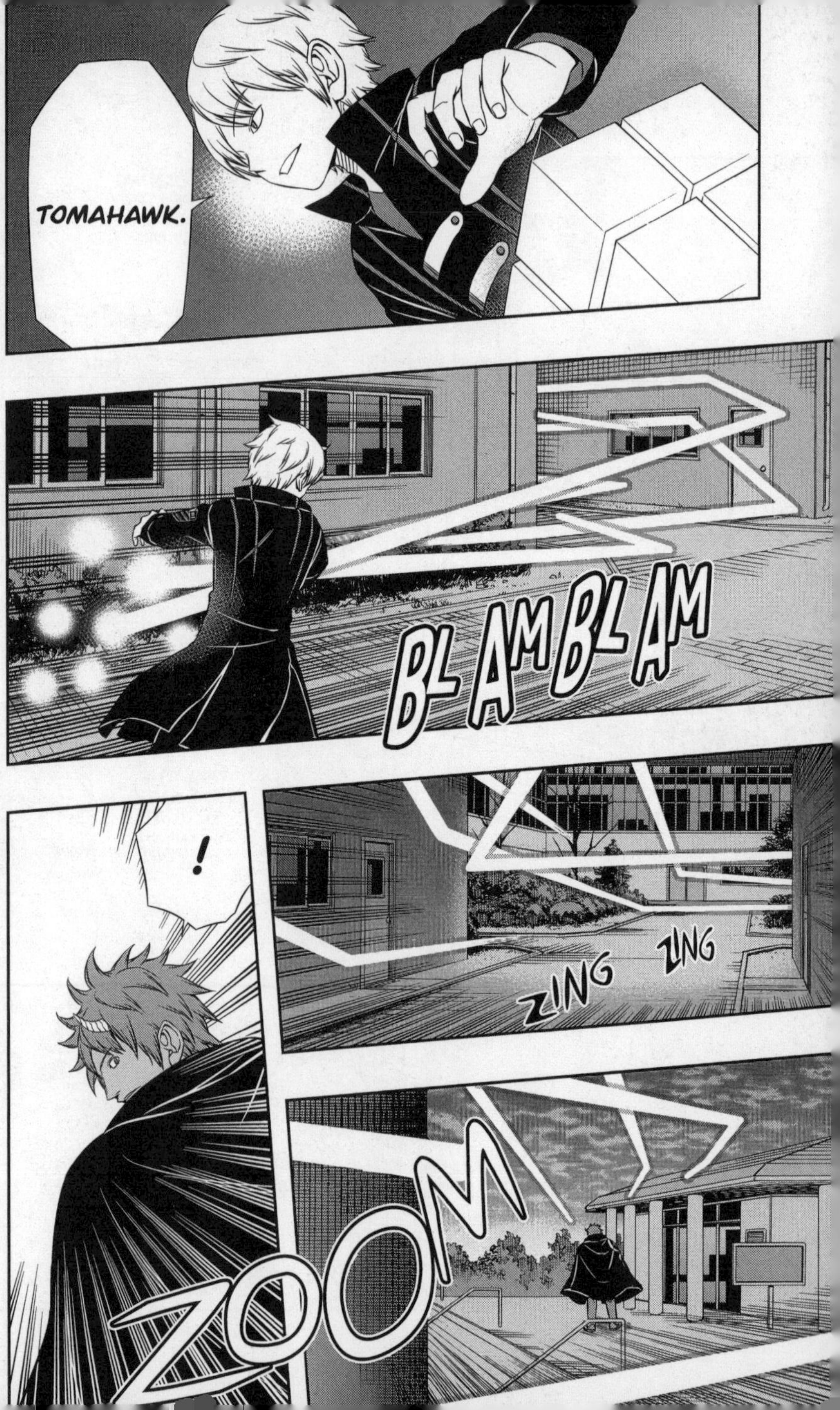
TOMAHAWK.
BLAM BLAM
ZING ZING
!
ZOOM

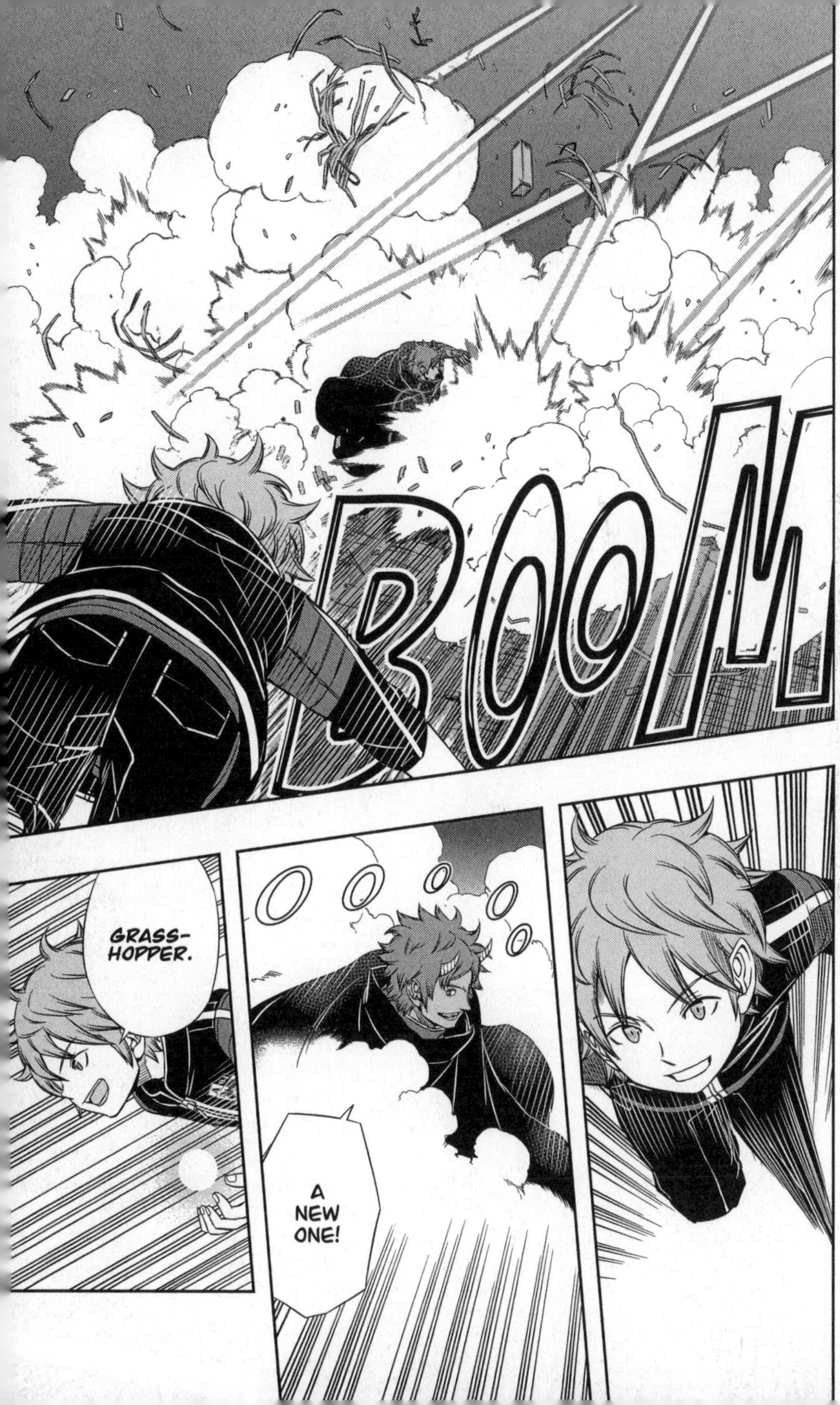
BOOM
A NEW ONE!
GRASS-HOPPER.

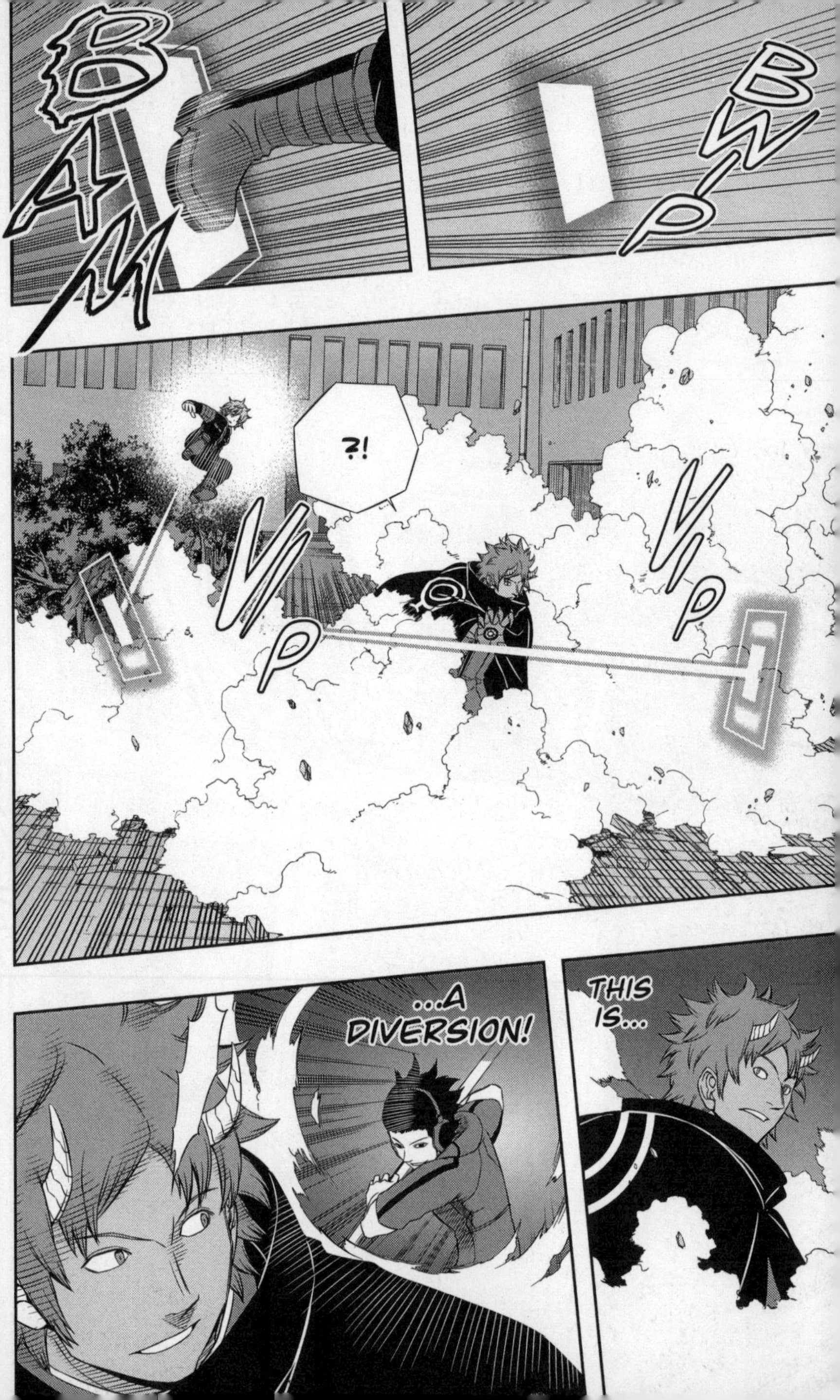
BWIP
BAM
VIP
?!
VIP
THIS IS...
...A DIVERSION!

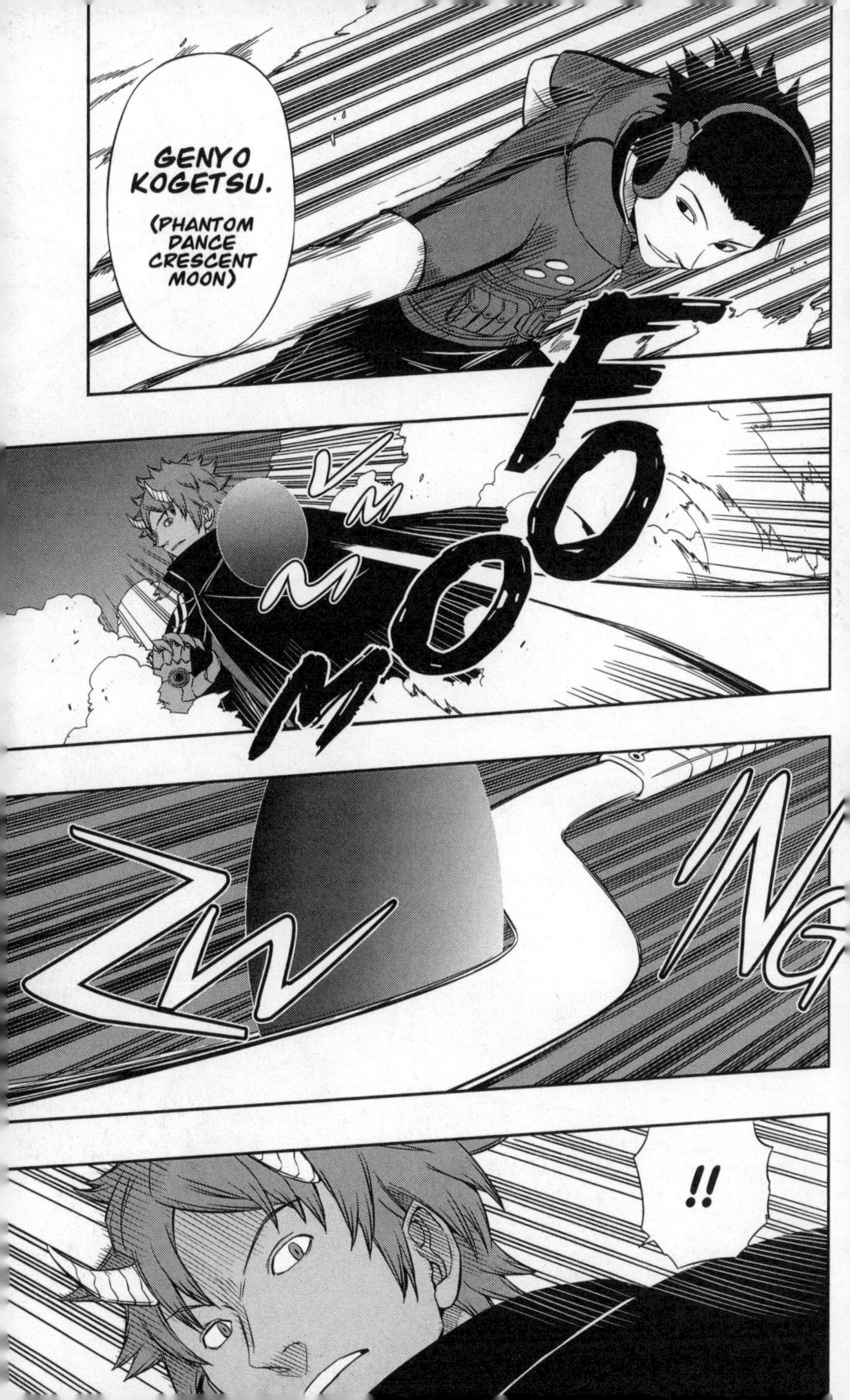
GENYO KOGETSU.
(PHANTOM DANCE CRESCENT MOON)
FOOOM
VMM
ZWNNG
!!

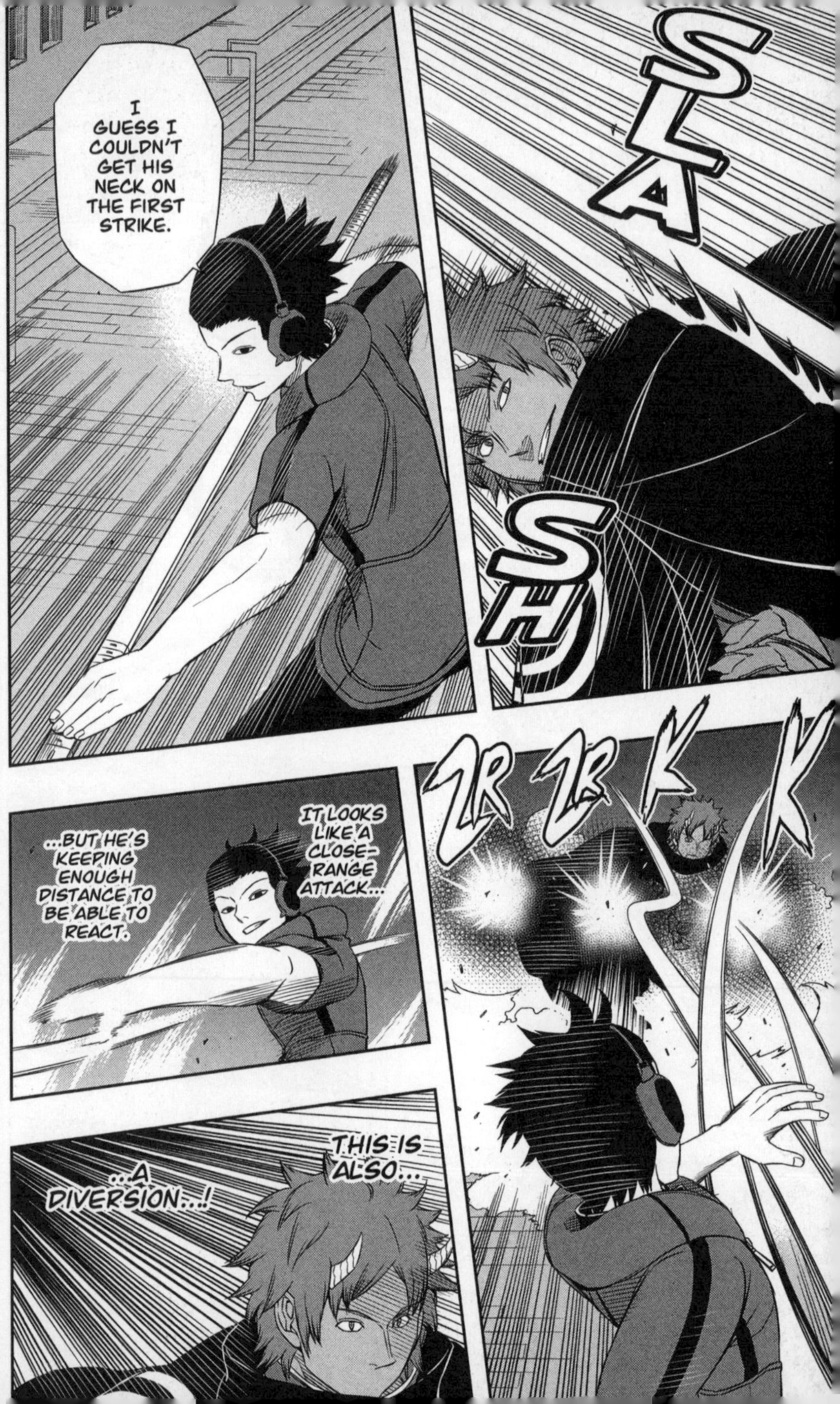
SLASH
I GUESS I COULDN'T GET HIS NECK ON THE FIRST STRIKE.
ZRZRKK
IT LOOKS LIKE A CLOSE-RANGE ATTACK...
...BUT HE'S KEEPING ENOUGH DISTANCE TO BE ABLE TO REACT.
THIS IS ALSO...
...A DIVERSION...!

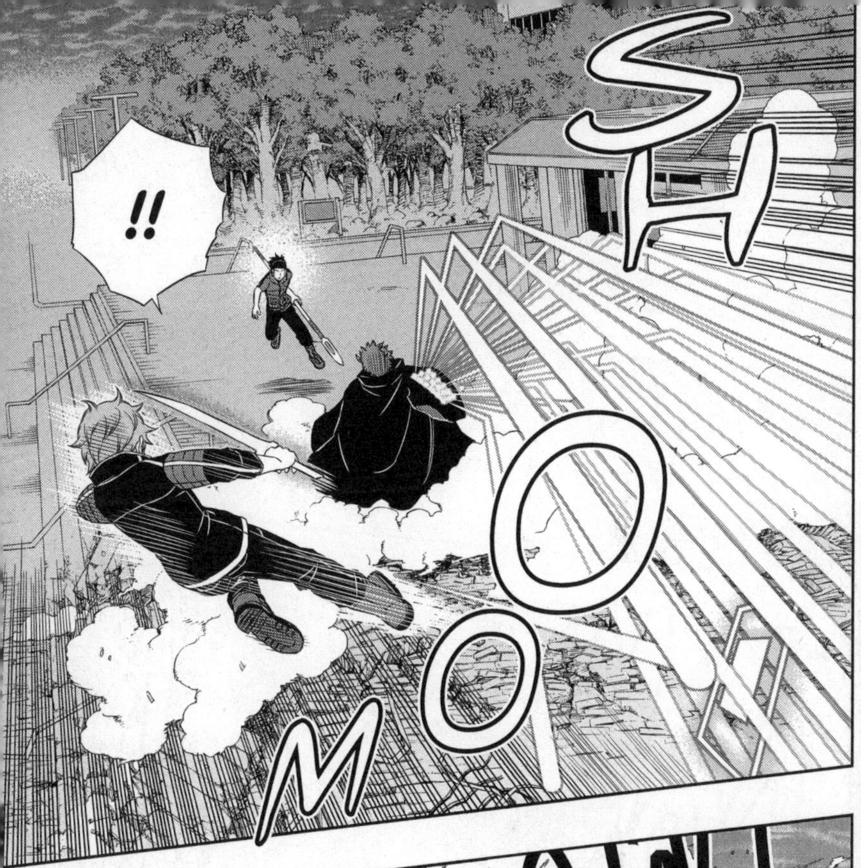
!!
SHOOM

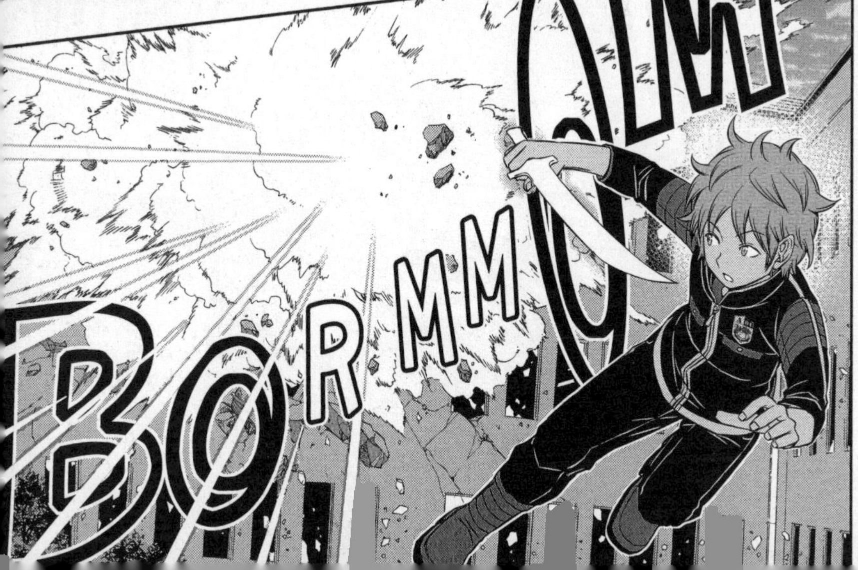
BORMMMOOM

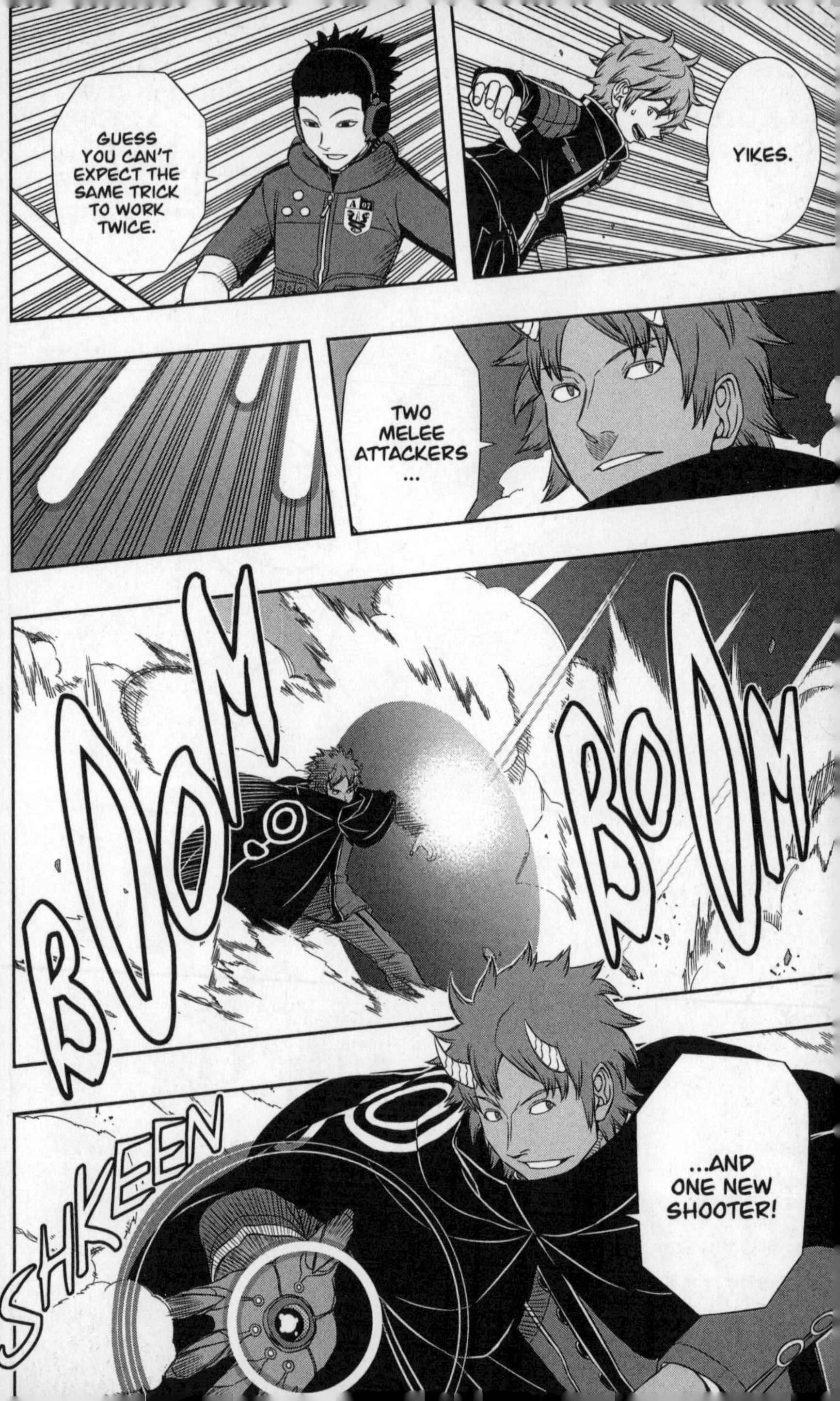
YIKES.
GUESS YOU CAN'T EXPECT THE SAME TRICK TO WORK TWICE.
TWO MELEE ATTACKERS ...
BOOM
BOOM
...AND ONE NEW SHOOTER!
SHKEEN

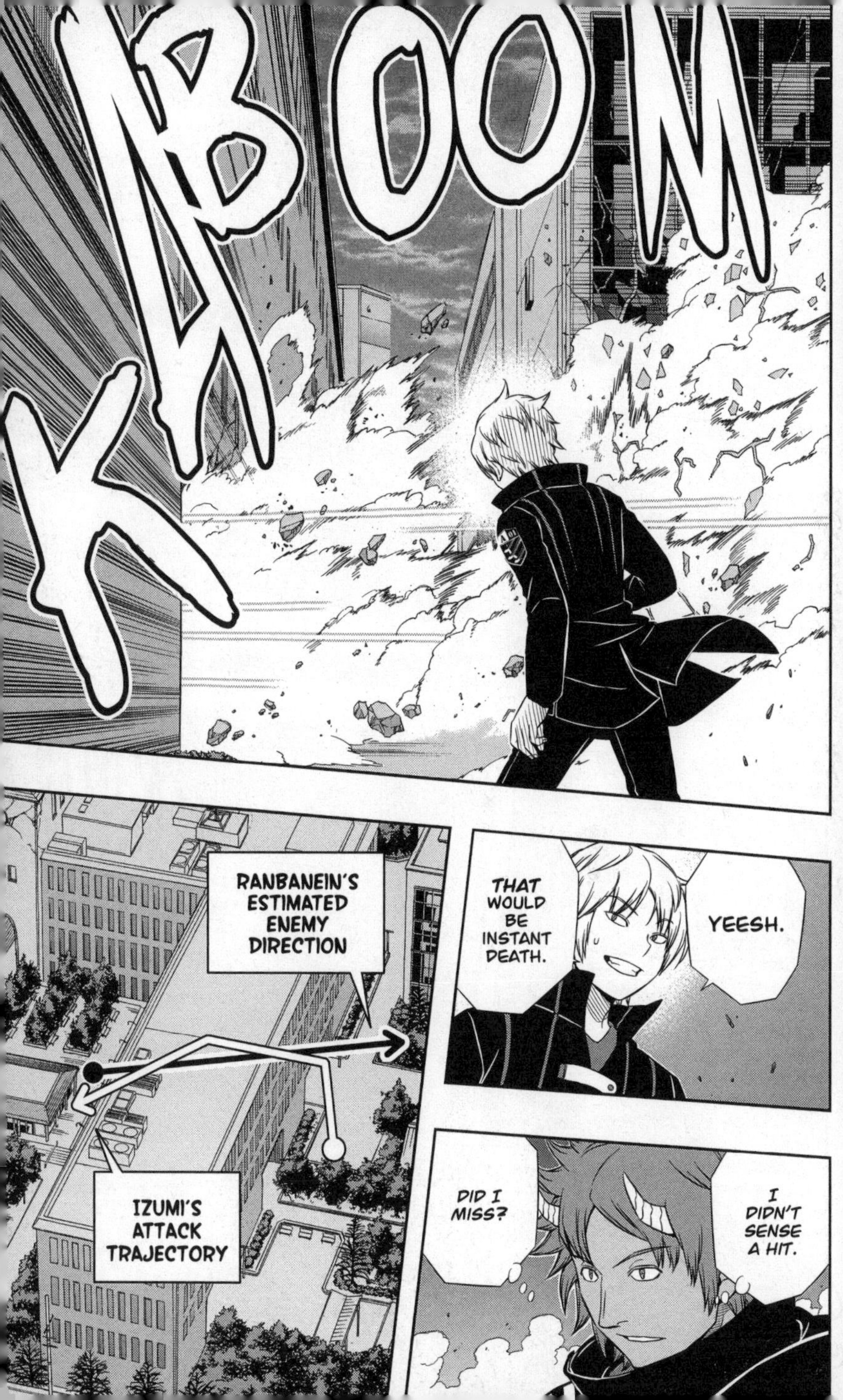
KABOOM
YEESH.
THAT WOULD BE INSTANT DEATH.
I DIDN'T SENSE A HIT.
DID I MISS?
RANBANEIN'S ESTIMATED ENEMY DIRECTION
IZUMI'S ATTACK TRAJECTORY

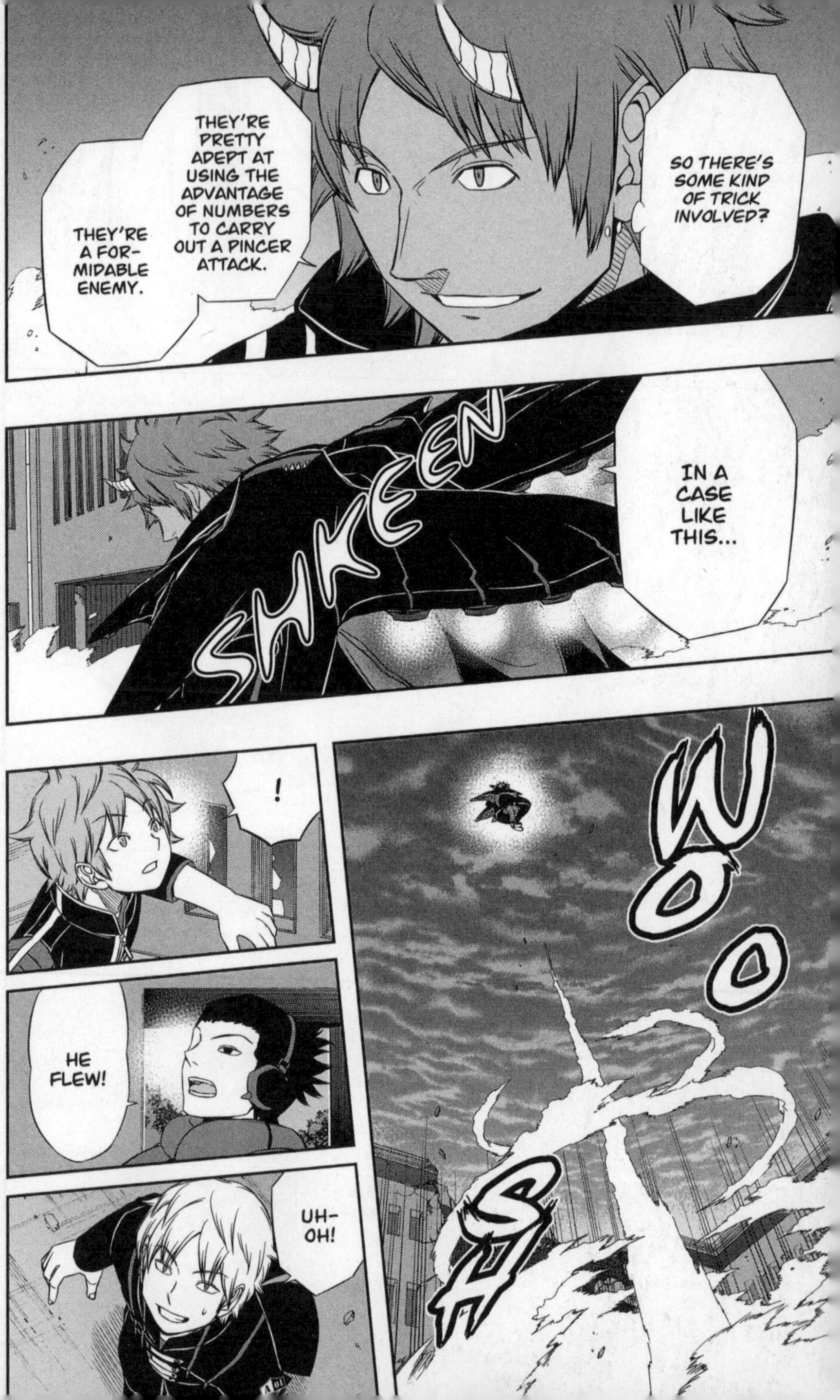
SO THERE'S SOME KIND OF TRICK INVOLVED?
THEY'RE PRETTY ADEPT AT USING THE ADVANTAGE OF NUMBERS TO CARRY OUT A PINCER ATTACK.
THEY'RE A FOR-MIDABLE ENEMY.
IN A CASE LIKE THIS...
SHKEEN
WOOO
SH
!
HE FLEW!
UH-OH!

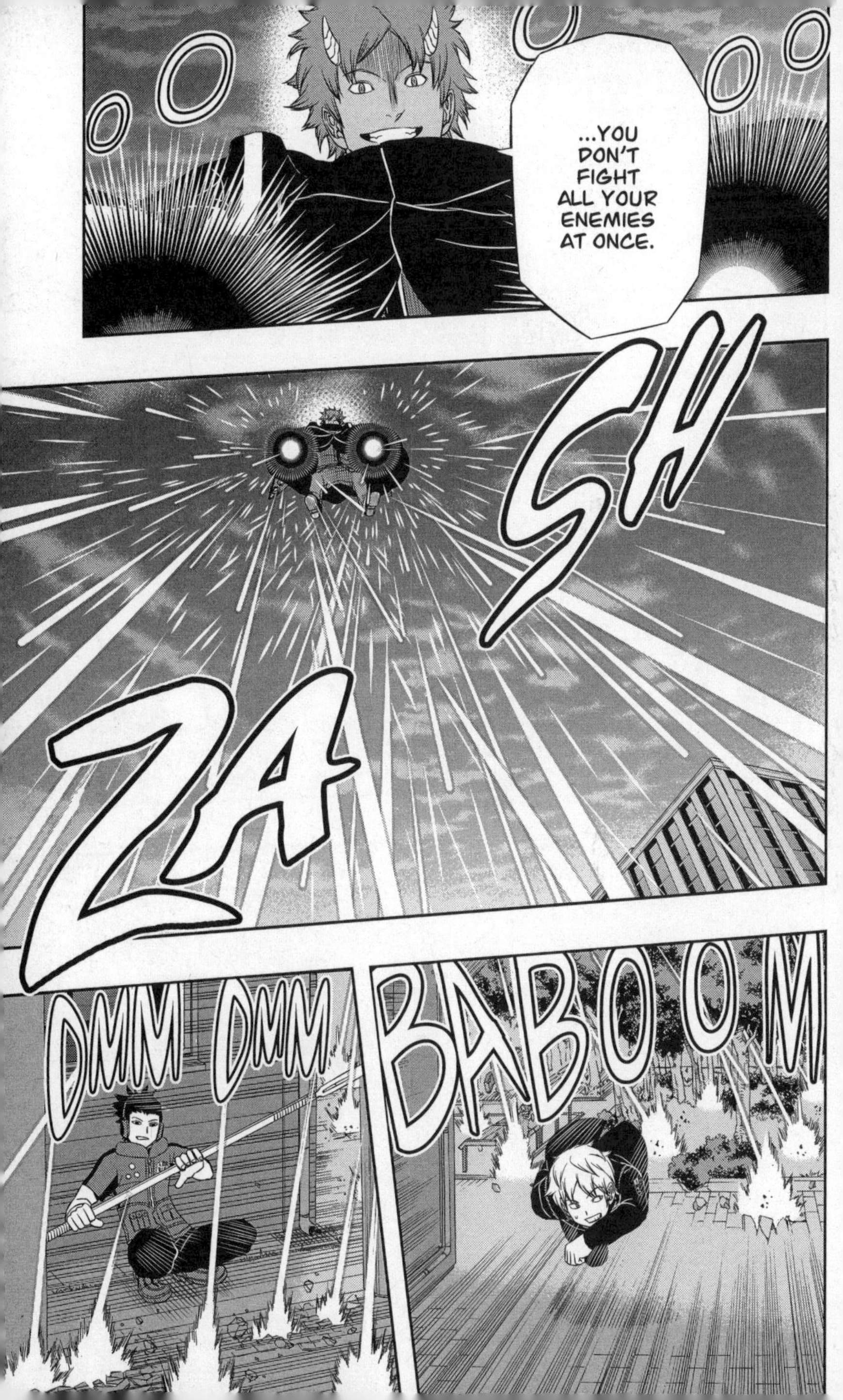
...YOU DON'T FIGHT ALL YOUR ENEMIES AT ONCE.
ZA
SH
BABOOM
DMM DMM

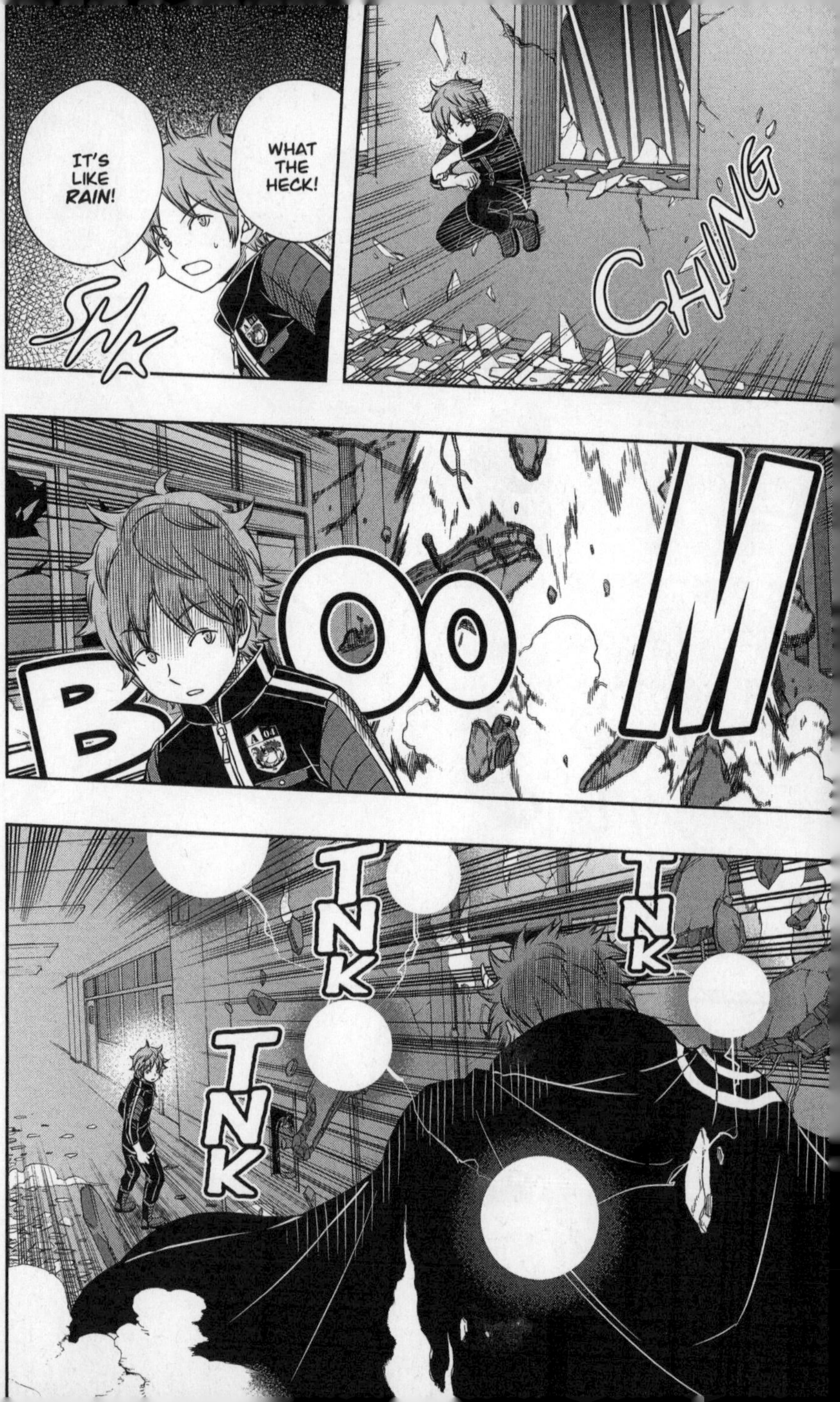
CHING
WHAT THE HECK!
IT'S LIKE RAIN!
SHK
BOOM
TNK
TNK
TNK

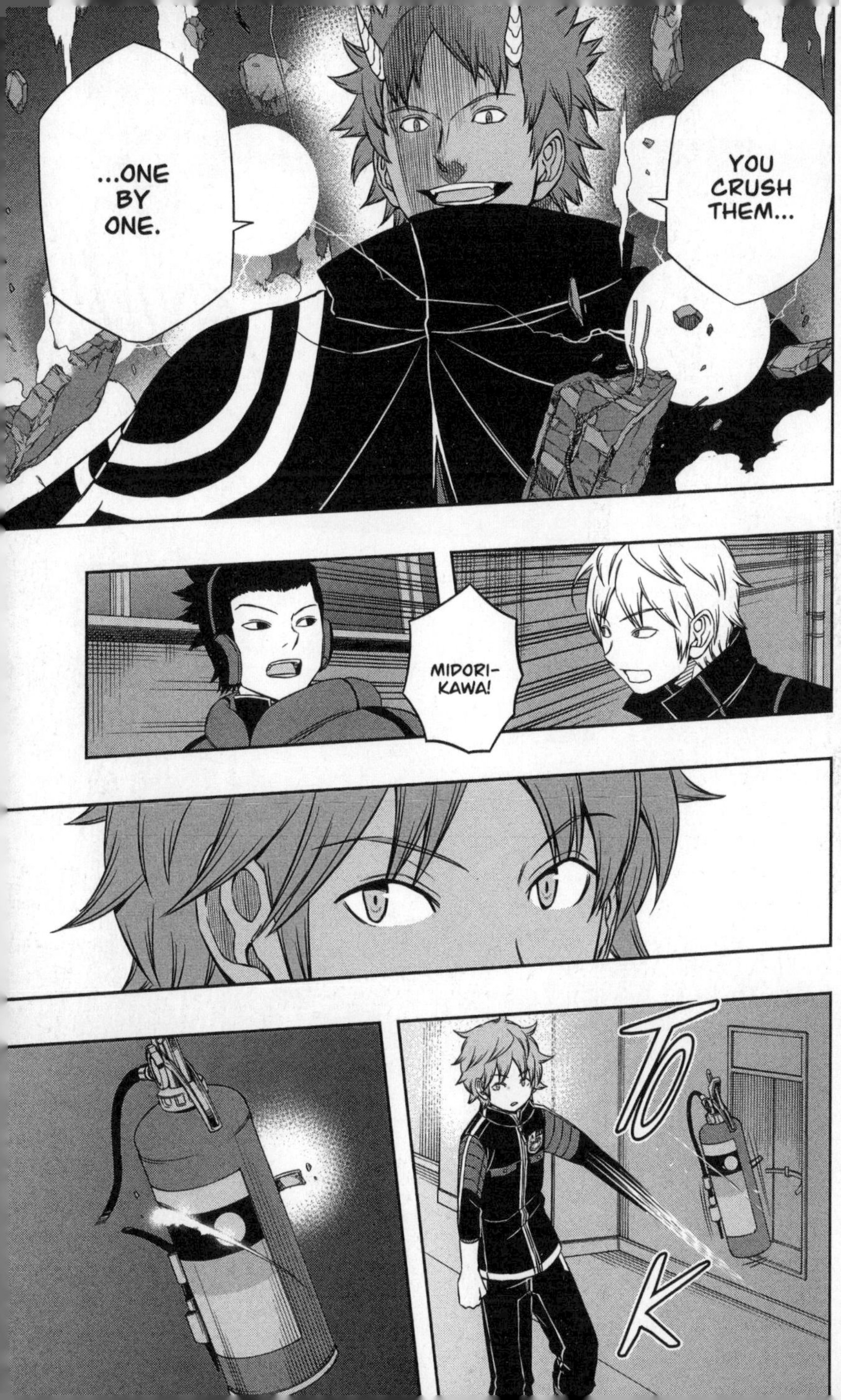
YOU CRUSH THEM...
...ONE BY ONE.
MIDORI-KAWA!
TOK

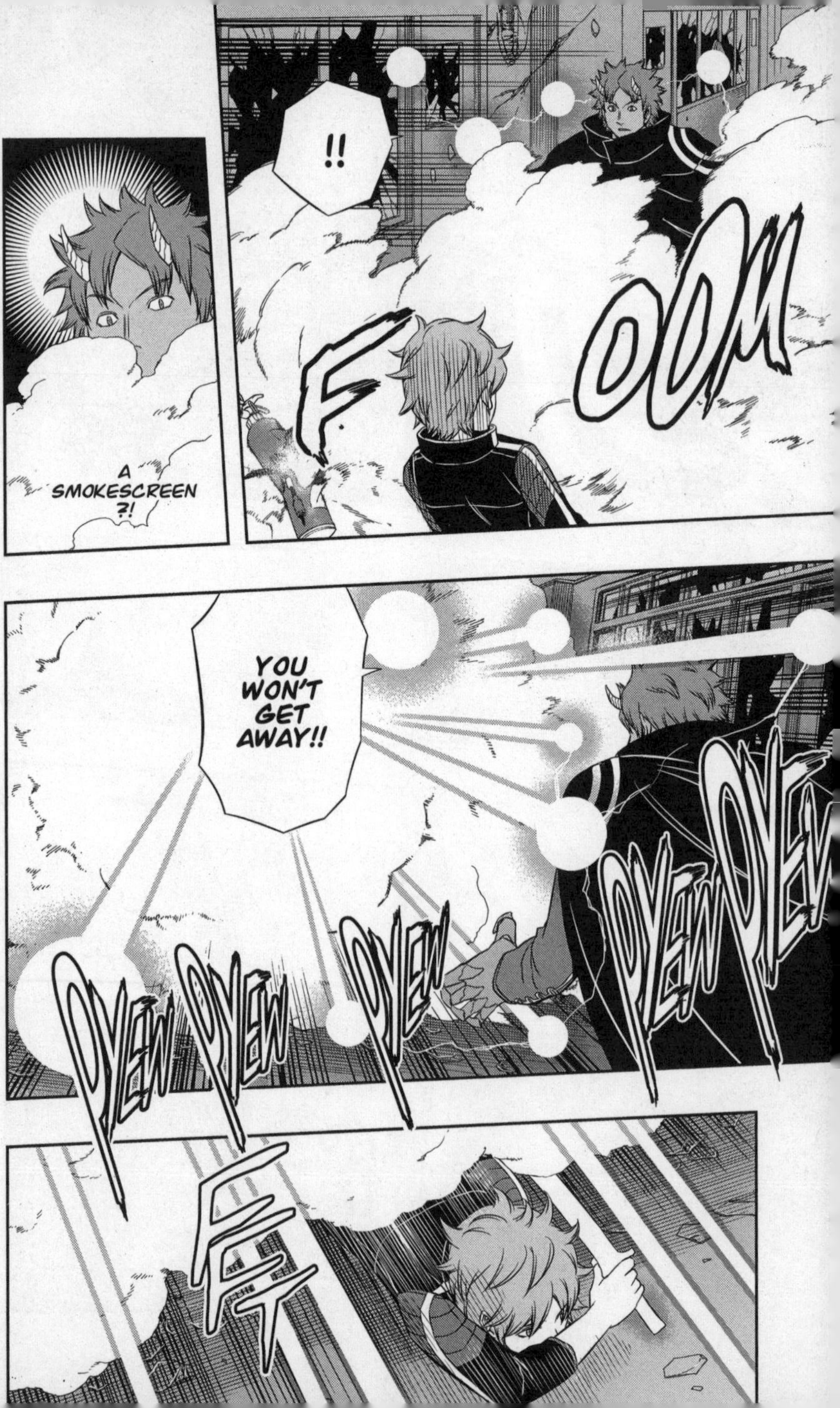
!!
FOOOM
A SMOKESCREEN ?!
YOU WON'T GET AWAY!!
PYEW PYEW
PYEW
PYEW PYEW
FFT

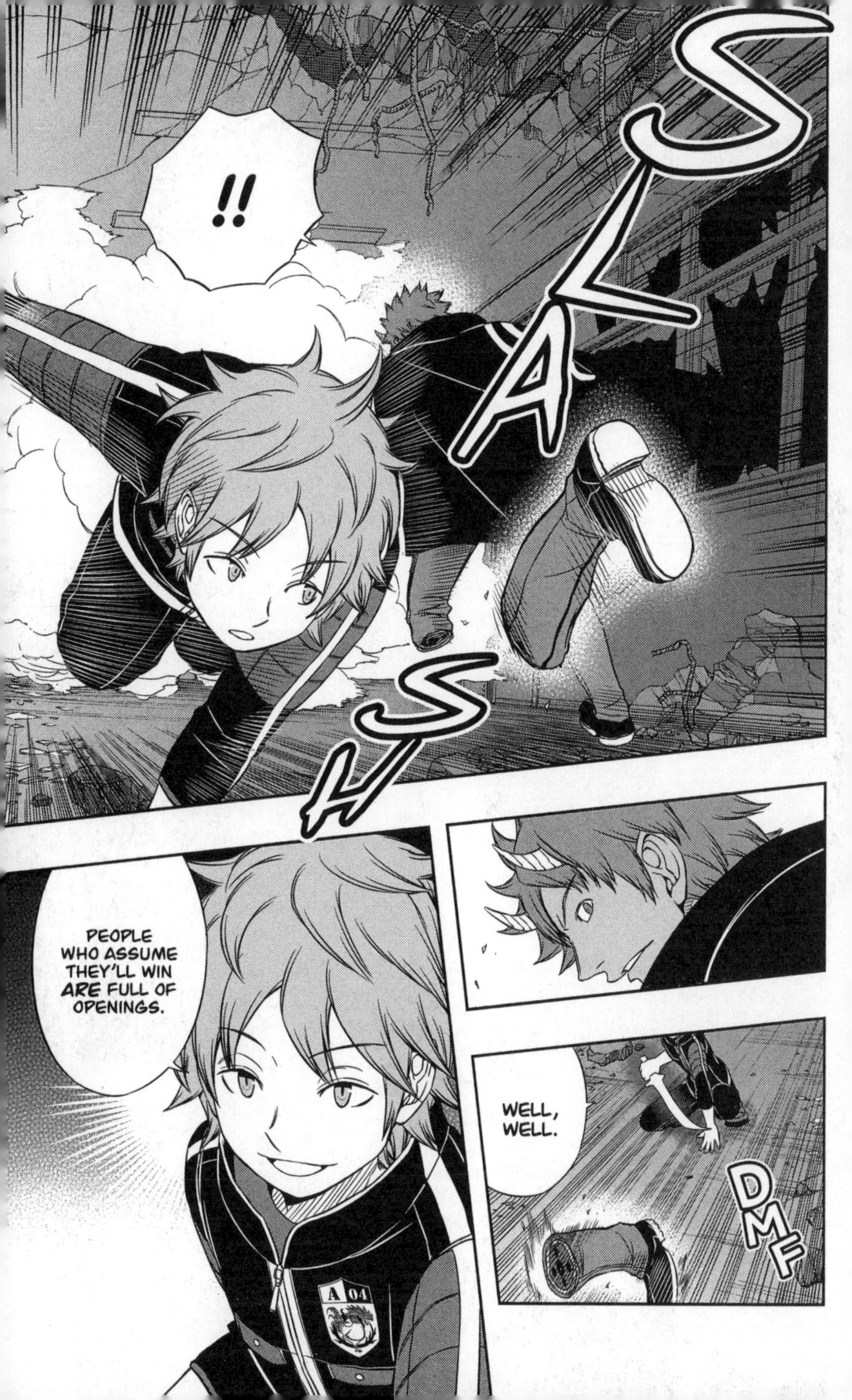
!!
SLASH
WELL, WELL.
DMF
PEOPLE WHO ASSUME THEY'LL WIN ARE FULL OF OPENINGS.

Trion Soldier
Neighbor Minion

Rabit [modded]
Trion soldier for capturing Trion users.

Rabits with added functions. They can use the same Trigger abilities as horned Aftokrator soldiers.

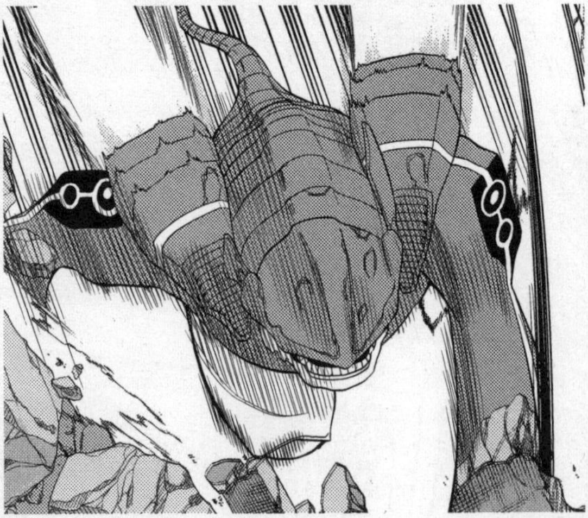

←Ranbanein type

Its main weapon is its high-power artillery. Its actions are bold, perhaps influenced by Ranbanein's personality. In fact, it's not really suited for capturing its targets.

↓ Enedora type

A meanie that uses liquification to surprise attack right in front of you. Is it my imagination or does it pose in a mocking way?

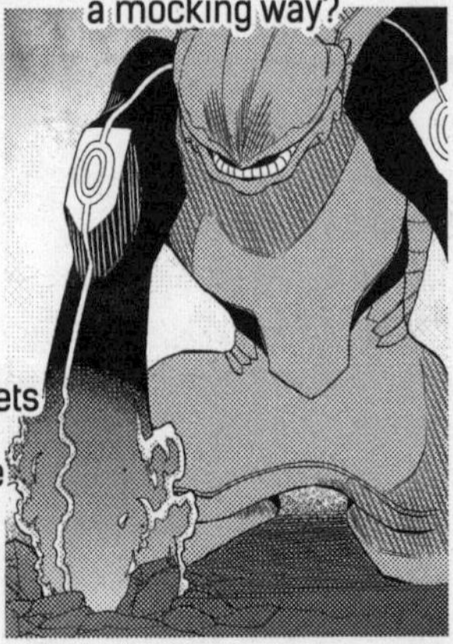

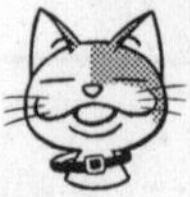

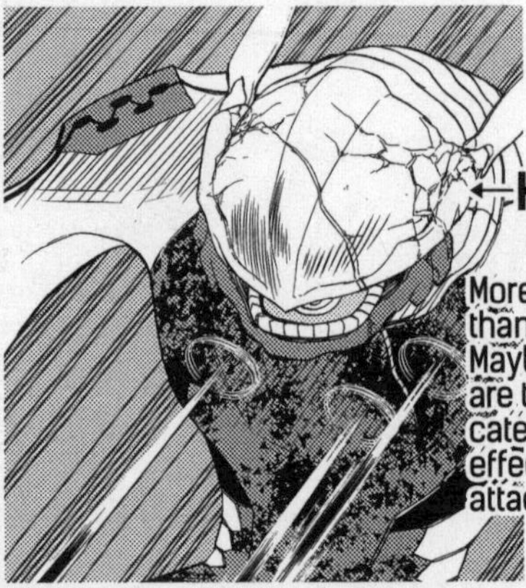

←Hyuse type

More defensive than the others. Maybe the magnets are too compli-cated for it to use effectively for attacks.

Chapter 60 Invasion: Part 10

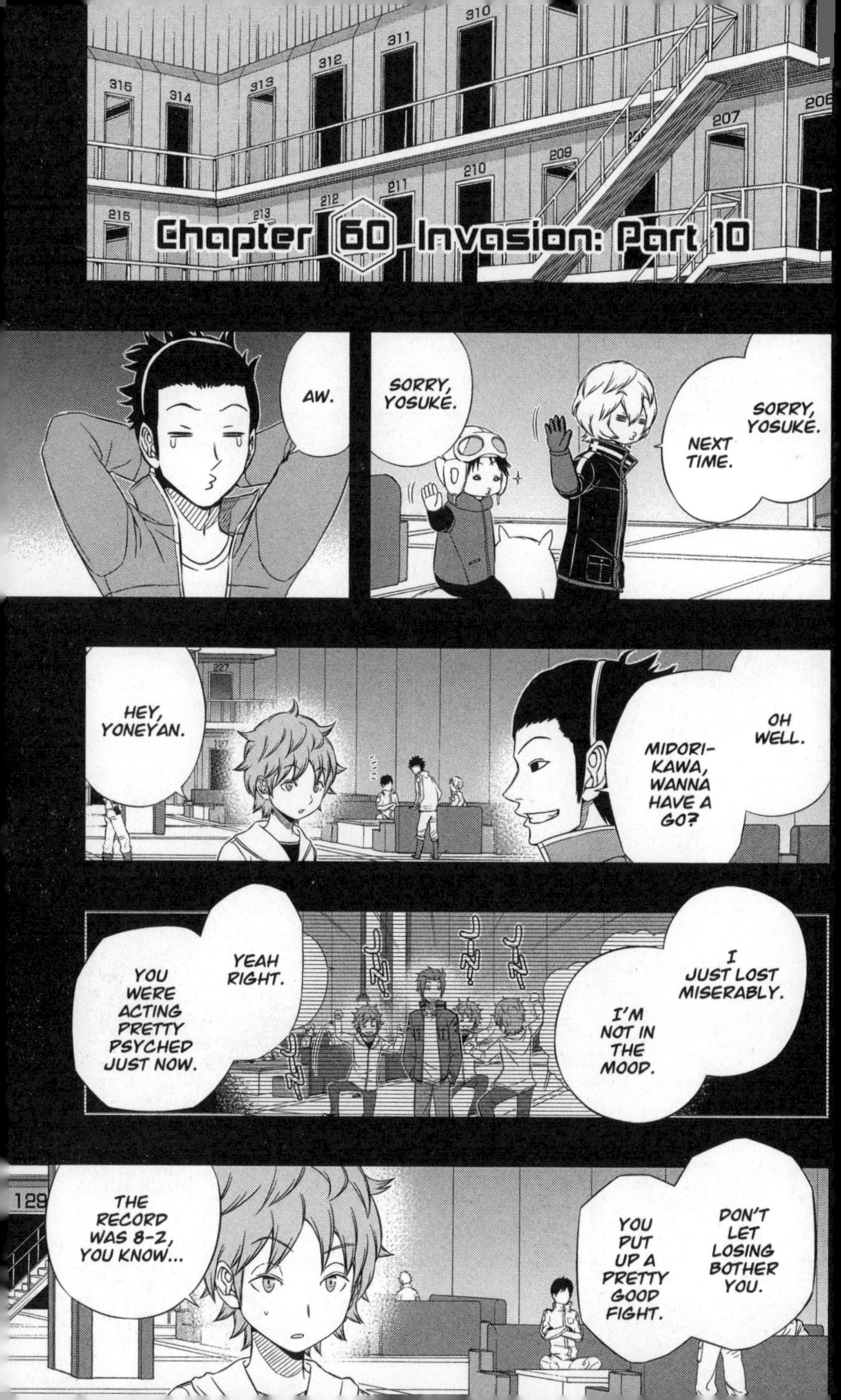

SORRY, YOSUKE.
NEXT TIME.
SORRY, YOSUKE.
AW.
OH WELL.
MIDORIKAWA, WANNA HAVE A GO?
HEY, YONEYAN.
I JUST LOST MISERABLY.
I'M NOT IN THE MOOD.
YEAH RIGHT.
YOU WERE ACTING PRETTY PSYCHED JUST NOW.
DON'T LET LOSING BOTHER YOU.
YOU PUT UP A PRETTY GOOD FIGHT.
THE RECORD WAS 8-2, YOU KNOW...

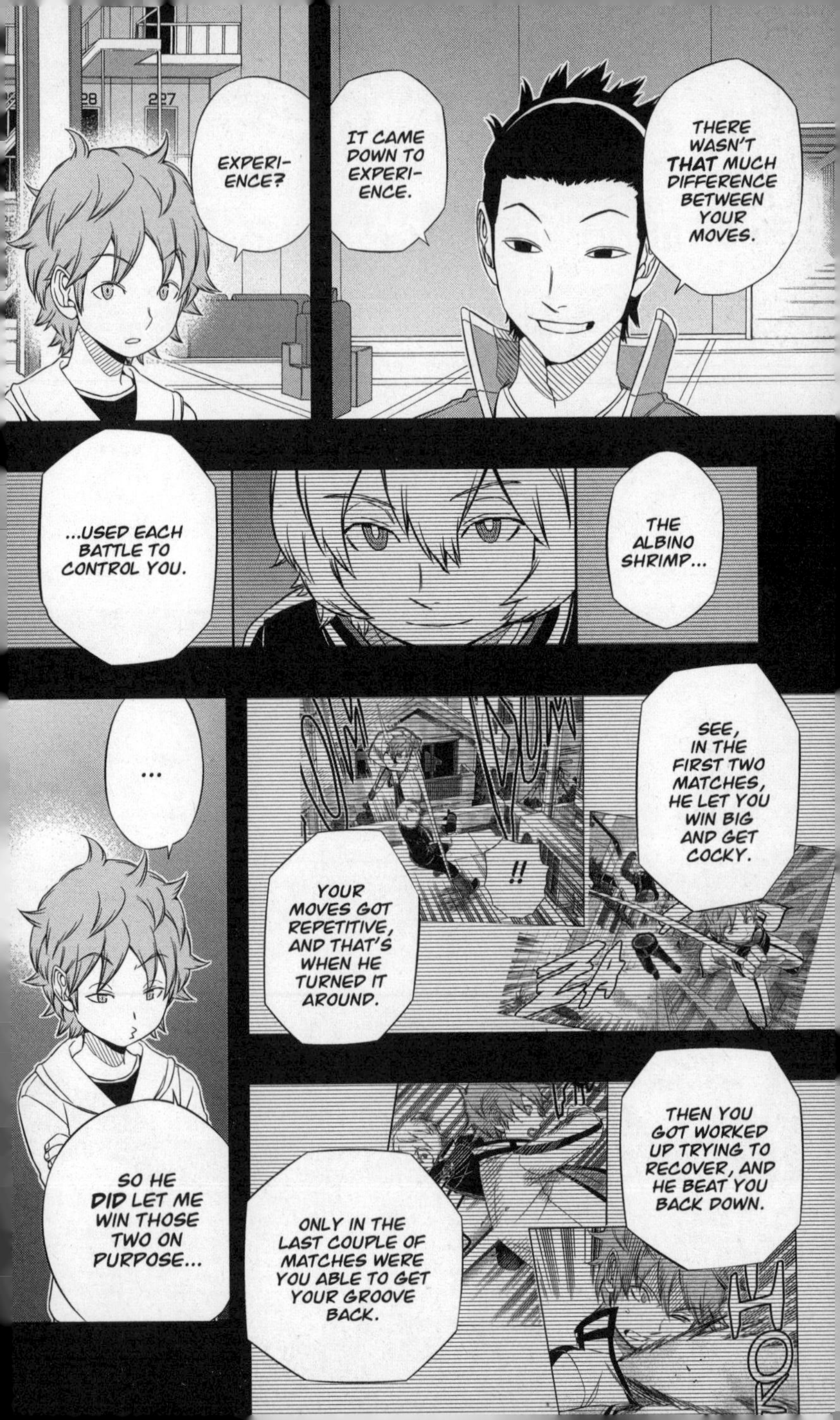
THERE WASN'T **THAT** MUCH DIFFERENCE BETWEEN YOUR MOVES.
IT CAME DOWN TO EXPERI-ENCE.
EXPERI-ENCE?
THE ALBINO SHRIMP...
...USED EACH BATTLE TO CONTROL YOU.
SEE, IN THE FIRST TWO MATCHES, HE LET YOU WIN BIG AND GET COCKY.
!!
YOUR MOVES GOT REPETITIVE, AND THAT'S WHEN HE TURNED IT AROUND.
THEN YOU GOT WORKED UP TRYING TO RECOVER, AND HE BEAT YOU BACK DOWN.
ONLY IN THE LAST COUPLE OF MATCHES WERE YOU ABLE TO GET YOUR GROOVE BACK.
...
SO HE **DID** LET ME WIN THOSE TWO ON PURPOSE...

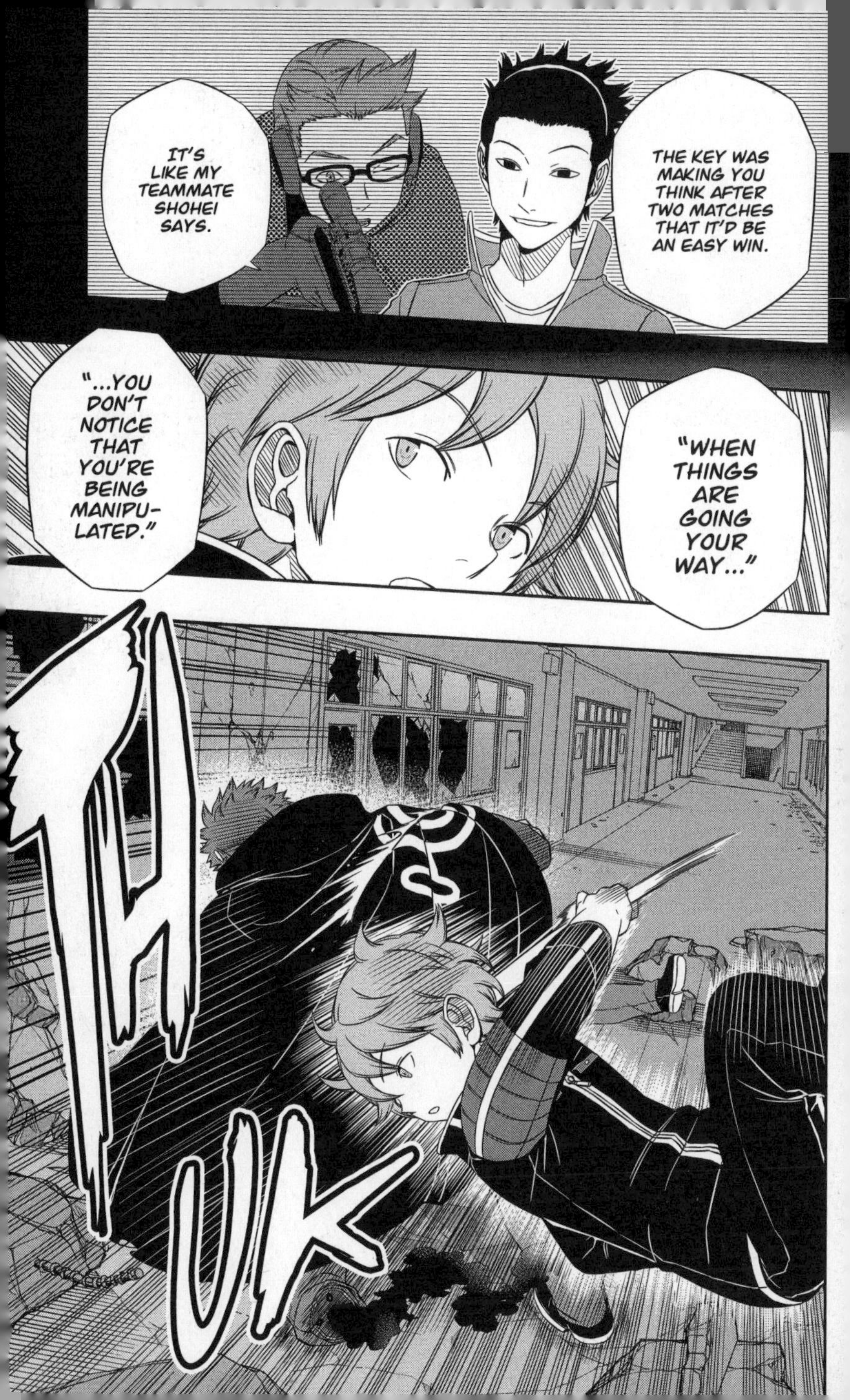
THE KEY WAS MAKING YOU THINK AFTER TWO MATCHES THAT IT'D BE AN EASY WIN.
IT'S LIKE MY TEAMMATE SHOHEI SAYS.
"WHEN THINGS ARE GOING YOUR WAY..."
"...YOU DON'T NOTICE THAT YOU'RE BEING MANIPU-LATED."
THUK

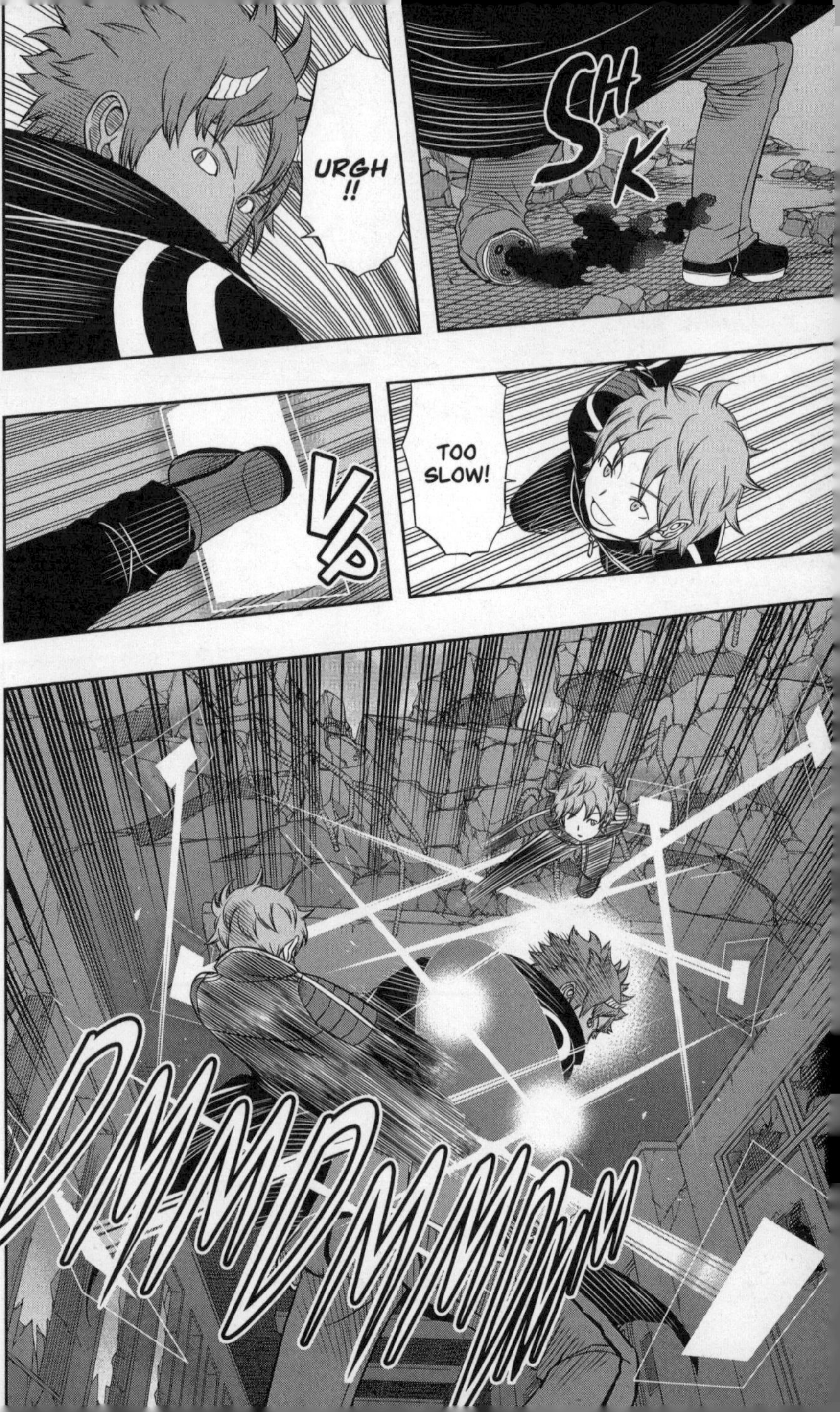
SHK
URGH!!
TOO SLOW!
VIP
DMMMMMMMM

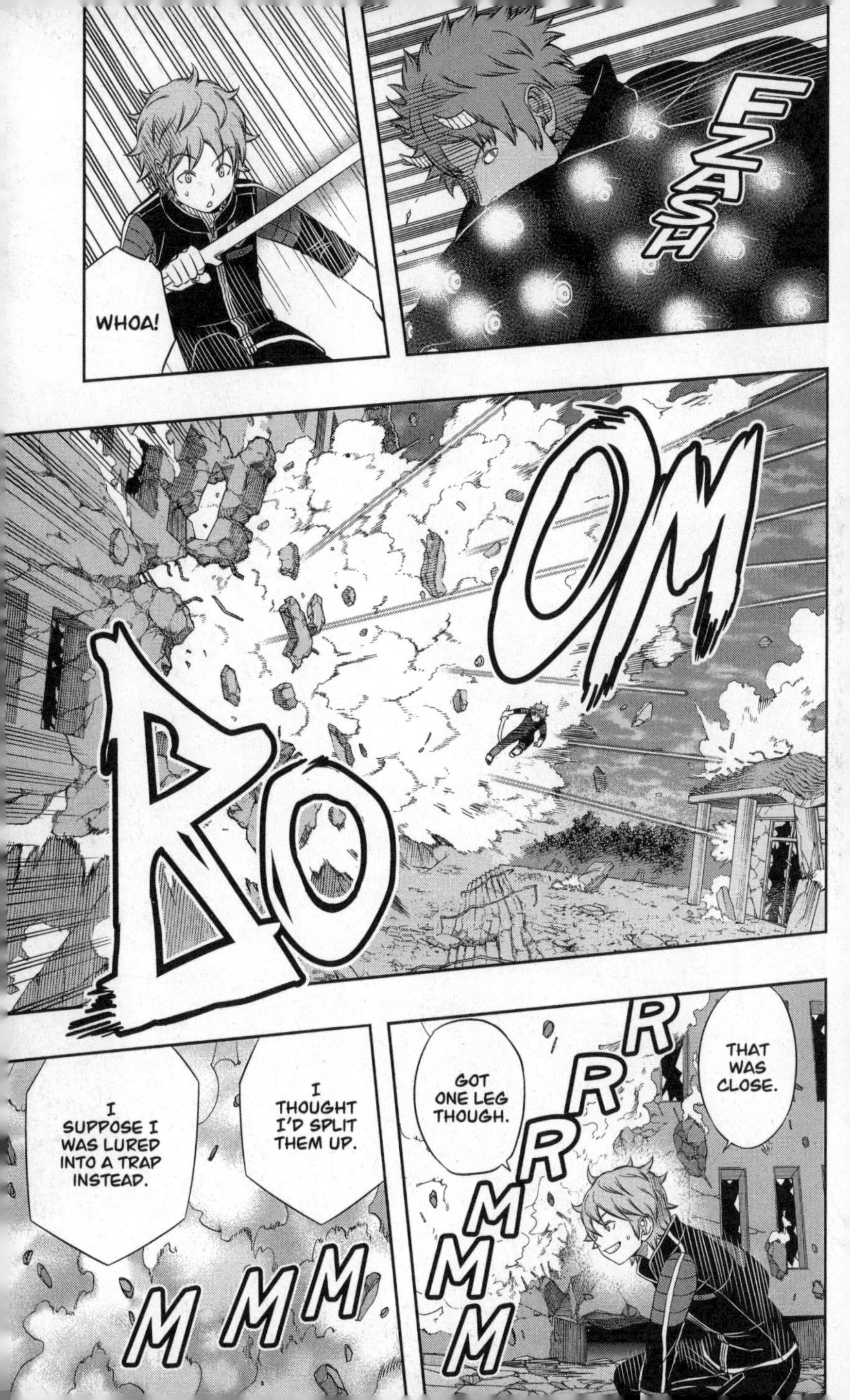
FZASH
WHOA!
ROOM
THAT WAS CLOSE.
GOT ONE LEG THOUGH.
RRRRMMMM
I THOUGHT I'D SPLIT THEM UP.
I SUPPOSE I WAS LURED INTO A TRAP INSTEAD.
MMM

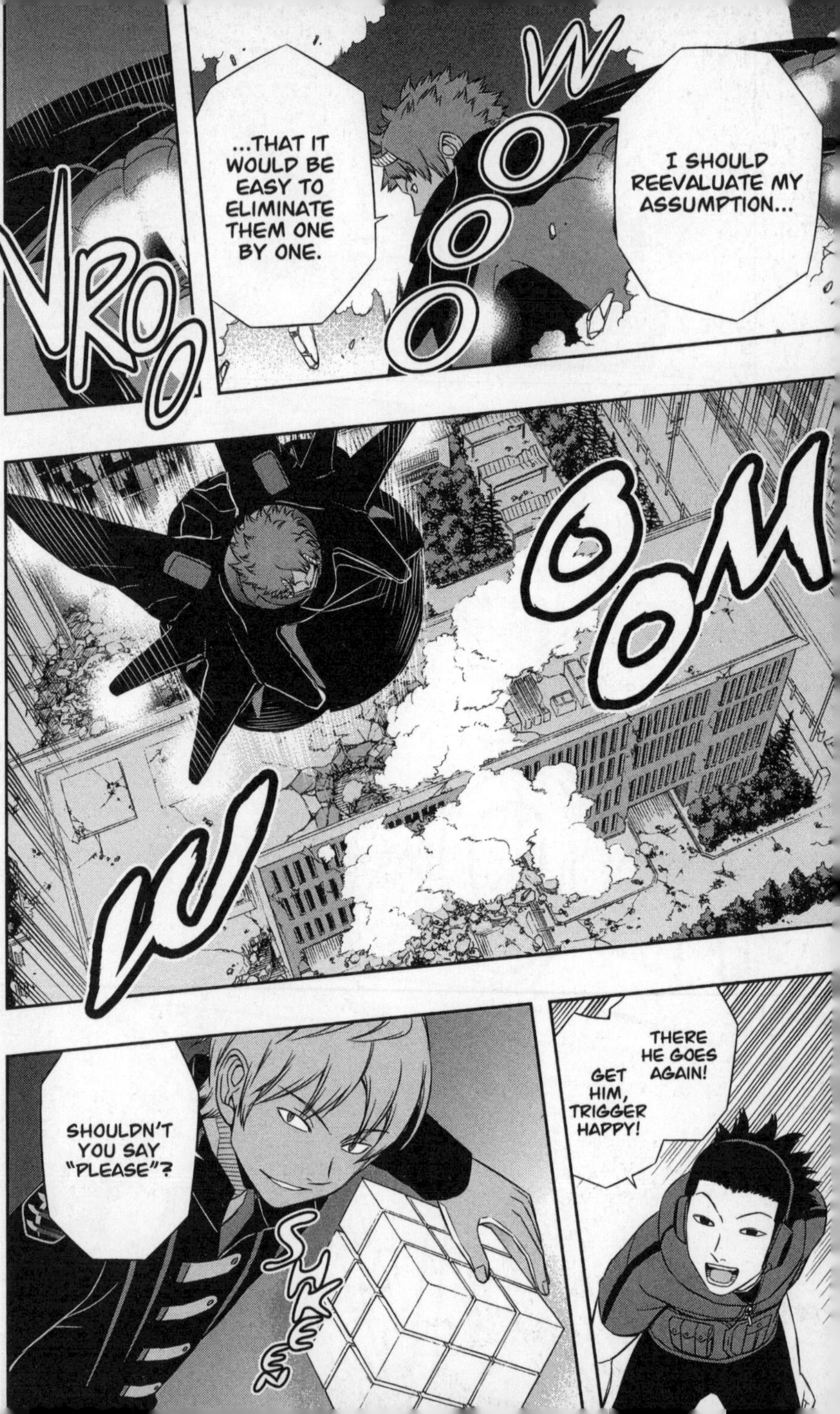

I SHOULD REEVALUATE MY ASSUMPTION...
...THAT IT WOULD BE EASY TO ELIMINATE THEM ONE BY ONE.
WOOOOO
VROOO
BOOM
THERE HE GOES AGAIN!
GET HIM, TRIGGER HAPPY!
SHOULDN'T YOU SAY "PLEASE"?
SHEEE

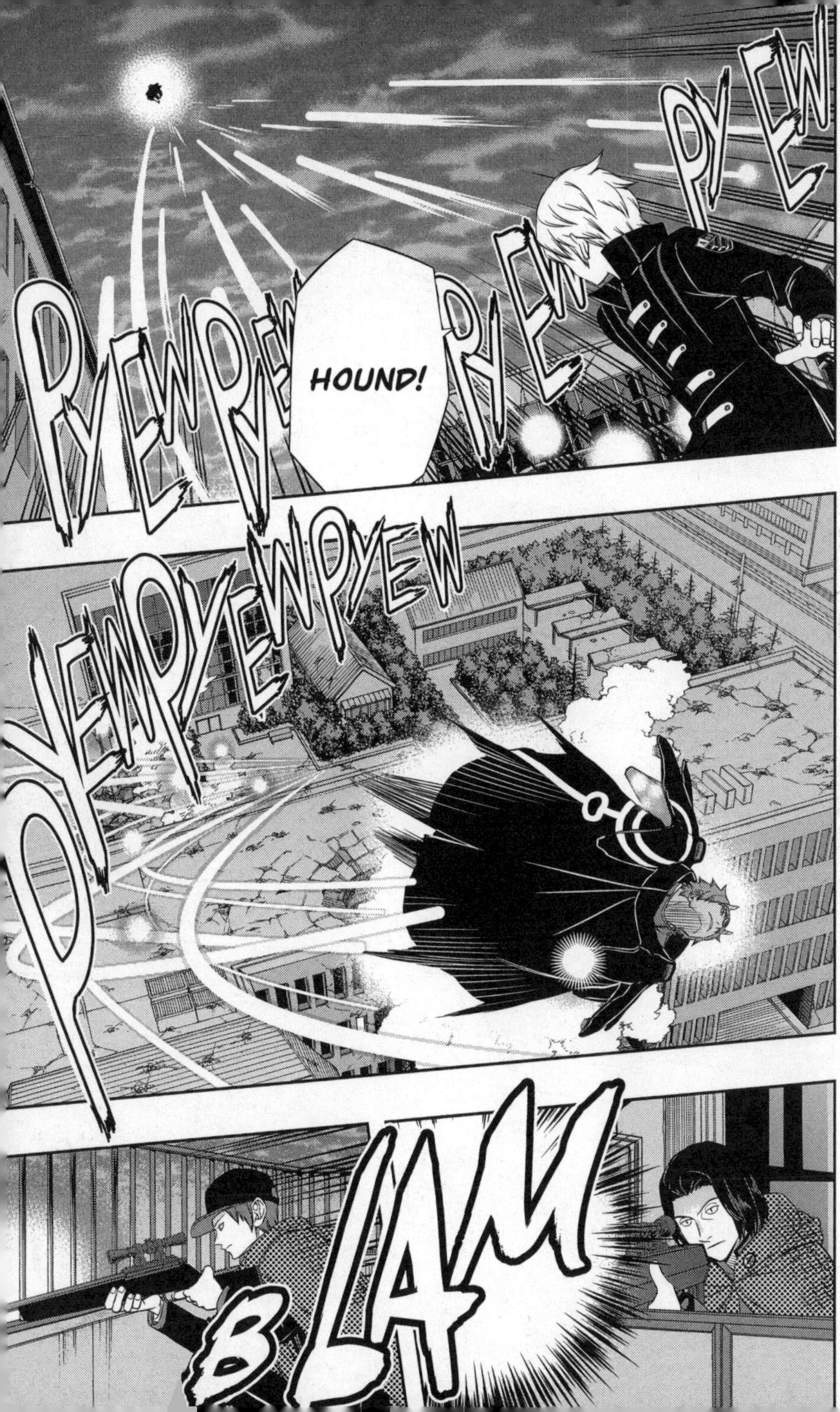
PYEW
PYEW
HOUND!
PYEWPYEW
PYEWPYEWPYEW
BLAM

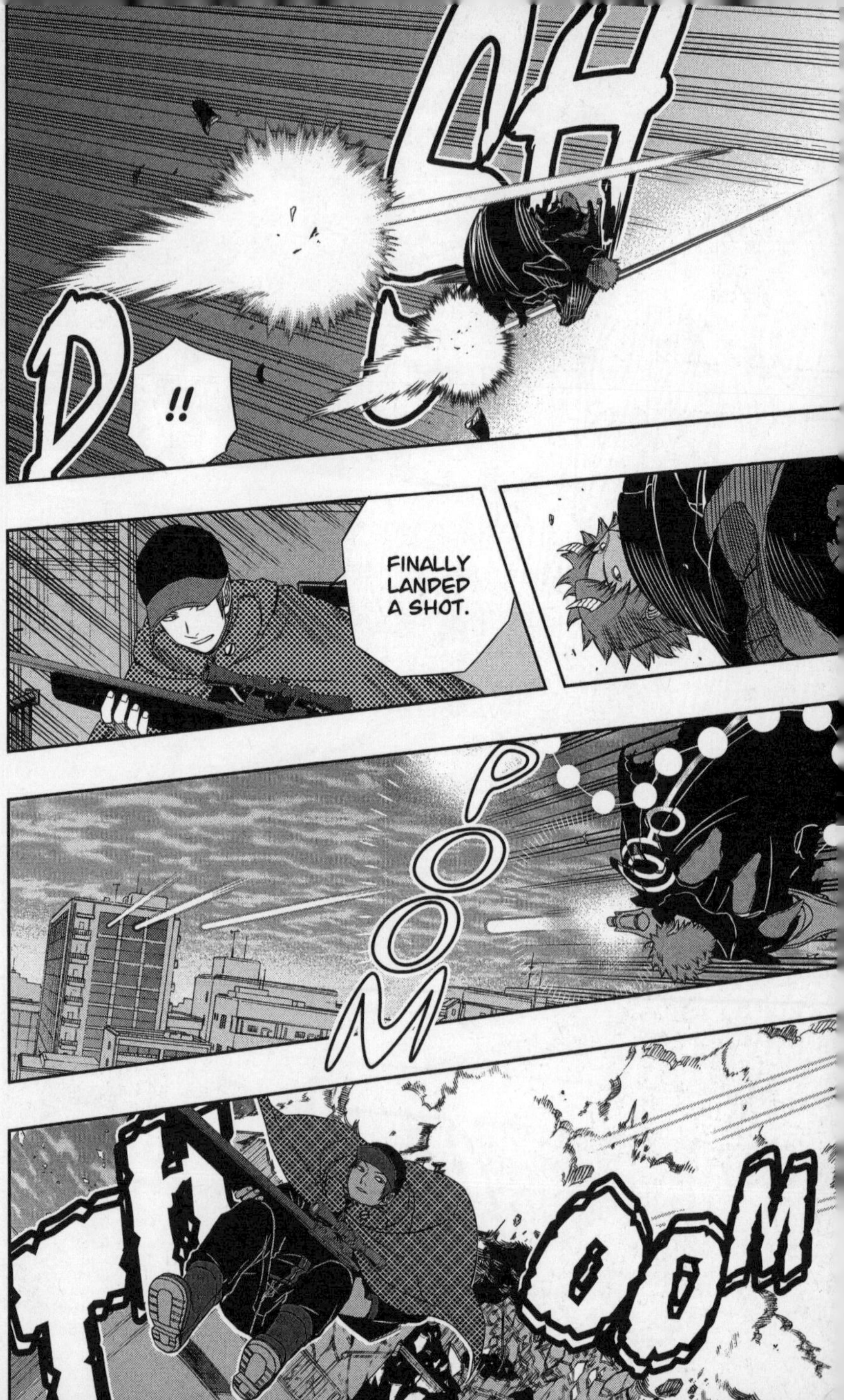
DOH
!!
FINALLY LANDED A SHOT.
POOOM
THOOM

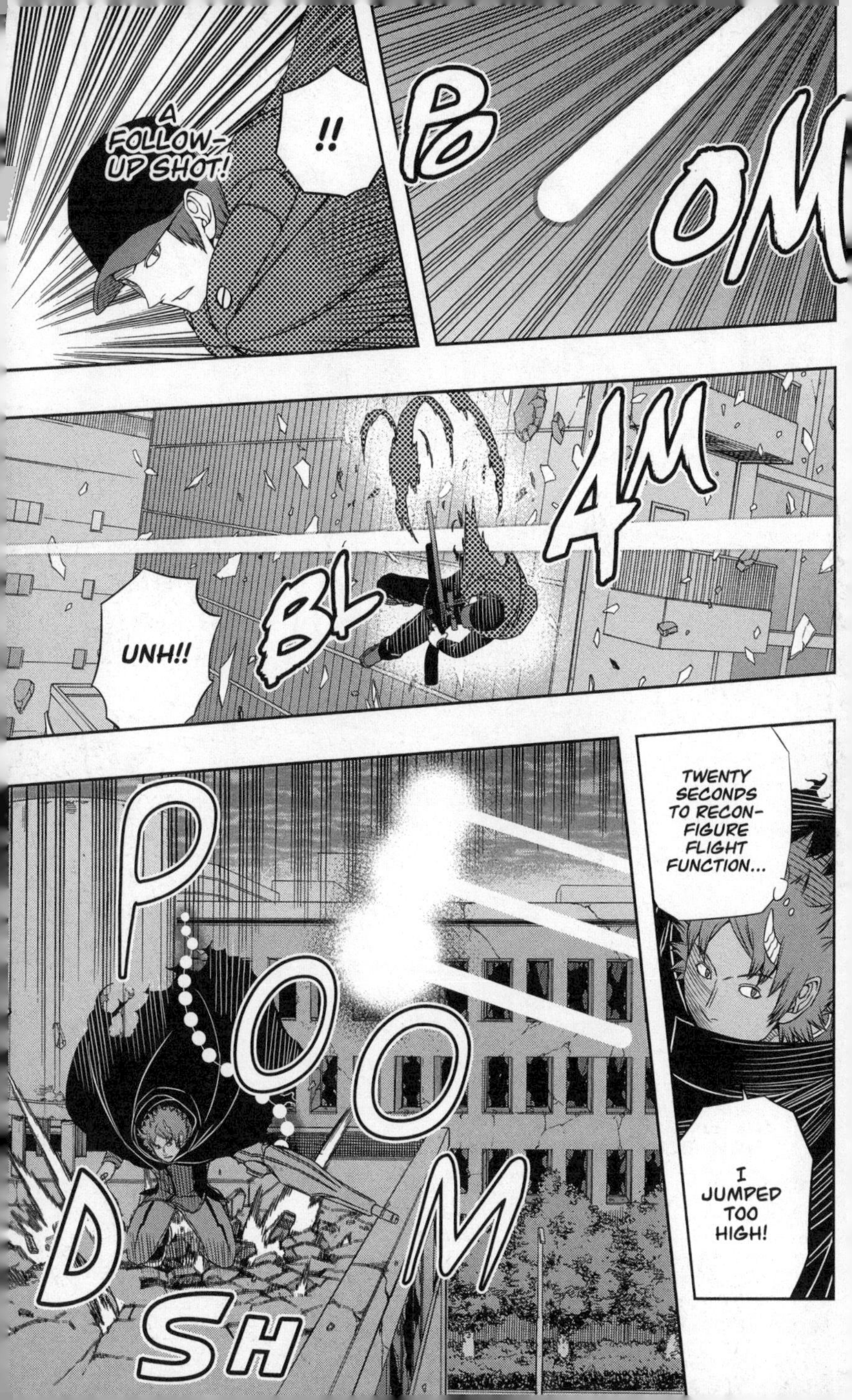
POOM
!!
A FOLLOW-UP SHOT!
BLAM
UNH!!
TWENTY SECONDS TO RECONFIGURE FLIGHT FUNCTION...
I JUMPED TOO HIGH!
POOM
DSH

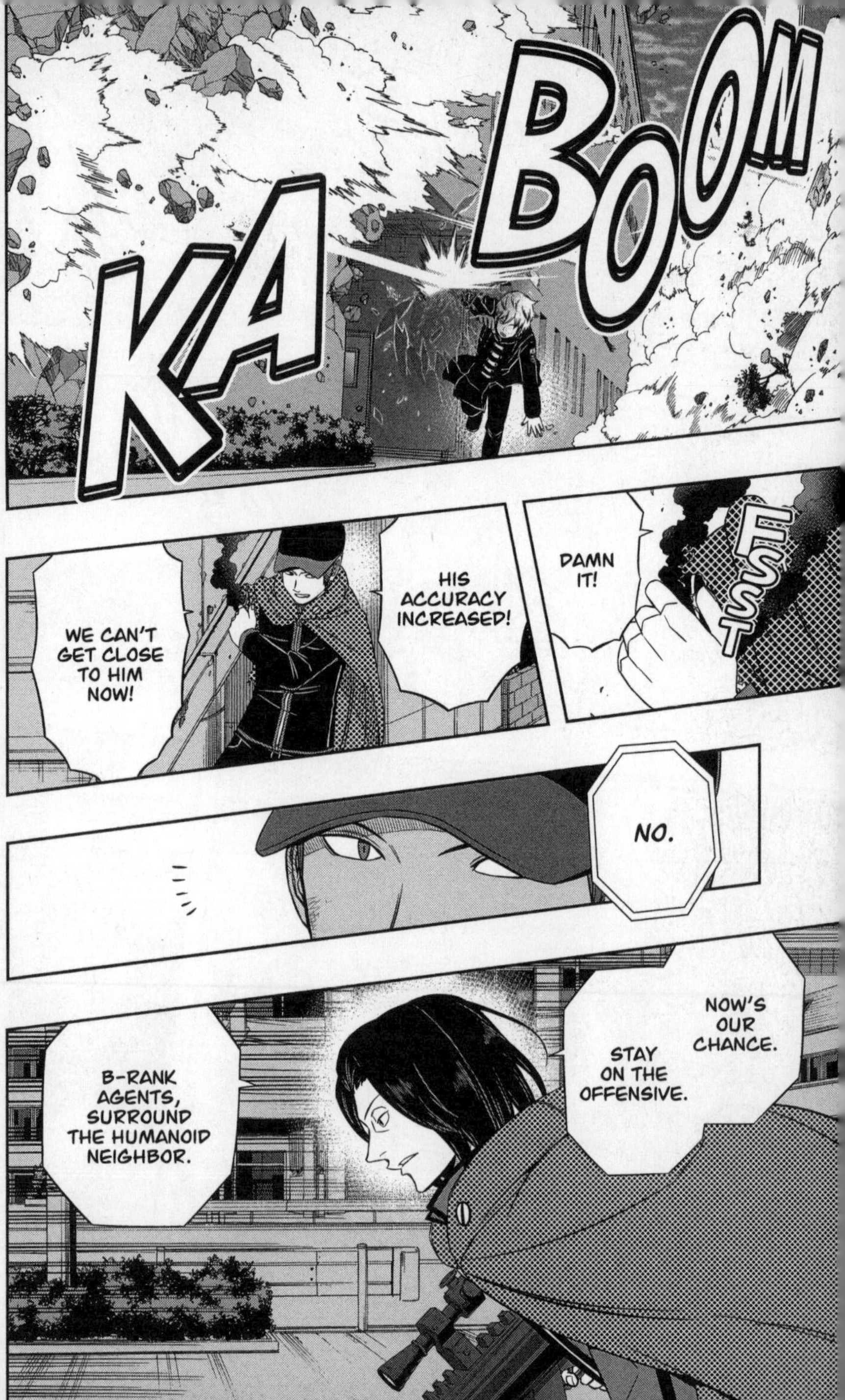
KA
BOOM
FSST
DAMN IT!
HIS ACCURACY INCREASED!
WE CAN'T GET CLOSE TO HIM NOW!
NO.
NOW'S OUR CHANCE.
STAY ON THE OFFENSIVE.
B-RANK AGENTS, SURROUND THE HUMANOID NEIGHBOR.

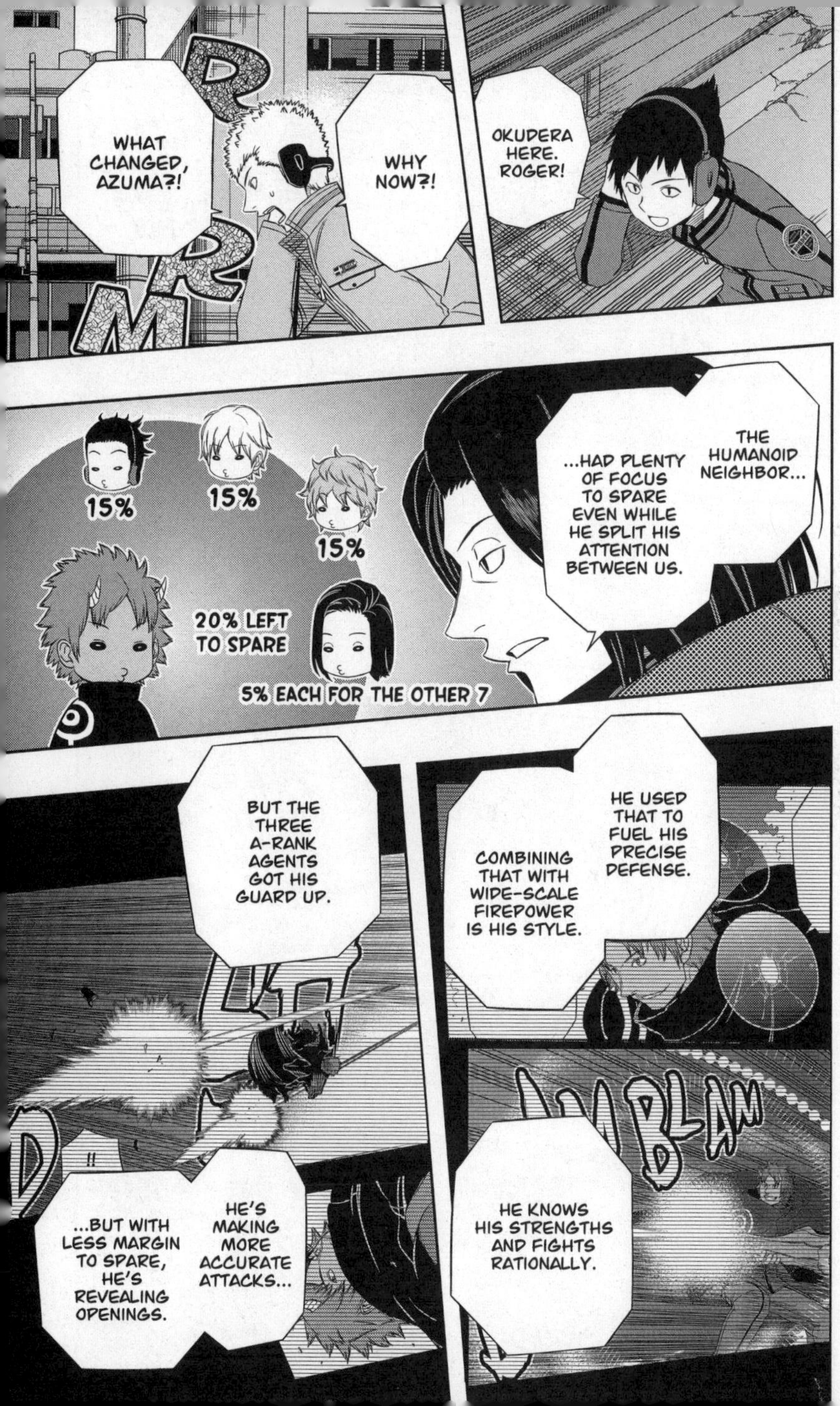
OKUDERA HERE. ROGER!
WHY NOW?!
WHAT CHANGED, AZUMA?!
THE HUMANOID NEIGHBOR...
...HAD PLENTY OF FOCUS TO SPARE EVEN WHILE HE SPLIT HIS ATTENTION BETWEEN US.
15%
15%
15%
20% LEFT TO SPARE
5% EACH FOR THE OTHER 7
HE USED THAT TO FUEL HIS PRECISE DEFENSE.
COMBINING THAT WITH WIDE-SCALE FIREPOWER IS HIS STYLE.
BLAM
HE KNOWS HIS STRENGTHS AND FIGHTS RATIONALLY.
BUT THE THREE A-RANK AGENTS GOT HIS GUARD UP.
!!
HE'S MAKING MORE ACCURATE ATTACKS...
...BUT WITH LESS MARGIN TO SPARE, HE'S REVEALING OPENINGS.

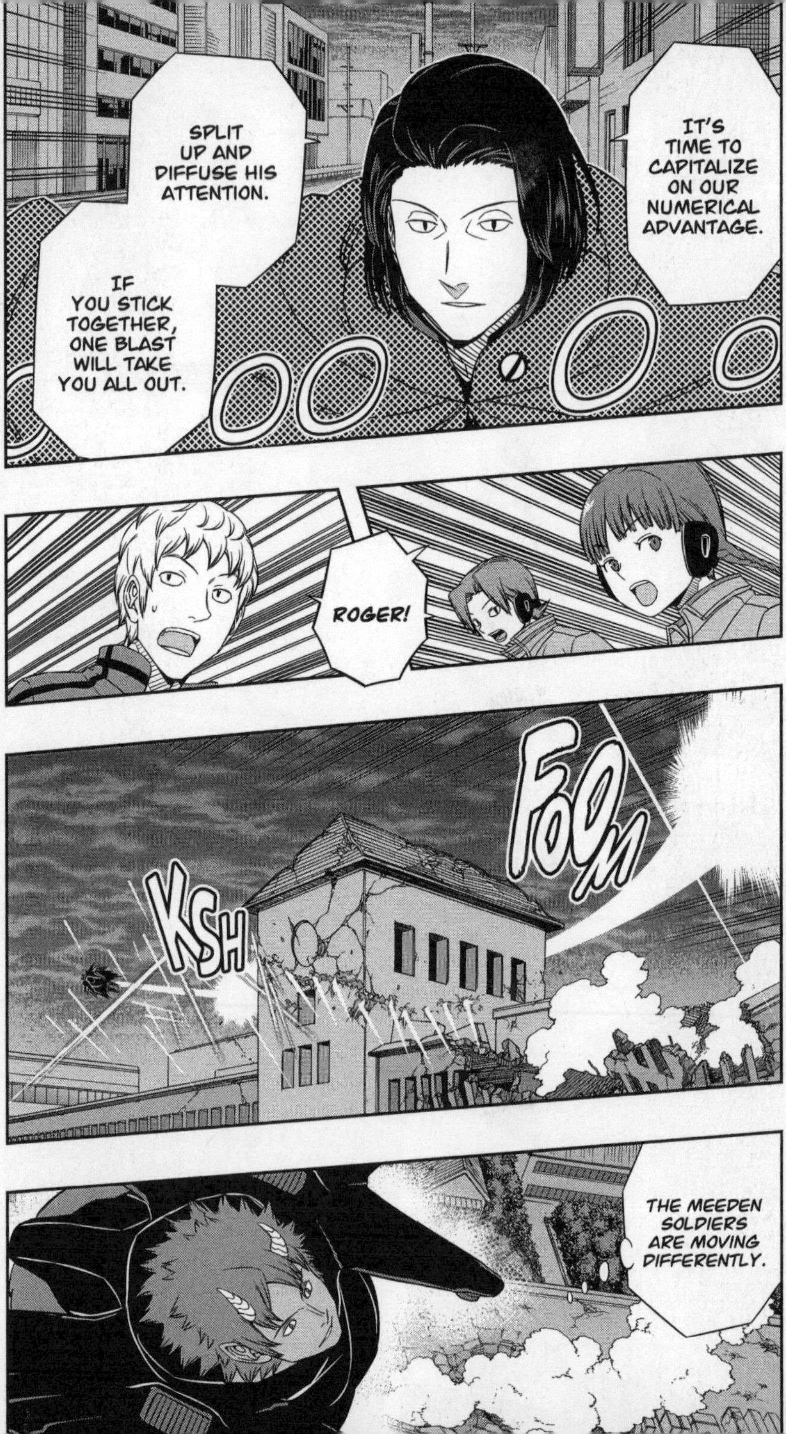
IT'S TIME TO CAPITALIZE ON OUR NUMERICAL ADVANTAGE.
SPLIT UP AND DIFFUSE HIS ATTENTION.
IF YOU STICK TOGETHER, ONE BLAST WILL TAKE YOU ALL OUT.
ROGER!
FOOM
KSH
THE MEEDEN SOLDIERS ARE MOVING DIFFERENTLY.

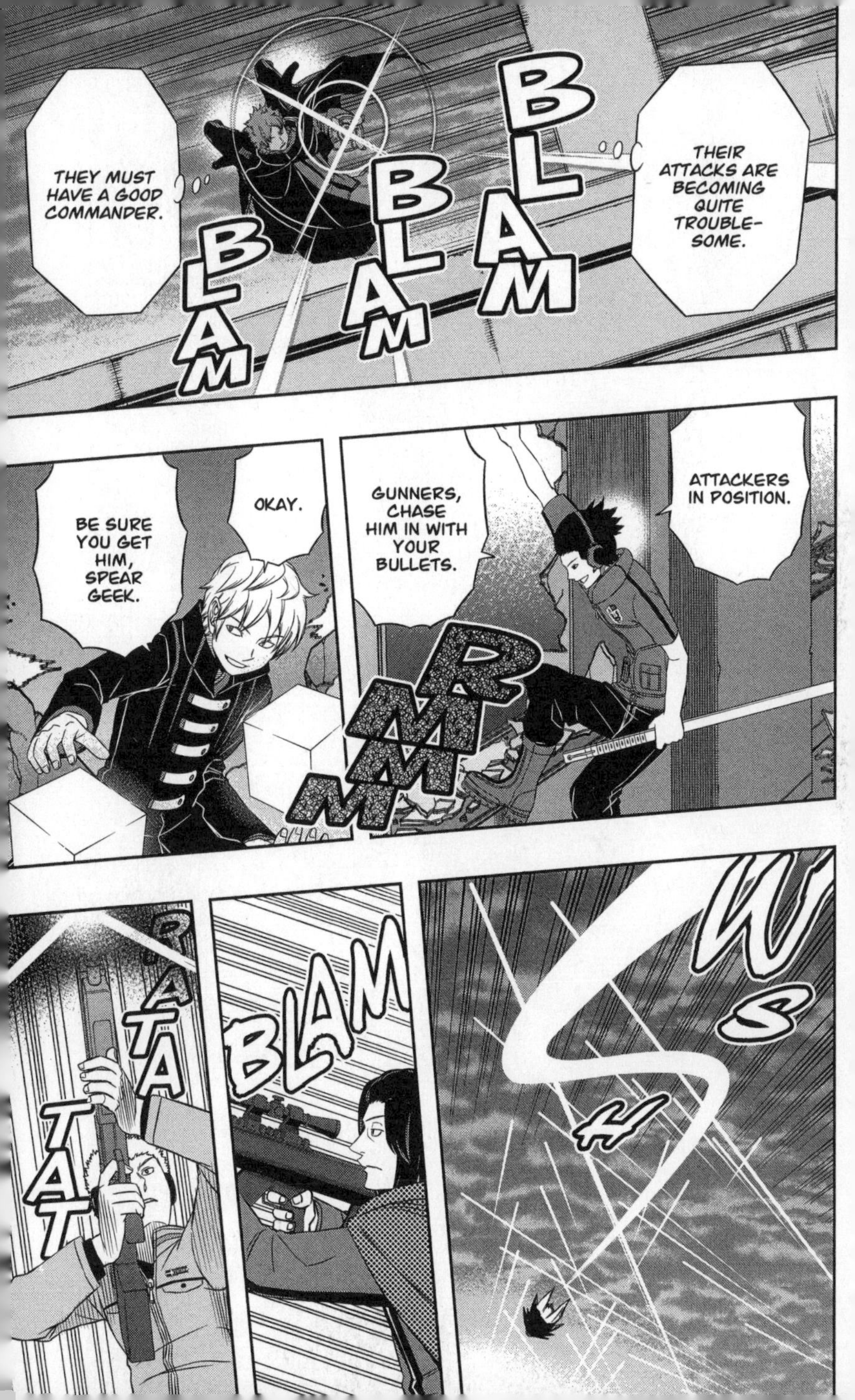
THEIR ATTACKS ARE BECOMING QUITE TROUBLE-SOME.
BLAM BLAM BLAM
THEY MUST HAVE A GOOD COMMANDER.
ATTACKERS IN POSITION.
GUNNERS, CHASE HIM IN WITH YOUR BULLETS.
RMMM
OKAY.
BE SURE YOU GET HIM, SPEAR GEEK.
WHSSH
BLAM
RATATAT

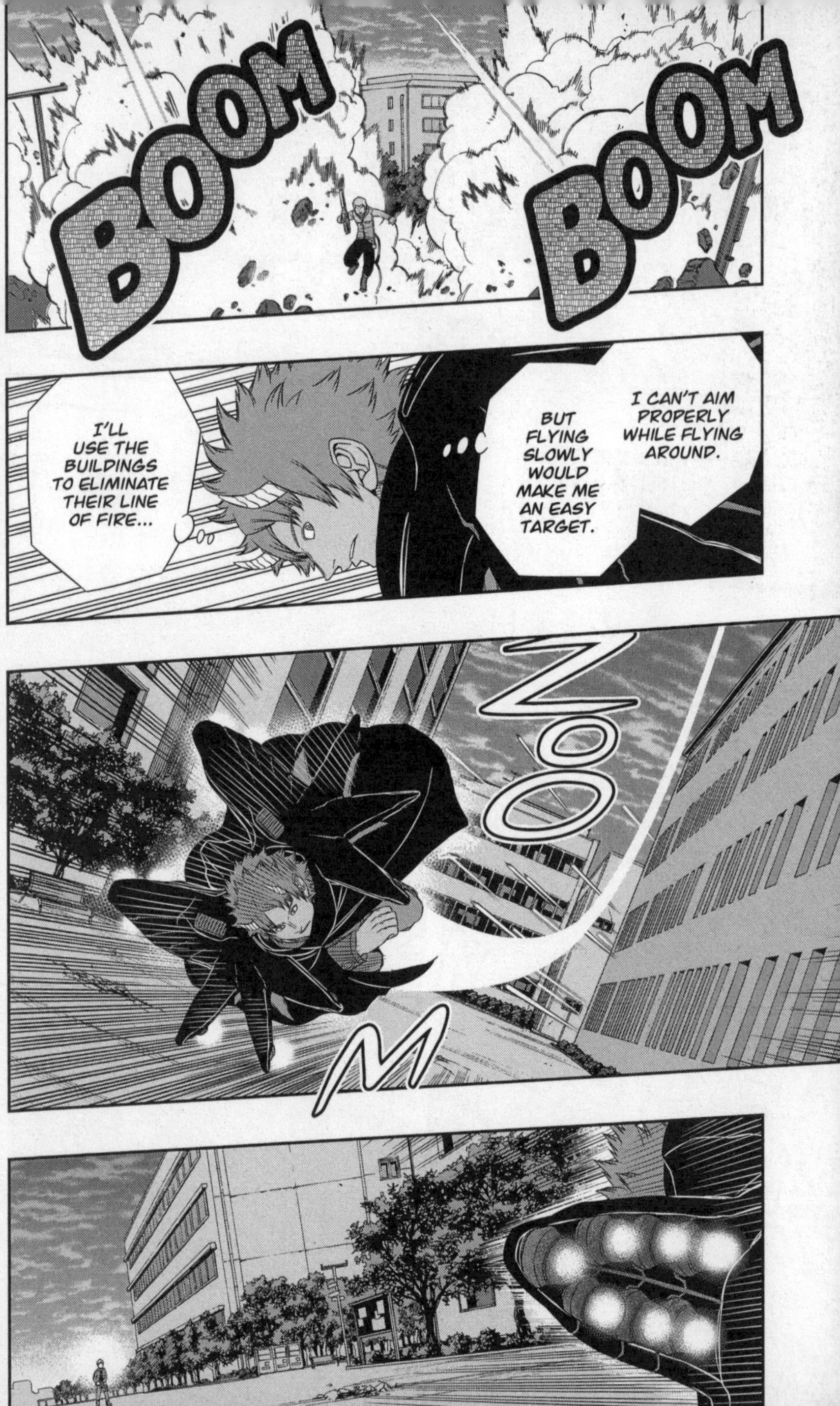
BOOM
BOOM
I CAN'T AIM PROPERLY WHILE FLYING AROUND.
BUT FLYING SLOWLY WOULD MAKE ME AN EASY TARGET.
I'LL USE THE BUILDINGS TO ELIMINATE THEIR LINE OF FIRE...
ZOOM

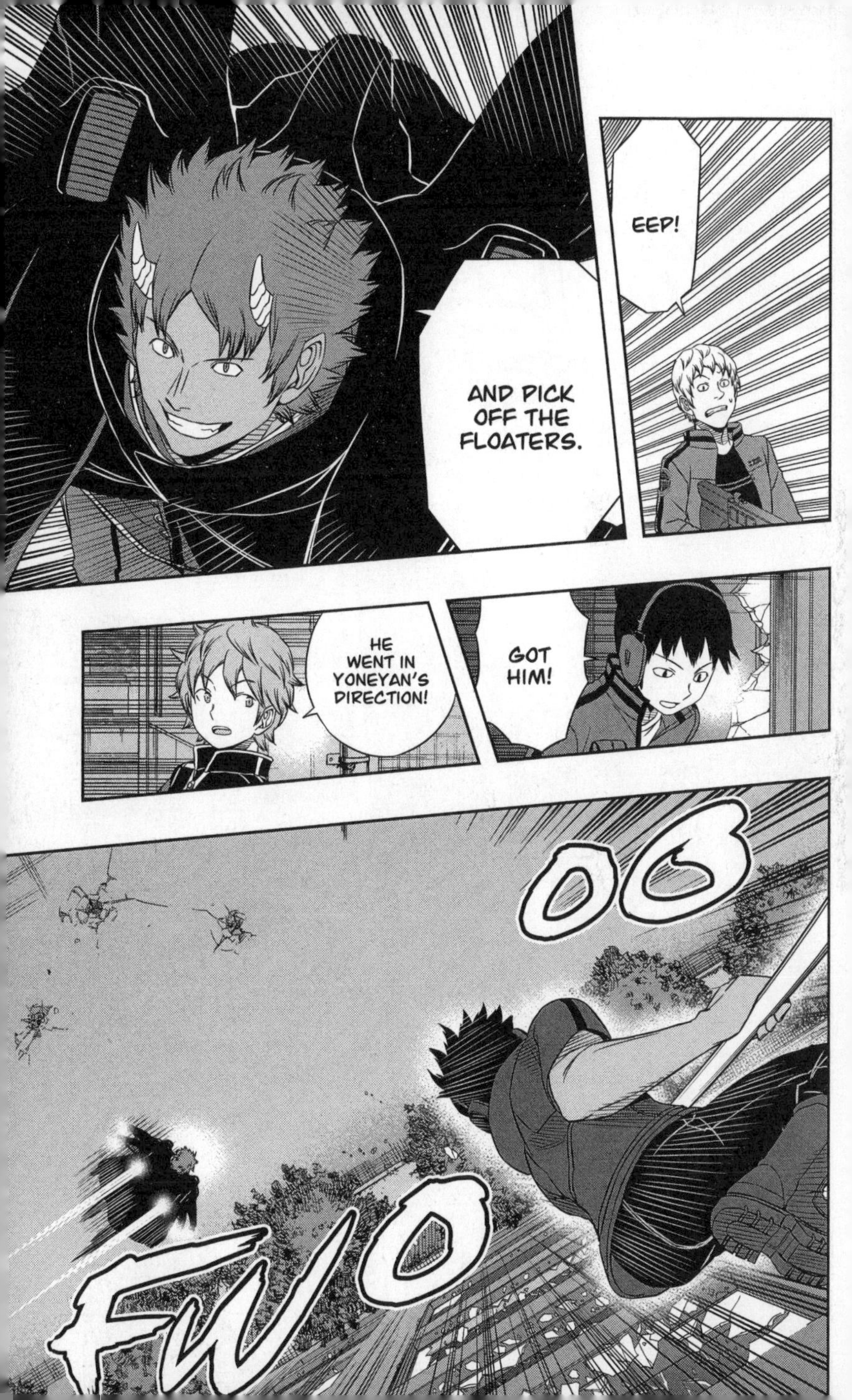
EEP!
AND PICK OFF THE FLOATERS.
GOT HIM!
HE WENT IN YONEYAN'S DIRECTION!
FWO
OO

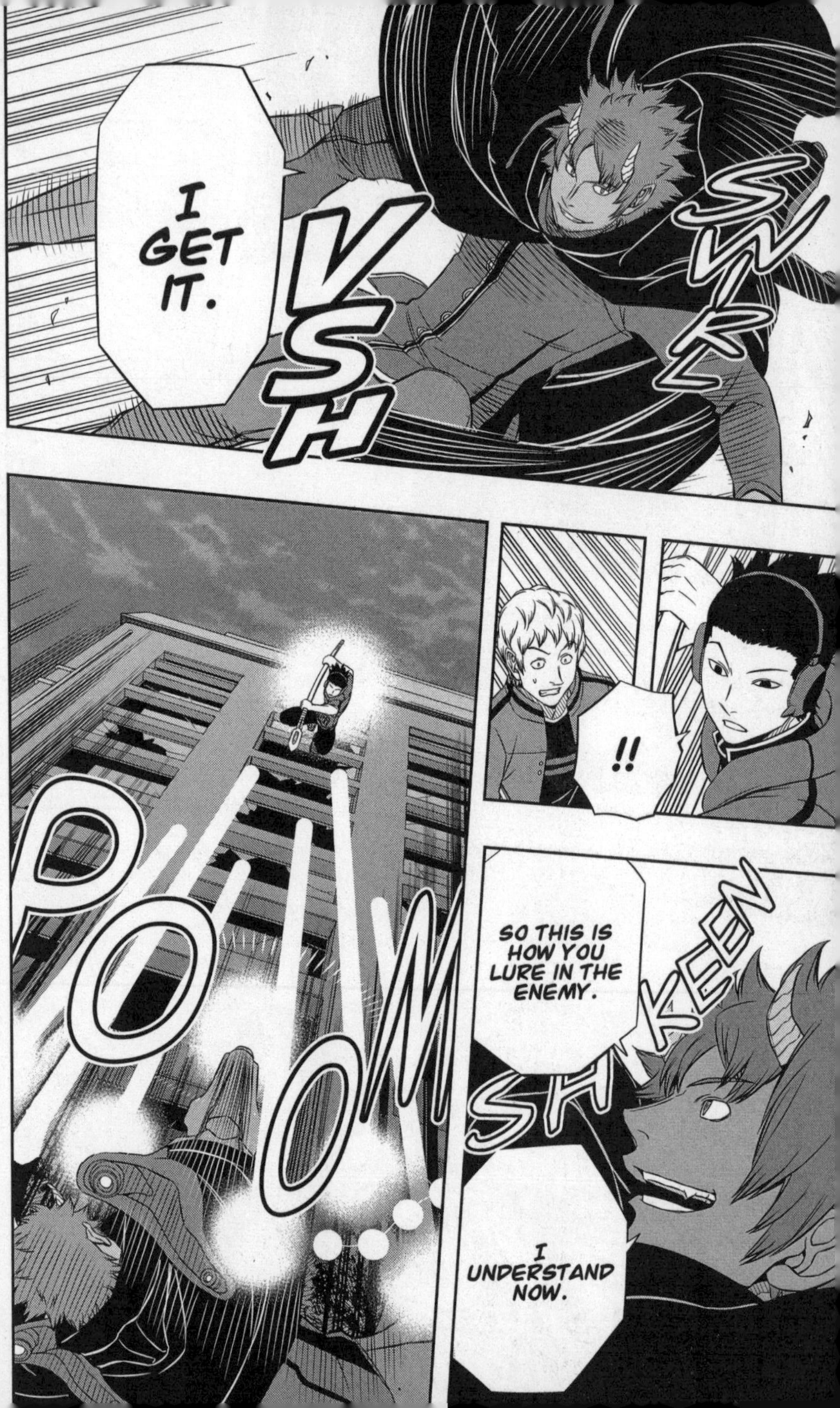
SWIRL
VSH
I GET IT.
!!
SO THIS IS HOW YOU LURE IN THE ENEMY.
SHKEEN
I UNDERSTAND NOW.
POOM

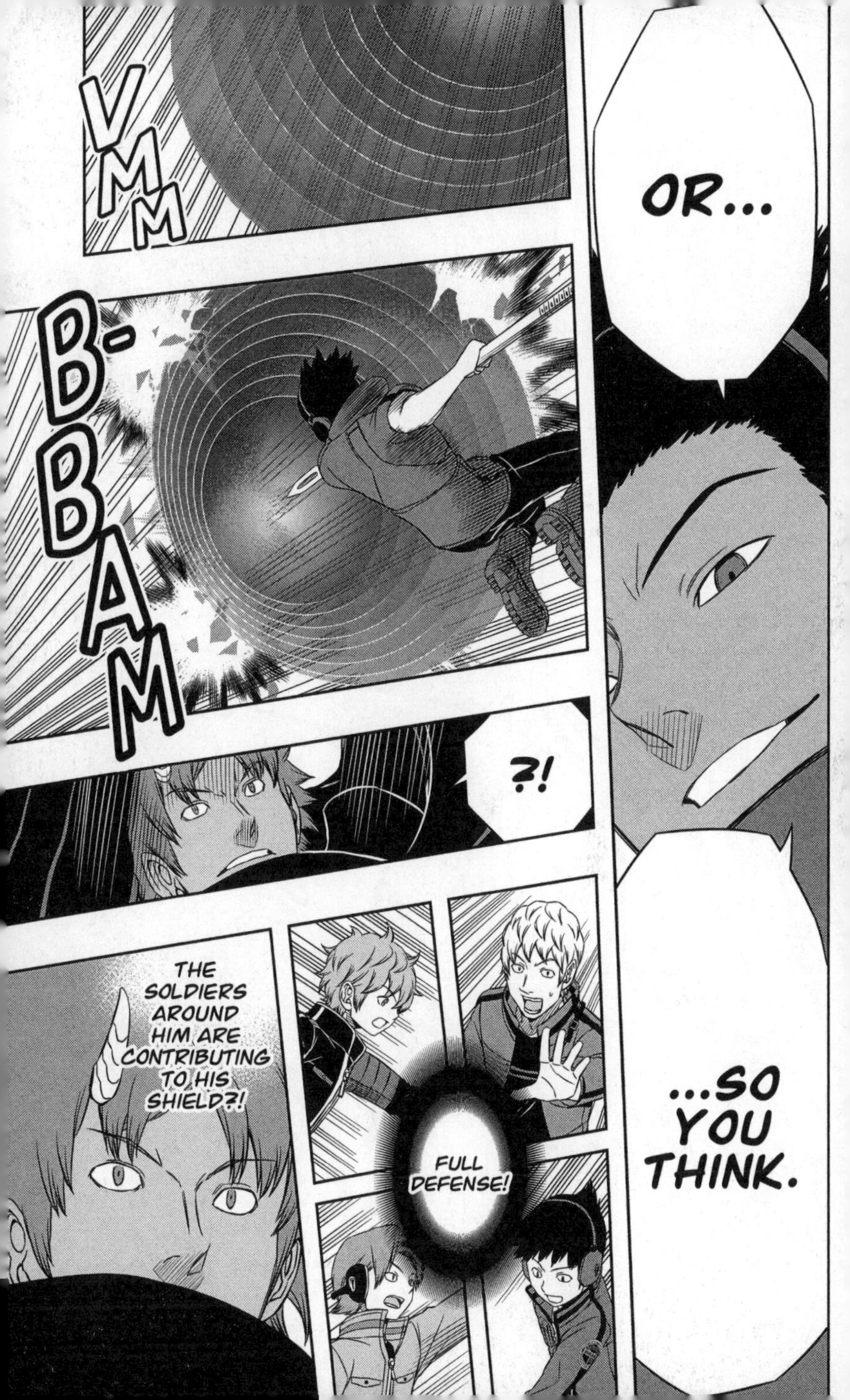
OR...
...SO YOU THINK.
VMMM
B-BBAM
?!
FULL DEFENSE!
THE SOLDIERS AROUND HIM ARE CONTRIBUTING TO HIS SHIELD?!

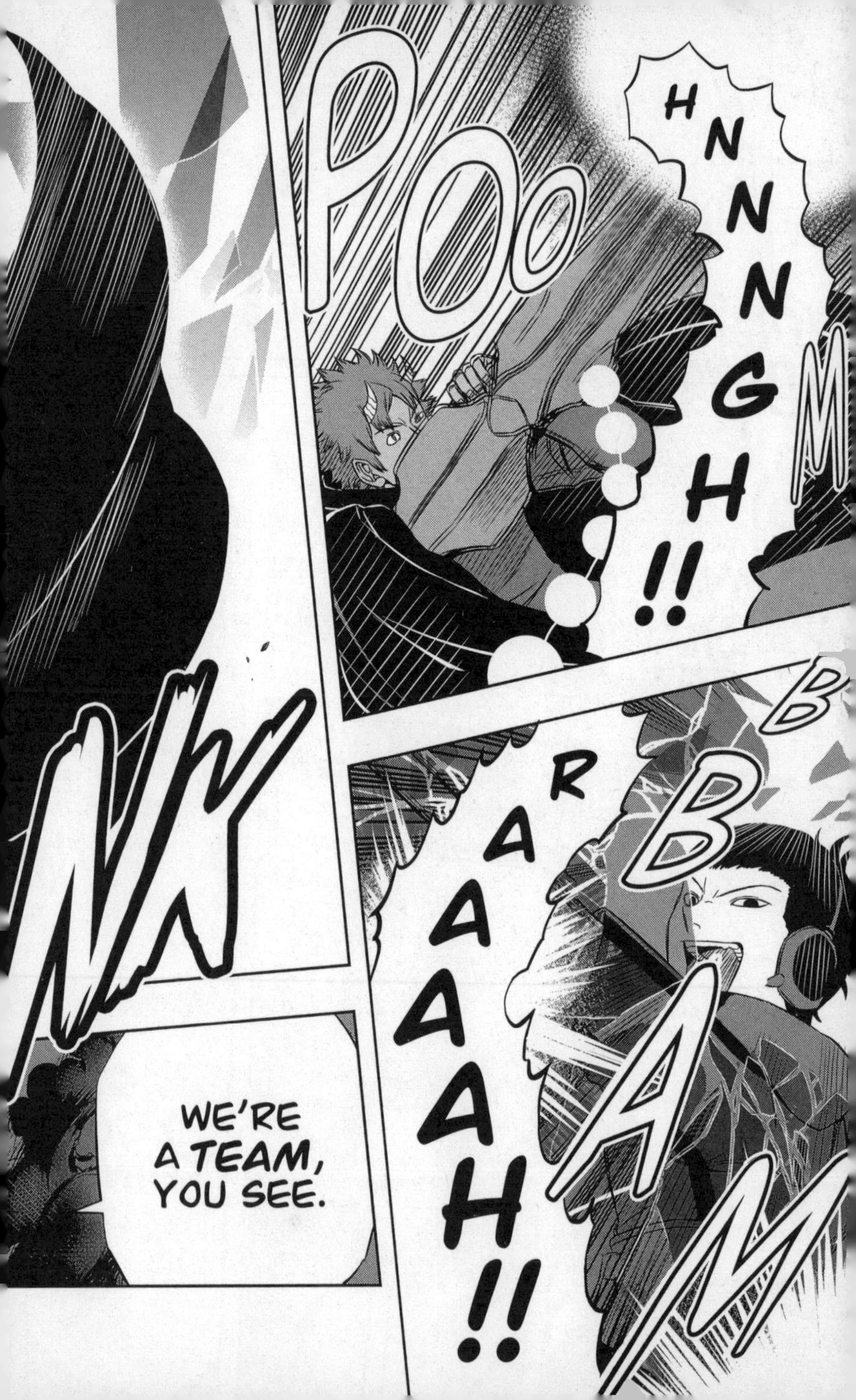
HNNNGH!!
POOOM
RAAAAH!!
BBBAM
WE'RE A TEAM, YOU SEE.

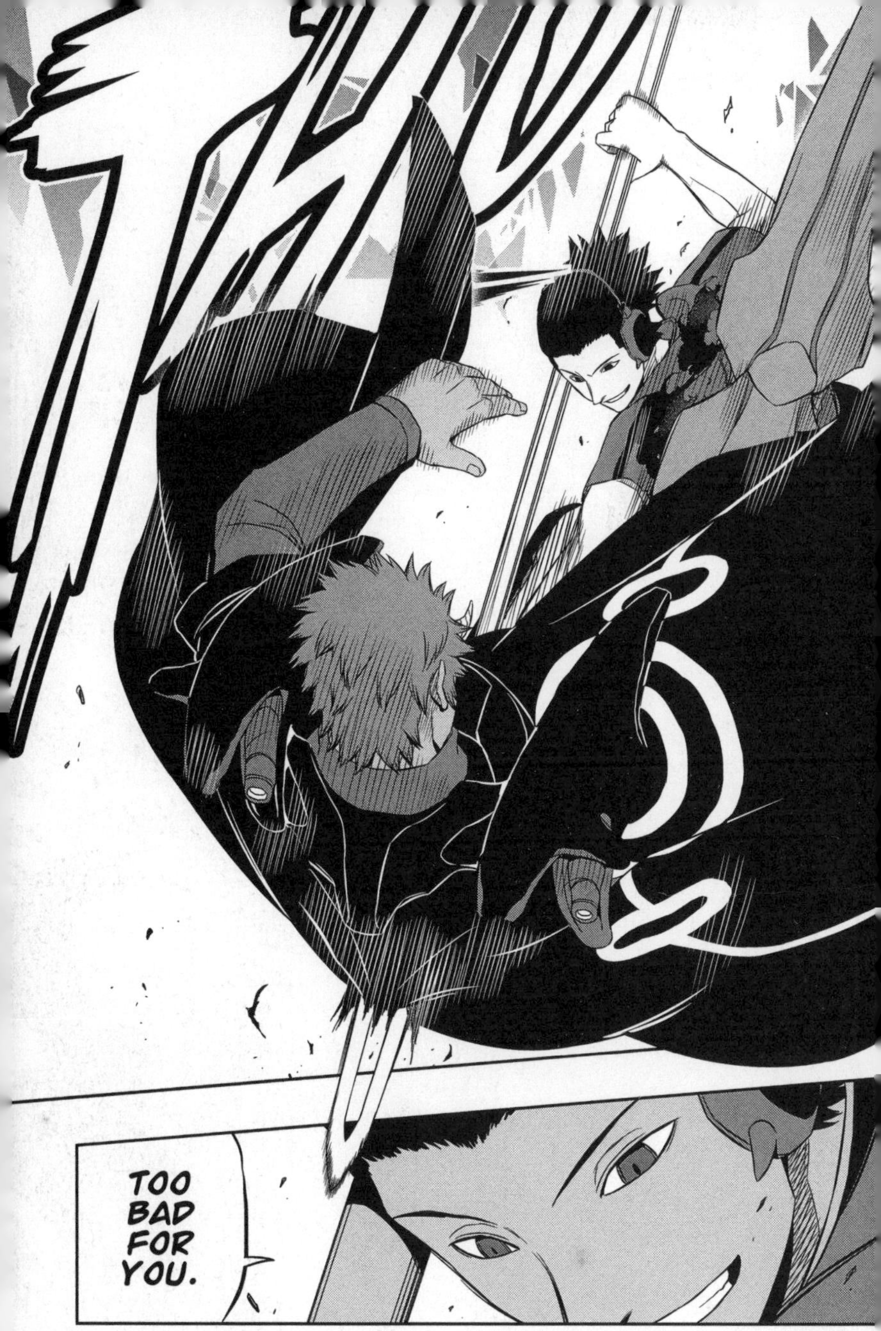
TOO BAD FOR YOU.

Ranbanein [Neighbor]

- 24 years old
- From Aftokrator
- Height: 6'7"
- Trigger: Keridón Thunder Feathers
- Likes: Battles with formidable foes, meat, wine, flying

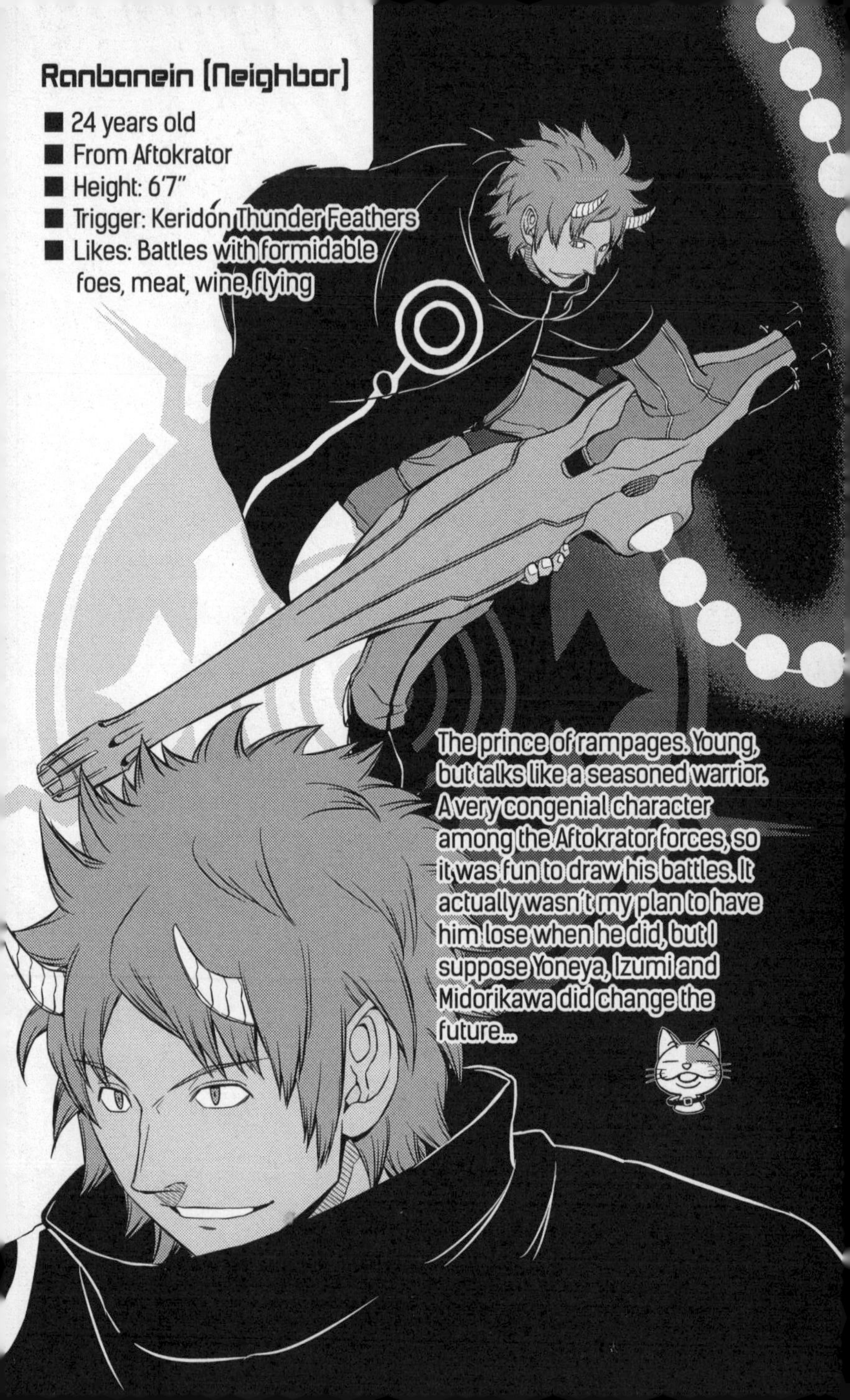

The prince of rampages. Young, but talks like a seasoned warrior. A very congenial character among the Aftokrator forces, so it was fun to draw his battles. It actually wasn't my plan to have him lose when he did, but I suppose Yoneya, Izumi and Midorikawa did change the future...

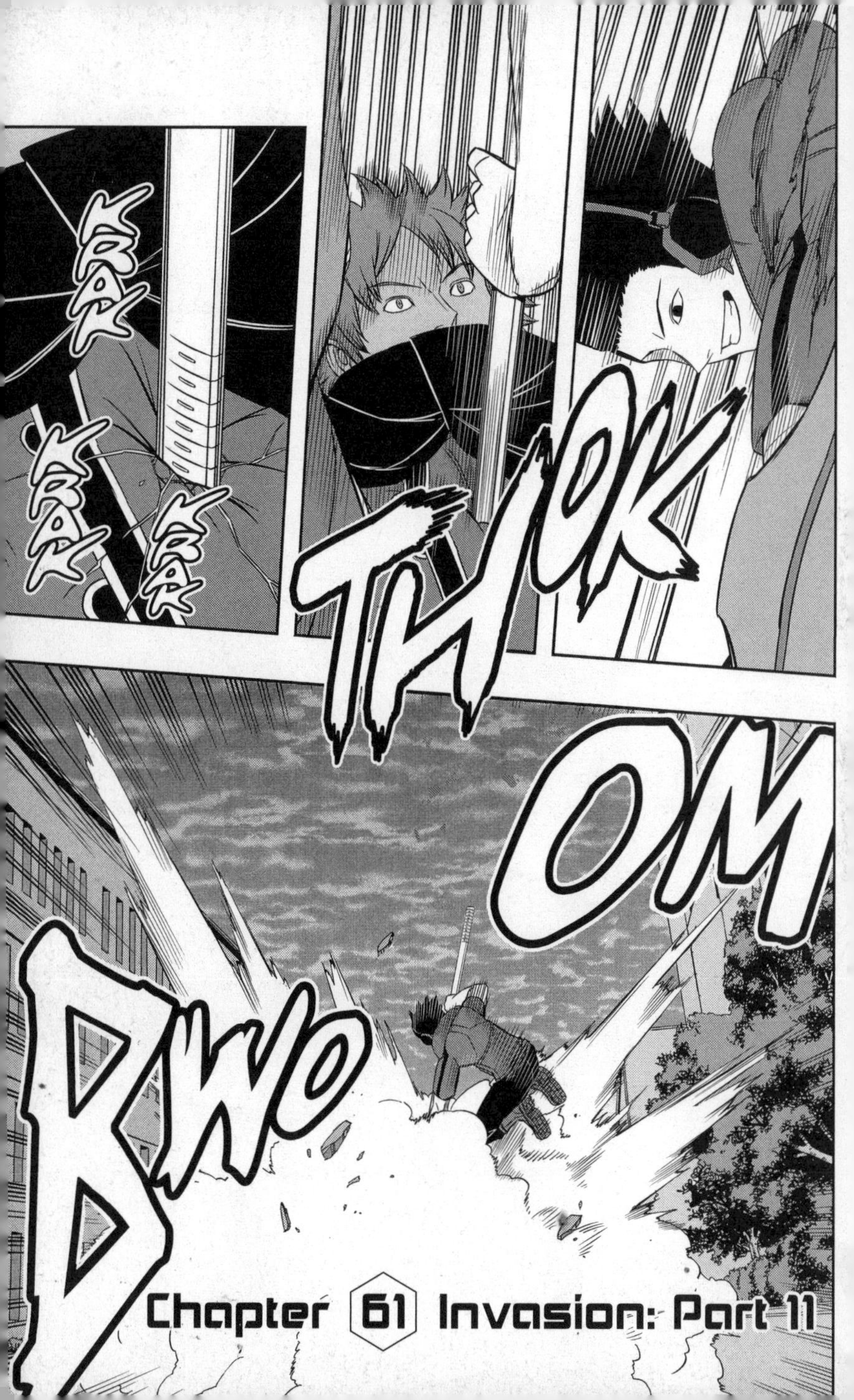
THOOK
KRAK
KRAK
KRAK
BWOOM

Chapter 61 Invasion: Part 11

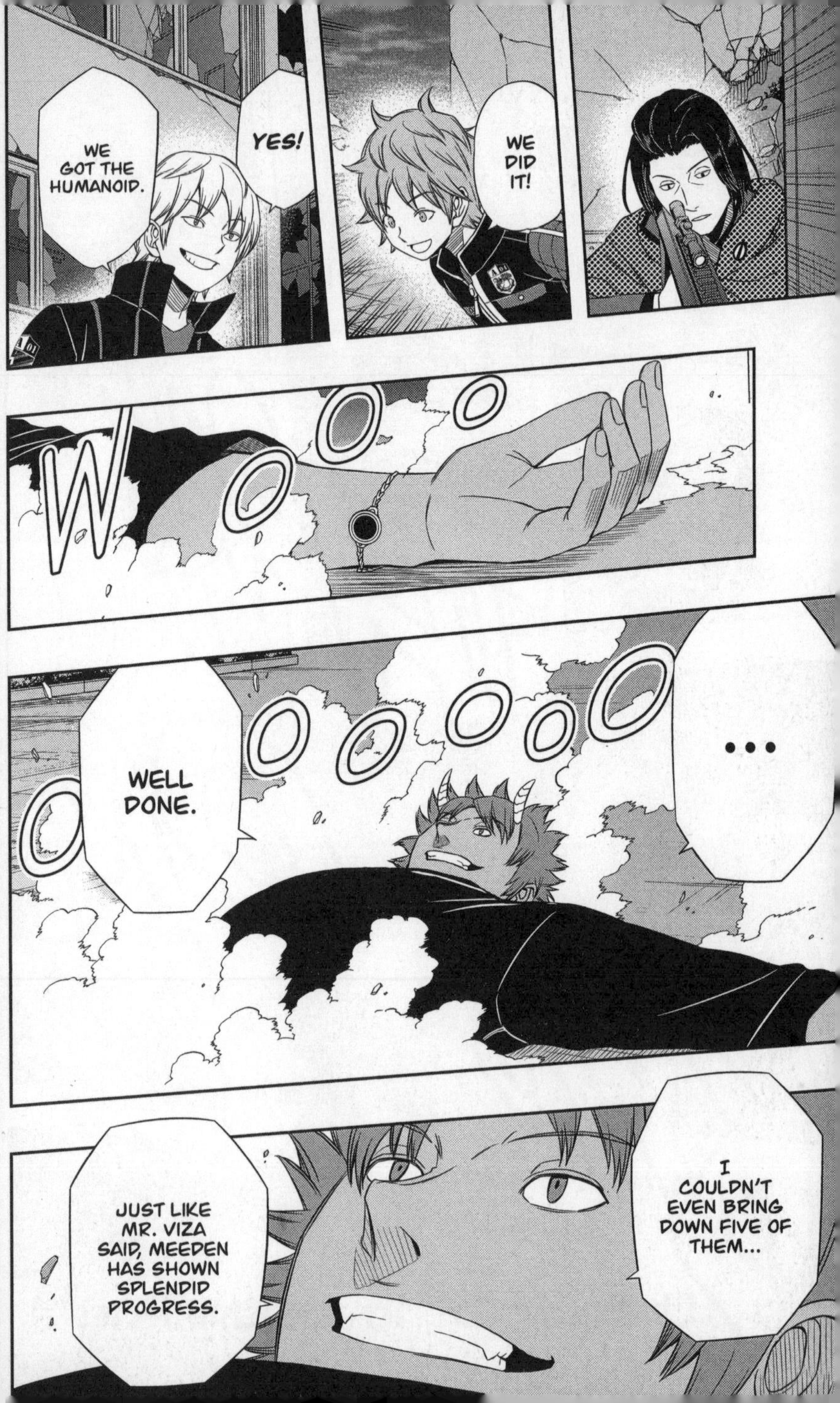
WE DID IT!
YES!
WE GOT THE HUMANOID.
WOOOO
OOOOOOO
...
WELL DONE.
I COULDN'T EVEN BRING DOWN FIVE OF THEM...
JUST LIKE MR. VIZA SAID, MEEDEN HAS SHOWN SPLENDID PROGRESS.

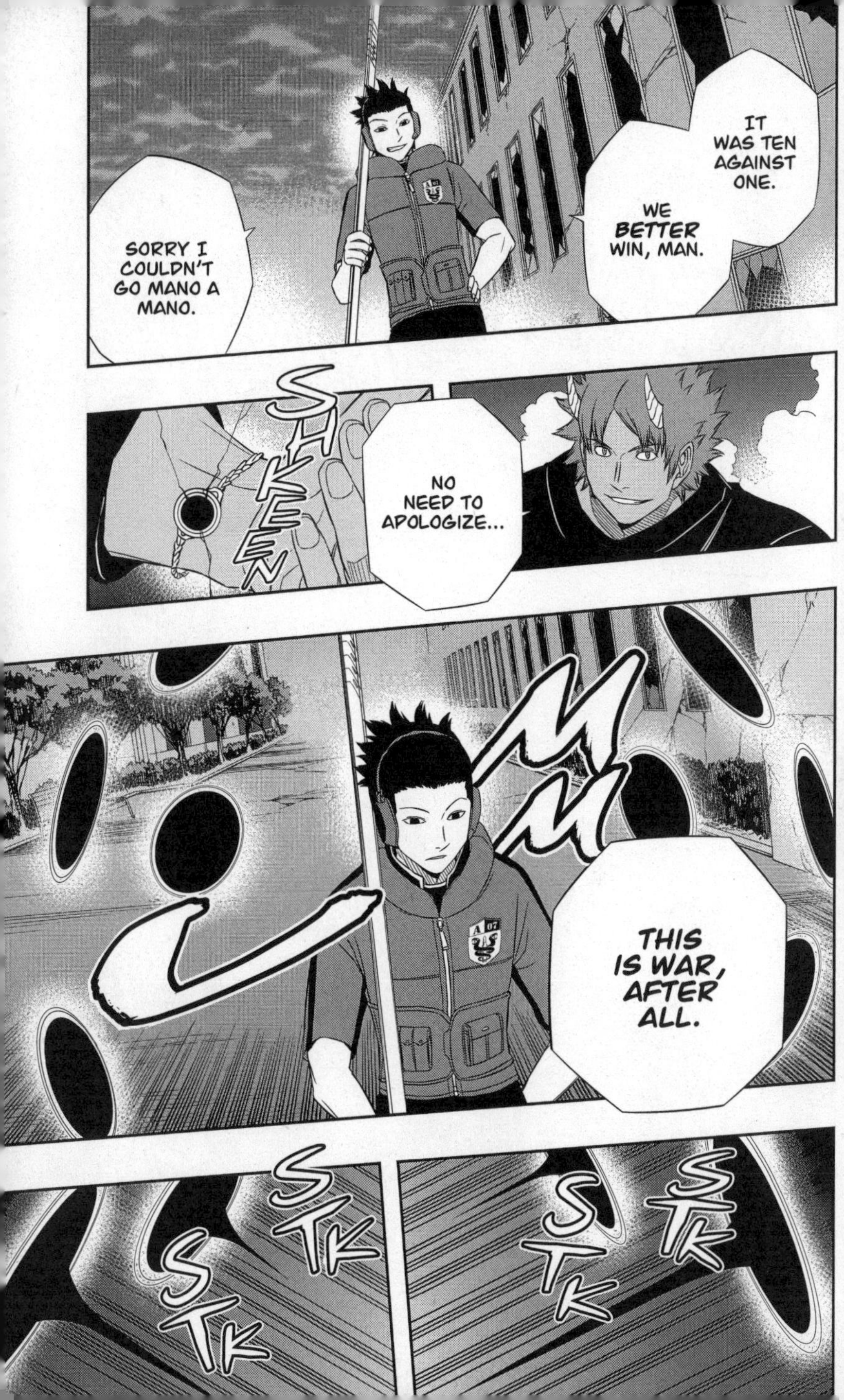
IT WAS TEN AGAINST ONE.
WE BETTER WIN, MAN.
SORRY I COULDN'T GO MANO A MANO.
NO NEED TO APOLOGIZE...
SHKEEN
MM
THIS IS WAR, AFTER ALL.
STK STK
STK STK

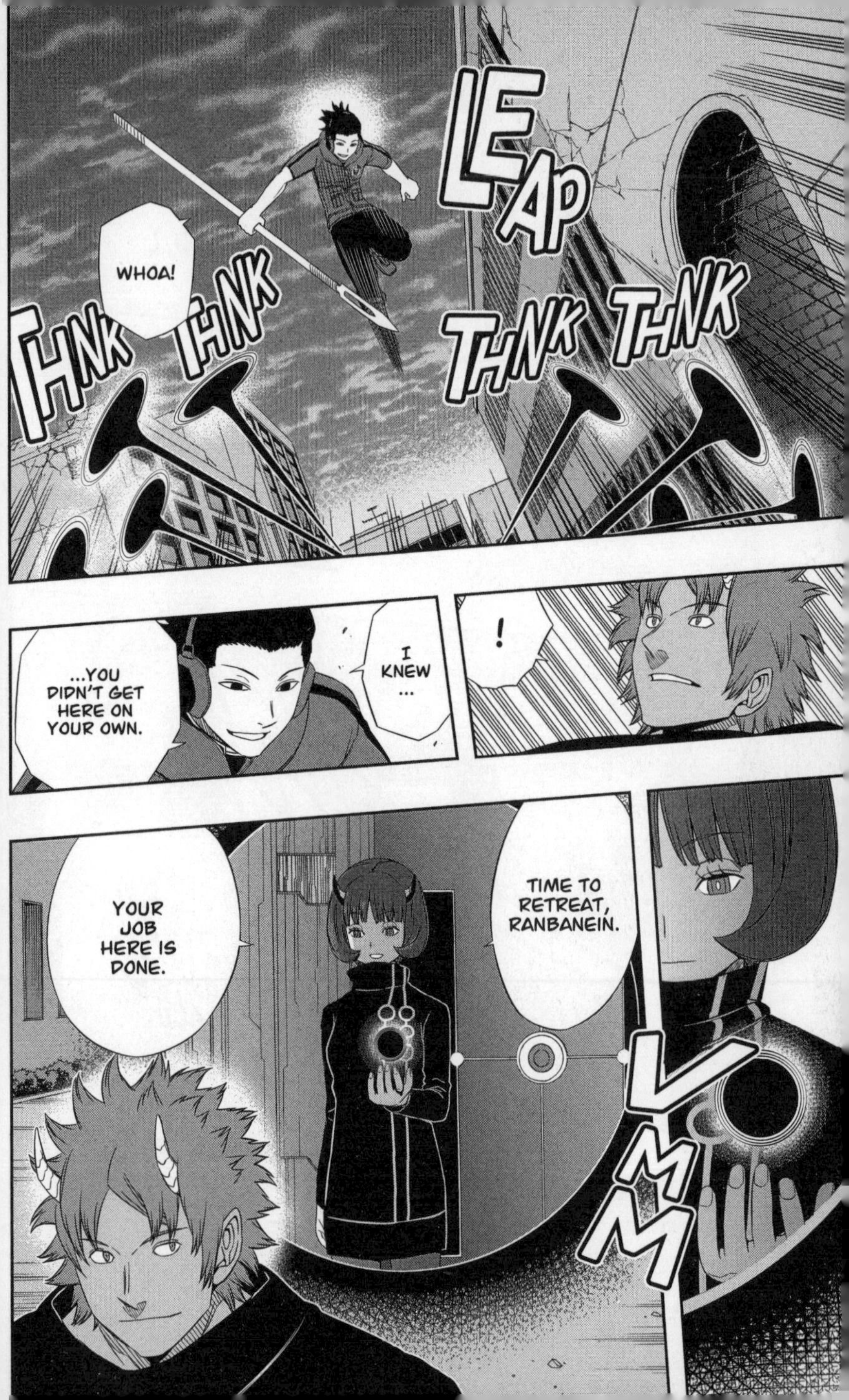
LEAP
THNK
THNK
WHOA!
THNK
THNK
!
I KNEW ...
...YOU DIDN'T GET HERE ON YOUR OWN.
TIME TO RETREAT, RANBANEIN.
VMMM
YOUR JOB HERE IS DONE.

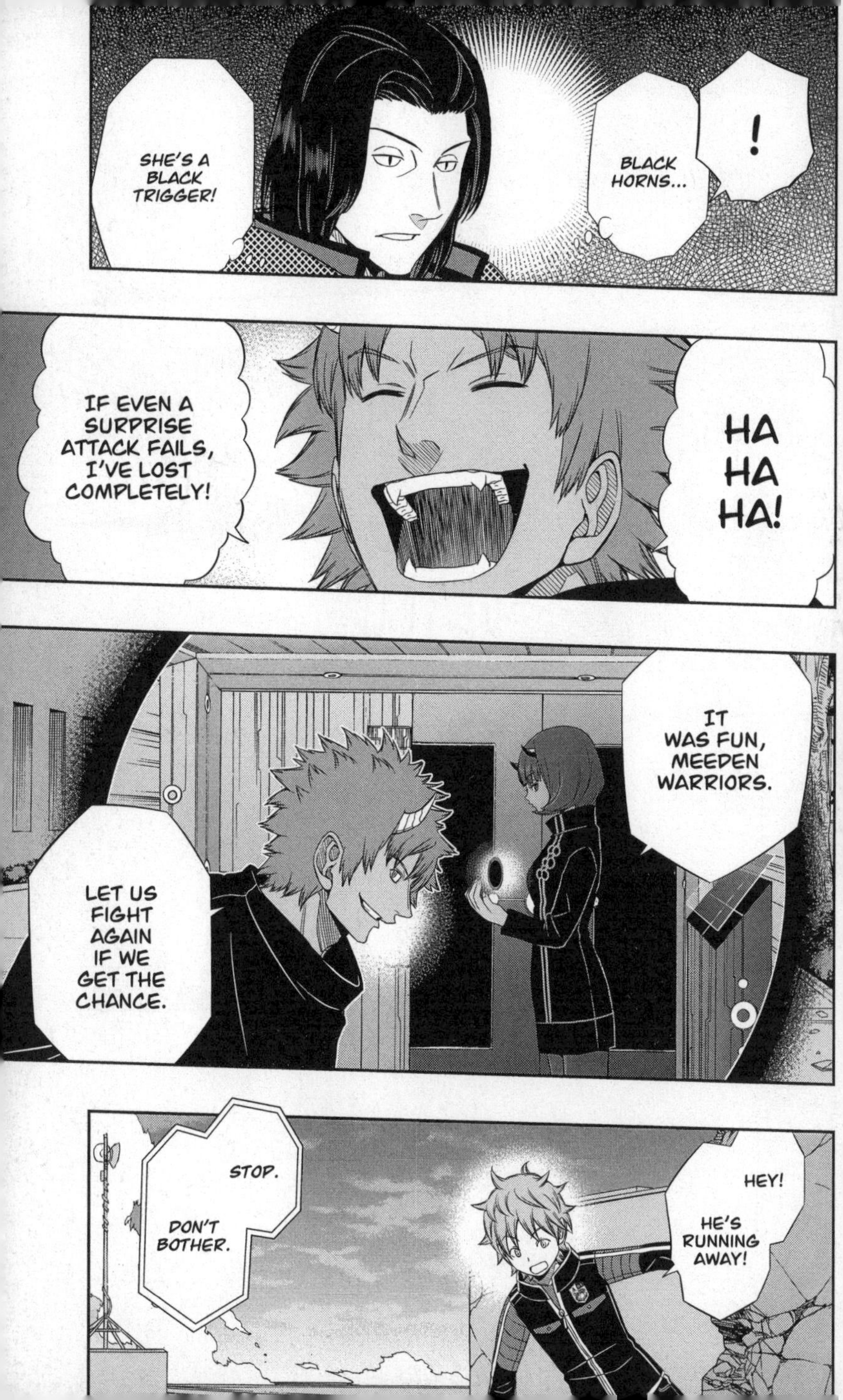
!
BLACK HORNS...
SHE'S A BLACK TRIGGER!
HA HA HA!
IF EVEN A SURPRISE ATTACK FAILS, I'VE LOST COMPLETELY!
IT WAS FUN, MEEDEN WARRIORS.
LET US FIGHT AGAIN IF WE GET THE CHANCE.
HEY!
HE'S RUNNING AWAY!
STOP.
DON'T BOTHER.

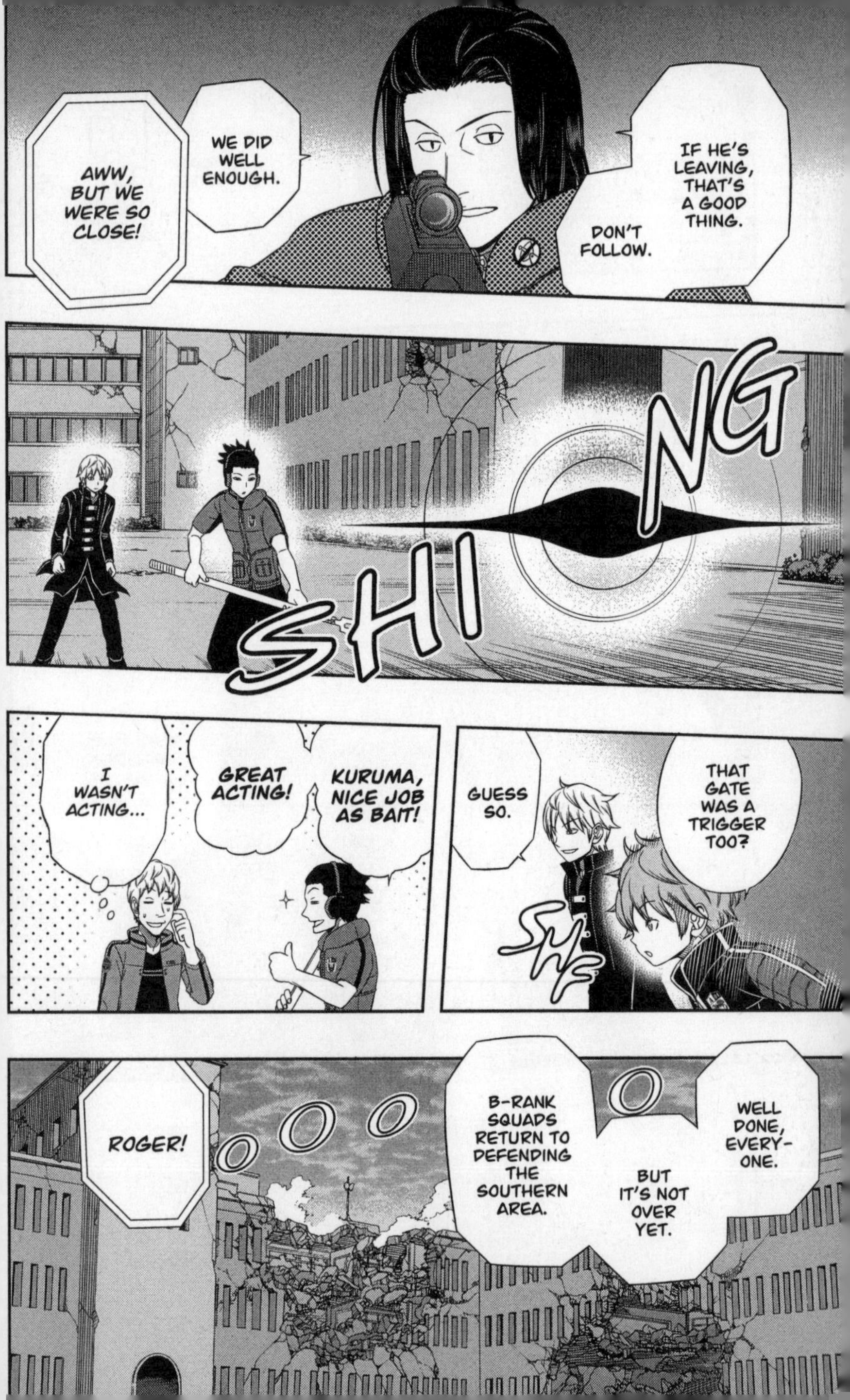
IF HE'S LEAVING, THAT'S A GOOD THING.
DON'T FOLLOW.
WE DID WELL ENOUGH.
AWW, BUT WE WERE SO CLOSE!
SHI NG
THAT GATE WAS A TRIGGER TOO?
GUESS SO.
SHF
KURUMA, NICE JOB AS BAIT!
GREAT ACTING!
I WASN'T ACTING...
WELL DONE, EVERYONE.
BUT IT'S NOT OVER YET.
B-RANK SQUADS RETURN TO DEFENDING THE SOUTHERN AREA.
OOOOO
ROGER!

READ THIS WAY

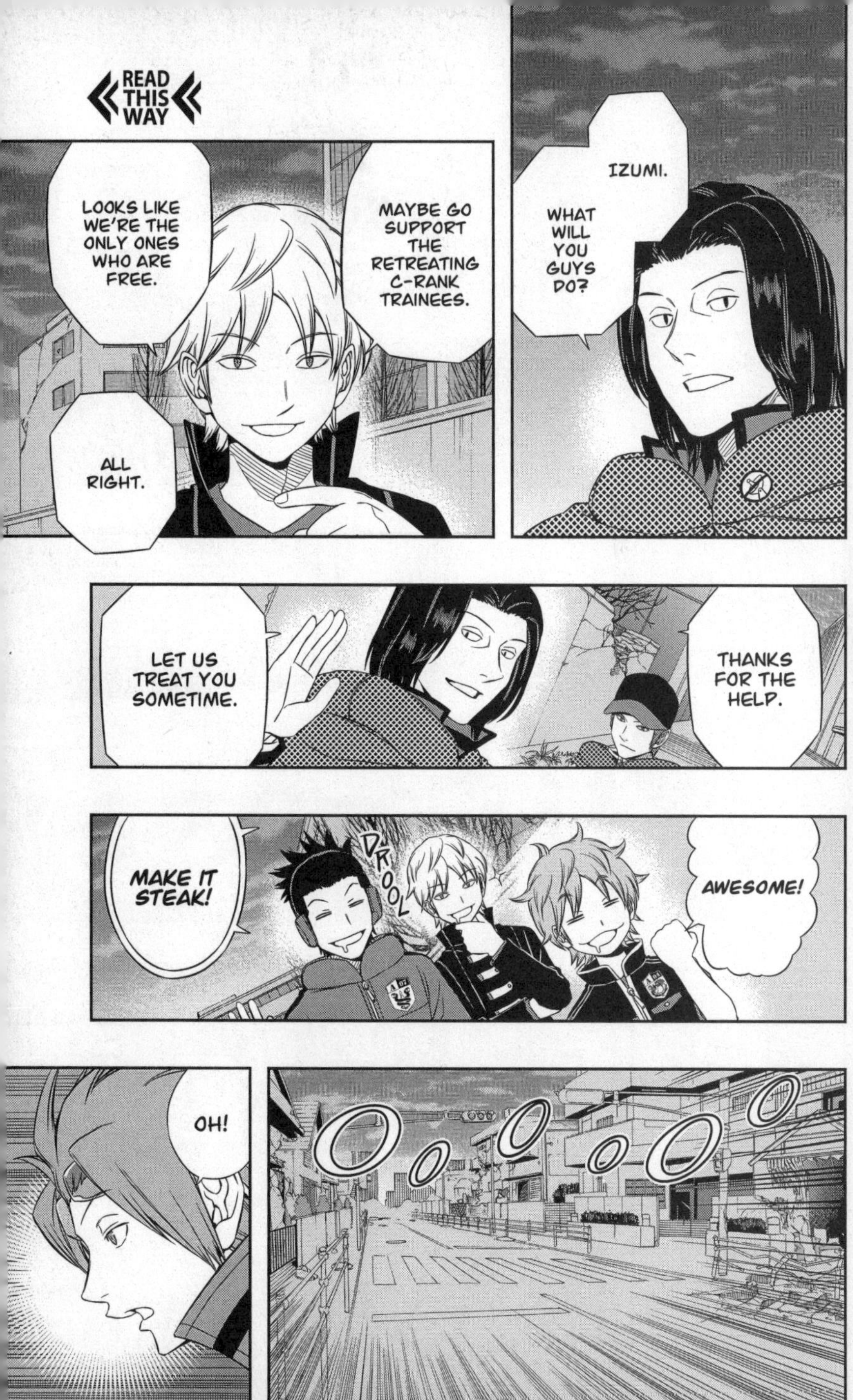
IZUMI.
WHAT WILL YOU GUYS DO?
MAYBE GO SUPPORT THE RETREATING C-RANK TRAINEES.
LOOKS LIKE WE'RE THE ONLY ONES WHO ARE FREE.
ALL RIGHT.
THANKS FOR THE HELP.
LET US TREAT YOU SOMETIME.
AWESOME!
DROOL
MAKE IT STEAK!
OOOOOO
OH!

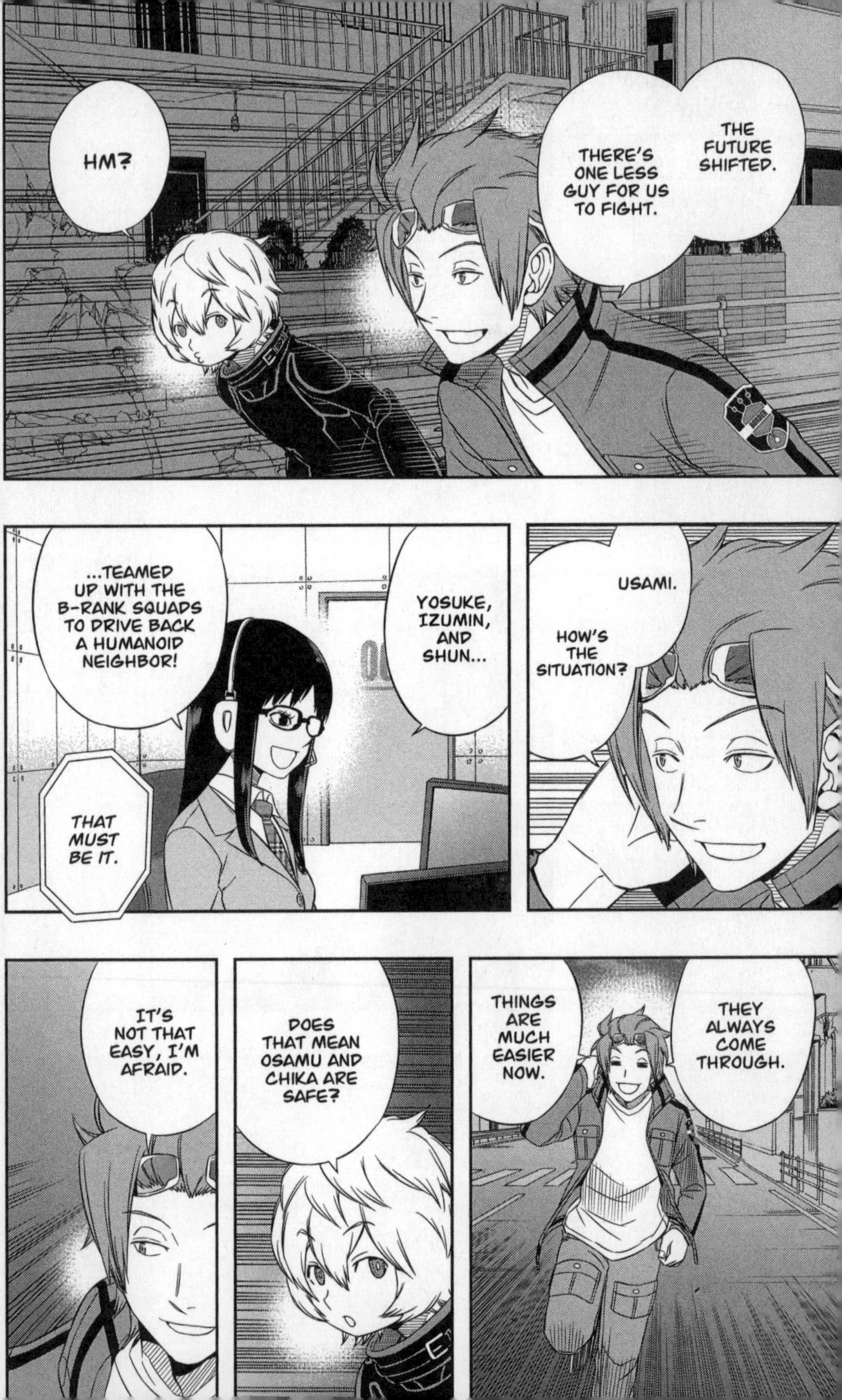
THE FUTURE SHIFTED.
THERE'S ONE LESS GUY FOR US TO FIGHT.
HM?
USAMI.
HOW'S THE SITUATION?
YOSUKE, IZUMIN, AND SHUN...
...TEAMED UP WITH THE B-RANK SQUADS TO DRIVE BACK A HUMANOID NEIGHBOR!
THAT MUST BE IT.
THEY ALWAYS COME THROUGH.
THINGS ARE MUCH EASIER NOW.
DOES THAT MEAN OSAMU AND CHIKA ARE SAFE?
IT'S NOT THAT EASY, I'M AFRAID.

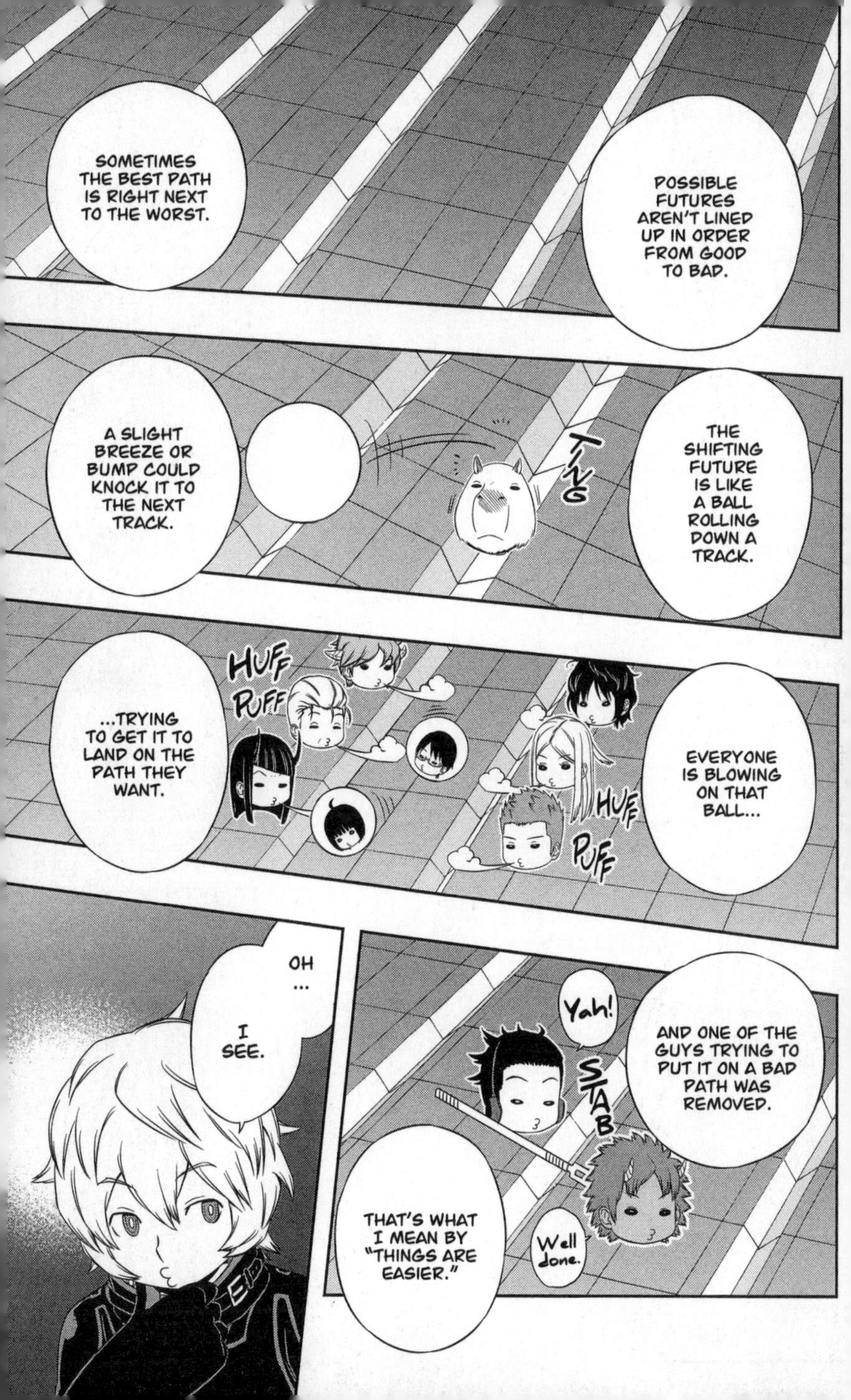
POSSIBLE FUTURES AREN'T LINED UP IN ORDER FROM GOOD TO BAD.
SOMETIMES THE BEST PATH IS RIGHT NEXT TO THE WORST.
THE SHIFTING FUTURE IS LIKE A BALL ROLLING DOWN A TRACK.
TING
A SLIGHT BREEZE OR BUMP COULD KNOCK IT TO THE NEXT TRACK.
EVERYONE IS BLOWING ON THAT BALL...
HUFF
PUFF
HUFF
PUFF
...TRYING TO GET IT TO LAND ON THE PATH THEY WANT.
AND ONE OF THE GUYS TRYING TO PUT IT ON A BAD PATH WAS REMOVED.
Yah!
STAB
Well done.
THAT'S WHAT I MEAN BY "THINGS ARE EASIER."
OH ...
I SEE.

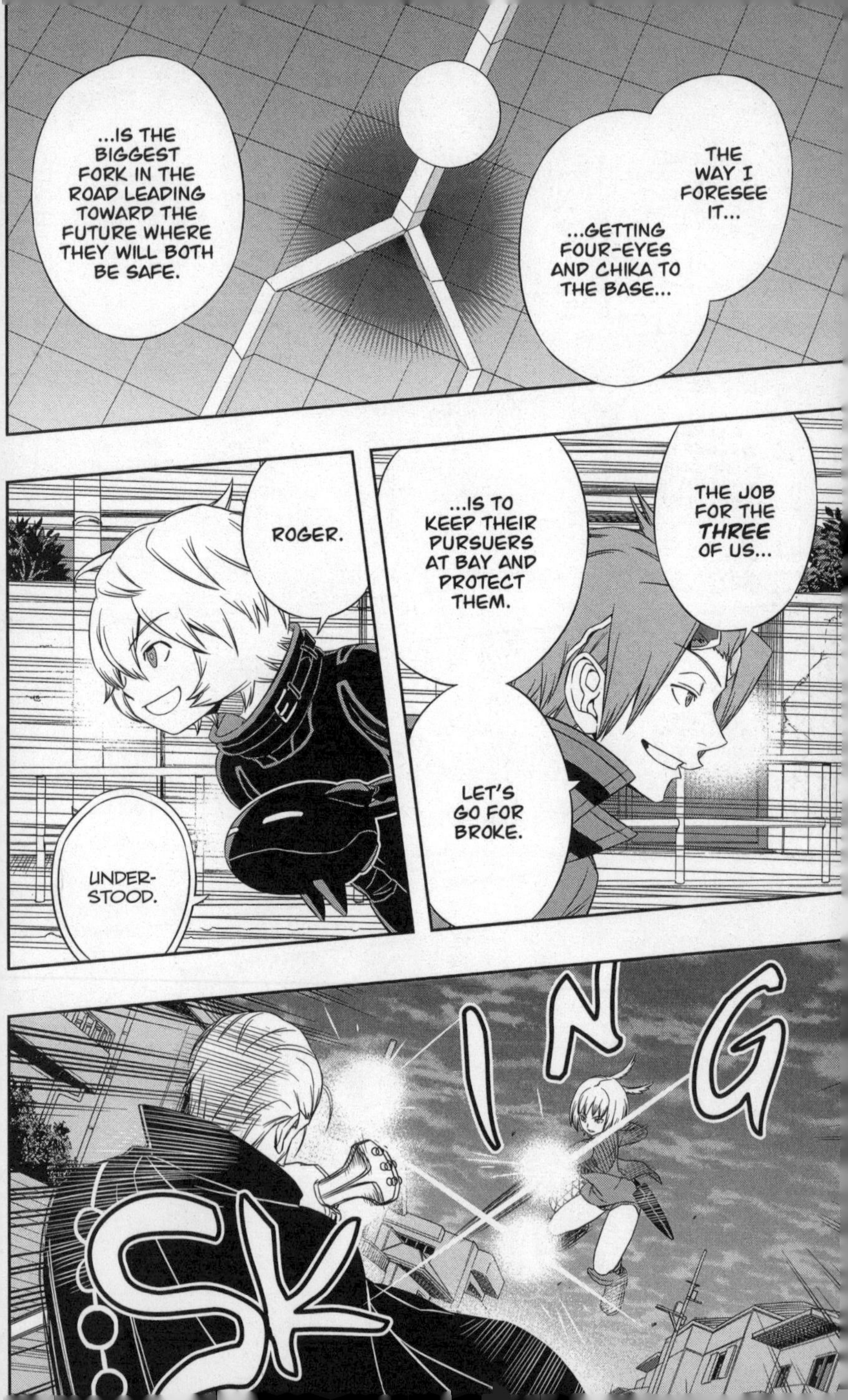
THE WAY I FORESEE IT...
...GETTING FOUR-EYES AND CHIKA TO THE BASE...
...IS THE BIGGEST FORK IN THE ROAD LEADING TOWARD THE FUTURE WHERE THEY WILL BOTH BE SAFE.
THE JOB FOR THE THREE OF US...
...IS TO KEEP THEIR PURSUERS AT BAY AND PROTECT THEM.
LET'S GO FOR BROKE.
ROGER.
UNDER-STOOD.
SKING

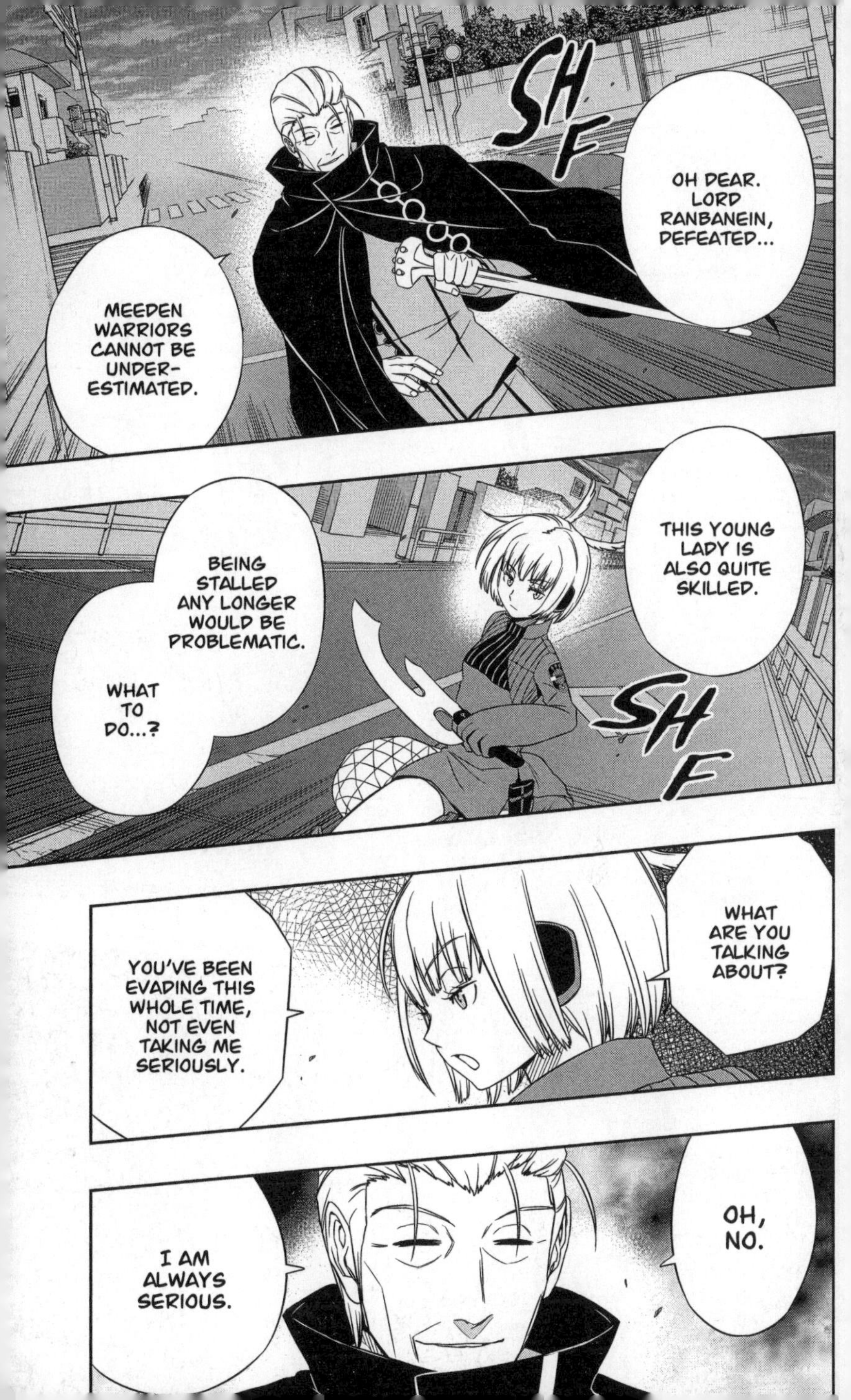
OH DEAR. LORD RANBANEIN, DEFEATED...
SHF
MEEDEN WARRIORS CANNOT BE UNDER-ESTIMATED.
THIS YOUNG LADY IS ALSO QUITE SKILLED.
SHF
BEING STALLED ANY LONGER WOULD BE PROBLEMATIC.
WHAT TO DO...?
WHAT ARE YOU TALKING ABOUT?
YOU'VE BEEN EVADING THIS WHOLE TIME, NOT EVEN TAKING ME SERIOUSLY.
OH, NO.
I AM ALWAYS SERIOUS.

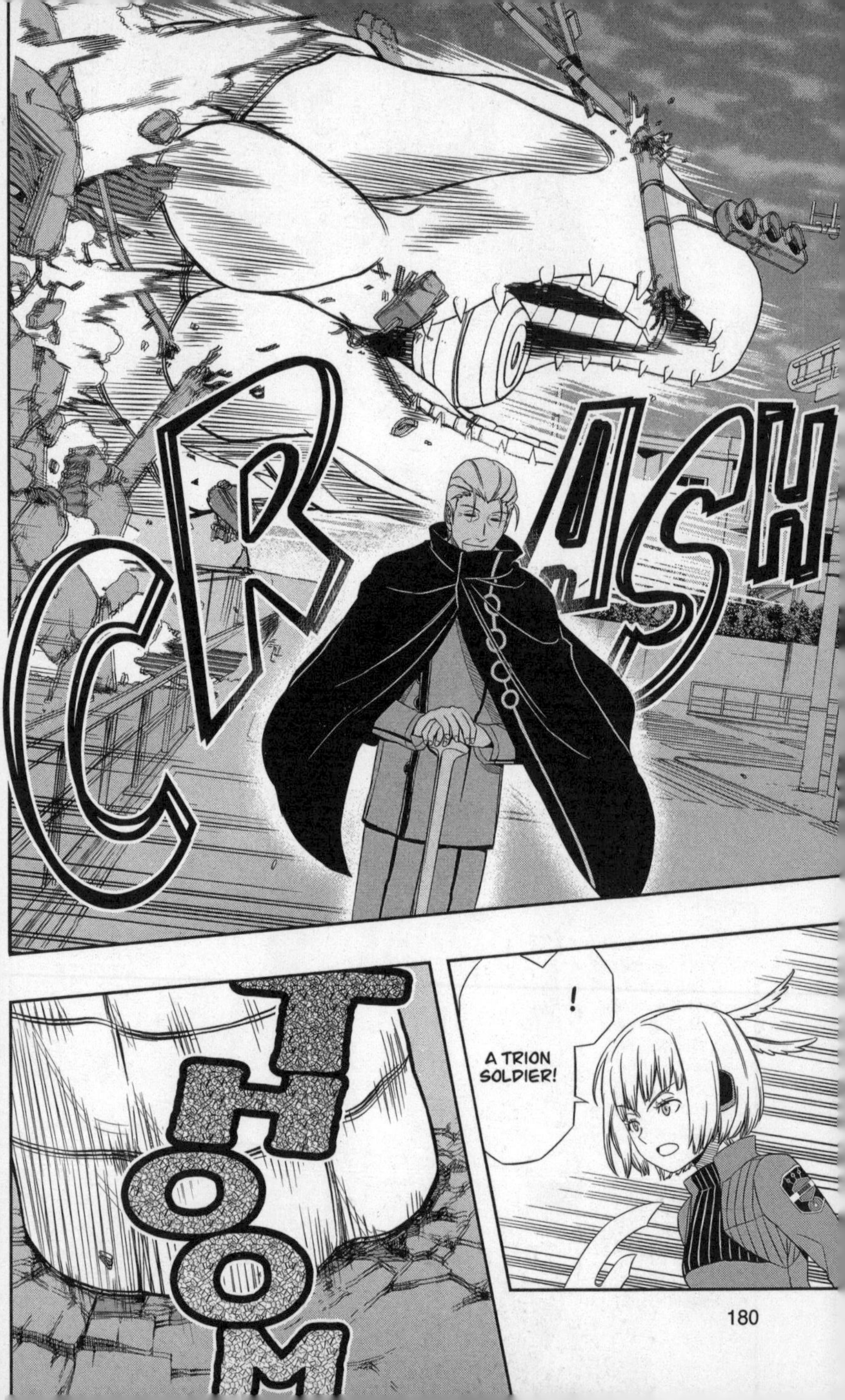
CRASH
!
A TRION SOLDIER!
THOOM

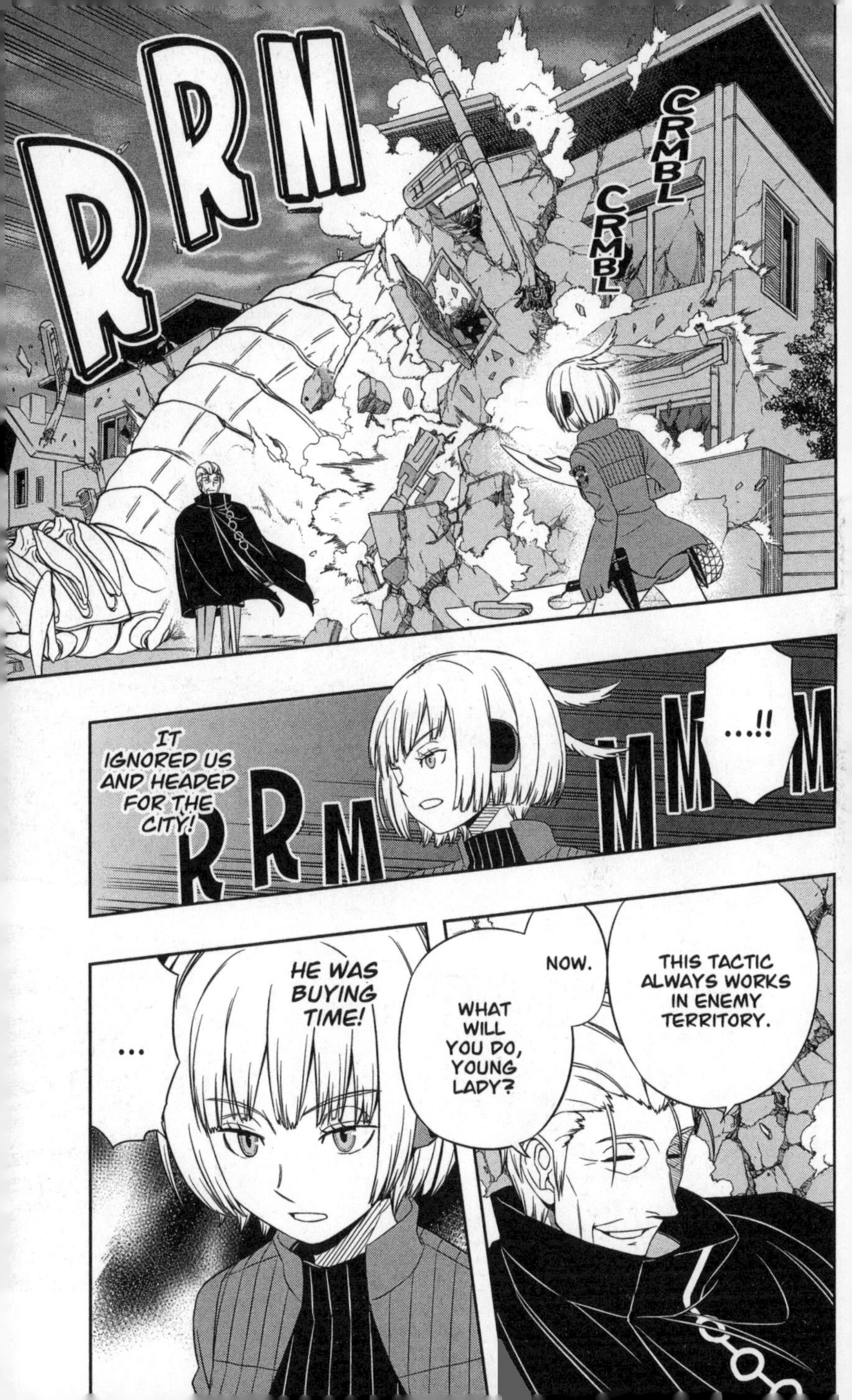
CRMBL
CRMBL
RRM
...!!
MMMM
RRM
IT IGNORED US AND HEADED FOR THE CITY!
THIS TACTIC ALWAYS WORKS IN ENEMY TERRITORY.
NOW.
WHAT WILL YOU DO, YOUNG LADY?
HE WAS BUYING TIME!
...

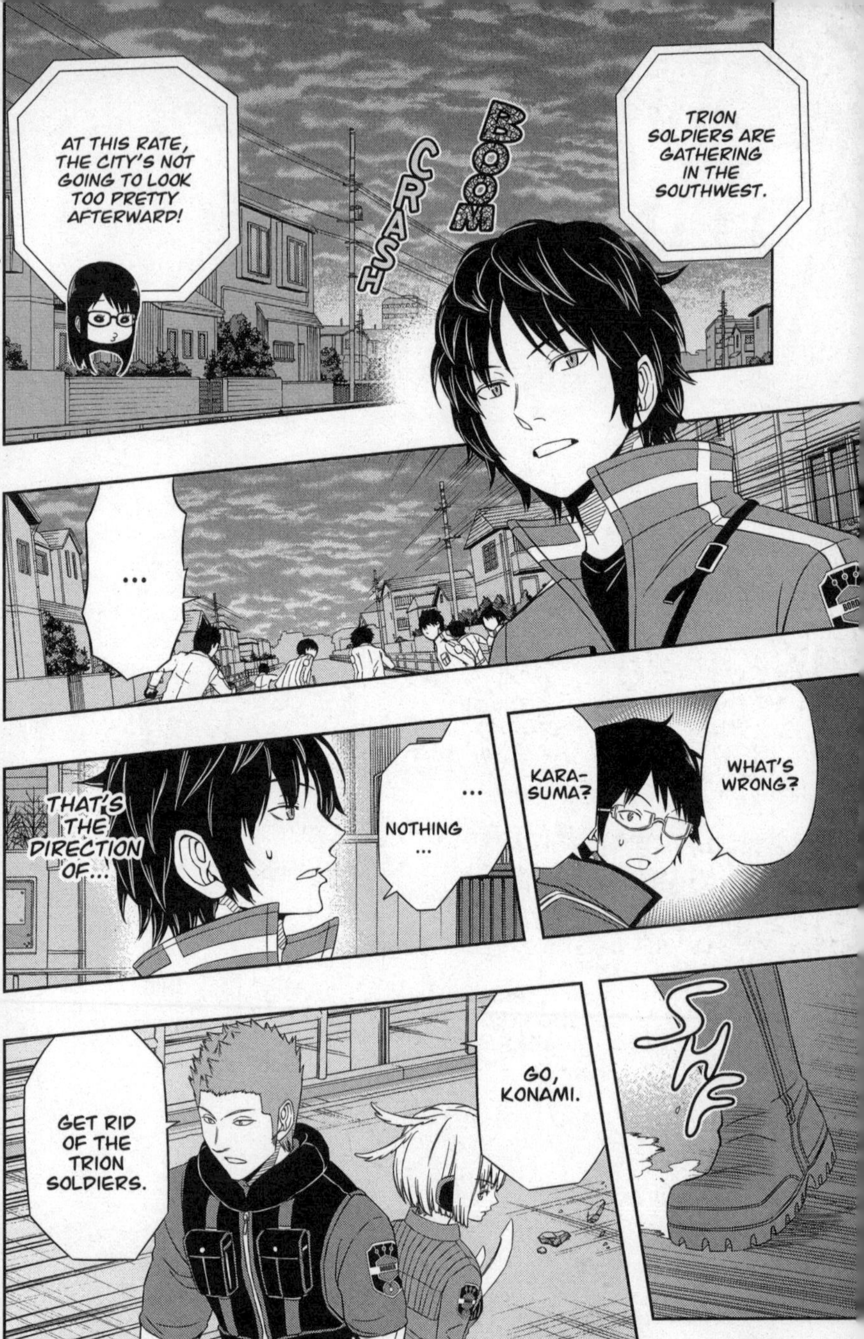
TRION SOLDIERS ARE GATHERING IN THE SOUTHWEST.
BOOM
CRASH
AT THIS RATE, THE CITY'S NOT GOING TO LOOK TOO PRETTY AFTERWARD!
...
WHAT'S WRONG?
KARASUMA?
... NOTHING ...
THAT'S THE DIRECTION OF...
GO, KONAMI.
GET RID OF THE TRION SOLDIERS.

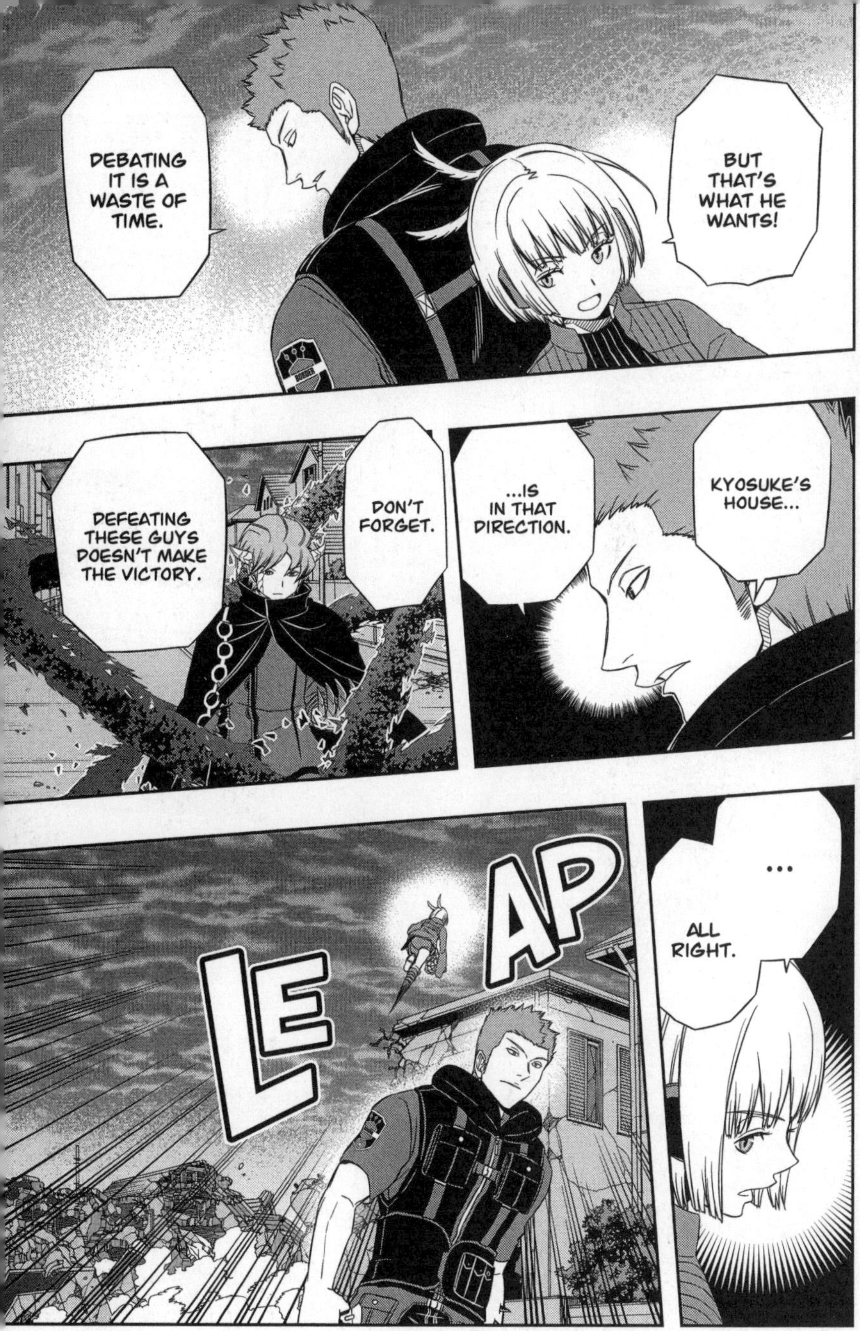
BUT THAT'S WHAT HE WANTS!
DEBATING IT IS A WASTE OF TIME.
KYOSUKE'S HOUSE...
...IS IN THAT DIRECTION.
DON'T FORGET.
DEFEATING THESE GUYS DOESN'T MAKE THE VICTORY.
... ALL RIGHT.
LEAP

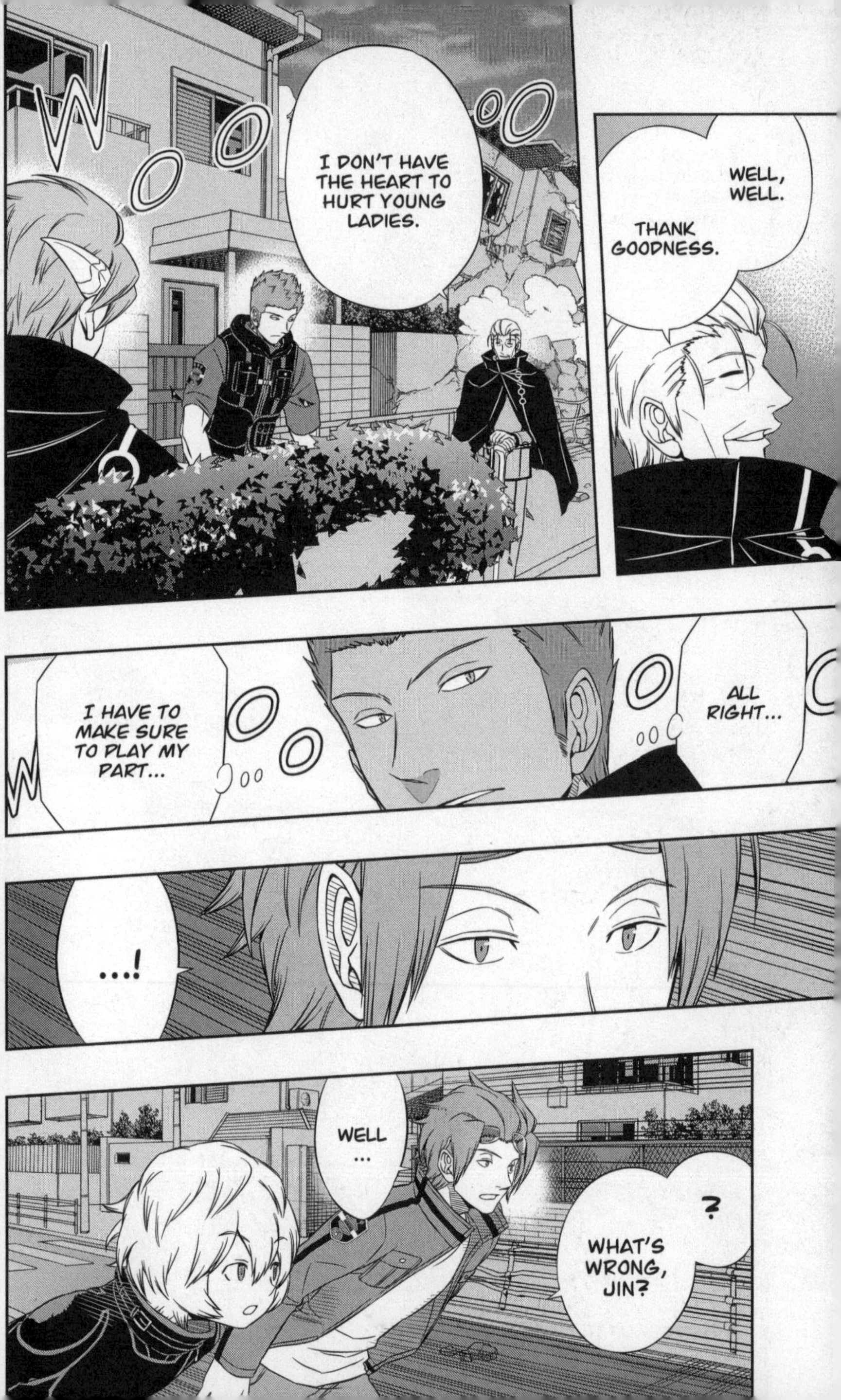
WELL, WELL.
THANK GOODNESS.
WOOOO
I DON'T HAVE THE HEART TO HURT YOUNG LADIES.
ALL RIGHT...
I HAVE TO MAKE SURE TO PLAY MY PART...
...!
?
WHAT'S WRONG, JIN?
WELL ...

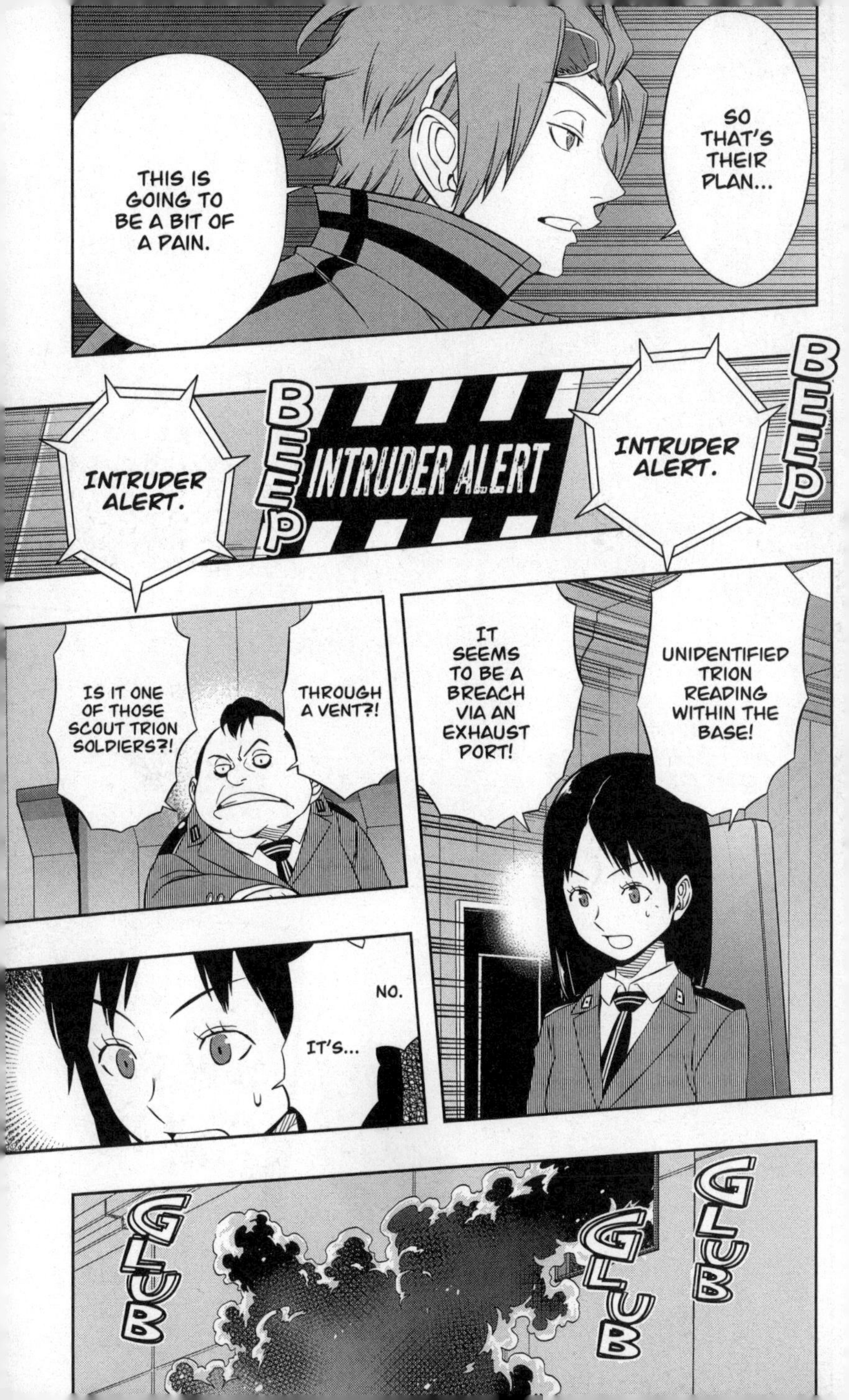
SO THAT'S THEIR PLAN...
THIS IS GOING TO BE A BIT OF A PAIN.
BEEP
INTRUDER ALERT.
INTRUDER ALERT
BEEP
INTRUDER ALERT.
UNIDENTIFIED TRION READING WITHIN THE BASE!
IT SEEMS TO BE A BREACH VIA AN EXHAUST PORT!
THROUGH A VENT?!
IS IT ONE OF THOSE SCOUT TRION SOLDIERS?!
NO.
IT'S...
GLUB
GLUB
GLUB

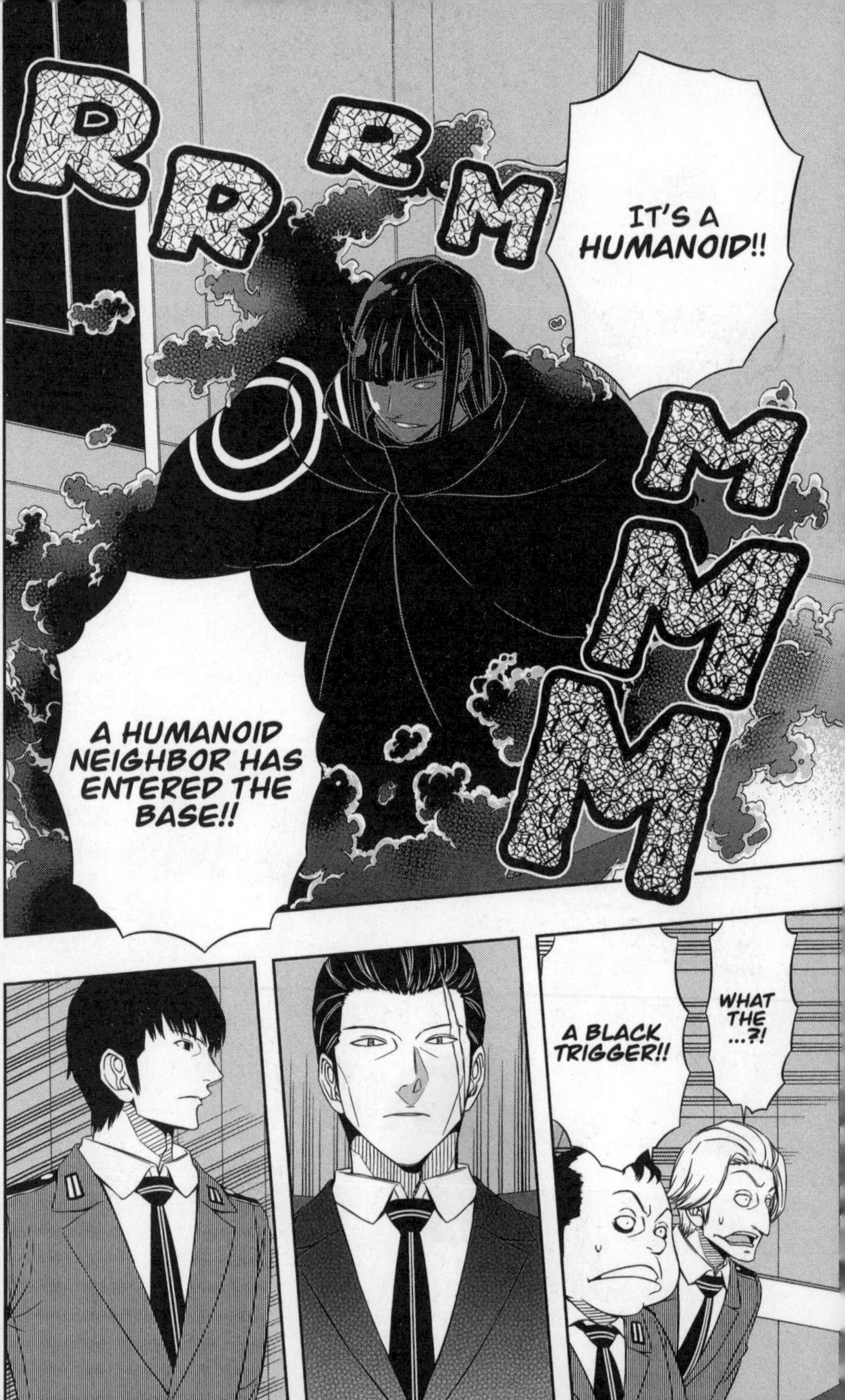
IT'S A HUMANOID!!
RRRMMMM
A HUMANOID NEIGHBOR HAS ENTERED THE BASE!!
WHAT THE ...?!
A BLACK TRIGGER!!

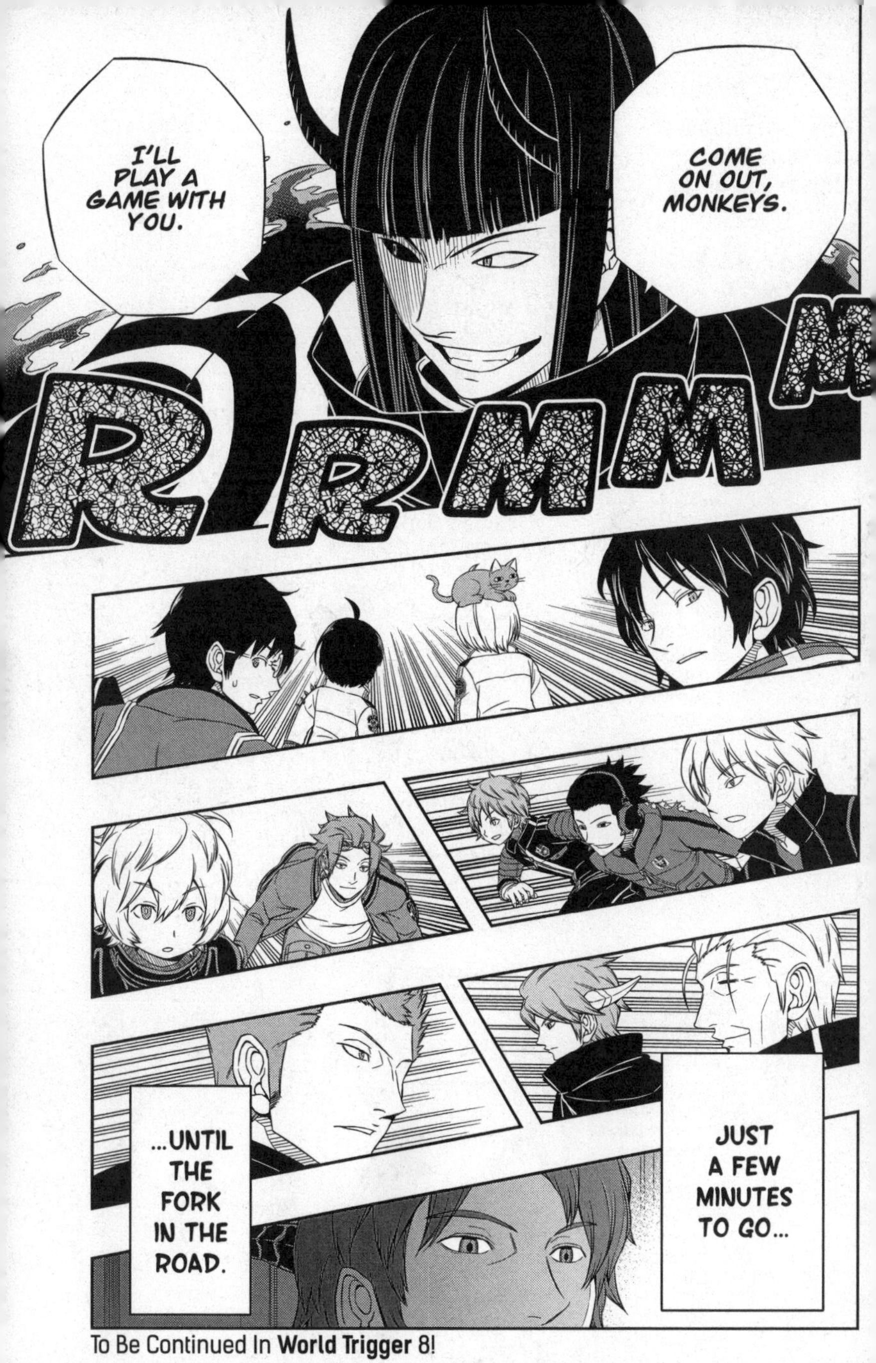
COME ON OUT, MONKEYS.
I'LL PLAY A GAME WITH YOU.
RRMMMM
JUST A FEW MINUTES TO GO...
...UNTIL THE FORK IN THE ROAD.

To Be Continued In **World Trigger** 8!

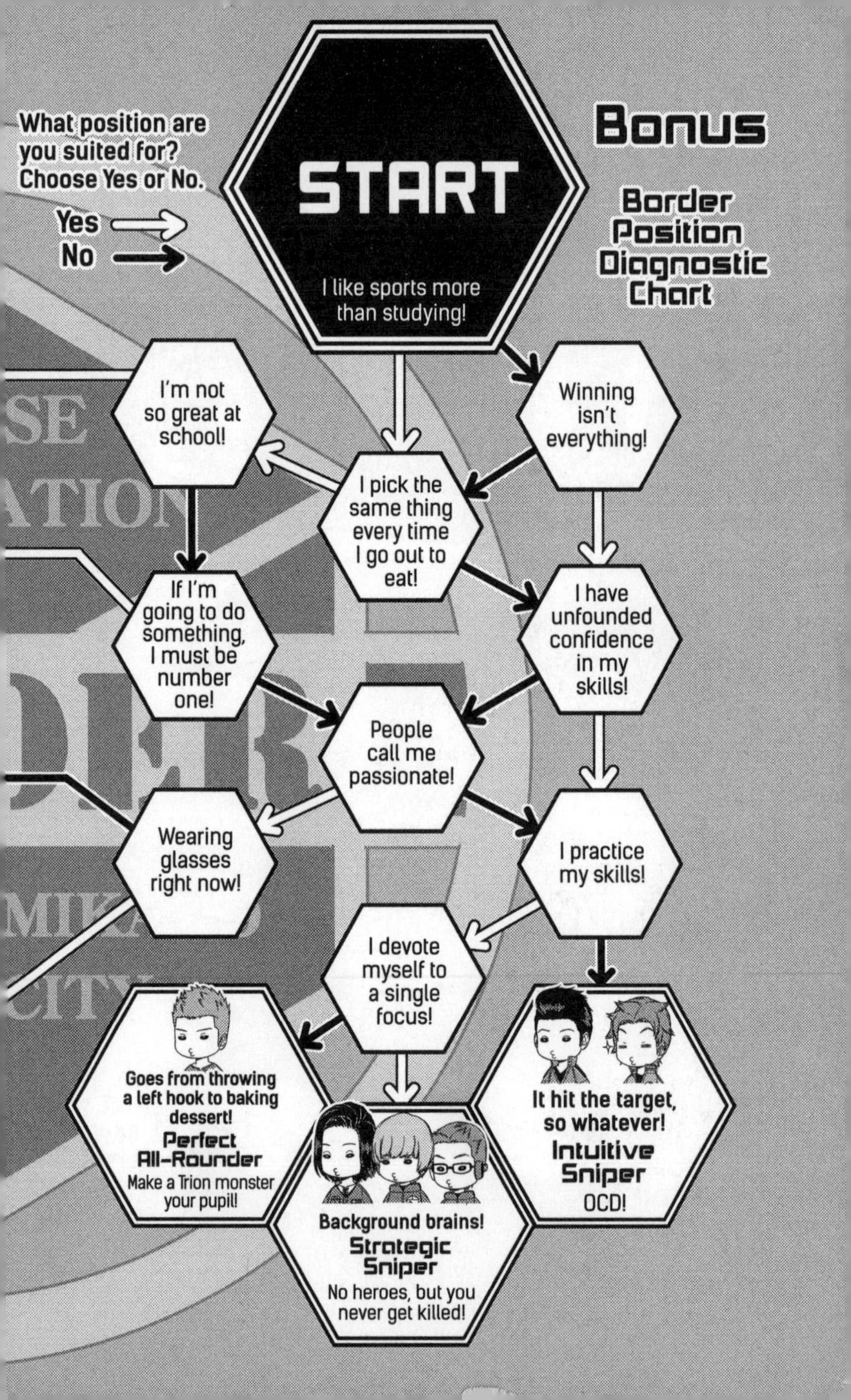
Bonus
Border Position Diagnostic Chart
What position are you suited for? Choose Yes or No.
Yes
No
START
I like sports more than studying!
Winning isn't everything!
I'm not so great at school!
I pick the same thing every time I go out to eat!
If I'm going to do something, I must be number one!
I have unfounded confidence in my skills!
People call me passionate!
Wearing glasses right now!
I practice my skills!
I devote myself to a single focus!
It hit the target, so whatever!
Intuitive Sniper
OCD!
Goes from throwing a left hook to baking dessert!
Perfect All-Rounder
Make a Trion monster your pupil!
Background brains!
Strategic Sniper
No heroes, but you never get killed!

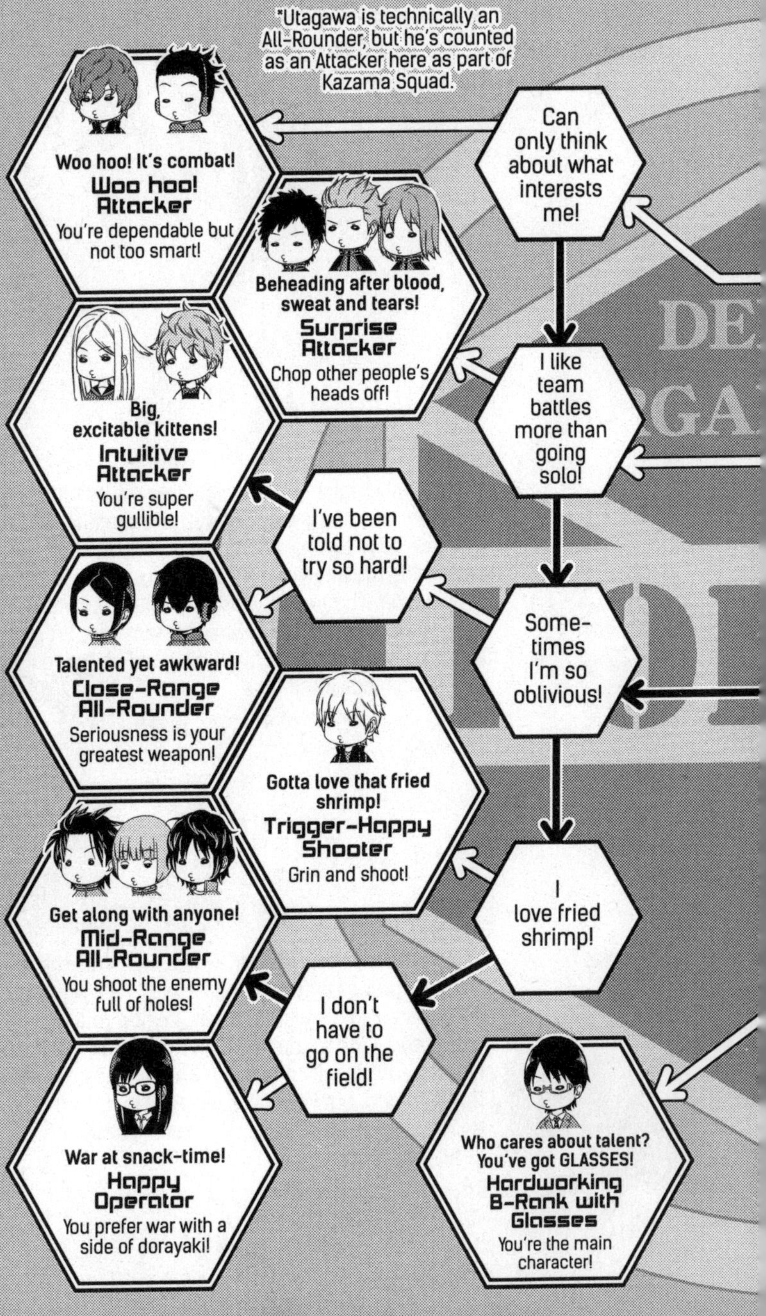
*Utagawa is technically an All-Rounder, but he's counted as an Attacker here as part of Kazama Squad.
Can only think about what interests me!
I like team battles more than going solo!
Some-times I'm so oblivious!
I love fried shrimp!
I've been told not to try so hard!
I don't have to go on the field!
Woo hoo! It's combat!
Woo hoo! Attacker
You're dependable but not too smart!
Beheading after blood, sweat and tears!
Surprise Attacker
Chop other people's heads off!
Big, excitable kittens!
Intuitive Attacker
You're super gullible!
Talented yet awkward!
Close-Range All-Rounder
Seriousness is your greatest weapon!
Gotta love that fried shrimp!
Trigger-Happy Shooter
Grin and shoot!
Get along with anyone!
Mid-Range All-Rounder
You shoot the enemy full of holes!
War at snack-time!
Happy Operator
You prefer war with a side of dorayaki!
Who cares about talent? You've got GLASSES!
Hardworking B-Rank with Glasses
You're the main character!

WORLD TRIGGER

Bonus Character Pages

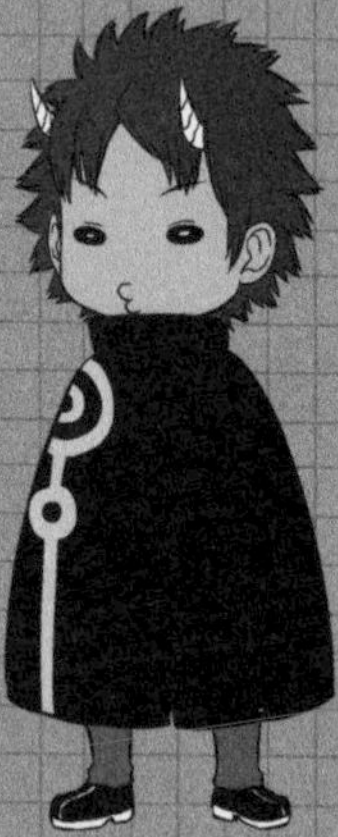

RANBANEIN

Jolly Jet-Gorilla

A genuinely trigger-happy triple threat of smiles, muscles and firepower. It's pretty fantastical to imagine guys like him flying all over Aftokrator. He was going to call Hyrein "brother," but official opinion is split over whether he would've called him "Bro-bro," "Brother dear" or "Brother mine." "Best brother in the whole world" is a bit of a long shot. My design inspiration was a red ogre.

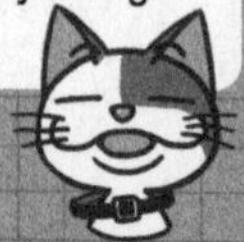

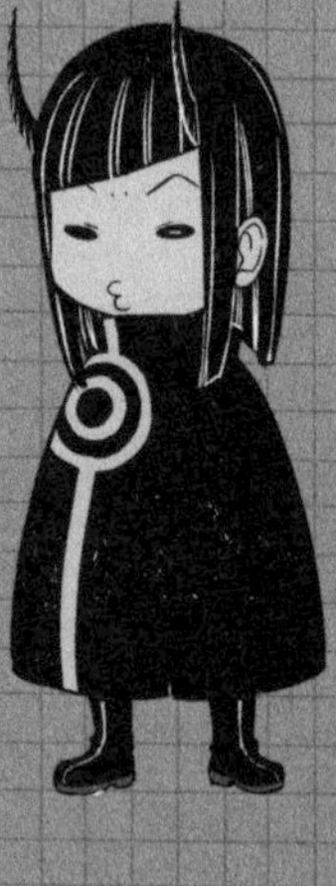

ENEDORA

#1 Adorable Moe Character

Along with the Rads and Mr. Kinuta, he's one of the "Three *World Trigger* Moe Characters." He's jiggling 24-7 thanks to his liquid Trigger; line up four Enedoras of the same color, and pop! They disappear. He was supposedly a nice kid before his horns were transplanted, but I doubt I'll ever get to draw that. My inspiration was the Hanya masks used in Noh theater.

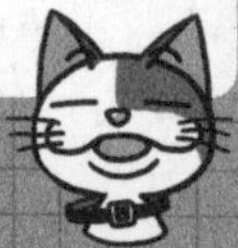

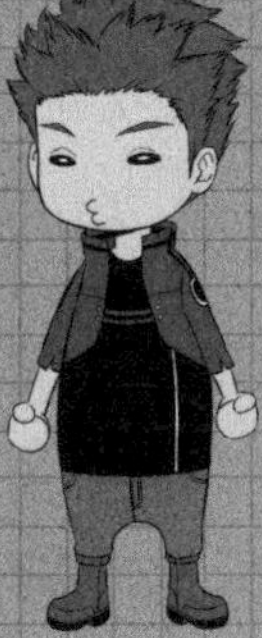

MURAKAMI

Twin Blade Top 5

Barely 18, he's a warrior who knows his position. He belongs to a minor branch and has a flaky captain, but he tries so hard that his forehead is all-out. Just like Reiji, Kazama and Kitora, people who are disciplined must want to expose their foreheads. I hope he interacts with Osamu and Yuma sometime.

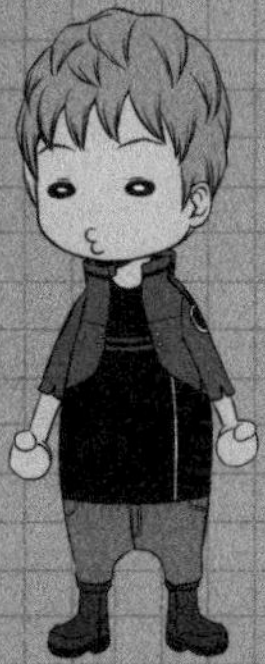

KURUMA

Bait Boy

He's like a fawn who strayed from his herd—a target for everyone. He comes from a rich family and grew up super spoiled, but he's a well-balanced person who's humble, not arrogant or selfish, and popular. He's never been angry in his life. His hair will soon become curly like the Buddha.

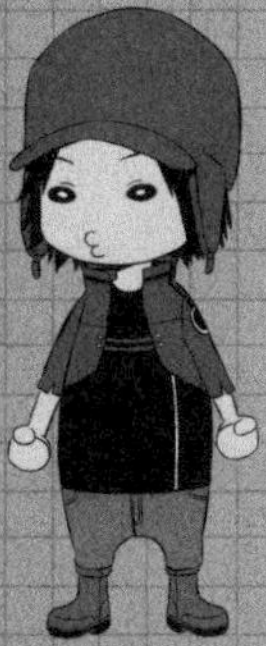

TAICHI

Swiss-Cheese Hat, Bottom Eyelashes

The unlucky Sniper who got obliterated when he followed Azuma. He tends to be clumsy, causing catastrophic damage while trying to do good, making him the true bane. He fiddled with a tropical fish tank and boiled the fish, but even though Kuruma shed tears of blood, he forgave him, forever earning Taichi's respect.

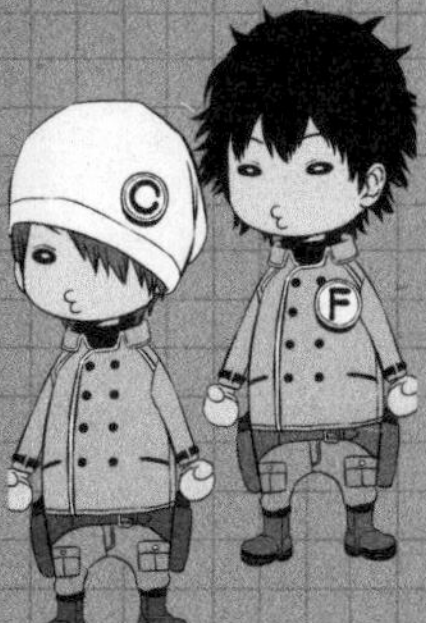

CHANO SQUAD

Two-Page Spread B-Rank

Redshirts with a lot of ambition who used up a two-page spread as they were getting defeated. It's the classic story of getting into a crisis because of dual-wielding pistols. This squad can turn any battle into a defeat. Also, I looked at my character data chart, and it said, "Makoto Chano: a tomboy." I realized that I could get into trouble and pretended not to have seen it.

YOU'RE READING THE WRONG WAY!

World Trigger reads from right to left, starting in the upper-right corner. Japanese is read from right to left, meaning that action, sound effects, and word-balloon order are completely reversed from the English order.

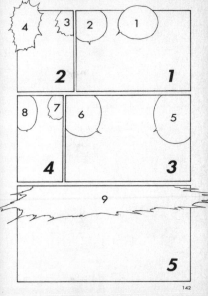

142